Out of Bounds

Out of Bounds

Academic Freedom and the Question of Palestine

MATTHEW ABRAHAM

B L O O M S B U R Y

NEW YORK · LONDON · NEW DELHI · SYDNEY

Bloomsbury Academic

An imprint of Bloomsbury Publishing Inc

1385 Broadway	50 Bedford Square
New York	London
NY 10018	WC1B 3DP
USA	UK

www.bloomsbury.com

Bloomsbury is a registered trademark of Bloomsbury Publishing Plc

First published 2014

Library of Congress Cataloging-in-Publication Data
Abraham, Matthew, 1972–
Out of bounds: academic freedom and the question of Palestine/by Matthew Abraham.
pages cm
Includes bibliographical references and index.
ISBN 978-1-4411-2723-5 (pbk.: alk. paper) – ISBN 978-1-4411-4254-2 (hardcover: alk. paper)
1. Academic freedom–United States. 2. Arab-Israeli conflict–Foreign public opinion, American. 3. Palestine–Foreign public opinion, American. 4. Intellectuals–Political activity–United States. 5. Intellectuals–United States–Attitudes. I. Title.
LC72.A416 2013
378.1'213–dc23
2013013604

ISBN: HB: 978-1-4411-4254-2
    PB: 978-1-4411-2723-5
    ePDF: 978-1-4411-3823-1
    ePub: 978-1-4411-9802-0

Typeset by Deanta Global Publishing Services, Chennai, India

Dedicated to the memory of Rachel Corrie,
who died in Rafch, Gaza on March 16th, 2003

CONTENTS

Acknowledgments viii

1 Introduction 1
2 The politics of perceiving Palestine 47
3 The case of Norman G. Finkelstein 59
4 The Question of Palestine and the subversion of academic freedom: DePaul's denial of tenure to Norman G. Finkelstein 79
5 Edward Said in the American imagination after 9/11 99
6 Noam Chomsky, intellectual labor, and the Question of Palestine 125
7 Recognizing the effects of the past in the present: Theorizing a way forward on the Israel-Palestine conflict 153
8 The perils of separation: Fouzi El-Asmar's *To Be an Arab in Israel* as an allegory of settler-colonial anxiety 183
9 Conclusion: What is next for academic freedom and the Question of Palestine? 199

Notes 207
Works cited 247
Appendix A 263
Appendix B 295
Appendix C 371
Index 375

ACKNOWLEDGMENTS

In writing *Out of Bounds: Academic Freedom and the Question of Palestine*, I have collected a number of intellectual debts to close friends, fellow travelers, and academic departments. I regret if I cannot name everyone here. The initial work for this book started with the help of a John C. Hodges Better English Fund Leave in the spring of 2006 at the University of Tennessee at Knoxville. I would like to thank Professor John P. Zomchick, the chair of the English Department, for his support during my two years at UTK. Perhaps one day he will be able to fully disclose why a John C. Hodges Better English Fund grant that was given to me for the summer of 2006 was mysteriously rescinded two months after it was awarded in writing under the cover of bureaucratic error. To my colleagues at DePaul University in Chicago: I am thankful for your efforts in supporting academic freedom and the exchange of important ideas during a difficult time in our institution's history. Although we have been forever changed by the events of 2006–07, I think we will eventually produce an accurate accounting of the specific political and financial pressures that were brought to bear on the "little school under the El." If *Out of Bounds* makes a minor contribution to the writing of that history, it will have served its purpose. May we resist the impulse to remain silent in the wake of controversy and attempted censorship!

To Michael Kleine, Professor of Writing and Rhetoric at the University of Arkansas at Little Rock, who set me on the course for an academic career, I offer my thanks and admiration. Without Michael's support during difficult times in the late nineties, this book may not have come to fruition. As a devoted teacher and friend, Michael has given me careful advice over the years with good doses of humor.

To Christine, my wife, I must give my unqualified thanks. To my son, Benjamin: May you question dogma and cant with persistence.

I wish to also thank my family for their love and support over the last several years. To my parents, Simon and Annie Abraham, thank you for allowing me to pursue my passion. To my siblings, Simon, Prema, and Jacob: thanks for being there. To Jim Buchanan and Caroline Roberts: you both are the best brother-in-law and sister-in-law for which one could possibly ask.

The following individuals have provided me with unqualified support and good advice over the last ten years: William L. McBride, Noam Chomsky,

Luciana Bohne, Peter Kirstein, John K. Wilson, Nate Roberts, Evan Lorendo, Gene Beiriger, Marcy Newman, Kim Petersen, Rima Kapitan, Victor Kattan, John Mearsheimer, Nate Roberts, James Holstun, Timothy Brennan, Keya Ganguly, Robert Jensen, Norman Finkelstein, David Klein, Mehrene Larudee, Harriet Malinowitz, Grant Farred, Lawrence Davidson, Stephen Bronner, Kurt Jacobson, and the editors of *Logos: A Journal of Modern Society and Culture, Cultural Critique, South Atlantic Quarterly*, and *Arab Studies Quarterly*. I would also like to extend a hearty thanks to Matthew Kopel, Kaitlin Fontana, Grishma Fredric, James Tupper, and the production team at Bloomsbury. To all of you, I offer my heartfelt thanks.

The arguments advanced in this book emerged from several different journal articles that were produced between 2003 and the present. Those articles appeared, or will appear, in the following journals/collections:

"The Rhetoric of Academic Controversy: Edward Said in the American Imagination after 9/11/01." *JAC: A Journal of Rhetoric, Culture, and Politics* 24.1 (2004): 113–42.

Review essay of Norman G. Finkelstein's *Beyond Chutzpah: On the Misuse of Anti-Semitism and the Abuse of History. Logos: A Journal of Modern Society and Culture* 4:4 (2005). http://www.logosjournal.com/issue_4.4/abraham.htm.

"The Perils of Separation: Fouzi El-Asmar's *To Be an Arab in Israel* as an Allegory of Settler Colonial Anxiety." *South Atlantic Quarterly* 7:4, special issue on "Settler-Colonialism." Eds. Aloysha Goldstein and Alex Lubin. Durham: Duke University Press, 2008, pp. 715–34.

"The Saidian Intellectual: Writing Between Culture and System" in *Truth to Power: Public Intellectually In and Out of Academe*. Eds. Silvia Nagy-Zekmi and Karyn Hollis. New Castle Tyne: Cambridge Scholarly Publishing, 2010.

"The Question of Palestine and the Subversion of Academic Freedom." *Arab Studies Quarterly*, Special issue entitled "Academic Freedom, Ideological Boundaries, and the Teaching of the Middle East." Tareq Ismael Terri Ginsberg, Hossein Khosrowjah, Rima Najjar Kapitan, and Gayatri Devi, Eds. 33/34, Fall 2011.

"Recognizing the Effects of the Past in the Present: Theorizing A Way Forward on the Israel-Palestine Conflict" (forthcoming, *JAC: An Interdisciplinary Journal of Rhetoric, Culture, and Politics*).

I wish to take this opportunity to thank the editors of these journals/collections for allowing me to reproduce versions of those original essays/chapters in a different form within this book.

CHAPTER ONE

Introduction

The great moral issue facing the world at the dawn of this millennium is whether Israel's attempts to protect itself against terrorism will result in a massive increase in worldwide anti-Semitism—anti-Semitism directed against the Jewish State itself, its supporters, and Jews throughout the world.

(ALAN DERSHOWITZ in *The Case for Israel*)

Out of Bounds: Academic Freedom and the Question of Palestine seeks to interrogate the degree to which academic freedom and the academic activities it supposedly protects are shaped and mediated by forces external to the university, specifically with respect to the Israel-Palestine conflict. More broadly, I am interested in assessing the social-political conditions informing and governing how the conflict is discussed, analyzed, and understood in various sites of concern, specifically within the US public sphere and among US intellectuals within and outside of the academy.

Out of Bounds focuses on the controversies that have enveloped the following scholars and activists: the Jewish thinker Norman Finkelstein, the late Palestinian critic Edward Said, American political dissident Noam Chomsky, the late International Solidarity Movement activist Rachel Corrie, and the Palestinian intellectual Fouzi El-Asmar. Finkelstein, the son of Holocaust survivors, has sought to expose how Zionist organizations have capitalized on Jewish suffering to immunize Israel—in its treatment of the Palestinians in the occupied territories—against international criticism. The various controversies that have surrounded Finkelstein—from his exposure of Joan Peters' *From Time Immemorial*, to his critique of Daniel Goldhagen's *Willing Executioners*, to his unstinting criticisms of Harvard Law Professor Alan Dershowitz's *The Case for Israel*—attest to not only the importance of his intellectual example but also the stakes involved in piercing the veil of misrepresentation and falsehood enveloping the Israel-Palestine conflict. That there are parties willing to distort the historical and diplomatic record, and to defame those who seek to correct those distortions, in an effort to preserve these misrepresentations and falsehoods that are so vital to securing crucial US support for Israel, suggests just how enormous a threat Finkelstein's critiques represent.

Edward Said, the distinguished professor of literature at Columbia University who is perhaps most famous for his trilogy (*Orientalism*, *The Question of Palestine*, and *Covering Islam*), was viewed as the most eloquent American spokesperson for the plight of the Palestinians living under occupation until his death in September of 2003. Said's family faced dispossession from historical Palestine in the wake of the *Al-Nakbah* (catastrophe) and Israel's creation. Chomsky, the most cited intellectual alive, has been actively engaged in the politics of the Israel-Palestine conflict for nearly 50 years, posing a consistent challenge to the subservience of the intelligentsia on the crucial issues pertaining to US and Israeli rejectionism.

Rachel Corrie died at the age of 23 on 16 March 2003, while defending a Palestinians home against demolition in Rafah, Gaza. Corrie's memorialization has been of intense concern and political struggle in the United States because she died at the hands of Israel's Defense Forces, the army of a US client state that the United States supports. While there has been substantial dispute as to the actual circumstances surrounding Corrie's death, to date there has been no official US government investigation into whether an Israeli Defense Force's bulldozer operator deliberately ran over Corrie as she defended a Palestinian home against demolition. Furthermore, Corrie's parents (Craig and Cindy Corrie) unsuccessfully brought a lawsuit against the Israeli government that lasted nearly 3 years. In the chapter devoted to the controversy around Corrie's legacy, I explore how the significance of Corrie's example even came to touch upon the professional politics of my own field, which is far removed from Middle East politics. Finally, Fouzi El-Asmar, a Palestinian Arab who now lives in the United States and continues to write about the plight of Israel's Palestinian citizens, authored *To Be an Arab in Israel*, a book that received considerable attention upon its publication in 1978 as a result of it showing the ugly underside of Israeli "democracy."

Each of these figures has become the focal point of intense controversy because of specific claims they have advanced in their scholarship, activism, and public advocacy about the Israel-Palestine conflict and its related issues. Indeed, each of them is the source of significant political anxiety in relation to the Israel-Palestine conflict, either because of what they represent or because what they have written as public intellectuals and advocates for Palestinian human rights. Clearly, not all of these figures are academic scholars, but each of them has confronted the politics of an intellectual culture committed to sustaining a silence around the Question of Palestine. While the cases of Jimmy Carter, John Mearsheimer and Stephen Walt, Joel Kovel, Joseph Massad, Nadia Abu-Haj, Sami Al-Arian, William Robinson, and Terri Ginsberg will be covered in a subsequent book, I think the dynamics of intellectual controversy currently enveloping the Israel-Palestine conflict can be captured in the small number of cases I have selected for treatment here.

The parameters of academic freedom

In investigating how the Question of Palestine has been approached, treated, and discussed within the US academy and beyond, one must develop some sense of what academic freedom is and how it came into being. Academic freedom has been called "a special concern of the first amendment" by Supreme Court Justice Louis Powell and constitutional law scholar Peter Byrne.[1] What Powell and Byrne mean by this is that the courts, specifically the Supreme Court, have never provided a firm, definitive, and satisfying definition of academic freedom, which leaves observers to wonder if academic freedom protects controversial lines of inquiry within the academy, such as those pursued by scholars advancing a Palestinian perspective in the context of the Israel-Palestine conflict. Indeed, a more conservative conception of academic freedom posits that academic freedom belongs to the university and not to the individual researcher. If the university has the freedom to decide who may teach, what may be taught, how it is to be taught, and who may be admitted for study, little room is left for the kinds of individual academic freedom allowing for the production of innovative and edgy scholarship. Part of the reason that no adequate and satisfying definition of academic freedom has been fashioned is a result of the unclear boundary between the academy and the world beyond the academy.

Creating a separation between the inside (the academy) and the outside (those sites beyond the academy within the public sphere) recognizes how academic utterances often find their conditions of justifiability in the very fact that they are academic utterances and not some other kind of utterance grounded in some other location. However, scholars who (as public intellectuals) consider controversial issues in their scholarship, or editorialize about such issues in their extramural statements in public forums, often become the targets of advocacy groups dissatisfied with a particular aspect of the scholar's critique—whether that critique be of American foreign policy in a particular region of the world or of some hot-button domestic concern such as gun control.

These external parties, especially since 9/11, have sought to restrict, and in some instances even silence, the critical speech of scholars seeking to articulate repressed viewpoints. The arguments driving such efforts frequently take the form of the following: X scholar has not complied with the norms of the academic profession in her treatment of Y issue. As a consequence, this scholar should be removed from the academy to protect students, the public, civil discourse, and the academic profession. In response to these intrusions into the academic space, members of the university community frequently invoke "academic freedom" to defend what they insist is their right to select the topics of their research, perhaps believing that the mere invocation of the phrase, and what it signifies, is enough to fend off the external attack.

Lamentably, academic freedom is not a principle that protects the individual researcher or teacher, but is instead a construct modulated by the boundaries between the inside and the outside of the academy, the boundaries shaping professional norms, as well as the boundaries between disciplines. The shapes of these boundaries are modulated by national crises (such as 9/11) *and* the concomitant expansion of the national security state, demographic trends, the forces of globalization, and in response to economic, political, and social exigencies.

It is a commonplace that academic freedom is central to academic life, as it is the very concept that distinguishes the university from other organizations in civil society; it emerges and takes shape out of a set of sharp restrictions, however. As Pauline Yu reminds us, ". . . academic freedom is not the defense of one point of view, whether politically correct or incorrect. Nor is it the defense of individual virtue or individual rights. It is, rather, a *corporate* freedom and a corporate obligation—the defense of the *collective* judgment of the academic community and its commitment to professional self-regulation according to disciplinary standards."[2] This definition of academic freedom, as a corporate freedom and a collective judgment, is the one currently animating contemporary debates about faculty rights and responsibilities.

To be accorded academic freedom, one must be able to articulate why one's work is academic as opposed to being merely relevant, interesting, or of political importance. Indeed, academic freedom is the freedom to pursue the academic profession within the bounds of the profession. As the *1915 Declaration of Principles on Academic Freedom and Tenure* notes, "The importance of academic freedom is most clearly perceived in the light of the purposes for which universities exist: (1) to promote inquiry and advance the sum of human knowledge; (2) to provide general instruction to students; and (3) to develop experts for various branches of public service."[3]

A dialectical relationship obtains between the adjective "academic" and the word "freedom." For example, as claims to freedom become larger and larger, the adjective "academic" in the phrase "academic freedom" loses its restrictive force. Conversely, as Stanley Fish makes clear, the claim that one is performing a legitimate academic task becomes increasingly convincing in proportion to the degree that one restricts one's freedom in performing that task. In other words, as Fish has noted, "*as bigger and bigger claims are advanced in the name of 'academic freedom', the less likely it is that one will successfully place one's work in a disciplinary framework.*" According to Fish, there are currently five versions of academic freedom that are operative at this historical moment. These are (1) It's Just a Job School; (2) The Common Good School; (3) The Uncommon Being School; (4) It's For Critique School; and (5) The It's For Revolution School. The It's Just a Job School believes that college professors are trained and paid to introduce students to recognized bodies of knowledge and nothing else. From this perspective, consciousness raising, political advocacy, and social transformation should be left to other professions, as they are not proper academic activities.

For the "Common Good" School, academic work acts as a corrective to the tyranny of public opinion, which is often hastily formed. While other professions may be responsive to the market or political forces or public opinion, the task of advancing knowledge within the academy is to follow the evidence wherever it leads, even if it results in the issuing of an unpopular discovery that is at odds with public opinion. Related to this view, the Uncommon Being School declares that since academics have to act as a check on the tyranny of public opinion, they require the extraordinary privileges that come with academic freedom. The "It's for Critique" School states that since academics are able to see through, and act as a check on public opinion, they should extend their commitment to critique to the norms governing their disciplines and the academic profession. All authority, even academic authority, is suspect in this view. Only by continually questioning norms will dissent be protected. Finally, the "It's For Revolution" School believes that the academy should serve as a training ground for revolution. This School already knows where the norms that the "It's For Critique" School seeks to interrogate come from. These norms come from the corrupt managers who serve in the corrupt institutions of a corrupt neoliberal society.

According to Fish, the movement from the most conservative to the most radical view of academic freedom—from the It's Just a Job School to the It's For Revolution School—will be marked by the transfer of emphasis from the word *academic*, which names the local and specific habitation of the asserted freedom, to the word "freedom," which does not limit the scope or place of what is being asserted at all. The concept of freedom is often understood as the absence of constraint, but such an understanding of freedom would be too broad if it were applied to the activities of academics. Some would limit academic freedom to professors who exercise functions that conform to a specific academic task [4] No one doubts that classroom teaching and research are activities where freedom is to be accorded at least to some extent. But what about the freedom to criticize one's superiors, or the freedom to configure a course in ways not standard in the department, or the freedom to have a voice in the funding of athletic programs, or in the decision to erect a student center, or in the selection of a President, or the awarding of honorary degrees, or the inviting of outside speakers to campus? Is academic freedom violated when faculty members have minimal input into, or are shut out from, these and other matters? What exactly is the scope of the freedom claim when one invokes "academic freedom"?

According to the AAUP's *1940 Statement of Principles on Academic Freedom and Tenure*, university professors are entitled to academic freedom in their teaching, research, and extramural utterance, with the understanding that when these professors write as citizens about matters of public concern, they will do so in ways that reflect well on the academic profession and one's academic institution. Avoiding sensational and intemperate expression when writing for the public is understood to be a part of one's academic responsibility. Beyond these restrictions, however, it is "not desirable that scholars be debarred from giving expression to their judgments upon controversial questions, or that their freedom of speech, outside the university, should be limited to questions falling within their own specialties" (299).

The *1940 Statement* does not directly address why academics should have these unusual protections that other citizens do not. Indeed, one must ask, "What is it about the nature of the academic enterprise that the AAUP's founders believed necessitated this special freedom? What justifies the academy's claim to this special freedom?" According to Matthew Finkin and Robert Post, authors of *The Common Good*, there are three principal threats to academic freedom: ecclesiastical authority, vested interests, and the tyranny of public opinion, with the latter two remaining the most visible threat in the present. With respect to scholars writing and speaking on the Israel-Palestine conflict, vested interests pose a particular difficulty as will become clear throughout the book.

At the turn of the nineteenth century and in the early twentieth, academics were at-will employees of the university, subject to dismissal if their scholarship or public utterances offended a powerful figure in the administration or on the board of trustees. The cases of Edward A. Ross, Scott Nearing, and Edward Bemis represent early test cases for academic freedom, and in each of these cases promising scholars were removed from their positions for offering up unpopular critiques of ruling interests. Ross, an economist, offended Dorothy Leland Stanford, the widow of the founder of Stanford University, with his advocacy of free silver and his public opposition to the use of immigrant labor in building California's railroads. Upon learning of Ross's positions, Mrs. Stanford simply insisted that Ross's employment contract not be renewed. Similarly, Scott Nearing, a talented economist, was summarily dismissed from the faculty at the University of Pennsylvania because his published views on American foreign policy met with the disapproval of Penn's Board of Trustees. Edward Bemis, a historian at the University of Chicago, made public statements about railroad monopolies, angering the University's founder, William Rainey Harper, who dismissed Bemis from his position in 1895.

Primarily because of the faculty outrage over the Ross dismissal at Stanford, Arthur O. Lovejoy and Edwin Seligman established the philosophical basis and material support for the American Association of University Professors in 1915. Lovejoy and Seligman recognized the distinctiveness of the academic task and the fragility of the protections afforded to it. As a result, they developed the concept of "academic freedom" to create a basis for shielding academic work from the influence and interference of non-academics. For the AAUP, professional self-regulation in the shape of professional norms and the placement of academic work within disciplinary frames would become the very conditions of possibility for invoking and justifying academic freedom.

Disciplinarity, the placement of one's work within a recognized body of knowledge, is the first step in laying claim to academic freedom. The protection of academic freedom, then, depends upon the maintenance and regulation of professional standards. In the absence of such standards, individuals would be licensed to pursue lines of inquiry based merely upon their individual preferences, making it nearly impossible to create and regulate a coherent body of disciplinary knowledge. Professional standards and norms establish the disciplinary matrix within which knowledge is created. Complying with these standards and norms, as a member of disciplinary community, is a coerced—but necessary—behavior if one is to obtain the privileges attached to the academic profession.

In the sense outlined above, academic freedom is a guild concept that emerges in relation to one's disciplinary and professional community. It's this understanding of academic freedom, as a guild arrangement whereby academics make judgments about other academics, which Stanley Fish endorses. It's the vocabulary of academic freedom—particularly its rhetoric of evenhandedness and tolerance—that Fish denounces as "a sham and a cheat," as this vocabulary is ultimately incapable of drawing distinctions between worthy and unworthy ideas and is insistent that every viewpoint at least deserves a hearing. This vocabulary contributes to the ideology of academic freedom, an ideology mediated by social conditions, political imperatives, and material transformations. This ideology is a rhetorical construct to the degree that it responds to material, political, social, and economic exigencies. How could it possibly be otherwise?

That the definitions of, and parameters afforded by, academic freedom are modulated by constraints such as institutional, professional, political, and social factors seems almost commonsensical. Academic freedom exists within universities, and as Cathy Chaput reminds us in her *Inside the Teaching Machine*, p. 54, "universities are local instantiations of national trends." It stands to reason that these national trends would condition the production of knowledge and its boundaries within the university, as well as conceptions of, and parameters for, academic freedom. The range of methodologies Chaput's Hermeneutics of Valuation brings together helps us to understand the blend of economic, political, and historical forces shaping the prospects of rhetorical intervention in the global public sphere:

Rhetorical Studies   Cultural Studies

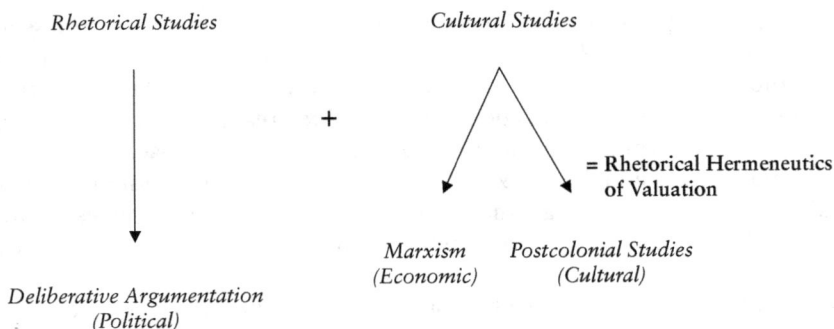

Deliberative Argumentation
(Political)

Marxism   Postcolonial Studies
(Economic)   (Cultural)

= Rhetorical Hermeneutics
of Valuation

FIGURE 1.1 (*Diagram adapted from Chaput's* Inside the Teaching Machine: Rhetoric and the Globalization of the US Public Research University. *Tuscaloosa: University of Alabama Press, 2008*), p. 8.

Chaput's Rhetorical Hermeneutics of Valuation brings together rhetorical, political, economic, and cultural frameworks to better explain how the concept of academic freedom responds to changes in conditions within local and national environments, adapting to these changes by expanding or restricting its boundaries and protections. The value of Chaput's model emerges in its bringing together of cultural studies, Marxist political economy, postcolonial studies, and rhetorical studies, enabling a fuller understanding of the variety of forces shaping conceptions of academic freedom. Academic freedom is frequently invoked in the belief that it is a neutral principle. The all-too-familiar feelings of disappointment and betrayal when academic freedom protections are denied to scholars pursuing controversial lines of inquiry is a result of not completely understanding that the conditions of possibility for academic freedom are based on—and emerge from—certain restrictions that are rhetorical, political, economic, cultural, professional, and disciplinary.

Over the years, as I have witnessed how frequently the academic freedom of researchers pursuing controversial lines of inquiry is violated by university administrations, I have noted how varied and complex the definitions of academic freedom have become. In debating whether academic freedom belongs to the university or to the researcher, or whether academic freedom only obtains for those who write and teach within a well-defined disciplinary framework, rather than to those who wish to engage political topics in their scholarship and extramural advocacy, it seems as if all of the fancy footwork done to explain academic freedom's conditions of possibility simply proves what we should have known all along: academic freedom cannot be grounded in principle, but must be viewed as a rhetorical and evolving construct that responds to the demands of the corporate state within which the university is situated.

Perhaps it would be best to dispense with increasingly novel conceptions and definitions of academic freedom, realizing that its contours are constantly evolving in response to global, political, social, economic trends while accepting the impossibility of grounding it in a principled way. The romanticized view of academic freedom which celebrates the heroic researcher's quest to speak truth to power on the most controversial issues of our time, a view that I (perhaps with many of you) am heavily invested in believing, will no longer do. The battles over academic freedom have shifted to battles over what constitutes the proper domain within one's discipline, as well as the etiquette required within the scholarly enterprise. Policing disciplinary borders and enforcing the supposed rules of etiquette guiding the academic profession have become the most effective ways to screen out certain lines of inquiry, as we will soon learn.

There is a great deal of law review scholarship covering the debate about whether or not academic freedom is an individual or an institutional right.[5] For my purposes, I am going to simplify this debate by simply stating that academic freedom is the freedom to pursue the truth within scholarship for the benefit of the public. The debates about institutional and academic freedom obscure what scholarship should be about: truth-telling and the betterment of society through the enlightenment of the citizenry about difficult issues. The insistence that academic freedom brings with it certain responsibilities seems to serve a normalizing function, an insistence that academic pursuits be conducted with a certain propriety, tone, and perhaps most importantly within certain ideological bounds. This requirement that scholars respect the dignity and feelings of others, while avoiding sensational and intemperate language, is actually an attempt to contain radical and unsettling thought.

Academic freedom, expertise, and democratic legitimation

As I mentioned previously with respect to the Common Good School's justification for academic freedom, one of the major arguments forwarded in defense of why academics need academic freedom is that the public good is served by the production of expert knowledge. The legitimation of democracy depends upon granting this expert knowledge more weight than that of lay opinion. When the AAUP was founded, lay opinion was positioned as the enemy of expert knowledge, a force capable of harming reasoned deliberations about important public problems. It is in this context, then, that academic freedom takes shape and meaning: academic freedom ensures that academics will be guided by the scholar's spirit instead of the tyranny of public opinion. As Dewey notes in his *The Public and Its Problems*, "Unless there are methods for detecting the energies which are at work and tracing them through an intricate network of interactions to their consequences, what passes as public opinion will be 'opinion' in its derogatory sense rather than truly public, no matter how widespread the opinion is" (177).

According to the *1915 Declaration of Principles*, "The lay public is under no compulsion to accept or to act upon the opinions of the scientific experts whom, through the universities, it employs. But it is highly needful, in the interest of society at large, that what purports to be the conclusions of such men trained for, and dedicated to the quest for truth, shall in fact be the conclusions of such men, and not echoes of the opinions of the lay public, or of the individuals who endow or manage universities" (*AAUP Redbook* 294). Furthermore, "The responsibility of the university teacher is primarily to the public itself, and to the judgment of his own profession; and while, with respect to certain external conditions of his vocation, he accepts a responsibility to the authorities of the institution in which he serves, in the essentials of his professional activity his duty is to the wider public to which the institution itself is morally amenable" (294). This duty to the wider public, and to the common good, is what opens up the possibility of academic work connecting to issues of public concern: "The liberty of the scholar within the university to set forth his conclusions, be they what they may, is conditioned by their being conclusions gained by a scholar's method and held in a scholar's spirit; that is to say, they must be the fruits of competent and patient and sincere inquiry, and they should be set forth with dignity, courtesy, and temperateness of language" (298). This quotation from the *AAUP Redbook* has in fact been seized upon by enemies of academic freedom within the Israel-Palestine conflict to marginalize those advancing a scholarly perspective favorable to the Palestinians.

To ensure that the academy would be allowed to regulate its affairs without the external interference of politicians, Boards of Trustees, and other interested parties, academics were expected to police each other, admonishing and guiding colleagues refusing to adhere to their professional duties. As the *1915 Declaration* notes, "If this profession should prove itself unwilling to purge its ranks of the incompetent and the unworthy, or to prevent the freedom which it claims in the name of science from being used as a shelter for inefficiency, or for uncritical or intemperate partisanship, it is certain that the task will be taken up by others who lack certain essential qualifications for performing it . . ." To fail to fulfill this duty would subject one's institution, discipline, and the whole academic enterprise to public scrutiny and disapproval.

Beyond complying with the dictates of professional behavior, professors are expected to meet the professional regulations mandated by their disciplines. Part of this obligation involves the responsible practice of placing one's scholarship within a recognized disciplinary framework. According to Robert Post, Dean of Yale Law School, the less one is able to situate one's discipline within a recognized body of knowledge, the less likely one will be able to derive the benefits of academic freedom. For Post, ". . . there is no warrant to depart from professional norms, since they provide the necessary constraining conditions and the standards according to which free inquiry is conducted, and establish the general framework of competence" (Butler, "Academic Norms, Contemporary Challenges," 112).

Since academic freedom is understood to be the right to purse the academic profession within the bounds of that profession, it is a professional freedom with severe limitations sharply limiting acceptable forms of inquiry. We have a paradox, then, in that if disciplinary norms enable academic freedom protections—keeping external parties at bay—and, if out of deference to these norms' ability to protect the academic enterprise, we refuse or are hesitant to question them, these norms themselves become obstacles to inquiry and innovation and ultimately threats to academic freedom. In other words, the conditions of possibility for claiming academic freedom protections have the potential to threaten academic freedom.

Judith Butler insists that we should be wary of positioning disciplinary and professional norms as ahistorical and unimpeachable sources through which to derive academic authority, as such norms are the products of history, preferences, exclusions, and constraints. These norms, by being norms, position dissenting positions as perspectives to be excluded or co-opted. As Butler explains, disciplinary norms themselves were at one time dissenting perspectives, perspectives that became norms as disciplinary practitioners came around to adopting them. Butler encourages us to think about how norms change, evolve, and adapt to historical, social, political, and institutional preferences in response to changing external conditions that are more often than not exercises of political power. Indeed, Butler's observations lead us to the Foucauldian truism that power and knowledge are inextricably intertwined, with those in power creating knowledge and naming it as objective.

If as Post suggests that one cannot lay claim to academic freedom without placing one's work within a recognized disciplinary framework, deriving from that framework the authority of its regulative unity or ideal, what happens to the whole enterprise of scholarly inquiry in the humanities and the social sciences, which depends upon challenging and blurring disciplinary boundaries themselves? Is this enterprise then a threat to academic freedom because it seeks to dissolve the armor of disciplinarity, the very justification for academic work that keeps external forces—eager to influence the academic enterprise—at bay? In other words, given the current threats to academic freedom, is it not best to dispense with efforts to question and challenge disciplinary norms in the interest of protecting the larger project of academic freedom, realizing at the same time that the enforcement of these norms poses a possible threat to the exercise of academic freedom?

Add to this paradox the fact that academic freedom is often viewed, from a legal standpoint, as being reserved for the university, as it is the academic institution that decides who has the right to teach, what may be taught, how it will be taught, and who will be admitted for study. Academic freedom has never really belonged to the intrepid individual researcher, but has rather been viewed as an institutional, corporate, and professional right. For example, the institution has the academic freedom to pursue affirmative action policies and to adjust its admission standards in the interest of diversity if it decides to do so. Of course, faculty members make decisions about curriculum, hiring, and evaluation, but these decisions are made in their capacity as disciplinary and institutional representatives. The contemporary debate about academic freedom revolves around these two distinct conceptualizations of academic freedom: first, as a right of the individual researcher; second, as a right that inheres within the university as an institution and the academic profession as a corporate body. These two conceptions are in direct tension with one another.

Heretical questions and the protection of tenure

Academic scholars consider academic freedom and tenure the cornerstones of the academic profession. Without the lifetime employment protections associated with tenure, academic scholars would not be able to enjoy academic freedom because they would be eternally and justifiably worried that their controversial research may offend a powerful party within or external to their universities, which could conceivably result in dismissal.

Socrates chose to drink hemlock in fifth-century B.C. Athens rather than to recant his supposedly heretical philosophical teachings. Galileo questioned the geocentric conception of the universe and faced excommunication from the Church, although he was later proven to be scientifically correct in forwarding a heliocentric model. What during Socrates's and Galileo's times were considered heresies—challenging state authority and asserting that the earth travels around the Sun—are now considered perfectly acceptable and correct positions. Socrates supposedly corrupted the children of Athens who heard his teachings about how a society should be organized, which in turn threatened those in positions of power. In speaking and writing about understanding of the earth's movement in relation to the Sun, Galileo met fierce resistance from church authorities who were positioned to destroy his reputation, regardless of how accurate Galileo's research may have been. Truth, then, was besides the point. The theory of planetary motion that Galileo espoused posed a challenge to state and ecclesiastical authority. Socrates' and Galileo's commitments to truth threatened the fabric of Athenian and Italian society, making them both dangerous men at key historical moments.

It is with such historical cases in mind, including the dismissals of Edward Ross, Scott Nearing, and Edward Bemis, that one can better understand the importance and purpose of academic tenure in the university system. Academic researchers need the protection of tenure and the academic freedom that accompanies it to publish the results of their research, even if those results are controversial or upset powerful parties within society. Without such protections, one might argue, academics would be forced to adopt the political fashions of the day to survive within their institutions, ultimately avoiding controversial positions in their scholarship that might jeopardize their careers. In theory, tenure provides the kind of economic and institutional protection required to safeguard the integrity of research, which is vital to the functioning of a free society. Whether tenure actually forwards this objective, the promotion of a free and open society where any topic can be researched and discussed, is certainly open to debate. Indeed, the tenure system in the United States has been the object of both unusual praise and scrutiny.[6]

Tenure, controversy, and the contemporary US academy

Academic decision-making around tenure and promotion is one of the most important processes within the university system. Protecting the integrity of this process should be of societal concern because tenure—at least in principle—provides academics with the protection to write about unpopular issues that have perhaps been misrepresented due to the power of special interests or the influence of various kinds of dogma. The general public has a vague sense that tenure provides job security to academics, enabling them to write and do research on potentially controversial issues without state or special-interest interference.

Tenure, as a literal property right, refers to the continuous contract rights that are granted to a probationary faculty member upon her demonstrating her fitness in the tenure and promotion process. Pre-tenure, a faculty member must satisfy the burden of proof demonstrating that she will continue to be a productive citizen of the university throughout one's career. It is not enough to complete the probationary period; one must demonstrate excellence in two of three areas with respect to research, teaching, and service. Since many faculty members often finish out their careers at the institution where they receive tenure, university administrations must be careful that they grant tenure to only those faculty members who demonstrate their capacity to contribute to their profession by doing research, publishing the results of that research, and teaching those results over an extended period of time.[7] In the absence of producing evidence that one is a productive scholar and teacher, it is difficult for a faculty member to receive tenure.[8]

While what I describe here is how the tenure and promotion process should generally should work—as a process where those who have worked the hardest and published the most should be rewarded with job security for their efforts—it is not the reality, especially for scholars who choose controversial lines of inquiry. Indeed, an excess of scholarly production cannot make up for the veritable sin that that an unpopular position or line of argument has been taken in the junior faculty member's scholarship. Of course, academic freedom should ideally protect any faculty member, regardless of rank, from capricious administrative decision-making in the event some individual or faction within or outside the university objects to the type of scholarship being produced. The ideal, however, is far away from the reality.

Those who defend the tenure system argue that it is the basis for freedom in research, which according to the AAUP's *1940 Statement of Principles on Academic Freedom and Tenure* is "fundamental to the advancement of truth." Furthermore, "Freedom and economic security, hence, tenure, are indispensable to the success of an institution in fulfilling its obligations to its students and to society."[9] Tenure, then, would seem to be a prerequisite for creating the conditions of a free and open society, where the only requirement for pursuing academic research is to pursue the truth wherever that pursuit may lead. However, there is evidence that suggests that tenure has neither enabled innovation nor emboldened academics to pursue controversial lines of research. It has instead contributed to the perception that the process leading up to a tenure decision is fraught with numerous ideological traps that make tenure increasingly difficult to achieve for talented young junior faculty members. If the tenure process actually acts as a litmus test to screen out those scholars who threaten a disciplinary consensus or social hegemony, then tenure itself may generally be said to protect only those faculty whose ideological commitments are consistent with a disciplinary or institutional status quo. While I cannot argue that this is always the true, it is perhaps the case, particularly in instances where a scholar is pursuing a deeply unpopular line of inquiry.[10]

The conferral of tenure and promotion upon a probationary faculty member is often viewed as the milestone of an academic career. Those who do not receive it are forced to leave the institution after a "terminal year," with their prospects of future academic employment severely limited. In this sense, the tenure and promotion year is a "do-or-die" situation, separating the worthy from the unworthy in the eyes of the university administration. This process forces the probationary candidate to face an audit performed by tenured colleagues within various levels of the institution. In essence, the process serves to evaluate faculty members in a relatively one-dimensional way, leveling a summative assessment of the candidate's performance over six years based upon standards and criteria that can shift without notice.

The degree to which bias can be expressed within the process and through the very tenure and promotion criteria around which academics plan their probationary periods is difficult to assess and sometimes impossible to prove. Although there are objective standards and criteria for assessing a candidate's teaching, scholarship, and service, these standards can be used to support subjective judgments about the quality of a candidate's scholarship. Some of the most intense struggles within academic departments revolve around strong disagreements among tenured faculty as to the relative contribution a junior faculty member's scholarship and teaching make to a field or a department's curricular coverage. At times, arguments questioning the relative merits of a candidate's scholarship can serve to cloak personal animus, racism, sexism, ageism, and, perhaps most frequently, disagreements with the political viewpoints expressed in the scholarship. Beyond gender and race discrimination, the most frequent and subtle type of discrimination exercised through the tenure and process is that which is based upon political viewpoint, particularly if the scholar expressing the viewpoint gains public prominence.

Noteworthy in this respect are the number of tenure and promotion cases involving scholars engaging the Israel-Palestine conflict which have received substantial press coverage largely because of the outside pressure placed upon the university's decision-making processes about these scholars' credentials. In principle, professors should never face professional retaliation or administrative censure in the pursuit of telling the truth.[11] However, this ideal state of affairs is increasingly distant from the present reality in the contemporary academy, where issues of societal concern are sometimes deliberately avoided precisely because they are difficult, divisive, and controversial. The Question of Palestine is one such issue. The Question of Palestine, another name for the Israel-Palestine conflict and the power of American Zionism, is "the last taboo in American life," to borrow a phrase from Edward Said.[12] The Question of Palestine is the last taboo in American life because the American public has been not only deprived of the relevant information about the conflict by its own government and media, but because people who have sought to bring the truth to light have been silenced in the course of seeking to reframe the Israel-Palestine conflict with respect to international law. What should be a straightforward approach to analyzing the conflict has become a veritable taboo, as many significant Americans such as Jimmy Carter have learned.

A taboo develops around a sensitive or controversial issue when the citizens of a country accept a troubling social hegemony as a result of a set of reinforcing assumptions, usually held by and endorsed by politicians and elites, which ultimately become easier to accept than to challenge. The US-Israel special relationship occupies a central place in American culture. Although being critical of this special relationship is consistent with principled political analysis, more often than not, citizens steer clear of issuing frank criticisms of Israel out of fear of being called "anti-Semitic." The special relationship is unlike any other in world history, with wide-ranging consequences for the Middle East and beyond. It is a hard to think of a world issue that is as important as the Israel-Palestine conflict for American citizens; indeed, accessing the facts about the conflict is not a difficult task as they are readily available—however, there has been a concerted effort to prevent the facts of the conflict from being widely disseminated in the public sphere.[13]

These "facts" include the following: (1) The United States and Israel have actively subverted a peaceful resolution of the conflict for over 40 years, while the Arab states and most of the world community have repeatedly recognized Israel's right to exist within its pre-June 1967 borders[14]; (2) Although it has posed as a "neutral broker" in the conflict, the United States has repeatedly sided with Israel by providing it with vital military, economic, and diplomatic support while denouncing Palestinian terrorism[15]; (3) The "peace process" has in no sense been about bringing peace to the Israelis and Palestinians, but in actuality has been committed to solidifying Israel's regional hegemony in the Middle East[16]; (4) Contrary to popular images of Palestinian intransigence in the face of Israel's "generous offers" of land for a state—such as Barak's offer to Arafat at the 2000 Camp David talks—the Palestinians have already given up 78 percent of their historical homeland and are merely seeking to hold on to under 80 percent of the remaining 22 percent[17]; (5) The historical roots of Zionism make clear that Israel's leadership since the state's founding has sought to either transfer its Palestinian citizens to the West Bank or to create a situation reminiscent of South Africa in which the Palestinians would live as third-class citizens in relation to the Israeli settler population.[18]

Because of the US government's tacit support of Israel's territorial ambitions, especially since 1967, and the US public's lack of knowledge about this support due to the avoidance of the mass media, it has been difficult to face and discuss the central facts about the Israel-Palestine conflict because of the intense psychological—nearly spiritual—connection between Israel and the United States. Hence, the facts are hidden to prevent the very people who should know about them, American taxpayers, from understanding their role in supporting Israel's ever-expanding militarism.

At this historical moment, there is no more controversial issue within the American public sphere than the Israel-Palestine conflict. Indeed, it is difficult to point to a more contentious issue within civil society, where it would seem that intense discussion about issues of the day would be encouraged and recognized as essential to the health of a democratic society. However, since the political interests and social forces surrounding the Israel-Palestine conflict exercise such a decisive hegemony over nearly every aspect of domestic life, it is important to understand that this issue is unique because of the stakes involved in its representations within the mainstream culture. In other words, since the United States plays such a vital role in the Middle East, and a nearly decisive role with respect to the Israel-Palestine conflict, it is important for US citizens to understand the specific ways in which propaganda has been deployed to mislead and deceive the public about Israel's military aims with respect to its neighboring states (Lebanon, Syria, Jordan, Iraq, and Iran). As I will seek to describe throughout this book, academics who have sought to correct illusions about the conflict have—at times—faced extremes of abuse and vilification.

While there are members of society, such as courageous journalists, positioned to speak and write with intelligence and originality on the issues of the day, the structure of the mass media has made it increasingly difficult for critical and hard-hitting views on the Israel-Palestine conflict to find a site of articulation outside of alternative news sources such as *Democracy Now*, *Dissident Voice*, *Counterpunch*, *Common Dreams*, and other online venues.[19] Ironically, alternative news venues often provide citizens with the vital background information and assumptions about important issues. These assumptions are rarely foregrounded in mainstream media coverage. This is especially true for US media coverage of the Middle East and definitely true of the mainstream media's coverage of the Israel-Palestine conflict.[20] Those who begin their scholarly line of inquiry with the assumptions articulated above appear bizarre and out of step with an accepted view, an appearance that stands as testimony to the power of American Zionism, which has structured public consciousness to reflexively support Israel's agenda in the Middle East.

Although the phrase "American Zionism" is never used in the mainstream media, its overwhelming force is evident in civil society.[21] The basic outlooks of the dominant institutions within the United States—social, economic, political, and educational—have been deeply touched by American Zionism, which can be briefly defined as the oneness of spirit and psychology that has obtained between the United States and Israel as settler-colonies. Just as the United States government removed the American Indians from the heartland of the country in the early twentieth century, the Israeli government is in the process of creating unbearable conditions for the Palestinians living in the occupied territories as part of a process that the late Baruch Kimmerling termed "politicide."[22] While the phrase "ethnic cleansing" may be judged to be unnecessarily provocative, it is as accurate to use it in the context of Israel-Palestine as it is to use it in the context of the removal of the Indians from the US mainland during the eighteenth and nineteenth centuries.

The psychological oneness that connects Israel and the United States through this settler-colonial past and present extends to the unprecedented military and diplomatic relationship that has developed between the two countries since the 1967 Six-Day War, when Israel proved its ideological serviceability to the United States in defeating the emergence of Pan-Arab nationalism in the form of Egypt's Gamal Abdel Nasser. Although this war has been described as an Israeli defensive war by Israel's apologists, the New Historians have conclusively determined, by examining the historical archives, that Israel attacked Nasser. It was after its impressive and lightning-fast victory in 1967 over Egypt, Syria, and Jordan that Israel would come to occupy a unique and privileged position in US Middle East policy, moving from a junior partner in the special relationship to a formidable ally whose diplomatic protection within the United Nations and the world community would become the United States' Achilles heel in the region.

The special relationship has been cultivated since Harry S. Truman's presidency, with American Zionists working extremely hard to solidify US and Israeli interests in the Middle East, or least arguing that they are the same. According to Mearsheimer and Walt's *The Israel Lobby and US Foreign Policy*, the United States' interests are no longer served by supporting Israel and that this support is the main reason the United States has a terrorism problem coming out of the Middle East. As Walt and Mearsheimer explained, the power of the Israel Lobby is the only plausible explanation for the United States' continued support of Israeli military aggression against the Palestinians and the Arab states.[23] These established scholars quickly found out that publishing this observation, along with ample empirical evidence, has the potential to create a major scandal within academia and far beyond.

Protecting Israel from criticism in the academy and beyond

The controversy that debates around the history and politics of the Israel-Palestine conflict generate can be attributed to the importance of the Middle East in world affairs. Various interest groups have a stake in preserving a certain narrative about the conflict, understanding that dominating public discourse is a key aspect of controlling the very policies that influence how events play out in the region. Leon Uris's bestselling book, *Exodus*, for example, was expressly commissioned by a New York public relations firm to bolster Israel's image in the United States. *Exodus* has played a key role in framing the ways in which many Americans conceptualize the Israel-Palestine conflict, with the virtuous Israelis living under siege not because of anything they have done or due to any Israeli wrongdoing, but because the villainous Palestinian Arabs do not respect Israel's right to exist as a Jewish state. In this sense, Israelis are portrayed as Ari Ben-Canaan (the protagonist in *Exodus*), struggling against the evil and indigenous forces of the Middle East. As Paul Findley, the former US Senator and Illinois congressman, writes in his *Deliberate Deceptions: Facing the Facts about the U.S.-Israeli Relationship*, "It is obvious that acceptance of fallacies about Israel is not a happenstance. It is the handiwork of many people applying their energy to the task with perseverance and commitment."[24]

One of the most prominent interest groups in the context of forwarding a specific image of Israel's role in the region is the American-Israel Public Affairs Committee, otherwise known as one of the central pillars of the Israel Lobby.[25] As Mearsheimer and Walt document extensively in their book, the American-Israel Public Affairs Committee and its many adjuncts exercise incredible power in shaping US foreign policy in the Middle East, punishing Congressional members who refuse to support Israel's territorial interests and aspirations, in addition to responding to and rebutting media coverage that is critical of Israel. The Lobby's influence extends to the academy, where its satellites monitor the production of scholarship on the Middle East, often marginalizing and spotlighting scholars who do not meet the necessary doctrinal constraints necessitating subservience to Israel's strategic goals in the region.[26] Although Mearsheimer and Walt make a few references in *The Israel Lobby* to academic figures such as Finkelstein, who have been subjected to unusual pressures because of their criticisms of Israel, they do not really go into much depth about specific tenure and promotion cases. To this end, *Out of Bounds* seeks to explore new terrain by—among other things—exploring how the academy has been structured to limit the kinds of arguments that can be successfully made and understood about the Israel-Palestine conflict. This is a very controversial claim, one that is likely to not be well received and strongly resisted; although I will provide evidence as to why I believe this observation is valid. *Out of Bounds*' main questions are as follows:

1   What influence does the Israel Lobby exercise upon a university's internal processes such as its tenure and promotion evaluation of a critic of Israel, when the critic has gained public notoriety because of his or her scholarship or extramural speech?

2   At this historical moment, are public intellectuals and activists able to maintain their independence from concentrated power when it comes to deliberating and weighing in on controversial issues such as the Israel-Palestine conflict?

3   What specific characteristics do those intellectuals who have resisted the veil of censorship that envelops the Israel-Palestine conflict have in common? How have they resisted the pressures and incentives to align with Zionist power?

These questions take on increased importance as the university becomes co-opted by Israel's US supporters. To understand how this co-optation has developed, we must turn to how intellectual restrictions developed around the Question of Palestine in the United States.

The penalties of speaking out

While the Bush administration's War on Terrorism ushered in a new era for the curtailment of civil liberties (as I discuss in Chapter 5), the dimensions of this war were not as severe as those in place at the time of McCarthyite scare of the 1950s. The academic blacklist, the restraints surrounding speech and scholarship, the fear of losing one's job for stating the wrong political views, etc., are more overtly a function of political litmus tests that have been established since 11 September 2001. One can no longer question the specifics of US foreign policy with the same confidence as in the past, assured that the protection of dissenting voices is a mainstay of US democratic society. This is particularly true with respect to exploring the roots of US foreign policy in the Middle East at this historical moment. One aspect of this US Middle East policy is unequivocal and unquestioned support for Israel, as a projection of US military, political, and cultural power as it acts as a Western bridgehead in the Middle East.

Since 1967, Israel has enjoyed a unique immunity in world affairs. This unique immunity has enabled Israel to use its military power in the Middle East to advance its regional goals, particularly with respect to its complete marginalization of the indigenous Palestinian population in the occupied territories, which has been conducted with crucial US support. This crucial diplomatic, and economic support that the United States provides to Israel emerges from the historic special relationship, which is on the verge of fraying. Nonetheless, this special relationship, unparalleled in modern history, continues to create extraordinary strain between the United States and its Arab allies. The intellectual dimensions of the special relationship have not been adequately theorized, leaving out a complete picture of how pervasively Israeli intelligence has penetrated the US domestic sphere, including the academy, as part of a widespread surveillance operation. An inadequate understanding of this Zionist surveillance of the US civil space makes the production of propaganda promoting Israel's illegitimate (meaning violent) suppression of the national aspirations of the Palestinian people all the more alarming. Academic scholarship has contributed to this disciplining of the American public space with respect to Israel's propaganda needs while marginalizing scholars who do not conform to the ideological line.

The academy's complicity in silencing the narrative of Palestinian oppression, and the relevant facts surrounding the Question of Palestine, has required the formation of an extensive belief system that has yet to be fully uncovered, interrogated, and explored.[27] The rise of American Zionism has conquered not only literal territory but also cognitive space. The US-Israel special relationship has "structured" perceptions quite effectively (like any good hegemony does), concealing the violence that has created the facts on the ground establishing reality in the occupied territories. In other words, the US-Israel special relationship could not have been built without academic assistance, surveillance, and censorship. That there is a relationship between intellectual labor and the material world was one of Marx and Engels' central insights in *The German Ideology*: "The ruling ideas are nothing more than the ideal expression of the dominant material relationships grasped as ideas; hence of the relationships which make one class the ruling one, therefore, the ideas of its dominance."[28] Foreign policy decisions are guided by the dominant material relationships that obtain within a society.

If foreign policy decisions are being made because of the flawed conclusions of politically motivated scholarship, or if such scholarship gains mainstream acceptance precisely because it coincides with the tyranny of public opinion, or the tyranny of an influential set of policymakers, one is left then to examine the relationship between the academy, governmental needs, and state aims. In other words, how do the political demands of a particular historical moment condition the production of scholarship about important foreign policy questions? For example, why did the US government turn to Bernard Lewis, Fouad Ajami, and Fareed Zakaria for their supposed expert advice about whether the United States would succeed in its invasion of Iraq and the prospects of a promising reconstruction? The answer is obvious: all three provided politically useful conclusions to the Bush administration as it pushed for the invasion. The quagmire and resulting civil war in Iraq led many people, even high-standing governmental officials, to question why the US government alleged that Saddam Hussein possessed weapons of mass destruction, when reliable evidence clearly suggested he did not, and grossly miscalculated the strength of the Sunni insurgency that erupted in June 2003 after major operations were declared to be over.[29] For example, retired US army generals, Anthony Zinni, William Odom, and John Battiste, questioned the Bush administration's judgment in pushing for the invasion, arguing that the administration's behavior ranged from "'true dereliction, negligence and irresponsibility' to 'lying, incompetence and corruption.'"[30] A more compelling explanation for the Bush administration's decision to push for the invasion can be found in the power of the Israeli Lobby.

How large of a role did the Israeli government, and the infamous Israel Lobby, play in moving the United States toward war in Iraq? Mearsheimer and Walt argued that the Lobby was a necessary but not in itself sufficient cause in the push for the United States to go into Iraq. In other words, in their view, absent the influence of the Lobby, the United States would not have invaded Iraq.[31] As they argued, drawing upon the views of Israeli military strategist Shlomo Brohm, Israel was happy to see the United States invade Iraq, with the understanding that the United States would next invade Iran and Syria. Scholars such as Fouad Ajami and Bernard Lewis, professors at Johns Hopkins and Princeton respectively, were key advisors to the architects of the Iraq war such as Paul Wolfowitz and Douglas Feith. Acting as long-time consultants to the State Department in the context of explaining Arabs and Arab cultures, Ajami and Lewis have often provided intellectual justifications for treating Arab peoples as simply standing in the way of modernization and Western development.[32] As Adam Shatz noted in his 2003 *Nation* article ("The Native Informant"), "Ajami's unique role in American political life has been to unpack the unfathomable mysteries of the Arab and Muslim world and to help sell America's wars in the region." This role has been adopted by many policy intellectuals within the beltway with respect to unifying Israel's strategic interests with those of United States.

The Project for the New American Century's connections to organizations such as the Washington Institute for Near East Policy (WINEP), the Jewish Institute for National Security Affairs (JINSA), and the American-Israel

Political Action Committee (AIPAC) confirmed that the United States and Israel sought to remake the world order through the flouting of international law and the use of Carl Schmitt's "The Law of Exception," whereby the strongest states are exempt from the regular conventions of the international community in times of crisis or social upheaval, for example 9/11. The promotion of democracy and the expansion of market economies in such contexts often serve as a useful pretext and cover for aims of war. Think tanks such as the American Enterprise Institute and Hoover Institution have been fighting Gramsci's "wars of position" for nearly two decades, creating the necessary epistemological frameworks through which the American public has comprehended the events of the last 30 years in the Middle East.

There has been deliberate obfuscation within mainstream academic scholarship about Israel's role in the region, and, contrary to perception, Israel's strategic aims have had a large influence on US foreign policy in the Middle East for some time. Israel is often presented as a gendarme of the United States, with the United States calling the shots about policy. One must entertain the possibility that Israeli governments since 1967, in conjunction with the Israel Lobby, have played a key role in determining US foreign policy in the Middle East. Central to this effort requires conflating Jews, Judaism, Zionism, and Israel, situating Israel as the spokesperson and defender of the Jewish people, while it in fact represents a site of extreme militarism and poses a danger to the ethical tenets of Judaism.

Jews, Judaism, Zionism, and Israel

Separating the history and events of the Holocaust from the history and events of the Israel-Palestine conflict is a difficult task. Since the Zionist movement was able to capitalize upon the suffering of European Jews during the Holocaust in brokering with the Great Powers for a Jewish state in Palestine, the history of Jews who suffered anti-Semitic persecution in Europe has been inappropriately fused with the history of Jews in Palestine. Zionism, which is incorrectly viewed as Jewish nationalism, promotes the linking of two Jewish histories—the history of Jews in Europe who suffered during the Holocaust and the history of those Jews who settled in Palestine and their descendants. Therefore, the effective bringing together of these two distinctly different sets of Jews through the prism of Zionism enables a productive conflation: There is only one way to be a true Jew—the Zionist way. The term "anti-Semitism," which was coined by Wilhelm Marr in the late 1800s, refers to the hatred European gentiles directed toward Jews. European anti-Semitism is distinct from Arab anti-Semitism because European anti-Semitism was/is based on Gentile repulsion, whereas Arab anti-Semitism is perhaps better described as springing from territorial displacement and religious difference. In the context of the Israel-Palestine conflict, however, hatred directed toward, and resistance against, Jewish occupiers of Palestinian land is viewed through the prism of anti-Semitism. The attempt to frame Palestinian resistance against territorial dispossession as being based in the same European anti-Semitism preceding Hitler's extermination program of the Jews of Europe is motivated by the Zionist goal of portraying the Palestinians as the Nazi's inheritors. Israel's apologists frequently cite the supposed connection between the Grand Mufti of Jerusalem and Hitler, arguing that the Grand Mufti traveled frequently to Germany to meet with the Führer about how to deal with increased levels of Jewish immigration to Palestine. However these apologists often avoid addressing the direct collaboration between Zionism and Nazism. In the United States, the avoidance of certain facts, along with the promotion of certain myths, can be attributed to the propaganda needs of American Zionism.

The domination of the American public sphere by American Zionism represents an impressive feat, unmatched in recent history. Zionism is frequently referred to as Jewish nationalism in that it provides the philosophical basis for the return to Zion, the historical home of the Jewish people, a return to the Second Temple destroyed by the Romans in 70 A.D. If we conceptualize Zionism as an attempt to advance Jewish chosenness, it is clear that within Zionism's discursive economy non-Jews are granted an antagonistic status. This view pervades Zionist thinking, which places Palestinian Arabs outside the realm of moral concern. How Zionism became such a powerful and all-encompassing ideology requires an extended analysis, focusing on its ability to influence the realms of foreign policy, domestic politics, mass culture, and the religious–political imagination of the entire West. The development and evolution of Zionism, as a discourse of power, into and throughout the intellectual and political domains of the United States represent an ideological triumph.

Apologists for Israel's territorial expansion and its conquest of the Palestinians in the occupied territories are trying to effect a transformation in thinking on several levels—social, political, epistemological, and theological. The revolutionary changes we have witnessed in our culture, particularly within academic culture (the Academic Bill of Rights, Campus Watch, David Project, Discover the Network, etc.) are directly tied to ensuring that criticism of Israel will rise to the level of a punishable offense. The wider assault on academic freedom, which has had particularly chilling effects on those interested in US foreign policy in the Middle East, is meant to limit the scope of acceptable academic inquiry. Professors who support the Palestinians of the West Bank and Gaza in their fight for self-determination make themselves particularly vulnerable inside and outside the university. The speed with which pro-Israel advocacy groups sprung up after the Second Intifada and 9/11 is quite remarkable. By converting the United States' war on terror to that of Israel's, these American Zionist groups enforce an acceptable "discursive code" concerning what Israel does to the Palestinians, almost always with US arms and munitions.

The United States public has yet to receive an honest and critical assessment of the deeply troubling ways the Israeli military has gone about sowing terror throughout the world, not just in the Middle East. As Benjamin Beit-Hallahmi's *The Israeli Connection* and Jane Hunter's *Israeli Foreign Policy* demonstrate, Israel's support of dangerous regimes in South America, South Africa, and throughout the Middle East suggests that Israel does the United States' military and intelligence work in various global theaters.[33] As Cheryl Rubenberg writes in her *Israel and the American National Interest*,

> The United States has realized two advantages from its close association with Israel: the collaboration between the Israeli intelligence service (the Mossad) and the Central Intelligence Agency, and Israel's battlefield testing of American weapons. The cooperation between the intelligence services has been extensive—throughout Europe, Africa, Asia, and Central and South America as well as the Middle East.[34]

These aspects of the US-Israel special relationship remain unknown within the US public sphere.

Policing the Question of Palestine

The academy is really the final site of contestation within which defenders of Israel's policies of brutal repression of the Palestinians in the occupied territories have yet to exert full control, hence the supposed controversies of the last 9 years at Columbia, Berkeley, Harvard, Yale, Duke, and many other campuses across the country. The little dissent against Israel's conduct in the Middle East, which has been registered mainly in Middle East Studies Departments, often by professors who are themselves of Arab or Arab-Palestinian descent, has attempted to resist and counteract the Israelization of the college curriculum, a process that seeks to maintain the dominance of Zionism's narrative about the Israel-Palestine conflict. The funding of Chairs in Holocaust and Israeli Studies by major benefactors has made it very difficult to bring the Palestinian viewpoint into the college classroom, as university administrators understand that the funding of these chairs and continued donor giving come with strings attached, even if ultimatums for the funding are never articulated. The infusion of Zionist money into US universities has had a detrimental effect on the prospects for open debate about the Israel-Palestine conflict, as this patronage inevitably requires presenting Israel in a positive light, no matter how terrible its misdeeds. Indeed, that there have been such widespread propaganda campaigns, directed at scholars of Palestinian origin such as Nadia Abu-Haj and Joseph Massad in attempts to deny them tenure, signals that Zionism is in crisis.[35] The merest crack in the consensus that US support for Israel is in the US national interest could jeopardize the dominance of Zionism's narrative.

Academic freedom and the Question of Palestine

Out of Bounds seeks to analyze how certain types of scholarship and political orientations toward the Israel-Palestine conflict are placed "out of bounds" with respect to academic freedom protections. Scholarship perceived as questioning the legitimacy of Israel as a "Jewish state" and characterizing Israel as engaging in a settler-colonial project in its dispossession of the Palestinian population living under Israeli occupation is frequently denounced as "unscholarly," "polemical," and "propaganda." My experience with this issue comes from observing, over nearly a 10-year period, the relentless attacks that have been directed against Norman Finkelstein's scholarship, which addresses the international consensus on the conflict and the United States' and Israel's rejection of that consensus, although Finkelstein has been subjected to techniques of academic mainstream media exclusion for almost 30 years. My question was a simple one: What is it that Finkelstein writes in his scholarship that necessitates such an adverse—and in my view—unfair reaction?

Finkelstein, who has never flinched in combating some of the most powerful cultural icons and academics in the world, is unrelenting in his critiques of Zionist Jewry, which plays a vital and supportive role in Israel's war of aggression against the Palestinians living under occupation. Finkelstein's journey has been unique, but also utterly predictable, as his challenge to the dominant frameworks governing how US citizens understand the conflict in the Middle East is in fact a wholesale rejection of a conventional wisdom that has obtained since Israel's creation in 1948. That framework has necessitated viewing Israel as a beleaguered country surrounded by a sea of Arab hostility that is not explained by what Israel does, but instead because of what Israel is as a Jewish state in the middle of the Islamic world.

An army of talented propagandists have defended Israel's settler-colonial project for the last 60 years through underhanded means. As M. Shahid Alam argues in his *Israeli Exceptionalism*, Israel's settler project was disguised as a national liberation movement for Jews. This Zionist masquerade which has not been entirely understood needs to be completely analyzed to fully comprehend the present historical predicament. The charade will continue until Israel has annexed the West Bank, at which time it will then formally declare what its borders are. Israel's violation of international law, with crucial US support, will continue as long as Israel can convince Western powers that it is in a war for its very survival. Israel will reject any and all calls for Palestinian statehood, as it and the United States did in September of 2011 at the United Nations. The only Palestinian state Israel will accept is one that it ultimately controls, as was the supposed Palestinian state that Yasir Arafat was offered at Camp David in September 2000. As Shlomo Ben-Ami has noted, in reflecting on why it is incorrect to view Arafat as the villain at Camp David, "If I were a Palestinian leader, I would have never accepted what was offered at Camp David," as it was in fact an Israeli matrix of control that would have considerably strengthened Israel's grip on Palestinian territory. Despite the misrepresentations of how the negotiations at Camp David actually played out in Dennis Ross's *The Missing Peace* and other accounts, Camp David's failure could not be blamed on Arafat. Furthermore, as even US negotiator Aaron David Miller has admitted, he and others on the US side far too often acted as Israel's lawyer.

The factual record, as discussed in Clayton Swisher's *The Truth About Camp David*, was distorted within the US media, in 2001 as the narrative of Arafat's intransigence in the face of Barak's supposedly generous offer at Camp David. According to Swisher, Bill Clinton and other US negotiators pinned the blame for Camp David's failure on Arafat, although they fully realized that Arafat (in fact, no Palestinian leader) could accept what Barak and Clinton offered, as Shlomo Ben-Ami has acknowledged. Although Ross, Martin Indyk, and several others have alleged that the blame for Camp David's failure could be laid at Arafat's feet, other prominent figures such as Jimmy Carter have stated quite the opposite.

The controversy around Camp David highlights, quite vividly, that knowledge claims (seemingly all knowledge claims) about the Israel-Palestine conflict are the objects of contention and controversy. The reason for this is a result of the frameworks used to interpret the action within the Israel-Palestine conflict. If one adopts the anti-colonial position, believing that Israel is engaged in a colonial war against the Palestinians, as a number of progressive thinkers have suggested, one draws on international law and human rights reports to condemn Israel's occupation. On the other hand, if one views Israel as engaged in a fight for its very survival against extremist groups such as Hamas, which are supposedly seeking to destroy it because it is a Jewish state—then, Israel is the ultimate haven for the Jewish people in the event of another Holocaust. These conflicting paradigms produce sharply divergent readings of the meaning of day-to-day acts of violence in the Middle East. We must analyze these divergent frameworks if we are to understand the pitched controversies that ensue when representations are made about questions of victimhood and justice in the Middle East. Depending upon the framework employed, either the Palestinians or the Israelis can be positioned as the ultimate victims, with justice residing with the favored party. It is in this context that debates about academic freedom in the Israel-Palestine conflict play themselves out.

Those who question and problematize the Jewish martyrdom/victim narrative find themselves facing serious barriers to the dissemination of their work. While Martin Kramer, David Horowitz, and Alan Dershowitz (and others) argue that the Left has created an environment within the academy that is completely anti-Israel, the reality is quite different: a number of Israel's supporters hold key academic and cultural positions, enabling them to control conversations about the Israel-Palestine conflict, blocking scholarly views that question Israel's dominance of the victim/martyrdom narrative to silence the Palestinian perspective. Israel must maintain its victim status; this is ensured by maintaining the "Israel under siege" paradigm. The notion that US Middle East Studies Programs are overrun by pro-Palestinian, anti-Israel zealots seeking to undermine the legitimacy of Israel at every available opportunity is simply false. In fact, the university setting is overwhelmingly pro-Israel, preventing the slightest understanding of the Palestinians' victim status in the conflict from developing. With respect to the Question of Palestine, various strategies of containment have attempted to turn the tables on critics of Israel. The most visible form of surveillance in this respect can be seen in the rise of the so-called new anti-Semitism, wherein charges of anti-Semitism are leveled against those who criticize Israel.

The New Anti-Semitism portrays scholars as anti-Semitic when they criticize Israel as the Jewish state, stigmatizing dissidents who are committed to questioning the United States' special relationship with Israel. Clearly, there are parties within the university who would prefer that the dimensions of the special relationship not be explored.[36] A number of watchdog institutions within the US public sphere seek to punish these dissident intellectuals who are attempting to pierce the veil of this veritable taboo surrounding the US-Israel special relationship. In brief, these watchdog organizations seek to curtail the American citizen's ability to comprehend and discuss the Question of Palestine.

Historically, Zionism and imperialism have worked hand in hand. Zionism has covered up its imperialist footprint, recasting itself as a liberation movement when it is in fact a colonialist one. This is the Zionist masquerade, an attempt to recast a colonial movement as a Jewish independence movement. Scholarship seeking to expose this masquerade will be deemed of bounds, hence the focus of this book: What are the scholarly protocols governing the production of academic views on the Israel-Palestine conflict? This is not so much a function of interrogating whether a scholarly etiquette surrounds scholarly discussion about the Israel-Palestine conflict as it is about interrogating how the cause of Israel (Israelism) came to achieve doctrinal supremacy within the dominant US academic institutions. Figures such as John Mearsheimer, Stephen Walt, and Ian Lustick—the author of *Trapped in the War on Terror* and *For the Lord and the Land*—have challenged the dominant narrative about the Israel-Palestine conflict, suffering a certain level of abuse and vilification as a consequence, even though their views are consistent with international law and the conclusions of Israel's New Historians and terrorism experts. This is a troubling paradox: what is in fact scholarly sound is controversial because public perceptions have been so thoroughly conditioned by propaganda designed to protect Israel's violations of international law. The discourse framing Palestinian resistance against Israel's occupation as legitimate is considered extremely dangerous to Israel's supporters, as it humanizes Palestinians and indicts Israeli actions as colonial actions. This framing is simply unacceptable to mainstream opinion. For example, Alan Dershowitz intones in his *The Case for Israel* that

> [t]hose who absurdly claim that the Jewish refugees who immigrated to Palestine in the last decades of the nineteenth century were the "tools" of European imperialism must answer the following question: For whom

were these socialists and idealists working? Were they planting the flag of the hated czar of Russia or the anti-Semitic regimes of Poland or Lithuania? These refugees wanted nothing to do with the countries from which they fled to avoid pogroms and religious discrimination. They came to Palestine without any of the weapons of imperialism. They brought with them few guns or other means of conquest. Their tools were rakes and hoes. The land they cultivated was not taken away from its rightful owners by force or confiscated by colonial law. It was purchased, primarily from absentee landlords and real estate speculators, at fair or often exorbitant prices.[37]

It is understood that Israel was advancing the imperial aims of one or more Great Powers. Why do Israel's apologists work so diligently to deny the connection to the Great Powers? It is essential to prove that Palestine was uninhabited and underdeveloped prior to Israeli colonization. If there are no Palestinian people, as demonstrated by "the recent in-migration" argument advanced by Joan Peters and others, then the Palestinian cause and its claims of injustice can be dismissed as illegitimate.

A great deal of scholarship has attempted to demonstrate that the Palestinians Refugee Question is contrived, that the Palestinian people are not a people, but simply a random assortment of Arabs that wish to express grievances against Israel, appropriate its wealth, and to destroy Israel as a Jewish State. It is for this reason that there have been such massive efforts to downplay or delegitimize the insights of Israel's New Historians. As Ephraim Karsh argues in his *Fabricating Israeli History*,

> My own research on the history and politics of the Middle East had led me to question some of the central claims of the "new historians," as well as the extent of their familiarity with the wider historical context of their research; but I ascribed these differences to contending approaches and interpretations—a common and constructive attribute of a scholarly discourse. The possibility of falsification of documentation by these revisionist historians had never occurred to me: not merely because of the presumed existence of elementary academic integrity, but also because such distortion would have undermined the foundations of scholarly and/ or scientific research, which must necessarily draw on earlier studies by way of accumulating an aggregate body of knowledge. (xviii)

Naturally, these revisionist views, as outlined in Ze'ev Sternhill *The Founding Myths of Israel* and Simha Flapan's *The Birth of Israel*, challenge the central founding histories about how Israel came into existence. Sachar and Lacquer, for example, tie Israel's birth very clearly to the condition of world Jewry in the wake of the Holocaust while completely downplaying the country's colonial origins. Acknowledging these origins would entail admitting that a grave injustice has been committed against the Palestinian population in and through the creation of the Jewish State. To avoid such a potential catastrophe, Israel's defenders are forced to point out that the Israel-Palestine conflict is the main front of the larger Arab-Israeli conflict. There are twenty-two Arab nations, as this argument goes, which should be able to accommodate the supposedly displaced Palestinian Arabs; therefore, surely there should be enough room in the Middle East for a tiny Jewish state, the bedrock of Western values in this vast sea of Arabia. The problem with this argument is that it denies the basic right of self-determination to the Palestinian, rejecting their agency as a people separate from other Arabs. While Zionism asserts that the rights of the Jewish people, wherever they might be, must take precedence over the rights of the indigenous population, Palestinian nationalism is (1) denied points of articulation and (2) is positioned as a negation of the Jewish state's supposed right to exist. Furthermore, Palestinian nationalism is often positioned in relation to Islamic extremism and terrorism.

In an inversion of reality, Palestinian rejection of Israel's right to exist as a Jewish State is posited as the sole reason for the lack of a resolution for nearly six decades of violence in the conflict. However, as Zalman Amit and Daphna Levi argue in their *Israeli Rejectionism: A Hidden Agenda in the Middle East Peace Process*, Israeli rejectionism has in fact been the norm, as Israel refuses to recognize the Palestinian leadership as a genuine partner, preferring instead to use its military dominance to reject the requirements of international law and the international consensus for a just resolution of the Palestinian Question. As they note,

> We were peripherally aware that the conquest of most of mandatory Palestine occurred at a high cost to the Jewish population. We were even aware of the fact that the war demolished the Arab community in the country and much of its population disappeared almost overnight. Along with the rest of our Jewish community, we convinced ourselves it was *entirely their fault. They* did not accept the UN partition plan; aided by the armies of five independent states, *they* attacked a one-day old state. We considered their defeat a justified miracle. Besides, we believed we never really forced them to leave. Their leaders had forced them to abandon their homes in order to return victorious accompanied by the armies of their brethren from the neighboring Arab countries.[38]

Although Amit and Levi were initially committed to defending the claims about the impossibility of a resolution with the Palestinians advanced by Zionist propaganda they were exposed to while growing up, they achieved an epiphany:

> The contention that Israel was the party opposed to peace, and had always been opposed to peace, initially sounded outrageous. But it was true, everything we had believed in since we joined the youth movement could not be true. It is difficult for adults to be forced to re-examine all their

past convictions, but all the indications pointed in this direction. When a historic opportunity presented itself to end the conflict and normalize its relationship with the neighbors, Israel sabotaged the opportunity. We had to face the possibility that Israel was simply not interested in making peace with its neighbors.[39]

Revelations such as Amit's and Levit's about the Israel-Palestine conflict, however, should not surprise us—they are the result of intellectual suppression and censorship in the public space.

Intertwined with the Question of Palestine is the question of intellectual freedom, the freedom to question what has previously been prohibited. Of course, within the academy, intellectual freedom is academic freedom, the freedom to pursue the academic profession within the bounds of the profession. However, as I discussed earlier, academic freedom has been redefined to protect the powerful, stigmatizing dissenting thought as unworthy of professional or institutional protection. This redefinition of academic freedom positions this dissenting thought as unprofessional and because it does not fall within disciplinary parameters it is un-disciplinary. This move to present dissenting thought as outside recognized bodies of knowledge and as "advocacy" is simultaneously a move to withdraw academic freedom protections from such thought. In other words, criticism of Israel and the legitimacy of Palestinian calls for self-determination cannot be considered accepted academic knowledge within the current discursive landscape, confirming Foucault's observation about how power, knowledge, and truth always work together.

As the American university has been put for sale to the highest bidder, this freedom to question troubling social hegemonies has been restricted by the profit motive, leading academics to take very conservative stances—or to completely avoid—controversial questions, especially on extremely sensitive topics such as the Israel-Palestine conflict, which has the potential to offend key donors to the university. Pro-Israel forces exercise extraordinary influence upon the contemporary American university, and as a result, can place pressure on a university to remove a scholar who becomes too outspoken about Palestinian self-determination. The attempts of pro-Israel advocacy groups to derail the tenure cases of Joseph Massad, Nadi Abu-Haj, and Norman Finkelstein are to the point. University administrators are well aware of how a single scholar writing and working on Israel-Palestine can be a point of friction for the public relations arm of the university. Subtle efforts are frequently undertaken behind the scenes to remove these scholars from the university. The public relations aspect of the university's ties with external constituencies cannot be underestimated, especially when it comes to appeasing key Zionist donors who are very sensitive about public criticisms of Israel. How an administration's concerns about these donors' sensitivities actually enter into actual decision-making is subtle and perhaps difficult to document. While the role of Zionist philanthropy in American politics and within mainstream institutions is well known, it is reticently discussed.

Many believe that the academy should represent and teach well established and accepted knowledge, knowledge recognized within a disciplinary framework. Interdisciplinary work that has express political goals can lead to the interference of lay boards and other external parties in university business, especially when the topic of the scholar's research or extramural utterance touches upon a particularly controversial issue, as the cases of Ward Churchill and Sami Al-Arian suggest. If the stakes are high enough, university administrators will act unilaterally to dismiss a faculty member with no regard for due process or faculty rights.

What use is academic freedom in this context if it cannot be deployed to protect the scholar advancing a dissenting position on a hugely crucial issue? The concept of academic freedom no longer enables advocacy and activism, as academic freedom belongs to the university to protect itself instead of to the scholar to pursue difficult lines of inquiry. To receive academic freedom protections, scholars must conduct recognized disciplinary work or they will be marginalized within the profession. This notion that academic freedom emerges in and through the collective body of a discipline has an inevitable tendency to contain and isolate dissident thought. Academic freedom is not about freedom at all, it's about conformity. There is a paradox here though: if there is a consensus on the resolution of the Israel-Palestine conflict, as yearly UN votes indicate, and if Finkelstein and others are simply reporting on and supporting the UN consensus, how can what they write be considered controversial, exotic, or representative of a dissident position? What they write about and advocate on behalf of must be rejected as bizarre. The demands of Israeli propaganda (hasbara) require that reality be turned on its head, necessitating the creation of an accepted framework that deems any and all criticisms of Israel as expressions of the New Anti-Semitism; a cottage industry has arisen to explain this New Anti-Semitism's rise. Indeed, this cottage industry is devoted to sowing confusion about the Israel-Palestine conflict, although none should exist.

An open debate about the Question of Palestine (the Israel-Palestine conflict) is important to the future of American democracy. This debate has not happened in our public sphere because open, frank discussions about the Israel-Palestine conflict and US Middle East policy have been out of bounds—nearly *verboten*—in the United States as a result of the highly effective special-interest group monitoring by American Zionist organizations.[40] A free and candid discussion about the historical and diplomatic dimensions of the Israel-Palestine conflict is in the best interest of our democratic process. To launch such a counter-hegemonic movement requires developing a full assessment of specific obstacles blocking an open consideration of the relevant issues in the Israel-Palestine conflict, especially the problem of Israeli rejectionism.

Beyond mainstream prohibitions on openly discussing the Middle East, there have been specific difficulties in studying and researching the Israel-Palestine conflict in the US academy, despite the principle of academic freedom. These challenges make the discursive terrain for those seeking to write critically about Israel-Palestine extremely hazardous and risky, resulting in a heavily slanted demand toward the needs of concentrated power; concentrated power firmly resides in the hands of Israel's supporters, Jewish and Christian. This pro-Israel bias heavily influences the operation of the American university, to an embarrassing degree. Administrative structures are heavily slanted toward pushing the pro-Israel line, largely because of the social-political power of American Zionist Jewry. While this might appear to be a bold claim, it is one that I firmly believe after several years of reflecting on, and being involved in, academic debates about the Palestinian predicament. Indeed, American democratic processes have been fundamentally corrupted by political groups bent on controlling the American citizen's access to important information about the Israel-Palestine conflict and the Middle East more generally.[41] This situation does not bode well for anyone, regardless of how one sees the truth in debates about the central issues around the conflict: Israel's demographic makeup, compensation and the Right of Return for Palestinian refugees, the living conditions of Palestinians living under occupation, expanding Israeli settlements, the legal illegitimacy of Israel's separation "barrier," and the status of East Jerusalem. Although these issues are of vital importance to the future stability of the Middle East and to the prospect of developing a long lasting peace between Israel and the Palestinians, Israel's supporters distort these important issues by insisting that Israel's security needs must take precedence over Palestinian human rights and a clear claim to redress for long standing injustices since Israel's founding.

Why is the Question of Palestine so difficult to discuss in a substantive and serious way in the United States?[42] Why are the relevant issues within the debate about the resolution of the Israel-Palestine conflict "out of bounds" so to speak? By "out of bounds," I mean the parameters informing debates about the Question of Palestine are quite different and more tightly regulated than the parameters structuring other types of debates about controversial issues of serious public concern. This difference is not merely a function of the fact that competing views about where the fault lies in the Israel-Palestine conflict are so opposed to one another, but more importantly because of the kinds of surveillance shaping the discussions themselves. Zionist students spying on professors, propaganda films designed specifically to target Palestinian professors in Columbia University's Middle East and Asian Languages Department, and Zionist administrators—who have an eye on their university's bottom line, particularly when it comes to appeasing the ideological views of major donors—seeking to remove faculty members who are outspoken critics of Israel, are very much a part of the contemporary academic landscape in the United States. This Zionist surveillance even extends to every aspect of the academic realm, where one would expect a greater tolerance of views about the conflict that do not conform to dominant narratives pitting the supposed Arab Goliath against the supposed little David of Israel.

Trapped in clichés

Clichés predominate in discussions about the Israel-Palestine conflict in the United States. Clichés such as "Israel has a right to exist" or "Until the relevant parties each agree to work toward peace, there can be no resolution of the conflict" are commonly uttered and—more importantly—believed as corresponding to the reality of what is propelling the conflict as it moves into its 67th year. We are told that Israel is in a fight for its very existence, subjected to defamation, demonization, and de-legitimization, and targeted for destruction—as the Jewish state. Even intellectuals, according to this line of thinking, have lost all sense of proportion and are zealous in their desire to condemn Israel while turning a blind eye to the transgressions of other states. The United Nations, the European states, and nearly one hundred and fifty countries are supposedly bent on tallying up Israel's wrongdoings. Israel's defenders insist that the political forces arrayed against Israel are anti-Semitic, suggesting that any attempts to frame concerns about how Israel's militarism affects the stability of the Middle East (or the pernicious effects of Israel's occupation on the aspirations of the Palestinians) are really manifestations of anti-Semitism. In such a context, the psychologies and motives of Israel's critics, Jewish and non-Jewish, are probed for anti-Semitic animus. What does it mean to say someone is a critic of Israel? What is one being critical of? Israel's existence? Its oppression of another people? Its people and institutions? Critics of Israel's critics never seem to articulate whether the criticism of Israel might in fact be justified.

One might point to the concept of academic freedom to explain why one would expect critical debate and uncensored commentary about the Question of Palestine in the US academy. However, this has not been the case in the United States due to the successful efforts of various constituencies within and external to the university; these constituencies have been committed to not only defaming those who seek to tell the Palestinian narrative of dispossession and loss, as well as Israel's large role in this, but seem bent on introducing false information into the debate to confuse the public. The reason critical discussions about the Israel-Palestine conflict are often placed out of bounds within the US public sphere is the result of the demands of Zionist power in the United States. This situation tells us as much about the political structures shaping public discourse in United States, as it does about the volatility of the Israel-Palestine conflict itself. While there has been ample discussion of the power of the Israel Lobby in the United States, less attention has been paid to how the American citizens' "structures of attitude and reference"[43] have been conditioned by factors within the domestic political sphere that produce sympathy for Israel's colonial-settler project.

While one might be tempted to simply identify Israel's positive portrayal within the US public space as resulting from a multipronged propaganda campaign to condition American citizens to adopt perspectives favorable to Israel's image. I think the processes informing the operation of Israeli propaganda is more subtle, operating at a subconscious level. From the time they are children, US citizens receive a multitude of messages through religious indoctrination, community affiliations, advertising, and film, leading them to identify Jews as "the chosen people," who deserve protection and respect.[44] As part of this cultural conditioning, Israel has come to represent the interests of the Jewish people, although it represents a Zionist, not a Jewish, project. Through this ideological conditioning process, the US public sphere has been primed to support Israel.[45]

A highly protective discourse has been created around—and about Israel—to hide the reality of its ethnic cleansing program against the Palestinians in the occupied territories. This discourse contributes to the creation of facts on the ground as Israel expands its settlement blocs, essentially fictionalizing the truth to serve a constructed image. This image obscures the brutality of Israel's occupation, the audacity of its military adventurism, Israel's deceptiveness as a rogue state, and the villainy residing at the heart of Zionism. Tell a lie often enough and it becomes truth—this has been the story of Zionism.[46]

As several authors, including Paul Findley, Alfred Lilienthal, and Stephen Green have amply demonstrated, Israel is also a distinct discourse in American life—a discourse nurtured and promoted by many tireless hands in government, media, and professional circles. As an object of devotion, Israel permeates a number of important spheres within US civil society, insidiously shaping policies and attitudes to ensure Israeli exceptionalism.[47] The ideological discourses around Israel subtly promote Zionist supremacy while also justifying Israel's settler-colonial project, placing both out of bounds for serious analysis and scrutiny. This protection has been taken to an almost unbelievable level. For example, federal law is now being marshaled to protect Israel against criticism, under the cover of shielding Jewish faculty and students against anti-Semitism.[48]

The question of motive

Far too often scholars who write about the Israel-Palestine conflict from a critical perspective, which is often interpreted as "pro-Palestinian," find their motives (political, psychological, etc.) questioned; as if simply expressing an interest in the topic somehow demonstrates someone's unconscious anti-Semitism. "Tendentious," "sloppy," "unbalanced," "partisan," "quotes taken out of context," "facts taken selectively and distorted" are the usual labels/ characterizations used to smear those writing about the relevant issues.[49] This is an unacceptable situation, contributing to the corruption of American public discourse. Creating impossible standards for those seeking to broach difficult and controversial issues about the US-Israel special relationship is not only undemocratic but is in fact part of a distinct strategy to prevent a discussion about the relevant issues from taking place.

The derogatory labels that have been applied to fair-minded individuals such as Jimmy Carter, Stephen Walt, and John Mearsheimer since the publication of their respective publications, *Palestine: Peace, Not Apartheid* and *The Israel Lobby and US Foreign Policy*, are not only libelous, but also indicative of a distinct strategy to block an open discussion about the parameters of Zionist power in the United States. What they report in their books about Israel's role in blocking the implementation of a comprehensive peace settlement in the Middle East is quite correct. The fact that they are correct leaves their detractors with only one strategy: smear the messenger.[50] In addition to being unjustly smeared as "anti-Semites," serious commentators on the Israel-Palestine conflict are inevitably framed as being "apologists for Islamofacism" by academic watchdogs such as Daniel Pipes, David Horowitz, and Steven Plaut, who frequently write for publications such as *FrontPage Magazine*.

With respect to developing an understanding of Islamic extremism and terrorism, inquiry has been foreclosed by those seeking to advance the argument that the enemy is irrational, incapable of being understood, and hopelessly committed to self-destruction. This characterization of Islamacist ideology, according to those who promote it, obviates looking at the Islamacists' professed motives for committing acts of violence and destruction since the motives themselves are spurious and largely irrelevant. In other words, there is no point in trying to rationally analyze why Islamicists do what they do since the whole religion is largely irrational. Academics seeking to find explanations for why Osama bin Laden and his followers sought to commit terrorism against the United States and its allies were portrayed as engaging in treason. Scholars who examine the professed reasons and motives for the 9/11 attacks are often viewed as agreeing with Osama bin Laden's critique of US foreign policy in the Middle East, particularly the United States' support for Israeli governmental policy in the occupied territories. Opening up possibilities and spaces for critique of US foreign policy in the Middle East poses a threat to the national security state, because if large numbers of the citizenry begin to question governmental policy in the region and refused to support its repressive policies, elite interests committed to supporting Israel's role in the global weapons industry would be threatened.[51]

Coming to consciousness about the Question of Palestine

Norman Finkelstein's tenure denial at DePaul University in June of 2007 left many observers of the American academic scene (as well as other

spectators) aghast at DePaul's seeming complete disregard for due process
and academic freedom protections that serious scholars are supposed to
enjoy. Despite overwhelming faculty support, Finkelstein was denied tenure
on indefensible grounds because of external pressures that should have been
ignored in any serious academic process. Alan Dershowitz, Frankfurter
Professor of Harvard Law, developed a keen interest in the outcome of the
case in late 2003, when Finkelstein publicized his critique of Dershowitz's
The Case for Israel on Amy Goodman's *Democracy Now* and other outlets.
Ultimately, Finkelstein published his critique of Dershowitz's *The Case for
Israel* in a book entitled *Beyond Chutzpah: The Misuse of Anti-Semitism and
the Abuse of History*, which was published by the University of California
Press. Dershowitz appeared to be seeking to prevent its publication, arguing
that the University of California Press did not use the usual peer-review
process in vetting it because it was ideologically invested in Finkelstein's
supposed Left critique of Israel's human rights record.[52]

The details surrounding Dershowitz's effort throughout the summer of
2005 to block the publication of *Beyond Chutzpah* at the University of
California Press were quite disturbing. Dershowitz seemed to be using his
position as a Harvard Law Professor to intimidate a well-respected university
press from printing and distributing a peer-reviewed book that offered up
a critique of Dershowitz's representations of Israel's human rights record.[53]
In addition to Dershowitz's inquiries about claims that were to appear in
Beyond Chutzpah, a New York law firm, Cravath, Swaine, and Moore sent
letters on Dershowitz's behalf insisting that it should be given the right to
inspect *Beyond Chutzpah* for the purpose of helping the press to remove
potentially libelous material harmful to Alan Dershowitz's reputation. One
must note the irony that Dershowitz, a noted civil libertarian, sought to
impact a press's decision to publish a book critical of his own *The Case for
Israel*. A little over a year later, in the fall of 2006, Finkelstein's tenure bid
would begin at DePaul.

The tenure case of a widely recognized scholar and the author of five
substantial books at a mid-level Catholic university was placed in jeopardy
because of the power of parties external to the university. In response,
DePaul's Faculty Governance Council called on Harvard's leadership to
rein in Dershowitz's effort to influence Finkelstein's tenure and promotion
process. While Dershowtitz's campaign against Finkelstein's tenure case
might have simply represented a unique set of circumstances surrounding
an academic process in one university, in my mind it signals something
far more problematic and perverse. The Finkelstein case established a
test case for how other scholars could be removed from universities and
the academic profession through external pressure and the tainting of
institutional personnel processes if their scholarship sufficiently threatened
a powerful interest group or individual. What did it mean that a renowned
Ivy League professor and a media superstar, who objected to the critiques
of his work by an untenured scholar at a far less prestigious institution,

could possibly play such an instrumental role in guiding that institution's decision-making in ending that scholar's career precisely along the lines he insisted it should?

Dershowitz invested substantial resources and effort into shaping Finkelstein's tenure case at DePaul University, suggesting that he was worried that if Finkelstein's critiques of his *The Case for Israel* and portrayals of Israel's human rights record in the book gained mainstream circulation and acceptance, it would be ruinous for his reputation. By portraying Finkelstein as a propagandist and not a scholar, insisting that Finkelstein's tenure case was not about academic freedom but about upholding academic and professional standards, and claiming that Finkelstein did not comport himself pursuant to the Association of American Universities' guidelines for professional conduct, Dershowitz avoided having to rebut the substance of Finkelstein's critique in *Beyond Chutzpah*.[54] Dershowitz effectively shifted the public's attention away from the main subject of Finkelstein's many books (Israel's human rights record, the use of Holocaust imagery and the charge of anti-Semitism to immunize Israel and its apologists from legitimate criticism, and the exposure of spurious scholarship on the Question of Palestine) to questions about Finkelstein's tone, civility, conduct, and persona.[55]

As one of Israel's strongest supporters in the United States, Dershowitz likely feared the prospect of *Beyond Chutzpah*'s publication, as the book revealed Dershowitz's attempt to present Israeli governmental policies—including extrajudicial execution, torture, and home demolition—in a positive light. In this context, Dershowitz noted that Israel possessed an admirable human rights record in light of the numerous internal and external threats it faces. Furthermore, Dershowitz concluded in *The Case for Israel* that, "When 'human rights' becomes a tactic, selectively and successfully invoked by the worst violators against those who make serious efforts to comply with the rule of law, human rights lose all objective meaning and their continued utility in the ongoing struggle for international justices becomes diluted" (231). In other words, those who accused the Israeli government of being one of the prime violators of human rights in the world today were in fact mounting a political attack against the legitimacy of the one modern democracy facing innumerable threats that makes a good-faith effort to comply with the rule of law. In fact, Dershowitz insisted that no modern democracy facing similar threats possessed a stronger commitment to the rule of law and the preservation of civil liberties as has Israel. As Dershowitz wrote in the introduction to *The Case for Israel*,

I prove beyond any shadow of a doubt that a pernicious double standard has been applied to judging Israel's actions; that even when Israel has been the best among the best in the world, it has often been accused of being the worst or among the worst in the world. I also prove that this double standard has not only been unfair to the Jewish state but that it has damaged the rule of law, wounded the credibility of international organizations such as the United Nations, and encouraged Palestinian terrorists to commit acts of violence in order to provoke overreaction by Israel and secure one-sided condemnation of Israel by the international community. (7)

In *The Case for Israel*, Dershowitz presents thirty-two questions—such as "Did Israel Start the Six-Day War?" "Was the Yom Kippur War Israel's Fault?" "Is Israel the Prime Human Rights Violator in the World?" "Is Settlement in the West Bank and Gaza the Major Barrier to Peace?" "Is the Israeli Occupation the Cause of All the Problems?" etc.—and answers each of them by absolving Israel of blame, seeking to prove that there is a massive conspiracy to unfairly paint Israel as a racist state operating outside of international law and human rights conventions. As Dershowitz notes in the conclusion of *The Case for Israel*:

> [It] is the thesis of this book that no nation in the history of the world that has faced comparable threats to its survival—both external or internal—has ever made greater efforts at, and has ever come closer to, achieving the higher norms of the rule of law. Yet no civilized nation in the history of the world, including totalitarian and authoritarian regimes, has ever been as repeatedly, unfairly, and hypocritically condemned and criticized by the international community as Israel has been over the years. The net result is that the gulf between Israel's *actual* record of compliance with the rule of law and its *perceived* record of compliance with the rule of law is greater than any other nation in history (222; emphasis in original).

The Case for Israel reads like a lawyer's brief exonerating a client who has been falsely accused of committing a crime, decrying that the client has been framed by the courts and the justice system. Indeed, Dershowitz sought to initiate a debate about Israel's human rights record, as well as the supposedly false accusations lodged against it, in the public sphere: "I welcome vigorous discussion about the case for Israel I make in this book. Indeed I hope to generate honest, contextual debate about an issue that has been polarized by extremist arguments" (8). It was in this context that Finkelstein's critique of *The Case for Israel* emerged. The public received a preview of what was at stake in this intellectual debate in September of 2003 when Finkelstein and Dershowitz debated the merits of the book on Amy Goodman's *Democracy Now*. During this debate and in public appearances afterward, Finkelstein called Dershowitz's *The Case for Israel* "a hoax plagiarized from another hoax," "a form of misleading and lying to the public," "a form of educational malpractice for which professors are rightly fired," and "a schmata (a Jewish rag)."[56] At that point, perhaps, Finkelstein's scholarship and reputation came into Dershowitz's crosshairs: Dershowitz was unlikely to tolerate this sort of challenge to his credibility as a commentator on the Israel-Palestine conflict.

Dershowitz may have realized that damaging Finkelstein's reputation would be a necessary step in protecting his own as a Harvard Law Professor and media pundit on current affairs. If DePaul granted Finkelstein tenure, Finkelstein's work on the exploitation of the Holocaust and Israel's human rights record would be given mainstream academic legitimacy, opening up the distinct possibility that the mainstream public would read Finkelstein's *Beyond Chutzpah* with interest given the author's credibility as a tenured professor. Perhaps realizing the detrimental effects for his own reputation if Finkelstein achieved tenure at DePaul, Dershowitz mounted sustained attacks against *Beyond Chutzpah* and Finkelstein in several venues. Dershowitz seemingly insisted that anyone who defended Finkelstein, his work, or his academic freedom was part of the "hard left"—a label apparently not requiring explanation or evidence, as insinuation and innuendo work within a public sphere where criticism of Israel can be portrayed as a form of social deviancy. The stigmatization of dissenting positions on the Israel-Palestine conflict, positions that are critical of the Israeli government's military policies and US support for those repressive strategies, becomes normal. As Finkelstein once noted. "When it's for the cause, anything goes," suggesting that propaganda efforts supporting the dictates of power do not have to meet the demands of elementary rationality. This predicament presents very real problems for understanding the United States' "terrorism problem," as Finkelstein explains in evaluating Osama bin Laden's publicized grievances against the United States, which insisted that Americans would not live in security until Muslims in the Middle East are able to:

> Why should Americans go on with their lives as normal, worrying about calories and hair loss, while other people are worrying about where they are going to get their next piece of bread? Why should we go on merrily with our lives while so much of the world is suffering, and suffering incidentally not with us merely as bystanders, but with us as the indirect and direct perpetrators. So that I think that you can summon up all the heroic and self-aggrandizing rhetoric you want, but there is a problem facing all of us now, and maybe it's about time that the United States starts having to confront the same sort of problems that much of humanity has had to confront on a daily basis for God knows how long.[57]

Finkelstein's reflections take us straight to the issue of Palestinian suffering and the direct role American citizens play in perpetuating it through their government's funding of Israel's occupation and increasing militarization. Within a cultural context so saturated with false information about the conflict, and due to a constant barrage of propaganda within the mainstream media rationalizing Israel's repressive policies against the Palestinians, a truth-teller who emerges on the scene to challenge seemingly impenetrable dogma poses an immense threat to the carefully constructed mythology.

Coming to the topic of the Question of Palestine

I came to learn of Finkelstein's reputation for exposing the falsehoods on the conventional wisdom on the Israel-Palestine conflict when I was a graduate student writing a Ph.D. dissertation on controversial academic scholarship and the US public sphere. Even pursuing a dissertation on the topic of Finkelstein's writings proved to be a controversial decision for me; there were those within my university who were unwilling to consider my inquiry "academic" or worthwhile.[58] As my dissertation director once noted, "Even if Chomsky and Finkelstein are telling the truth about the Israel-Palestine conflict, the weight of the scholarly apparatus will prove insurmountable." The message was clear: regardless of what the truth about the Israel-Palestine conflict might be, it didn't matter because of the strength of pro-Israel special-interest groups in the United States who were devoted to defending Israel's image. As the argument went, these special-interest groups determine the lenses through which Americans come to understand the conflict, even if these lenses stand in opposition to international law and the international consensus on the resolution of the Question of Palestine. While such descriptions of Zionist power in the United States may seem conspiratorial, I would allege that they are in fact *understated*.

Despite various subtle warnings that I would ultimately hurt my academic career if I persisted in studying Finkelstein's work and intellectual example, I decided the potential costs were worthwhile to address issues about conscious censorship around the Israel-Palestine conflict, issues that academics seemed to be deliberately avoiding. Gathering evidence of Finkelstein's effective exclusion from the academic scene proved to be difficult. For example, there were those unwilling to divulge information about the real reasons for Finkelstein's dismissal from Hunter College in New York where Finkelstein was an instructor in the political science department, a position he held for nearly 10 years before receiving a severe salary cut upon the publication of *The Holocaust Industry: The Exploitation of Jewish Suffering*. It became clear to me, upon making various inquiries within Finkelstein's former department, that the true reasons for his departure from Hunter College were not being disclosed. The academic structure has ways of dealing with trouble makers that threaten it, as I came to learn in a couple of different institutions. Many well-meaning people communicated to me that supporting Finkelstein's academic freedom or advocating on his behalf would not help my academic career. Despite these warnings, I felt it important to support Finkelstein on principle, especially when Dershowitz began a campaign to seemingly marginalize him with the academic community. Dershowitz responded to those supporting Finkelstein's academic freedom and producing critical commentary about his *The Case for Israel*, including individuals who wrote positive review essays of *Beyond Chutzpah*.[59]

It is difficult to convey how politically and emotionally charged the environments within which Finkelstein's interventions on the Israel-Palestine conflict take place are. It is hard enough for those writing on controversial issues, such as the influence of the Israel Lobby in the United States, to be taken seriously. This is a result of the doctrinal constraints governing the production of knowledge claims about the Middle East. The Israel-Palestine conflict, however, plays out on a discursive terrain several orders of magnitude more volatile than any other public issue. In Finkelstein's case, because he is Jewish and the son of Holocaust survivors, the stakes are enormous for Israel's supporters since Finkelstein's identity lends significant credibility to his criticisms of Israel. Finkelstein's critics claim either that he is a self-hating Jew, or that he can't really be considered Jewish and should be condemned as an anti-Semite. The stridency of some of Finkelstein's critiques, his sometimes intemperate language, and his portrayals of figures such as Elie Wiesel, Abe Foxman, Jerry Kosinski, and others—whom he argues are part of The "Holocaust Industry"—might lead one to wonder if he goes too far in his criticisms. Finkelstein's supposed lack of academic couth became the basis for Dershowitz's attempt to influence Finkelstein's tenure decision at DePaul. The fact that a relatively vulnerable institution, without the financial backing to fend off powerful interest groups, succumbed to outside pressure to end Finkelstein's academic career reveals a lot about how power works in the US academy.

That a Harvard Law Professor sought to affect a tenure case at another institution, in a clear attempt to protect his own reputation, seemingly threatening to besmirch a Catholic institution as anti-Semitic to protect himself from criticism, suggests that the American public sphere has been structured in such a way to block the Palestinian permission to narrate. Dershowitz insisted that Finkelstein was denied tenure because of a lack of scholarship and unprofessionalism.[60] Finkelstein's scholarship, because it explored not only Dershowitz's possible scholarly derelictions, but more importantly Dershowitz's seeming avoidance of international law with respect to the conflict, did not meet the demands of the reigning propaganda system. This requirement, that scholarship touching upon an issue so central to US foreign policy interests conform to mainstream views, reveals that even the most rigorous scholarship on the conflict is often portrayed as bizarre and bigoted—even if it accords within the assessments of the world's leading authorities on the Israel-Palestine conflict, as Finkelstein's scholarship does. As the attempts of Israel's defenders to attack Richard Goldstone have proven, no one is immune from the Lobby's relentless campaign of defamation when Israel's right to use state terrorism is called into question. Richard Goldstone, who authored the Goldstone Report examining Israel's invasion of Gaza in December of 2009, was quickly vilified by leading American Zionists, despite the facts the he identifies himself as a Zionist, comes from a long-time Zionist family, and has relatives who live in Israel.

The Finkelstein case established a pattern for how other scholars could be removed from universities and the academic profession through pressure and tainting of internal processes. Professors such as Joseph Massad, Nadia Abu-Haj, Joel Kovel, and Juan Cole faced threats to their tenure promotion process, positions, and appointments due to the outside interference of Zionist organizations. In fact, critics of Israel are held to different standards of evaluation within the academic process, which are often changed at the last minute to justify dismissal, within the US academy. The strategies within the academy to contain critical thought about the Israel-Palestine conflict are well honed, often drawing on baseless accusations against one's supposed "uncollegiality," "activist impulses," "advocacy," and "misguided scholarship"—all of which are convenient smokescreens to avoid having to deal with the substance of one's academic critique of Israel. The academic profession in the United States does not want to face the implications of its own complicity in squelching critical discussions about the heavy price Israel has inflicted on the Palestinians, not only because of the profession's self-professed commitment to academic freedom, but because one might ultimately reach the conclusion that academic freedom has never existed with respect to the Question Palestine—only cynicism, *Realpolitik*, political manipulation, and intense surveillance of the Palestinian predicament within scholarship.

Principles such as academic freedom are usually understood to be invariable, consistent, and continuous. University administrations, however, currently use academic freedom as a rhetorical device, allowing it to be manipulated in the context of creating pretexts for dismissal if the political exigence is clear. Institutions invent new criteria to exclude critics of Israel from the due process protections that are afforded to all other faculty. To understand why critics of Israel are treated as they are within the academy, one must understand that academic freedom must adjust to institutional demands instead of to the needs of individual researchers who need protection from repressive cultural/institutional forces. Academic freedom, then, does not protect the dissenting, critical scholar, but instead protects the institution; it is frequently deployed to justify administrative wishes in the context of personnel and programmatic decisions. Standing in opposition to a prevailing orthodoxy—such as US support for Israel—frequently incurs the displeasure of powerful parties outside of the university; this is most certainly the case for scholars writing critically about the Israel-Palestine conflict.

The use of the charge anti-Semitism as a political weapon against Israel's critics has been quite effective. In this context, anti-Semitism represents something so nebulous and shape-shifting that the lack of evidence for its actual existence becomes the basis for asserting that it has gone underground, is an undeniable unconscious force, and can just easily be said to be present, even when it is completely absent. That the politics of anti-Semitism has taken on the status of a mystery religion, enabling a perverse form of state worship in service to Israeli exceptionalism and Zionist chauvinism is extremely troubling and stands at the heart of the continuation of the Israel-Palestine conflict.[61] This continual insinuation that the person offering up a critique of Israel is an anti-Semite creates a very difficult situation for those seeking to write critically about the conflict, discouraging all but the most intrepid from venturing into this hazardous political environment out of fear of professional exclusion. As Finkelstein's example suggests, a commitment to truth-telling comes at a very steep price few are equipped to pay. That a small number of courageous individuals have risked their professional careers and livelihoods to tell this truth warrants a full analysis. The silencing of these critical voices is not only bad for American democracy, but also bad for democratic deliberation and the prospect of building a comprehensive peace in the Middle East. If think tanks such as the Washington Institute for Near East Policy, the Jewish Institute for National Security Affairs, and the Saban Center for Middle East Policy are manipulating and deceiving American citizens and politicians about what Israel's militarism bodes for the future of the Middle East because of the steady diet of propaganda they produce that passes for fact, then not only are citizens and politicians receiving a distorted view of the roots of the conflict, but they are being denied the basic information that would allow them to comprehend why anti-Americanism has become so rampant in the region; this distorted view is one that we are obligated to resist regardless of the professional and personal price we may pay for doing so. Such distortions, whether about Palestinian nationalism or Israeli's supposed commitment to peace, produce a destructive form of popular knowledge compounding several deliberate deceptions.

For example, that DePaul denied Finkelstein tenure for the very reasons Dershowitz claimed it should have (lack of professionalism, lack of scholarship, *ad hominem* attacks) demonstrates Dershowitz's concerns coincided with the interests of the Israel Lobby, providing an example of the Lobby's pervasive influence within academia, the one space that—at least in theory—is supposed to be free from external political pressure. In other words, while Dershowitz's efforts to shape DePaul's decision on the Finkelstein tenure case were the most public and relentless instances of outside interference over an extended time period, Dershowitz's efforts should not be viewed as that of one individual, but of a whole set of political concerns associated with what James Petras calls the "Zionist Power Configuration." Naturally, these sorts of assertions are often greeted by radical skepticism: "How can you prove that there is such an influence at work to make life difficult for critics of Israel? What is your evidence?"; "Isn't to mention pro-Israel influence in the academy to invoke the very anti-Semitic tropes that are reminiscent of the *Protocols of the Elders of Zion*?" "Anti-Semitism is an unconscious psychological force that permeates every society, so even if you disclaim any anti-Semitic animus, you are unaware of how your critiques and the words you use to conduct it are in fact anti-Semitic." That critics of Israel face these unanswerable questions and vague assertions suggest that no amount of evidence will convince these skeptics that the discourse around Israel has stifled debate about the Middle East in the United States.

A cottage industry has emerged insisting that critics of Israel are not motivated in their critiques out a concern for Palestinian human rights, or any other humanitarian reason. Instead, Robin Shepherd, George Gilder, Robert Wistrich, Jeffrey Herf, Neil Lochery, George Harrison, and others argue that these critiques emerge and take shape, first and foremost, within the discourse of historical anti-Semitism, perhaps unwittingly to the critics themselves.[62] While recognizing that temperate and rationale criticism of Israel cannot be characterized as anti-Semitism, these authors insist that so much discussion of Israel in these days is mired in a discourse that paints Israel as a "pariah state," "the Third Reich reincarnate," and "the greatest human rights violator in the world," that it is impossible to believe that Israel's critics are simply criticizing the Jewish state without also (by implication) criticizing Jews. As Shepherd points out in his *A State Beyond the Pale: Europe's Problem with Israel*, the Holocaust and Israel are the most significant developments in Jewish life in the twentieth century; to attack the legitimacy of Israel is to attack the Jewish people.[63]

What writers such as Shepherd are doing is to shield Israeli actions from critical scrutiny by changing the subject of discussion. The subject shifts from Israel's treatment of the Palestinians, to the motivations of Israel's accusers. It is the classic thief, thief technique (if you are caught with your hand in someone's pocket, point hysterically in the other direction and cry, "Thief, thief!" in a desperate attempt to change the topic from your villainy to someone else's supposed transgression): it suggests that Israel's defenders cannot reply to the substantive critiques being offered, providing instead complex psychological explanations about why Israel is being portrayed the way it is internationally. Demonizing the critics, instead of rebutting their criticisms, becomes the only remaining option—if you can't respond to the message, blame the messenger for producing it due to his unrecognized identity conflicts, unconscious bigotry, and hidden political allegiances with Israel's enemies. Each of these attempts to malign Israel's critics seeks to avoid the indisputable and uncomfortable reality about Israel's illegal actions threatening the stability of the Middle East. Lamentably, many Jews believe that their own identity is under attack when Israel is criticized. David Solway's *The Big Lie: On Terror, Anti-Semitism, and Identity* is one such book in this genre committed to privileging Jewish suffering and channeling it into a defense of Zionism. Solway writes:

> While I maintain that the Palestinian claim to historical title is shaky if not apocryphal, and that, despite the stridency of Palestinian spokesmen and the ignorance of their Western backers, the territory in question was never licitly "Palestinian" to begin with, I must also acknowledge that sixty years of collective suffering, economic mendicancy, and political

displacement have created a feeling of both resentment and solidarity that cannot be easily overlooked. Along with this feeling go the presumption of historical empowerment and the belief in a homeland that inevitably transform themselves into a deep political conviction that can no longer be rationalized away or scumbled out of the picture. As a result, whether or not the Palestinians may be construed as constituting a legitimate nation—and the historical documentation makes it clear that they cannot—they have nevertheless in the course of the last two generations developed the conviction of nationhood that, as such, is now a "fact on the ground" there is no way of circumventing. They have, so to speak, established squatter's rights. (112)

Furthermore, Solway concludes:

As I have contended throughout, and as Joan Peters has shown in her *sedulously* researched *From Time Immemorial*, the case for Israel is far stronger than the case for Palestine, especially if we recall that the British census reports during the Mandatory period were regularly falsified to create the impression of a massive and indigenous presence that did not exist, that the whole of Palestine, both what is now Israel and what is now Jordan, was originally intended by the League of Nations as an indivisible Jewish homeland and that the Jewish state was officially recognized by the United Nations. (197, emphasis mine)

Both of these paragraphs disqualify Solway from being considered a serious commentator on the Israel-Palestine conflict, yet Solway's views continue to circulate as truth in the US public sphere. First of all, Joan Peters' *From Time Immemorial* has been thoroughly discredited as a serious source on the Israel-Palestine conflict. Second, the racist assumptions informing Solway's evaluation of Palestinian territorial claims to what is now occupied territory verges on the bizarre. Solway confidently asserts that any future Palestinian state will descend into chaos and violence because Palestinians are inherently incapable of governing themselves. Here is his characterization of "Palestine":

Infested with terrorist organizations and militant factions, wholly reliant on immense infusions of foreign aid, lacking a functioning infrastructure as well as reliable control over the instruments of violence, given to summary executions, prone to the extremes of mob psychology, and without genuine historical legitimacy founded in *veridical* memory, it is moot whether what we call "Palestine" may be considered as even a *potential* state, let alone a tenable economic and political entity. (108, emphasis in original)

Only in a public sphere committed to upholding such willful misrepresentations of the Israel-Palestine conflict could Solway's reflections pass as serious commentary.

CHAPTER TWO

The politics of perceiving Palestine

Since September 11 there has been a concerted effort by a small but well-funded group of people outside academia to monitor very carefully what all of us are saying, ready to jump on any sign of deviation from what they see as acceptable opinion. It's an attack on academic freedom, and it's not very healthy for our society.

(ZACHARY LOCKMAN, qtd. in Phillip Weiss's "Burning Cole")

The sad fact is that if someone displays the slightest degree of independent thought on the subject of US-Israel relations, they'll get falsely smeared.

(STEPHEN WALT on the attempts to derail Senator Chuck Hegel's bid to become Secretary of Defense, "The Art of Smear")

As I suggested in the previous chapter, the Israel-Palestine conflict is subject to so much controversy because competing parties possess strong and varying convictions about who in fact are the victims and who in fact are the victimizers in the conflict. As a result of a badly misinformed public sphere within the United States where an image upheld by a constant stream of propaganda, a carefully crafted image of who is at fault in the conflict, has been substituted for the reality. The radically different frameworks within which the conflict has been placed depend upon narrative structures seemingly at complete odds with one another.[1]

One narrative structure situates Zionism as the savior of the Jewish people against historical anti-Semitism in the wake of the Holocaust, while another narrative situates it as a chauvinistic, ethno-religious ideology that is responsible for the persecution of the Palestinians living under Israeli occupation. The latter description positions Zionism as the proximate cause of the unrest in the Middle East. The rancor and vehemence with which these competing narratives are offered up by participants in the strenuous debates about the Israel-Palestine conflict to question the legitimacy of both of these dominant narratives are startling. Before accepting or refuting one or the other of these dominant narratives, one must become knowledgeable about the historical evidence either supporting or negating the legitimacy of Zionism as a nationalist project. Readers interested in the historical background behind the rise of American Zionism in the US public sphere should consult the following excellent studies: Kathleen Christison's *Perceptions of Palestine*, Lawrence Davidson's *America's Palestine: Popular and Official Perceptions from Balfour to Israeli Statehood*, and Peter Grose's *Israel in the Mind of America*.

The Israel-Palestine conflict seems to sweep up those who venture into it within a maelstrom of controversy and partisanship—even when those who seek to remain neutral in arbitrating the competing claims between Israeli and Palestinian nationalism inevitably find themselves accused of picking sides. I have observed that participants, in debates about the conflict, have a tendency to accuse those on the other "side" of bad faith and moral dereliction. The stridency and righteousness with which these accusations are advanced speak to the stakes of the debate itself. In making various claims about the conflict, partisans often claim to be speaking truth to power.[2] Indeed, they claim to be speaking from a marginalized and lonely position, the truth of which has yet to be recognized because of powerful propagandistic forces seeking to divert the public away from the relevant issues. For example, those on the Left have long maintained that the charge of anti-Semitism as deployed by Israel's defenders is part of an organized effort to distract the public's attention away from Israel's violations of international law.

This accusation implicates a number of different Jewish organizations such as the Anti-Defamation League, the American Jewish Committee, and the World Jewish Congress as seeking to reframe Israeli wrongdoing by accusing Israel's critics such as Norman Finkelstein as being motivated by anti-Semitic animus.[3] In other words, since these organizations have difficulty in rebutting the factual assertions of Finkelstein and many others about the conflict, it is simply easier to depict anyone who criticizes Israel's behavior as "anti-Semitic," since in this facile formulation anyone who criticizes Israel (as the supposed state of the Jewish people) is in actuality criticizing Jews in their quest for national determination. In conjunction with other elements of the Israel Lobby, these organizations seek to stifle discussion of the historical and documentary record because this record clearly places Israel in the wrong. As a result of this predicament, Israel's defenders must make the person forwarding the relevant information about the conflict the subject of discipline and abuse.

For one group, whose adherents typically describe themselves as "anti-Zionists," the Israeli government with key US support has been, and continues to be, engaged in a program of ethnic cleansing of the Palestinians living in the West Bank and Gaza. According to this perspective, Israel seeks to *either* transfer its own Arab citizens, who constitute a little over 20 percent of its population, because they constitute a "demographic time bomb" posing an existential threat to Israel's character as a Jewish state out of Israel, *or* create an apartheid state modeled on the South African model with all Palestinians— including those who are currently Israeli citizens—living in the West Bank or Gaza.[4] These views are often attributed to figures on the so-called academic Left and even to some political commentators on the far Right.[5] This perspective about Israel's strategic ambitions is controversial within the US public sphere precisely because they place into question Israel's claims to moral exceptionalism within world affairs, suggesting that Israel is in no sense committed to peace with the Palestinians or its Arab neighbors.

In contrast, supporters of Israel contend that Israel faces a double standard, which subjects it to criticisms that no other country facing similar threats has ever had to answer to. Ultimately, these supporters allege that those directing such criticisms toward Israel—whether about Israel's human rights record in the occupied territories or the increased building of settlements in the West Bank—must be motivated by overt or latent anti-Semitism.[6] In their *Uncivil University: Politics and Propaganda in Higher Education*, Tobin et al. ask,

> Are the policies of Israel questioned, debated, and criticized more often, or sometimes singled out as compared to other countries? Is a passionate Israel critic outraged about the policies of Israel, but not of Iran or North Korea? Is criticism aimed at Israel about human rights violations from an individual or group that has no concern for repression in Cuba or Burma, or the abrogation of a free press in Russia? What if someone is obsessed with the Israeli treatment of Palestinians but has nothing to say about the horrors that occur in Sudan? Is a group passionate about the social status of Palestinians, but is oblivious about the untouchables in India or the lack of women's rights in Saudi Arabia and Iran?

They conclude that "[i]t is the double standard and hypocrisy that together distinguish anti-Israelism from legitimate questions about Israeli government policies."[7] Because of these complicated aspects of the Israel-Palestine conflict, debate about the relevant issues is controversial—marked by much debate, angst, and a hesitation to even enter the discursive arena around issues relating to Israel and the Middle East.[8] In fact, there is a lack of debate about the Israel-Palestine conflict precisely because the parties on both sides of the issue refuse to talk to each other, opting instead to talk past each other.

Several powerful and overlapping discourses have even made it difficult to discuss the Israel-Palestine conflict within the American university system, where one would expect that controversial topics could be discussed openly and not suppressed for fear of offending constituencies either within or outside the university.

Academic freedom and the prospects of debate

Does the principle of academic freedom structure debates about the Israel-Palestine conflict, protecting dissenting positions and enabling academic intellectuals to debate the relevant issues without constraints or the fear of professional repercussion? In actuality, academic freedom has been used to perversely limit debate about the Israel-Palestine conflict, with Israel's defenders claiming that their academic freedom is infringed upon whenever the Israeli government is subjected to criticism in classrooms, academic articles, and lecture auditoriums.[9] Such criticisms exhibit, according to this perspective, a lack of balance and manifest an ideology of hatred directed against Jews.[10] Academic freedom and free speech have been redefined to explicitly classify criticism of Israel on college campuses as a form of harassment against Jewish students and faculty, a formulation which requires conflating Judaism, Zionism, and Israel.[11] According to this line of thinking, certain academic fields require greater oversight and public accountability, with outside groups—mostly Zionist organizations—arguing that they should determine whether a campus's programs are contributing to an environment hostile to Jews.[12] As Tobin et al. maintain, "Anti-Semitism and anti-Israelism are more than mere ideologies or political positions: they are twin expressions of institutionalized prejudice. They have become, in some cases, pervasive on the campuses of many universities, the strongest indication of how much civilization has been discarded in contemporary higher education."[13]

If it is the case that anti-Semitism and anti-Israelism have become intertwined, as Tobin et al. suggest, one must ask to what extent criticisms of Israel possess within them criticism of Jews *qua* Jews. In other words, if criticism of Israel is merely a fashionable and supposedly acceptable way to engage in anti-Semitism, there must be a way to prove that those doing the criticizing of Israel are manifesting anti-Semitic animus instead of expressing concerns about human rights, regional stability, Palestinian self-determination, etc. If Israel were not the Jewish State, but instead the Catholic State, would those who currently criticize Israel be equally compelled to criticize Israel's occupation and its dealings with the Palestinians? Frequently, critics of Israel point to the historical example of the South African apartheid government in the 1980s to rebut the charge that they have selectively targeted Israel for boycott, criticism, etc. As this argument goes, if it was proper to boycott and criticize South Africa in the 1980s for its apartheid regime, it is equally appropriate to now boycott and criticize Israel in the present because of its continued occupation of Palestinian land. By this logic, a country is being criticized for what it does, not because of the religion or ethnicity of the dominant group within the country. Israel's supporters reject this comparison, claiming that Israel is not an apartheid state, but is instead a country fighting for its very survival against Islamic terrorist groups seeking its destruction, and that professions of anti-Zionism are really expressions of anti-Semitism. Other scholars, however, have gone so far as to allege that the charge of anti-Semitism is a public-relations device that Israel's apologists use to distract attention away from the historical and diplomatic record, a record which raises serious questions about Israel's true commitment to following international law in the region.[14]

Israel is granted extraordinary immunity in world affairs as a result of its unique status as a holy state, that is, a state not bound by conventional norms of behavior because of its ideological serviceability to concentrated power. This immunity is challenged whenever academics subject Israel's human rights record or military aggression to scrutiny. The increasing amount of criticism Israel has faced from the international community and within American academia signals that Israel (and the United States) can no longer hide what it has done to Palestinian civil society in the West Bank and Gaza. The usual charge that critics of Israel are motivated by anti-Semitism is no longer as effective a weapon in distracting the public from the relevant criticisms of Israel's behavior. As Walt and Mearsheimer point out in *The Israel Lobby and US Foreign Policy*, "The obvious reason is that increasing numbers of people recognize that this serious charge keeps getting leveled at individuals who are not anti-Semites but who are merely questioning Israeli policies or pointing out that the lobby promotes policies that are not always in the U.S. national interest."[15] As the history of Israel's treatment of the Palestinian people becomes more widely known, it will become increasingly difficult for Israel's defenders to employ underhanded tactics to silence critics who are motivated by a concern about US national interests and the stability of the Middle East. Walt and Mearsheimer note the following in the conclusion of *The Israel Lobby*:

> To foster a more open discussion, Americans of all backgrounds must reject the silencing tactics that some groups and individuals in the lobby continue to employ. Stifling debate and smearing opponents is inconsistent with the principles of vigorous and open dialogue on which democracy depends, and continued reliance on this undemocratic tactic runs the risk of generating a hostile backlash at some point in the future.[16]

To gain an understanding of what motivates those who defend Israel's actions against the Palestinians, and its contributions to reducing Middle East stability more generally, we must examine what is known as the Question of Palestine, one of the most intractable questions in human history.

The Question of Palestine consists of a distinct set of propositions about an area in the Middle East represented by present-day Israel and the occupied territories, the West Bank and the Gaza Strip. Despite this naming of a specific geographic location, the Question of Palestine identifies the significance of Palestine in worldwide affairs as a site of social, religious, and political strife. The Question of Palestine entails many questions about nationalism, national belonging, colonialism, Jewish and Palestinian history, suffering, dispossession, and exile. If we speak of a Palestinian Question, recognizing how Israel's creation in 1948 resulted in the creation of Palestinian refugees and these refugees' quest for the world's recognition of their injustice, it is impossible not to identify how Israel's creation was an attempt to end the Jewish Question after the Holocaust. As Edward Said notes in his *The Question of Palestine*, "Here, then, is another complex irony: how the classic victims of years of anti-Semitic persecution and the Holocaust have in their new nation become the victimizers of another people, who have become, therefore, the victims of the victims."[17] Historically, the Jewish Question refers to the many solutions offered by Jewish leaders to end discrimination against Jews in Gentile societies and is an acknowledgment of the key role anti-Semitism has played in defining Jewish identity in the diaspora.

This relatively small land area known as Palestine has received an inordinate amount of Western academic and governmental analysis for the last 50 years because of the region's significance to Christianity, Judaism, and Islam. Said documented this interest extensively in his *Orientalism*, where he set out to show that Western understandings of the East depend upon stereotypes of its inhabitants as backward, incapable of civilization, and degenerate. The basis for most of the scholarship about the East has been filtered through the prism that Said describes, providing an extremely distorted and fundamentally incorrect view and understanding through which to frame Islam and the people and cultures of the Middle East. As Said explained,

> Orientalism is, above all, a discourse that is by no means in direct, corresponding relationship with political power in the raw, but rather it is produced and exists in an uneven exchange with various kinds of power, shaped to a degree by the exchange with power political (as with a colonial or imperial establishment), power intellectual (as with reigning sciences like comparative linguistics or anatomy, or any of the modern policy sciences), power cultural (as with orthodoxies and canons of tastes, texts, and values), power moral (as with ideas about ideas about what "we" do and what "they" cannot do or understand as "we" do).[18]

These discourses of power continue into the present, perpetuating ignorant analysis and commentary by a group of neoconservative scholars who are attempting to carry out a revolution of sorts in the type of relationship the United States and Israel will have with the Arab world for years to come.

One should include in this group figures such as Martin Kramer, Daniel Pipes, Steve Emerson, David Horowitz, Fouad Ajami, Stanley Kurtz, Charles Krauthammer, and Bernard Lewis. Kramer, for example, argues in his *Ivory Towers on Sand* that Edward Said's *Orientalism* exercised a pernicious influence on Middle East Studies during the 1980s and 1990s, lulling American academics into a sense of complacency about the real dangers of militant Islam. Pipes contends that militant Islam has swept across the United States and poses a threat to American citizens that has yet to be taken seriously by government officials.[19] Each of these figures contends that the Arab world is incorrigibly corrupt with respect to its political structures and incapable of repairing its social ills without Western intervention. Additionally, academics are accused of being apologists for Arab failures, for example, the deprivation of rights for women, terrorism, resistance to modernity, etc., while condemning the United States' and Israel's colonial endeavors in the region. To better understand the ideological stakes in preserving a modern commitment to the White Man's Burden in the Middle East, it is necessary to acquire some historical understanding of the Holy Land's significance.

The Holy Land, as the region represented by Israel is often called, brings together three major religions—Christianity, Judaism, and Islam—and is considered the homeland of the Jewish people. Palestine, as this land was once called, is also the land of Canaan, where nearly four million Palestinians live in various states of dispossession, statelessness, and existential alienation because Israel symbolizes the destruction of the Palestinian population in 1948, when hundreds of Palestinian villages were razed by Zionist forces such as the Haganah and the Stern Gang. The means employed to disband the Palestinian population were harsh, ruthless, and decisive, as nearly 800,000 Palestinians were turned into homeless wanderers in the months leading up to May of 1948. This history, which was at one time contested, no longer seriously is because of the work of Israel's New Historians, who have revolutionized our understanding of how the removal of the Palestinian population and its culture were at the heart of Zionist planning and strategy since the days of Jabotinsky and Ben-Gurion.[20]

US support for Israel fulfills several strategic goals in the Middle East. First, Israel acts as a military and cultural outpost against the rise of Arab nationalism, ensuring US and Israeli control of the region through military force. This military force plays a key role in helping the United States secure the stupendous energy reserves throughout the Middle East and West Asia—particularly in Saudi Arabia, Kuwait, the United Arab Emirates, Afghanistan, and Iran—for US profits instead of for the indigenous population. It is not a surprise, then, to learn that much of what US citizens know about Israel and its dealings with Arab populations, particularly the Palestinian population with which it has dealt so harshly, has been shaped and controlled in the United States by groups sympathetic to the Zionist project. Given the religious significance of the holy sites in Jerusalem to Christians, Jews, and Arabs, and the extremist passions ownership of these sites often inflame, the region is often described as a "tinderbox."[21] This descriptor of the region as a "tinderbox" indicates that the Israel-Palestine conflict may very well be the proximate cause of a nuclear war, and all that entails for the region and the world, a testament to the importance and significance of accurate representations of contemporary Middle East history, particularly for those who play more than an insignificant role in funding the state within the region responsible for the vast majority of the violence.[22]

Despite the attention academic and government analysts have paid to the Middle East, a serious set of dangerous misassumptions inform their work, which often passes as "mainstream." While there has been a scholarly consensus on how to resolve the Israel-Palestine conflict, it has been effectively overwhelmed by a barrage of propaganda, which has made it difficult to distinguish between reality and illusion. Why, for example, is there so little public awareness within the US about the relevant international law surrounding the conflict? UN 242, 194, 338, and other legal protocols are never mentioned in mainstream media coverage of the conflict, yet people are led to believe that "fault" resides equally between the Israelis and the Palestinians. UN 242 prohibits the acquisition of land by force, while 194 takes up the Palestinian refugee problem, with 338 seeking the implementation of 194.[23]

Since it is intolerable to claim that the United States and Israel have blocked a comprehensive peace settlement in the Middle East since 1967, the scholarly record must be presented as exotic and radical, when it in fact documents a steady diet of misrepresentation about the United States' role in supporting Israel's illegal military occupation despite the United States' posturing as a "neutral broker," as well as its hypocritical stance on Palestinian terrorism, which must be described by the doctrinal system as a threat to Israel's "right to exist," something no state claims a right to in the international system. The phrase "Israel's right to exist," if it were accurately used by the Western media, would add a few words: "Israel's right to exist as crazy state, which poses a constant danger to the region and the world."[24] In its current doctrinal usage, it refers to "Israel's constant vulnerability due to its existence in the midst of Arab hostility and how this necessitates the world suspending all moral and common sense in judging Israel's military actions in the region." Israel has still not declared its borders, has no bill of rights, and has no constitution. The diplomatic record, which documents nearly 46 years of US and Israeli rejectionism, has been desperately avoided by US supporters of Israel; it must be, so that the real story of Israel's illegal acquisition of Palestinian land can be described under such mantras as "security needs" and "Israeli defense against terrorism." These ruses must be preserved to ensure that Israel will be considered the David in a sea of Arab Goliaths, when it fact the opposite is true. This startling discrepancy between image and reality is particularly striking because the mainstream media in the United States so effectively blur the line between truth and fiction.

The very parameters governing the types of knowledge that can enter the debate are strictly controlled by a host of watchdog organizations, academic and cultural. For example, defining what constitutes "terrorism," which is inevitably always tied to Palestinian retaliation against Israeli military strikes, versus what constitutes "resistance" is crucial to controlling the terms of debate in the conflict, especially in the United States. If Palestinian resistance to Israeli land appropriation and annexation were properly labeled as "legitimate resistance," as it is, Israeli settler colonialism could not be described as occupation necessary for Israeli security. The terrorism industry—Steve Emerson, Claire Sterling, Judith Miller, Bernard Lewis, Fouad Ajami, etc.— ensures that Islamic terror remains in front of American audiences, even though state-sponsored terrorism is, by many more orders of magnitude, a far more destructive and frequent phenomena. State terror, however, rarely ever counts as "terror" because the strong control the doctrinal system, and in Noam Chomsky's words, "their terror doesn't count as terror."[25]

Academic treatments and discussions about Israel's human rights record have generally been highly protective of Israel's military history, the conditions under which Israel was founded, and its real commitments to peace. I would invite those who are interested in examining at Israel's commitment to peace to look at Alfred Lilienthal's massive book *The Zionist Connection*, which details how badly the Israel-Palestine conflict has been misrepresented in elite circles due to conscious censorship and under threats of professional silencing. For academics, speaking truth to power on Israel-Palestine can lead to underemployment, blacklisting, exclusion from certain professional circles, and vilification within one's community. While these academics are often labeled "anti-Semitic," they are doing nothing more than bringing attention to the conflict's diplomatic and historical record. Speaking out on the Question of Palestine, at this historical moment, is something academics are loathe to do—and rightly so. The professional payoffs are nil, the penalties heavy, and the repercussions far reaching. Untenured academics, who have become too active in writing and speaking about Israel's human rights record and the US-Israel relationship, have been summarily dismissed from their positions.[26] In response, many people shrug their shoulders, state that there's little point in getting involved in such a highly charged issue when the chances of changing anyone's mind are so small. But, clearly individuals are motivated and inspired to speak out and enter the fray despite the daunting odds.

Even established scholars like Mearsheimer (a distinguished professor at the Univ. of Chicago) and Walt (the Robert and Renee Belfer Professor of International Affairs and academic Dean of the Kennedy School of Government at Harvard) were subjected to abuse and vilification after the publication of their supposedly controversial article entitled "The Israel Lobby" in the *London Review of Books* in March 2006. In this article, they questioned whether US support for Israel's occupation and military adventurism is in the American interest, going so far as to ask whether the United States has a terrorism problem in the Middle East largely because of its support of Israel.[27] A firestorm of criticism was lodged against these two establishment scholars by insiders within the academic community when this article became a book, proving that no one can be protected from being tarred with the brush of anti-Semitism when it comes to criticizing Israel's regional policies in the Middle East and US support for these policies.[28]

"The Israel Lobby," which drew the usual reactions from Zionists such as Alan Dershowitz, marked an important moment in discussions of the Israel-Palestine conflict in that Walt and Mearsheimer hold prominent academic positions, teaching at Harvard and the University of Chicago, respectively. Neither Walt nor Mearsheimer could be described as "radical" or "leftists," making the appearance of their article in the *London Review of Books* even more prominent, and confirming the suspicion that any discussion of the special relationship between the United States and Israel or the existence of an Israeli lobby will inevitably lead to denunciations against those advancing the argument, no matter what their credentials. Originally, Walt and Mearsheimer wrote the article ("The Israel Lobby") for *The Atlantic*, a monthly magazine known for its Zionist sympathies, which decided not to publish it after initially soliciting the manuscript.

To understand why this article was so controversial, one must first examine the specific arguments being advanced by Walt and Mearsheimer and the precious cultural assumptions about Israel challenged by these arguments. Their main argument was not that the Israel Lobby controls US Middle East policies, but instead that the Lobby exercises a great deal of influence over those policies, creating a situation where the United States often pursues objectives within the region that are contrary to its own interests: "The bottom line is hard to escape: although America's problems in the Middle East would not disappear if the lobby were less influential, US leaders would find it easier to explore alternative approaches and be more likely to adopt policies consistent with American interests."[29] The US-Israel special relationship has no parallel in world history, involving billions of dollars in yearly military and financial support for Israel's military adventurism, over 100 billion dollars since 1967. In addition, the United States provides diplomatic cover for brazen and repeated violations of international law as Israel continues its assault against the Palestinian population. Walt and Mearsheimer explain that US support for Israel must stop if Israel continues its annexation of the West Bank, from which Israel will conduct further expansion throughout the Middle East:

> If Israel remains unwilling to grant the Palestinians a viable state—or it tries to impose an unjust solution unilaterally—then the United States should curtail its economic and military support. It should not do so because it bears Israel any ill will but because it recognizes that the occupation is bad for the United States and contrary to American political values. Consistent with the strategy of offshore balancing, the United States would base its actions on its own self-interest rather than adhere to a blind allegiance to

an uncooperative partner. In effect, the United States should give Israel a choice: end its self-defeating occupation of the West Bank and Gaza and remain a close ally, or remain a colonial power on its own.[30]

Israel's expansionist plans, which run deeply through Zionist thinking and planning, neither known about or discussed in the United States. Oded Yinon, Israel Shahak and Noam Chomsky have been warning about Israel's territorial ambitions since the early eighties.[31] The primary reason there have been so few voices speaking out about these hugely relevant issues, which have far-reaching consequences for the Middle East, can be attributed to the effectiveness of charging anyone who brings attention to the relevant information with anti-Semitism.

Even former President Jimmy Carter, the one President who has done the most to ensure Israel's security, was accused of harboring anti-Semitic animus when his *Palestine: Peace Not Apartheid* was released in 2006. *Palestine: Peace Not Apartheid* merely recounted the diplomatic record around the Israel-Palestine conflict since Carter's Presidency, whiles insisting that Israel's refusal to dismantle settlements in the West Bank was the main obstacle to achieving peace in the Middle East. That a former American President would voice this view was too much for some US apologists for Israel who are used to dominating the parameters of the debate.[32]

Unsurprisingly, the world of academic grant making has been subjected to the unusual political litmus tests associated with Zionist censorship of supposedly anti-Israel views, which usually means anti-Zionist views, as pro-Israel advocacy groups seek to derogate the limits of expression about the Israel-Palestine conflict. As Scott Sherman's *Nation* article, entitled "Target Ford," documented, the grant-making world has been corrupted by the power politics governing understandings of the Middle East conflict in the United States.[33] For example, Ford Foundation grant recipients now must sign an agreement pledging not to engage in research or activities that would result in the destruction of any state—a clear reference to one state in particular, Israel. This change in grant-making language has had a chilling effect on the types of research activities scholars can pursue. To argue, for example, that Israel should become a bi-national state, which would disturb its Jewish character, would technically exclude someone from receiving a Ford Foundation grant because one would in effect be arguing that Israel does not have a right to exist as a state devoted to the preservation of a Jewish majority.

The international law expert, Francis Boyle, writes: "I have been accused of being everything but a child molester because of my public support for the Palestinian people. I have seen every known principle of academic integrity and academic freedom violated in order to suppress the basic rights of the Palestinian people. In fact, there is no such thing as academic integrity and academic freedom in the United States when it comes to asserting the rights of the Palestinian people under international law."[34] Boyle really does bring us to the main issue: if academic freedom does not exist to protect those seeking to promote discussion of one of the most important and explosive issues of our day, then can academic freedom really be said to exist at all? Academic freedom cannot exist outside of an institutional context and the constraints that govern such contexts. Nor can it exist as a metaphysical concept or a neutral principle untouched by the power relations that are present at any historical moment. Academic freedom, however, is an ongoing project that requires continual commitment and a dedication to protecting embattled scholars seeking to challenge the reactionary forces within our culture.

CHAPTER THREE

The case of
Norman G. Finkelstein

*Professor Finkelstein specializes in exposing spurious
scholarship on the Arab-Israeli conflict. And he has a very
impressive track record in this respect. He was a very promising
graduate student in history at Princeton, when a book by Joan
Peters appeared, called From Time Immemorial, and he wrote
the most savage exposition in critique of this book. It was a
systematic demolition of this book. The book argued, incidentally,
that Palestine was a land without a people for people without
a land. And Professor Finkelstein exposed it as a hoax, and he
showed how dishonest the scholarship or spurious scholarship
was in the entire book. And he paid the price for his courage, and
he has been a marked man, in a sense, in America ever since.*

(AVI SHLAIM ON NORMAN FINKELSTEIN,
9 May 2007 interview on *Democracy Now*)

*As a strong supporter of freedom of speech and a lifetime practi-
tioner of freedom to criticize, I would certainly never prevent the
expression of any views regarding Israel, but I am also a strong
believer in the reality that words matter and that unreasoned condemnation can sometimes come with a heavy price.*

(ALAN DERSHOWITZ, *The Case for Israel*)

Introduction

To date, perhaps the most significant academic freedom case involving a scholar focusing on the Israel-Palestine conflict is Norman Finkelstein's denial of tenure at DePaul University in 2007.[1] I saw this case up close and as a faculty member at DePaul.[2] In 2000, Finkelstein, a Princeton educated political scientist, became the object of international notoriety with the publication of his book the *Holocaust Industry: The Exploitation of Jewish Suffering*, in which he argued that US defenders of Israel's military adventurism in the Middle East have blackmailed the international community with the moral capital and sympathy that was created in response to the Holocaust. The son of Holocaust survivors, Finkelstein has been relentless in his exposure of what he believes to be the manipulative use of the Holocaust in the context of the Israel-Palestine conflict, claiming that American Zionist Jewry has used the Holocaust to immunize Israel against international criticism in its continued human rights violations against the Palestinians living in the West Bank and Gaza.[3]

Finkelstein came to Harvard Law Professor Alan Dershowitz's attention in September of 2003, when Finkelstein alleged that Dershowitz's bestselling book, *The Case for Israel*, was a "spectacular hoax" because it relied upon evidence and arguments from Joan Peters' *From Time Immemorial*, a book that Finkelstein carefully demonstrated to be fraudulent nearly 20 years earlier.[4] The public spectacle began in September of 2003 when Finkelstein squared off in a debate about *The Case for Israel* on Amy Goodman's show *Democracy Now*.[5] During that debate, Finkelstein vowed to provide documentation, which would disprove Dershowitz's insistence that he was the target of a simple *ad hominem* and bigoted attack, alleging that *The Case for Israel* was "a fraud concocted from another fraud": a reference to Joan Peters' *From Time Immemorial* which sought to prove, in the words of Golda Meir, that there are in fact "no Palestinians."[6] One of the interesting rhetorical feats that apologists for Israel's colonial behavior have relied upon over the last 30 years involves arguing that Palestinians were relatively recent in-migrants to the area once called Palestine, which became Israel in 1948. By virtue of this argument, Israel committed no wrongdoing upon its creation and there was no moral issue involved in driving out Palestinians from the new Jewish state because they were random Arabs who could live in any of the 22 Arab countries in the Middle East and were not a distinct national group. This argument is precisely the one Peters made in 1984 and with Dershowitz seemingly drawing on it in *The Case for Israel*. Like Peters, Dershowitz argues that an exchange of populations occurred between Jews and Arabs, whereby Jews living in various Arab countries made their way to Palestine, while Arabs left what would eventually become Israel. This demographic feat is reproduced in Dershowitz's *The Case for Israel* in support of his argument that Israel did not engage in ethnic cleansing between 1947 and 1949.

In his *Democracy Now* debate with Dershowitz on 24 September 2003, Finkelstein argued not only that Dershowitz had borrowed material and arguments from Peters' *From Time Immemorial*, but that he had done so to bolster a book that essentially ignored the findings of major human rights organizations and Israel's New Historians, a group of scholars including Benny Morris and Avi Shlaim, who have shined new light on Israel's founding and commitment to solidifying peace in the region.[7] These New Historians argue, based upon the archival material released in the last 20 years by the Israeli government, that Israel deliberately sought to expel the Palestinians from Israel proper as part of a larger effort to secure its own military hegemony in the region. According to New Historians such as Morris and Shlaim, Israel's birth was far from pure, involving the Haganah's and Irgun's unspeakable acts against the Palestinian population, which included mass killings, the bombings of homes as part of a widespread campaign of terror, and the rapes of thousands of Palestinian women. This attempt to drive the Palestinian population out of what would eventually become Israel was successful, emboldening Israel's soon-to-be prime ministers to commit to what Livia Rokach would come to label "Israel's sacred terrorism."[8] Dershowitz largely avoided the findings of these New Historians, particularly the scholarship of Illan Pappe, who has demonstrated Israel's commitment to a carrying out a program of ethnic cleansing against the Palestinians.[9]

Finkelstein's larger claim was that Dershowitz sidestepped the findings of major human rights organizations such as Amnesty International and B'tselem because they did not support Dershowitz's contention that no other country has responded as well to Israel to internal and external threats while maintaining a firm commitment to adhering to the rule of law and preserving democratic principles. Israel has long been called "the only democracy in the Middle East," although its Arab citizens largely have second-class status and are often viewed as a potential threat to Israel's character as a Jewish state. According to Finkelstein, either Dershowitz was wrong or the human rights organizations were involved in a massive anti-Semitic conspiracy— there could be no third explanation. The implications of this debate about Dershowitz's specific assertions about Israel's human rights record, the conditions under which Israeli courts seemingly condone torture, as well as the kinds of evidence Dershowitz brought to bear on these issues, were profound and extended over nearly 5 years.

Dershowitz attempts to influence publication of Finkelstein's *Beyond Chutzpah*

Dershowitz's interest in Finkelstein increased when Finkelstein declared his intention to publish his findings about *The Case for Israel* in a book that was to be called *Beyond Chutzpah: The Misuse of Anti-Semitism and the Abuse of*

History. In this book, Finkelstein called into question Dershowitz's reputation as a serious commentator on the Israel-Palestine conflict. Dershowitz claimed that the University of California Press was publishing *Beyond Chutzpah* because it is a hard-left press that agreed with Finkelstein's politics, insisting that the outside reviewers UCP solicited to review Finkelstein's manuscript concurred with Finkelstein's positions because they were virulent critics of Israel.[10] Ultimately, the Press was able to withstand Dershowitz's attempts to influence the publication of the manuscript, but the pressures placed on it to abandon the project were relentless. Dershowitz even sought to get the University of California's Board of Regents to stop publication of the book, but the Board took no action. Despite Dershowitz's efforts to enlist his help, California's governor Arnold Schwarzenegger refused to get involved, stating that given the academic freedom issues surrounding the case it would be inappropriate to use his authority to prevent publication of the book.[11]

It is almost unheard of for an academic to write a letter to the governor of a state enlisting his help in preventing the publication of another academic's book, a book which had received the imprimatur of a prestigious university's editorial board and been vetted by six internationally recognized experts on the US-Israel-Palestine conflict. But that seems to be what Dershowitz did when he wrote a "polite note" to Schwarzenegger in May of 2005 seeking Schwarzenegger's help in separating UC Press from the lies of "an academic hit-man" and "full-time malicious defamer."[12] Dershowitz alleged that Finkelstein's published criticisms of prominent Jewish Americans, including Stuart Eizenstat, Dennis Ross, Edgar Bronfman, Israel Singer, Abe Foxman, Elie Wiesel, and Dershowitz himself, were beyond the pale of what should pass as legitimate scholarship. In addition, Dershowitz conveyed this view to UC press with phone calls and letters throughout the spring and summer of 2005 in an apparent campaign, intimating that he would sue the press if certain defamatory accusations—that he did not write and perhaps did not even read *The Case for Israel*—were not removed.[13] While these accusations were relatively minor in comparison with Dershowitz's omission of the relevant diplomatic and historical record about the conflict, the essence of the debate became embroiled around minutiae pertaining to correct citation protocols.

While claiming that his real intention was never to block publication of the book—("I want it to be published so that it will be demolished in the court of public opinion")—Dershowitz clearly sought to create a situation in which any press entertaining the publication of *Beyond Chutzpah* would be placed in the crosshairs of potentially lengthy and ruinous litigation.[14] For instance, Dershowitz wrote to Colin Robinson, an editor at the New Press, which initially expressed an interest in publishing *Beyond Chutzpah*, about supposed inaccuracies in the manuscript. Dershowitz claimed that upon receiving this letter New Press dropped the book. Robinson countered this, pointing out that it was Finkelstein who withdrew from the contract, using an "opt out" clause, when it became clear that Dershowitz's letters, inquiries, and legal threats would delay publication.[15] As Lynne Withey, UC executive press director, noted in the midst of the controversy, "He doesn't want the book published."[16] As Dershowitz stated in one of his many public complaints, "It is shocking that a university press would hide behind academic freedom in defending its decision to publish such trash by an author of such low scholarly repute."[17] "This is not about academic freedom," Dershowitz continued—"the University of California Press is free to publish whatever it chooses. It is about academic standards. Plainly, the University of California Press's decision to publish Finkelstein's drivel was influenced largely by sympathy for his radical ideology."[18] Dershowitz claimed that his goal in contacting UC Press was "to eliminate as many of the demonstrable falsehoods as possible" in *Beyond Chutzpah*.[19]

Why was *Beyond Chutzpah* so controversial?

The publication of Finkelstein's *Beyond Chutzpah: The Misuse of Anti-Semitism and the Abuse of History*—the much-awaited sequel to his controversial *The Holocaust Industry: The Exploitation of Jewish Suffering*—represented a curious moment in US intellectual history. The main title of the book, "Beyond Chutzpah," appropriated the title of Alan Dershowitz's bestselling book, *Chutzpah*—a reference to the Yiddish term which means to be pushy or assertive ("assertive insistence on first-class status among our peers" (*Chutzpah* 9).[20] To go "beyond chutzpah" means that one has entered a realm of absolutism, intolerance, and fanatical devotion. One who has gone "beyond chutzpah" cannot hear well-meaning criticism, even when it is well warranted as a result of blind faith in an ideal and a belief in one's own goodness—a clear reference to Philo-Semitic doctrine in its supposed protection and promotion of Jews and Jewish interests.

 Beyond Chutzpah is divided into three main parts. The first part examines the rise of the so-called New Anti-Semitism, examining its use as a political weapon by US supporters of Israel to accomplish three basic goals:

a   distract the public from examining the historical and diplomatic record, which confirms that Israel has never been interested in having peace with its Arab neighbors (particularly the Palestinians). In fact, right-wing elements within the Israeli government fear a cessation of the conflict, which might lead to a comprehensive peace settlement that has been supported by an international consensus for 44 years. This implementation has been blocked by the United States and Israel;

b   creates controversy where no real controversy exists to confuse and
    obfuscate the conflict's roots, that is, Israel's systematic removal
    of the Palestinian population of the West Bank and Gaza from the
    beginning of Zionism's entry into Palestine; and

c   employs holocaust imagery and rhetoric which casts Jews, not
    Palestinian Arabs, as the victims at the present historical moment—
    suggesting that Israel, as a haven for all Jews in the event of another
    holocaust, must be defended at all costs no matter how indefensible
    its behavior.

The second part of the book, and perhaps the most important, focuses on
the Israeli government's forty-four year commitment to implementing the
removal of the Palestinian population from the occupied territories and
the apartheid practices it has instituted against the Palestinian Arabs in
the form of torture, targeted assassination, administrative detention, home
demolition, the use of Palestinian civilians as human shields, illegal seizures
of land and water aquifers, and the unequal application of the law in the
territories. As Ze'ev Schiff, a celebrated Israeli military correspondent, has
confirmed, Israel as a matter of policy has long targeted the Palestinian
civilian population—in fact, the IDF has drawn no distinction between
Palestinian combatants and Palestinian civilians. Much of the evidence for
this claim can be found in the writings and diaries of Moshe Sharett, Moshe
Dayan, and Ben-Gurion, where these leaders reveal Israel's real territorial
ambitions and attitudes toward the Palestinians.[21] Using the findings of
mainstream human rights organizations such as Amnesty International,
B'tselem (an Israeli organization), Human Rights Watch, as well as
Palestinian human rights organizations, Finkelstein provided a near point-
by-point rebuttal of Dershowitz's *The Case for Israel*, revealing that there
truly is very little quality control regulating the production of "scholarship"
about the US-Israel-Palestine conflict in the United States. Otherwise, how
could *The Case for Israel* have been showered with so much praise by US
cultural elites when it is so at odds with what is found in the writings of
Israeli prime ministers, military historians, and scholars?[22]

   The third part of *Beyond Chutzpah* contains the appendices documenting
that Dershowitz derived material from Peters' *From Time Immemorial*
without proper attribution in his *The Case for Israel*; misrepresented the
history of the conflict and recent "diplomatic efforts" such as Sadat's
offer of peace in 1971 and the Camp David meeting between Clinton,
Barak, and Arafat in 2000; and distorted the positions of his key nemesis,
Noam Chomsky, who has favored a resolution of the conflict according
to the international consensus. Dershowitz claimed that Chomsky's thirty-
eight year position as his own while portraying Chomsky as an "extremist"
for rejecting what Dershowitz stated he has supported all along—a two-
state solution.

Dershowitz's *The Case for Israel* and Joan Peters' *From Time Immemorial*

Twenty-two of the fifty-five footnotes in the first two chapters of *The Case for Israel* come *From Time Immemorial*, although Dershowitz cited the primary sources and the page numbers that Peters listed. References to the original sources show that Dershowitz reproduced Peters' research as his own—often with comical results. In advanced page proofs of *The Case for Israel*, it is clear for all to see that Dershowitz directed his research assistant, Holly Beth Billington, to cite various obscure nineteenth-century sources back to the primary sources instead of to Peters' *From Time Immemorial*, where he originally found them. Drawing upon the *Chicago Manual Style* and a statement from the former President of Dartmouth College, Robert O. Freedman, Dershowitz insisted that he cited the sources correctly. However, as Alexander Cockburn pointed in his response to Dershowitz in the pages of *The Nation* in October of 2003, the *Chicago Manual of Style* specifies the following rules for indicating that one has found a primary source within a secondary source: "Quoted in. To cite a source from a secondary source ('quoted in') is generally to be discouraged, since authors are expected to have examined the works they cite. If an original source is unavailable, however, both the original and the secondary source must be listed" (727). In the exchange with Cockburn in *The Nation*, Dershowitz cited the *Chicago Manual of Style* as providing the following instructions: "With all reuse of others' materials, it is important to identify the original as the source. This ... helps avoid any accusation of plagiarism.... To cite a source from a secondary source ('quoted in ...') is generally to be discouraged ..." As it turns out, the sentences preceding the ellipsis appearing in a section of the *Chicago Manual* entitled "Citations Taken From Secondary Sources" are separated from the sentences following the ellipsis between "plagiarism" and "To cite"—in a section entitled "To Cite a Source from a Secondary Source"—by 590 pages. Furthermore, the phrase "the original" in this context refers not to the primary source but to the origin of the borrowed material—in this case Peters' *From Time Immemorial*. It is clear that neither Dershowitz nor his research assistants checked the primary sources in Peters' *From Time Immemorial* when, for example, Dershowitz cited the 1996 edition of Mark Twain's *Innocents Abroad*. Here is the citation as provided in *The Case for Israel*: "Mark Twain, *The Innocents Abroad* (New York: Oxford University Press, 1996), pp. 485, 508, 520, 607–8."[23] These pages, which Dershowitz listed as coming from this edition, correspond to the pages of the 1881 edition of *The Innocents Abroad* that Peters relied upon. This discrepancy is corrected in the paperback edition, along with all the other 21 other misattributions Finkelstein highlighted.[24]

Despite all the contrived controversy, Finkelstein claimed that the Israel-Palestine conflict—at least within serious scholarly treatments—is fairly straight forward from the standpoint of the historical and diplomatic record.[25] Finkelstein attempted to prove that Israel's apologists, in an attempt to obfuscate the roots and real grievances within the conflict, employ the charge of anti-Semitism to question the credibility and motivations of anyone who focuses on the following:

1 Israel's human rights record, particularly with respect to Israel's use of torture and the Israeli Defense Force's use of Palestinian civilians as human shields in combat operations;

2 Israel's unequal application of the law between Israeli settlers and Palestinians living in the occupied territories;

3 Israel's numerous violations of international law;

4 The key role US intellectuals play in making excuses for 1–3.

Employing the charge of anti-Semitism against critics of Israel to distract people from these important issues, Finkelstein argued, has become transparent. *Beyond Chutzpah* made that case that it is high time to call this public relations strategy what it is: a blatant attempt to silence individuals seeking to restore the integrity of the historical and diplomatic record while twisting the memory of Jewish suffering to serve the political ends of Zionism, political ends many Jews have fiercely resisted since the beginnings of the Zionist movement.[26]

As Finkelstein recounts in the book's introduction, he reached a personal milestone in the course of writing *Beyond Chutzpah*. Nearly twenty years earlier, he came upon Peters' *From Time Immemorial*, a book that sought, in light of Israel's public relations disaster in Lebanon after Israel's 1982 invasion, to shore up the faith among the Zionist faithful by insisting that Palestinians do not—and have never had—a valid moral, diplomatic, or legal claim about land dispossession against Israel. In fact, in Peters' world, the Palestinian claims of injustice and dispossession were manufactured to advance the political objectives of the Arab states against Israel. Finkelstein's decision to publicly expose *From Time Immemorial* as a "threadbare hoax" was a definite turning point in his life and academic career. Indeed, as Finkelstein reflects in the book's first few pages, his work has since that time been in one way or another connected to the US-Israel-Palestine conflict.

The importance of *Beyond Chutzpah*

Finkelstein has long been known as an intellectual who shatters favored pieties, and as a result, often faces extraordinary barriers in reaching a mass audience.[27] As a Jew and the son of Holocaust survivors, Finkelstein has been challenging the US Zionist establishment in one way or another since his parent's passing. For most of his adult life, he had been preparing to write *Beyond Chutzpah*, a book unsettles conventional knowledge—the *Exodus* version of history—about the conflict. When it was published in 2005, the book possessed the potential to change the very nature of the debate on the conflict because of its commitments to seemingly long-lost intellectual ideals such as truth, intellectual honesty, integrity, the historical record, and "speaking truth to power"—even when speaking truth to power leads to one's ostracism and perpetual underemployment.[28]

Finkelstein's most serious indictment in *Beyond Chutzpah*, however, was not necessarily of Alan Dershowitz; instead, he goes much further, exposing much of the US intellectual culture and the cultural institutions within the United States that have actively conspired in blocking an accurate rendering of the historical and diplomatic record on the conflict. As Finkelstein notes,

> The point, of course, is not that Dershowitz is a charlatan. Rather, it's the *systematic institutional bias* that allow for books like *The Case for Israel* to become national best sellers. Were it not for Dershowitz's Harvard pedigree, the praise heaped on this book by Mario Cuomo, Henry Louis Gates Jr., Elie Wiesel, and Floyd Abrams, the favorable notice in media outlets like the *New York Times* and *Boston Globe*, and so on, *The Case for Israel* would have had the same shelf life of a publication of the Flat-Earth society.[29]

Cuomo, Gates, Wiesel, and Abrams provided positive blurbs for *The Case for Israel* in mainstream media outlets, indicating that they believed the arguments in the book to be serious and corroborated by evidence within scholarship and the historical and diplomatic record. With increased attention being brought to Israel's violations of Palestinian human rights in the European press since the beginning of the Second Intifada in September of 2000, US supporters of Israel sought to blame the poor reputation Israel was developing in the international community on the rise of a New Anti-Semitism. As this line of thinking went, Israel had been targeted for criticism not because of what it does to the Palestinians in violation of international law, but because of a resurgent wave of anti-Semitism that has roots in age-old hatreds of the past. Israel's critics, then, were hiding their thinly veiled animus toward the Jewish state behind anti-Zionist arguments and were not motivated by humanitarian they purported to be. To draw this equation between anti-Semitism and anti-Zionism, Israel's supporters have sought to make the argumentative leap that criticism of Israel as the Jewish state is anti-Semitic precisely because Israel is the home of all Jews for all time. However, this argument does not work since there are many anti-Zionist Jews who reject Israel's attempts to speak in the name of Judaism. The traditional response to this problem has been to label anti-Zionist Jews as "self-hating Jews," which requires a suspension of rationality and sound judgement.[30]

Just as he described what he termed "the Holocaust Industry," in a book of that title, creating a distinction between the holocaust (the historical event) and the Holocaust (the ideological creation carefully nurtured by Israel's apologists to immunize the Israeli government against the international community's condemnation of the occupation of the Palestinian population in the West Bank and Gaza), Finkelstein alleges that there's anti-Semitism, an age-old form of prejudice directed against Jews that any decent person would be opposed to and dedicate their life fighting against, and then there's "anti-Semitism"—the latter being an ideologically serviceable mystery religion which accrues considerable benefits for the Israeli government in its oppression of the Palestinians living in the occupied territories. Finkelstein goes even further, claiming that the New Anti-Semitism ends up coddling Zionist Jews, particularly American Zionist Jews, protecting them from much-deserved scrutiny in their advocacy for special dispensations as oppressed "chosen people," while in fact being the most privileged ethnic group in the United States. As he writes:

> Legitimate questions can surely be posed regarding when and if Jews are acting as people who happen to be Jewish or acting "as Jews," and, on the latter occasions (which plainly do arise), regarding the actual breadth and limits of this "Jewish power," but these questions can only be answered empirically, not *a priori* with politically correct formulae. To foreclose inquiry on this topic as anti-Semitic is, intentionally or not, to shield Jews from legitimate scrutiny of their uses and abuses of formidable power.[31]

Finkelstein determines that Abraham Foxman, Phyllis Chesler, Gabriel Schoenfeld, Elie Wiesel, Alan Dershowitz, and a whole host of others—who Finkelstein derisively labels as "the Holocaust Industry"—have been sowing confusion as to what at issue in the conflict, with the sole aim of shielding Israel from worldwide scrutiny as it continues its effort to undermine international law, with crucial US support.

In various ways, throughout *Beyond Chutzpah*, Finkelstein demonstrates that the very logic behind the charge of "the New Anti-Semitism" falls apart when it is subjected to analysis. It is, according to Chesler's *The New Anti-Semitism*, anti-Semitic to associate all Jews with Israel ["Anyone who does not distinguish between Jews and the Jewish state is an anti-Semite"], but according to Chesler it is also anti-Semitic not to do so ["American and Diaspora Jews" must understand that "Israel is hour heart and soul . . . we *are* family" (Chesler's emphasis)].[32] The charge of anti-Semitism, and the concomitant fear of being labeled an anti-Semite, has led far too many people to stop thinking for themselves, leading them to rely upon necessary political results instead of serious investigation and analysis. If the charge of anti-Semitism can be used so widely, to denounce anyone who challenges so-called Jewish interests,—which usually means one has simple criticized the Israeli government's occupation policies—what has been constructed but a new form of totalitarianism? Finkelstein's larger question is this: When will the antics parading as serious arguments cease and some semblance of rationality set in, so discussions about the Israel-Palestine conflict may be conducted in a serious way? For far too long, high theater has confused the central issues.

The power of the New Anti-Semitism

As Finkelstein explained, each time the Israeli government faces a public relations problem, usually in the form of international condemnation for its military exploits, a new alarm is raised about anti-Semitism being on the rise. This strategy was apparent after the 1982 Lebanon War and in light of the Sabra and Shatila massacre, a massacre committed by Lebanese Phalangists under Israeli supervision, as well as during the First and Second Intifada. A more fundamental question arises in this context: How is it that the anti-Semitism of the Nazis has been transferred to the Palestinians living in the occupied territories? This transfer is a part of Zionism's deal, representing one of the Holocaust Industry's greatest triumphs and requiring a good deal of historical reckoning.[33] A lachrymose narrative has been accepted as "standard history," whereby the hatred that Palestinians direct toward Jewish occupiers must be understood through the lens of anti-Semitism. As Joseph Massad claims:

> While much of Israel's violence is "explained" by the pre-Israel status of European Jews, Palestinian violence is also viewed hermeneutically through the status of those same Jews, the status of the Palestinians as products of their own separate history being deemed irrelevant. After all, "[t]he only history is white." Israel's actions, however, are believed to stem from the status of those Jews who arrived on the shores of Palestine after fleeing the Nazi regime and the holocaust, only to be confronted by another violence anti-Semitic campaign, this time by Palestinian Arabs and Arabs from neighboring countries intent on expelling them from their last and only haven. Thus, Israel's violence, regrettable as it may be, is in effect viewed as self-defensive in nature. In the same vein, Palestinian violence, which was/is in self-defense against foreign invaders, is also "explained" out of context as part of this anti-Semitic campaign against Jewish refugees. All discourse involving Palestinians and Israel has been and continues to be situated within the bounds of these hermeneutical axioms—whereby, among other qualifiers, Jews are *always* refugees fleeing the holocaust when, in fact, they need to be viewed in the context of two separate histories and discourses.[34]

Unfortunately since Israel's triumph against Egypt's General Abdul Nasser in the Six-Day War, the historical record has been so polluted by Holocaust propaganda, propaganda meant to highlight Jewish suffering to the exclusion of the suffering of other ethnic groups, that any critical discussion of Israel has been a near impossibility. Finkelstein lays the vital ground for a rational discussion about Israel, the US-Israel special relationship, and Israel's 46 years of oppression against the Palestinians. To these ends, Finkelstein shows that there's nothing new about the New Anti-Semitism. He demonstrates a clear connection between the manipulation of the specter of a New Anti-Semitism by Israel's apologists, who seek to distract the public from the international consensus, and Israel's increasingly aggressive military behavior. Ultimately, the New Anti-Semitism is about denying the reality of the conflict through the perversion of Jewish History.

Exposing a systemic bias

In its exploration of how the frequently employed charge of anti-Semitism serves elite interests, along with its in-depth analysis of Alan Dershowitz's problematic distortions in *The Case for Israel*, *Beyond Chutzpah* demonstrated—that when it comes to discussing, covering, and unashamedly misrepresenting the specific facts of the Israel-Palestine conflict—certain US intellectuals set a new benchmark. As Finkelstein explained, *Beyond Chutzpah*'s "substantive aim was to use *The Case for Israel* as a peg to explore crucial aspects of the Israel-Palestine conflict."

> If truth and justice are the most potent weapons in the arsenal of the oppressed, the manifold reports of these human rights organizations are the most underutilized resource for a just resolution of the Israel-Palestine conflict. It appears that they are rarely read and almost never cited. And it is mainly because these uniquely authoritative publications lie around collecting dust that apologists can propagate so much mythology about Israel human rights record. Were their findings widely disseminated, Israel's occupation would clearly be morally indefensible.[35]

In this sense, *Beyond Chutzpah* went to the real source of the problem— pro-Zionist, American Jewish abuse of power in supporting Israeli aggression against the Palestinians suffering under occupation. Finkelstein intrepidly asks, Do American Zionist Jews, qua Jews, lend the societal benefits of their ethnic privilege to advance Israel's morally-bankrupt agenda toward increased militarization and the annexation of the West Bank? If the voting behavior of the US Congress and its genuflection to AIPAC is any indication, the answer is obviously "yes." However, Israel serves strategic interests for the United States in blocking the growth of Arab nationalism and the greatly feared Pan-Arab movement; it cannot obviously be described as just an object of pro-Zionist Jewish American devotion. Israel, in some sense, occupies a central place in the US imagination in its aspirations to be a beacon of light in the wilderness. To push the point even further, Israel and the United States are one.

Nonetheless, one must wonder whether or not Finkelstein—in this book of nearly three hundred and twenty pages—merely proved a truism: power politics determines the rules and the discourses through which to apprehend reality, even when those rules and discourses defy elementary logic, downright commonsense, and the never-read findings of Amnesty International, B'Tselem, and Human Rights Watch. While there has been international condemnation of the Israeli government's illegal occupation and oppression of the Palestinians in West Bank and Gaza for nearly forty six years, Israel's occupation has continued because Israel is militarily and diplomatically supported by its superpower patron, the United States. US and Israeli elites have found it more than worthwhile to ignore the moral and legal prohibitions against ethnic cleansing (there is no more accurate phrase) of the Palestinians while cashing in on the benefits of a desperate *real politick*.

Finkelstein's thorough descriptions of just how problematic the so-called New Anti-Semitism is—in such books as Foxman's *Never Again?*, Chesler's *The New Anti-Semitism*, Schoenfeld's *The Return of Anti-Semitism*, and the vast majority of the contributions to Ron Rosenbaum's *Those Who Forget*—proved the seeming futility of confronting powerful individuals and organizations on these issues, as the spinning of information can deter all but the most intrepid researcher. Despite the international consensus on the illegality of Israel's occupation, and the widespread anti-Arab sentiment that exists worldwide, Foxman, Chesler, Schoenfeld, and most of the contributors to the Rosenbaum collection attempt the more-than-slightly-difficult task of turning reality on its head: Jews are victims, never victimizers; Israel is vulnerable; the Arab world's resistance and anger toward Israel can only be blamed on an inexplicable anti-Semitism; anyone who disagrees with them is an anti-Semite. In this context, even one-time close allies can be characterized as turn coats, as Leon Wieseltier (*The New Republic* editor) was for not adequately toeing the party line. This proves, as Finkelstein notes, how the revolution can indeed devour its children when the party and that party line are thrown into jeopardy (*Beyond Chutzpah* 40). Foxman, Chesler, Schoenfeld, and Dershowitz avoid dealing with the real anti-Semitism—primarily their own—because they are so committed to defending Israeli military actions against criticism while theorizing about the New Anti-Semitism. The label "anti-Semite," if it is to remain coherent and remain true to its historical roots, should also apply to those who claim that Israel speaks on behalf of all Jews, particularly diaspora Jewry; it clearly does not.

This is a direct throwback to the darkest days of Stalinism, when those criticizing the Soviet regime were, by virtue of this fact alone, branded "objective" abettors of fascism, and dealt with accordingly. One day it's the uniqueness of and universality of theological absolutism; the next day it's the uniqueness and universality of the Holocaust. *The constant is the totalitarian cast of mind, and attendant stigmatizing of dissent as a disease that must be wiped out by the state.* (*Beyond Chutzpah* 49; emphasis mine)

Sadly, Finkelstein's historical analogy proved itself to be accurate, providing a refreshing glimpse into the standards governing US intellectual life. In his book, *The Case for Peace*, Dershowitz claimed that he seeks to expose those extremists who are "more Israeli than the Israelis" and "more Palestinian than the Palestinians." That Alan Dershowitz posed as an objective party, employing the discourse of reason, factuality, and legitimacy to foist an extremely problematic and troubling text such as *The Case for Israel* on the public requires extended reflection. As Finkelstein noted in the *Beyond Chutzpah's* conclusion, Alan Dershowitz did not make the case for Israel; he was in reality laying the ground for its destruction through his seeming re-descriptions of Israeli torture of Palestinians as justified security measures, as well as his condemnation of the Israeli peace movement, the International Solidarity Movement, and those fighting to broaden civil liberties in Israel. Playing the part of the prototypical "tough Jew,"[36] Dershowitz seemingly sought to undermine international law as it applies to the Israel-Palestine conflict.

Conclusion

I reviewed Finkelstein's *Beyond Chutzpah: The Misuse of Anti-Semitism and the Abuse of History* in the October 2005 issue of *Logos: A Journal of Modern Society and Culture*, which stirred Dershowitz, among others, to write a complaint letter to the *Logos* editors.[37] I stated in my review essay that Israel's apologists have systematically distorted the diplomatic and historical record with respect to Israel's occupation of the West Bank and, until recently Gaza, because the facts plainly do not correspond with the requisite propaganda image. Israel and the United States have blocked a diplomatic settlement of the conflict for nearly 46 years. If to express this truism makes one "an anti-Israel activist," then so be it. As I explained at that time, those interested in fully rounded scholarship on the diplomatic and historical record, however, would do well to consult and consider Ilan Pappe's *The Making of the Arab-Israeli Conflict*, Naseer Aruri's *Dishonest Broker: The Role of the United States in Palestine and Israel*, Steven Spiegel's *The Other Arab-Israeli Conflict: Making America's Middle East Policy from Truman to Reagan*, Charles Enderlin's *Shattered Dreams: The Failure of the Peace Process in the Middle East*, and Noam Chomsky's *The Fateful Triangle: The United States, Israel, and the Palestinians*.

Israel's 42-year occupation of the Gaza Strip was illegal according to international law. What is ambiguous or erroneous about that? According to the Fourth Geneva Convention, it is illegal for an occupying power to transport its population into occupied territory. The removal of Israeli settlers from the Gaza Strip brought Israel into some compliance with international law, although human rights organizations such as B'tselem have since labeled Gaza as the world's largest "open-air prison."[38]

Israel is only a "democracy" to the extent that it is "a democracy for Jews," with its 1.5 million Palestinians considered a demographic time bomb that threatens Israel's "Jewish character." According to Zionist thinking, as Yosef Gorny powerfully demonstrates in his *Zionism and the Arabs, 1882-1948: A Study of Ideology*, the Palestinian-Arab population has long posed the main obstacle to the creation and maintenance of an exclusively Jewish state. Yehoshua Porath points out in his two-volume work on Palestinian nationalism, and as Benny Morris has confirmed in his inexhaustible *The Birth of the Palestinian Refugee Problem Revisited*, Palestinian resistance to Zionist conquest arose out of a fear of territorial displacement and not, as is frequently assumed and rhetorically insisted, because of Arab anti-Semitism. By the main tenets of Zionist thinking Israel's Arabs are a cancer on the larger body politic that must be removed either by transfer or by the creation of an apartheid state; these Arabs within Israel are second-class citizens in an "Israeli democracy." Fouzi El-Asmar's *To Be an Arab in Israel* is a powerful and moving testimony of the effects of "Israeli democracy" on the Palestinian Arab. *To Be an Arab in Israel* forms the basis for a separate chapter of this book.

In addition to these three main points, I responded to Dershowitz's argument about the circumstances preceding the University of California Press's publication of Finkelstein's *Beyond Chutzpah*. Dershowitz wrote the following in his letter to the *Logos* editors:

> In order to deflect attention away from their lack of academic standards and hard-left anti-Israel bias, Finkelstein and his publisher have lied about the issue of academic freedom. Nobody has ever tried to censor Finkelstein's drivel. He can always publish it with presses that acknowledge their anti-Israel bias. The issue is, and has always been, one of academic standards: how could the University of California Press publish a work so lacking in standards, so filled with misquotations, falsifications, and faked data by a failed academic with a well-deserved reputation for the "pure invention" of his sources? No objective university press would have published this sequel to a book the *New York Times* called a "variation on the anti-Semitic forgery, the *Protocols of the Elders of Zion*."[39]

Most interestingly, Dershowitz claimed that he never tried to block publication of Finkelstein's *Beyond Chutzpah*, seeking only to ensure that it met the requisite standards for publication at a well-known academic press. The controversy, according to Dershowitz, was not one about academic freedom but instead about academic standards. Dershowitz's statements were clearly red herrings: First, why did he hire the New York law firm, Cravath, Swaine, and Moore, to write intimidating letters about the anticipated content of *Beyond Chutzpah* to employees at the University of California Press if he was not seeking ultimately to interfere with the book's publication? Dershowitz claimed that he did so to ensure that demonstrable falsehoods, such as that he did not write or even possibly read *The Case for Israel* before its publication, would be removed.[40] Such charges did not appear in *Beyond Chutzpah* because Finkelstein focused on documenting how Dershowitz's refusal to seriously contend with and rebut the findings of human rights organizations about Israel's treatment of the Palestinians in the occupied territories, as well as the insights of mainstream scholarship, revealed some troubling aspects of US intellectual culture. Furthermore, as *The Case for Israel* was lauded as an important book constituting required reading for citizens and politicians, Finkelstein asked some hard-hitting questions about the mainstream intellectuals and the institutions that house them. Under these circumstances, it is quite understandable why Dershowitz took an interest in the publication of *Beyond Chutzpah* by the University of California Press.

Clearly, the University of California Press, and not outside parties, should decide if a manuscript meets its high standards for publication; it has a rather good track record in this regard. In other words, the Press did not need Dershowitz's assistance in assessing the merits of *Beyond Chutzpah*. Six experts on the US-Israel-Palestine conflict, experts in Israel and the United States, twenty faculty members on the editorial board of UC Press at the University of California at Berkeley, and several libel attorneys determined that *Beyond Chutzpah* was suitable for publication.

When Dershowitz could not prevail upon the editorial board, he then appealed to Governor Arnold Schwarzenegger to prevent publication of the book. Dershowitz's continued repetition of spurious charges, such as that the University of California Press published Finkelstein's *Beyond Chutzpah* because of the Press's well-known anti-Zionist and anti-Israel bias, betokened little more than lapses into demagoguery. It was indeed interesting to see how Dershowitz sought to establish himself as the determiner of appropriate standards for publication of a book critical of him at a university press on which he does not sit on the editorial board. One might conceivably turns the tables and ask how Wiley & Sons could publish *The Case for Israel* and then, less than 2 years later, publish Dershowitz's *The Case for Peace*, an equally problematic book. An answer to this state of affairs is offered in *Beyond Chutzpah*: "The point, of course, is not that Dershowitz is a charlatan. Rather, it is the systematic institutional bias that allows books like *The Case for Israel* to become national best sellers" (17; emphasis in original). While Finkelstein's assessment of US intellectual culture might seem too sweeping, it is important to keep in mind that AIPAC mailed every member of Congress a copy of *The Case for Israel*, an indication of the Lobby's interest in ensuring that those voting for continued military and economic aid for Israel possessed the "appropriate" facts. As Finkelstein notes, "American Jewish organizations reportedly earmarked a copy for every Jewish high school graduate and widely distributed it on college campuses, while the Israeli Foreign Ministry purchased thousands of copies for worldwide distribution, Israeli embassies stockpiled it, Israeli information officers used it as a basic text, and Israel's Mission at the United Nations distributed hundreds of copies to U.N. ambassadors and officers" (*Beyond Chutzpah* 89). It is clear that the Dershowitz constructed image of Israel in *The Case for Israel* was rather to amiable to elite interests.

Dershowitz's criticisms of Finkelstein's supposedly polemical style and his specific public allegations about *The Case for Israel*, as well as Dershowitz's steady campaign to interfere with the publication of *Beyond Chutzpah* at the University of California Press during the summer of 2005, contributed to my own realization that something was amiss: when it comes to debating the specifics of the US-Israel-Palestine conflict, Israel's apologists must engage in antics rather than serious analysis. Avoiding the facts and side-stepping the implications of international law necessitate the use of creative methods of avoidance. In other words, controversy must be created where no real controversy exists to avoid the following inconvenient facts: Israel's occupation of the West Bank is illegal according to the Fourth Geneva Convention and UN Security Council Resolution 242; Gaza, after "disengagement," has been left as an open-air prison, where 1.2 million Palestinians are experiencing near complete social and economic suffocation; the nearly four hundred thousand settlers in the West Bank and around East Jerusalem are violating international law; Israeli settlement blocks on the West Bank (Ariel, Maale Adumim, and Gush Etzion) have been expanding since the so-called disengagement and are cutting off East Jerusalem from the rest of the West Bank.

Harvard Middle East Studies expert Sara Roy claims that, "Whatever else it claims to be, the Gaza Disengagement Plan [was], at heart, an instrument for Israel's continued annexation of West Bank land and the physical integration of that land into Israel."[41] Israel and the United States, despite being at the forefront of seeking "peace in the Middle East," have actively worked against "peace" in the meaningful sense; US intellectuals have been complicit in concealing the Israel's military force's brutal treatment of the Palestinian population of the occupied territories for nearly 46 years; elite intellectual opinion in the United States has tolerated and has provided ideological cover for the intolerable conditions within which occupied Palestinians live, conditions ultimately endangering Israeli security.

In his *An Israeli in Palestine*, Jeff Halper indicates that all the energetic discussion about the creation of a Palestinian state always avoids a crucial issue: viability.[42] The inevitable question, "Will the Palestinians be allowed to construct a viable Palestinian state?" is disingenuous because the prospect of Palestinian statehood will seemingly always be framed as a threat in relation to Israeli security. There is a clear scholarly consensus on how the Palestinians living under occupation have been treated by the Israeli Defense Forces, as well as a consensus among human rights organizations about Israel's human rights violations. However, Dershowitz, who was seemingly not interested in investigating scholarship or the findings of human rights organizations, sought to present Israel as a country with an unparalleled human rights record. He accused me in my review essay of simply repeating Arafat's "bantustan accusation," when exactly the same language is used by Meron Benevisti to describe what is happening in the West Bank. As Benevisti noted, "the goal of disengagement is to improve the demographic situation by removing a million and a half Palestinians from Israeli control and thereby reducing the danger that the country will cease to be a Jewish state" and that "[t]he bantustan model for Gaza, as depicted in the disengagement plan, is a model that Sharon plans to copy on the West Bank."[43] However, this is not the first time that Dershowitz has attempted to portray human rights organizations, even Israeli human rights organizations, as being politically motivated by an anti-Israel agenda. For example, in 1970 Dershowitz, in an article for *Commentary* entitled "Preventive Detention," described Israel's imprisonment of the Palestinian political activist Fouzi El-Asmar as a legitimate form of preventive detention because El-Asmar represented a terrorist threat. However, El-Asmar was actually imprisoned for his political activism against Israel's occupation, not because he represented an actual terrorist threat.

In his response to Dershowitz's "Preventive Detention," an article which appeared in the December 1970 issue of *Commentary*, Israel Shahak, a survivor of the Nazi Holocaust, wrote: "Mr. Dershowitz is not really important in himself, but unfortunately his attitude is typical of several American Jews I have encountered in Israel: their real liberalism is, and always was, a fake . . ." (37). In his letter to the editors of *Commentary*, Shahak concluded with a serious warning to "American Jews":

> You cannot continue in this way. You now have the same choice that was once given you on Mount Carmel: "How long will ye halt between two opinions? If the LORD be God, follow Him, but if Baal, follow him" (Kings I, 18:21). And similarly now: If you believe in the same justice for Arabs that you demand for yourselves and for your brothers in the USSR, raise your voices and fight for the human rights of the Arabs in Israel in exactly the same way: If not, go and worship military force, bow low to Phantoms and tanks, accumulate money—and go to hell. (37–8)

Shahak's powerful words are as relevant now as they were over 30 years ago. On 29 November 2005, Dershowitz, in a debate with Noam Chomsky at Harvard's Kennedy School of Business, intoned "Thank God Israel has to make peace with the Palestinians and not the professors."[44] Academics, particularly those who read scholarship and the hundreds of reports that have been issued by B'tselem, Amnesty International, and Human Rights Watch, are capable of stating the facts and are indeed a threat. Dershowitz contended that my "intemperate use of language," "wild historical fabrications," and "parrot[ing] of so many demonstrably false accusations" "made it difficult to write a rebuttal against a writer whose own article readily discredits itself." One example of my "wild historical fabrications," according to Dershowitz, was my claim that American Jewish Zionists blocked the immigration of Jewish DPs (displaced persons) to the United States in the aftermath of WW II. In his recent book, In *The Shadow of the Holocaust: The Struggle Between Jews in Zionists in the Aftermath of World War II*, Yossef Grodinsky documents quite carefully the coercive efforts the Zionist movement employed to bring Jewish DPs to Palestine at the end of WW II.

Dershowitz expressed astonishment that I would label Israel "a crazy state" and "not a democracy." As I wrote in my review essay, the term "crazy state" is a term of art within the international relations literature. It was developed by an Israeli scholar, Yeheskel Dror, in a book entitled *Crazy States: A Counterconventional Strategic Problem*. Those interested in the topic should also read Chomsky's *The Fateful Triangle* (Chapter 7, Section 4.2.2) about the grave threat Israel poses to the world if it chooses to exercise its Samson Option. Chomsky writes:

> The growing threat has been recognized within Israel. Yaakov Sharett writes that the greatest danger facing Israel now is the "collective version" of Samson's revenge against the Philistines—"Let me perish with the Philistines"—as he brought down the Temple in ruins, killing more Philistines than he had during his lifetime. He cites the [Moshe] Sharett diaries, the entry just cited [where M. Sharett "recorded in October 1955 his fear concerning Defense Minister Pinhas Lavon of the Labor Party. Lavon, he wrote, 'has constantly preached in favor of acts of madness and taught the army leadership the diabolic lesson of how to set the Middle East on fire, how to cause friction, cause bloody confrontations, sabotage targets and property of the Powers [and perform] acts of despair and suicide'"], where Defense Minister Lavon is quoted as saying: "we will go crazy ('nishtagea') if crossed." ... This 'Samson complex' is not something to be taken lightly. Aryeh (Lova) Eliav, one of Israel's best-known and most influential doves, writes that the attitude of "those who brought the 'Samson complex' here, according to which we shall kill and bury all the Gentiles around us while we ourselves shall die with them," is a sign of the same sort of "insanity" that was manifested in the violent counter-demonstration in which Emil Grunzweig (a mathematics teacher from Kibbutz Revivim, was killed by an Israeli Army assault grenade while participating in a Peace Now demonstration calling upon Ariel Sharon to resign as the Kahan Commission had recommended)—and is a phenomenon of some significance in contemporary Israel. (467–8)

Neve Gordon, in his November 2000 *Nation* review of Finkelstein's *The Holocaust Industry*, aptly wrote:

> Informing Finkelstein's analysis is a universal ethics, which echoes Arendt's important claim that Eichmann should have been sentenced for his crimes against humanity rather than his crimes against the Jews. His book is controversial not entirely because of his mistakes or his piercing rhetoric but because he speaks truth to power. He, and not the Jewish organizations he criticizes, is following the example set by the great Jewish prophets.[45]

Much the same can be said about the motives and means of *Beyond Chutzpah*. Finkelstein's exposure of Dershowitz's scholarly derelictions should prod us to ask serious questions about US intellectual culture and, more importantly, ourselves. That Finkelstein's case against Dershowitz was so well documented proves that something has gone seriously awry in the quality-control mechanisms governing our culture's understanding of the US-Israel-Palestine conflict. That Dershowitz went to such great lengths to criticize anyone who wrote even a faintly positive review of *Beyond Chutzpah* attested to his underlying desperation. That mainstream US intellectuals timidly avoided denouncing Dershowitz's *The Case for Israel* and *The Case for Peace* while simultaneously not defending and praising the courage of Norman Finkelstein and critical books such as *Beyond Chutzpah*, reveals the extent to which power politics can corrupt our perception and moral sense.[46]

CHAPTER FOUR

The Question of Palestine and the subversion of academic freedom: DePaul's denial of tenure to Norman G. Finkelstein

I have a sinking feeling about the damage this [Finkelstein's tenure denial] will do to academic freedom . . .

(RAUL HILBERG, *Chicago Sun Times*, 10 June 2007)

Through a strange concatenation of events, DePaul University has become a battle ground for two things: 1) academic freedom; 2) hideous forty-year occupation of the Palestinians by the Israeli government, supported by US taxpayer dollars.

(NORMAN FINKELSTEIN *848*, Chicago Public Radio, 15 June 2007)

Historically, university administrations have insisted upon protecting the concept of academic freedom, as it is the centerpiece of the university's mission and functioning. At the same time, no university administration has ever owned up to a violation of academic freedom, or admitted that academic freedom was at issue, in the context of the dismissal of a controversial faculty member (see Schrecker 1986, 1999). In defending their decisions to terminate or deny tenure in controversial cases, universities simply claim that other plausible reasons—beyond the scholar's research area or provocative extramural speech—existed for the dismissal or tenure denial (see Schrecker 2010). This "other reasons" approach to sidestepping a university's obligation to promote academic freedom, for scholars advancing particular political viewpoints, becomes particularly problematic with respect to denying basic due process protections to scholars writing critically about the Israel-Palestine conflict.

Within the current political landscape of the US academy, academic freedom has been largely redefined to protect Israel's defenders against serious and substantive criticism, producing the unfortunate result that supporting Palestinian human rights in scholarship can be portrayed as "advocacy," "partisanship," and "political posturing" (see "AAUP Statement," 2004; Hollinger 2005). Despite all of the seemingly fancy rhetorical footwork about what academic freedom is and how it should be conceptualized, a university depends upon it in justifying to the public its existence as an intellectual testing ground. Regardless of how one defines academic freedom, all would agree that, without academic freedom, a university cannot theoretically represent itself as a serious experiment station for examining the most important and controversial ideas of our time. Universities have an obligation to defend academic freedom to create the conditions of possibility that are necessary for experimentation and the discovery of knowledge. Unfortunately, as the denial of tenure to the embattled political scientist Norman Finkelstein at DePaul University in June 2007 amply demonstrated, this commitment to academic freedom is transient at best.

Despite the sound and the fury around his tenure denial in June of 2007, Finkelstein ultimately praised DePaul University upon reflecting on the unique set of pressures that eventuated in his unjust dismissal:

> For the record, I did not begrudge DePaul's decision to deny me tenure. It has always been my belief that no one except me should have to bear the costs of my political convictions. *The sustained pressures exerted on a middle-tier Catholic institution vulnerable to charges of anti-Semitism would probably have proven intolerable.* It was also an institution that performed a creditable public service, attracting a morally impressive student body from which I greatly benefited during my last days there and to whom I will be eternally grateful (emphasis added). (Finkelstein 2008–09)

Well-known public intellectual, the author of several recognized books, and one of the most effective of DePaul's professors, Finkelstein possessed an envious academic record by any standard. It is quite clear Finkelstein should have easily received tenure and promotion to Associate Professor of Political Science at DePaul University in 2007 under any reasonable process free from external pressures. The process, however, was anything but reasonable and untainted (see "Middle East Studies," 2007). Indeed, a review of the relevant documents in the Finkelstein tenure case leads one to a clear and simple conclusion: DePaul's stated reasons for denying Finkelstein tenure and promotion cannot be reconciled with the factual record. These reasons were contrived to construct a transparent pretext for dismissing an outspoken critic of US and Israeli Middle East policy. As Noam Chomsky noted on *Democracy Now!* in May of 2007 shortly before DePaul announced its final decision, "It's amazing he [Finkelstein] hasn't had full professorship a long time ago" (Goodman 2007).[1]

The fact that Finkelstein was not only denied tenure, but done so in violation of the most fundamental aspects of academic due process (as I will explain), strongly suggests that critics of Israel, and their well-vetted scholarship, not only are deprived of basic academic freedom protections, but that academic freedom does not exist for them as either an individual right or within the context of institutional, disciplinary, or professional norms.[2] Indeed, it appears that academic freedom can easily be deployed as a rhetorical device in service of a distinct political program if the situation requires it (see Fish 1994, 2001). In other words, academic freedom provides substantive protections to scholars when the viewpoints they espouse are endorsed by those holding the reins of power. In those instances, academic freedom becomes largely irrelevant since those viewpoints do not need protection because they coincide with, and do not threaten, concentrated power.

Ironically, DePaul justified Finkelstein's tenure denial on the grounds that it posed a distinct threat to academic freedom and public discourse. DePaul's Dean of the College of Liberal Arts and Sciences noted in his assessment of Finkelstein's tenure application: "I see this [Finkelstein's "apparent penchant of reducing an argument and oppositional views to the inevitable personal and reputation damaging attack, demeaning those with whom he disagrees"] as a very damaging threat to civil discourse in a University and in society in general. Such inflammatory polemics in no way further the civil discourse and serious intellectual inquiry that the Academy stands for to say nothing for the deeply shared DePaul University and Vincentian value of 'personalism'—respect for the dignity of the individual" (see "College Personnel Committee," 2007). In his relentless questioning and deconstruction of the motives and strategies of some of Israel's most persistent defenders (Alan Dershowitz, Daniel Goldhagen, and Elie Wiesel), Finkelstein represented a threat to "civil discourse" and "serious intellectual inquiry that the Academy stands for" (ibid.).

Scholars writing on the Israel-Palestine conflict find themselves frequently placed in the crosshairs of extremely powerful interest groups devoted to protecting Israel from criticism due to its human rights record.[3] These groups are willing to engage in the most underhanded strategies to defame its political opponents. The pattern is clear: an extremely accomplished scholar on the conflict becomes the object of a national campaign launched by pro-Israel partisans to distract the public from the critique of Israel the scholar offers. When the strength of the scholarly record is strong and irrefutable with respect to the usual evaluative grounds, and the teaching record impeccable, the university administration has to manufacture a way to drive the faculty member out of the university without exposing itself to costly liability. This is not an easy task, although the academic structure can always accommodate (and effectively hide) politically discriminatory reasons for terminating a faculty member, making those reasons appear plausible within a supposedly objective process. So it was with Finkelstein's tenure denial, as Finkelstein was constructed as an enemy of academic freedom instead of as someone who was denied basic academic freedom protections. Academic freedom, the freedom to pursue controversial lines of inquiry as part of one's research, was seemingly redefined to protect Israel's staunchest defenders against substantive criticism of their apologetics.

The redefinition of academic freedom ("defending the free inquiry of associates," Holtschneider denial letter) to protect a powerful special-interest group (apologists for Israel's militarism, occupation of Palestinian territory, etc.), whose interests could be jeopardized by serious criticism, is unprecedented, providing a new model for containing and marginalizing progressive social thought.[4] Finkelstein's tenure denial presented an important test case for the real enemies of academic freedom, those seeking to make public criticism of Israel's human rights record tantamount to a speech crime (see D. Cole 2003; J. Cole 2005; Sherman 2005). That these enemies succeeded in ensuring that DePaul would deny Finkelstein tenure and promotion should be of grave concern to critical intellectuals interested in sustaining an open debate about the historical and diplomatic record on the Israel-Palestine conflict in the US public sphere (see Williams 2007a). An examination of the specific aspects of the case will set the stage for a more in-depth analysis of the behind-the-scenes maneuvering and politics informing DePaul's decision to deny Finkelstein a lifetime position at the University.

The facts of the case

Despite a 9 in favor, 3 against vote at the departmental level, a 5 in favor, 0 against at the College level, the Dean of Liberal Arts, Charles Suchar, withheld his support of Finkelstein's tenure application. Ultimately, Suchar claimed there was confidential information driving the administration's decision-making, in an attempt to justify his refusal to support the recommendations of two different faculty bodies (the political science department and the College Personnel Committee).[5] After the University Board on Promotion and Tenure (DePaul's highest level committee in the tenure and promotion process) recommended by a vote of 4 in favor, 3 opposed to deny tenure, DePaul's President, Father Dennis Holtschneider, accepted that recommendation (see Holtschneider 2007).

The Board pointed to supposed shortcomings in Finkelstein's scholarship that were identified by the three members of DePaul's Political Science

Department who had issued a minority report and voted against granting tenure, specifically citing concerns about the "accuracy of some of the evidence [Finkelstein] uses in his scholarship and the cogency of some of his arguments" (Birmingham 2007). Citing "broader expectations and professional standards by which DePaul faculty are obliged to comport themselves as members of the academic profession and as members of the DePaul intellectual community," "the UBPT expressed several concerns touching upon [Finkelstein's] scholarship, specifically what they consider the intellectual character of his work and his persona as a public intellectual" (Holtschneider 2007).

Furthermore, the Board noted that "Criticism has been expressed for his inflammatory style and his personal attacks in his writings and intellectual debates. These concerns are relevant to [the UBPT] in the recognition that an academic's reputation is intrinsically tied to the institution of which he or she is affiliated. It was questioned by some whether Dr. Finkelstein effectively contributes to the public discourse on sensitive social issues." Those who questioned whether Finkelstein effectively contributes to the public discourse on sensitive social issues, of course, remain unidentified, although it is not difficult to figure who these individuals and organizations might have been (see Dershowitz n.d.; Plaut 2007c). Alan Dershowitz, several Zionist watchdog organizations, including the Anti-Defamation League and American Jewish Committee, possessed a vested interest in seeing that DePaul would deny Finkelstein tenure. Finkelstein's devastating critiques of American Zionism, US support for Israel, Israel's human rights record, and the various absurd apologetics offered in defense of all three were threatening to the nearly totalitarian grip of Zionist power. How often do the feelings and sensitivities of one's political opponents become the operative and legitimate grounds upon which to deny tenure? If one's political opponents possess sufficient political power, the rules of the game clearly are up for sale to the highest bidder.

What does one make of the fact that, as Finkelstein's case moved up through DePaul's institutional hierarchy, his scholarship was subjected to criticisms about its tone, style, and etiquette, instead of its substance, as well concerns about how DePaul's reputation might suffer if tenure were granted? Concerns about the accuracy of the evidence Finkelstein's used in his scholarship were clearly a red herring. The only logical inference to be drawn is that DePaul recognized the distinct problems that would arise if Finkelstein were to become a tenured faculty member for a nearly 30-year career. Perhaps according to the logic of those opposing Finkelstein's tenure bid, Finkelstein's presence on the DePaul faculty would have undoubtedly inhibited the university's long-term institutional growth, for example financial donations to the University, international institution building, and external partnering (Abraham 2007). While one cannot not know with certainty if threats to withhold financial contributions to DePaul were the driving motivation for DePaul's administration decision to deny Finkelstein tenure, or if parties interested in the decision promised to give substantial financial support to the University in return for Finkelstein's tenure denial, there can be little doubt that long-term institutional growth was at issue.[6] The University Board on Promotion and Tenure may have come to its decision by considering how Finkelstein's presence at DePaul would ultimately effect this long-term institutional growth, a consideration that DePaul was well within its legal rights to entertain. In a rarely referenced portion of Chapter 4 of DePaul's Faculty Handbook, captioned as "Reappointment and Separation," one finds the following statement: "The University reserves the right to use the widest latitude, within the bounds of academic freedom, as it determines which faculty to retain. . . ."[7] Since academic freedom had to be respected in advancing arguments against Finkelstein's tenurability, DePaul's administration simply redefined the parameters of academic freedom. At the conclusion of the process in June 2007, DePaul's President Dennis Holtschneider explained, "Some will consider this decision in the context of academic freedom. In fact, academic freedom is alive and well at DePaul" (Grossman 2007).

DePaul likely knew that this battle would ultimately be won on legal grounds, not ethical grounds, as it created specific arguments about Finkelstein's unsuitability for a tenured position at DePaul because his persona and scholarship stood at odds with the Catholic institution's Vincentian mission.

In invoking the institution's mission ("preserving the God-given dignity of the intellectual"), emphasizing distinctive aspects of DePaul's character (Vincentian personalism), and portraying Finkelstein as a threat to the academic freedom of others (not "defending and respecting the free inquiry of associates"), DePaul established the necessary legal grounds upon which to carry out the tenure denial. That DePaul's Office of the General Counsel played a larger role in shaping the rationales offered to justify the outcome in the Finkelstein's tenure case, as opposed to the input of any faculty body, gives us some insight into the current political landscape within the contemporary academy (see Schrecker 2010).[8] Within this environment, truth and the development of a critical perspective are very much beside the point.

The Dershowitz factor

Finkelstein's prospective tenure bid at DePaul became the object of Alan Dershowitz's interest in late 2003. Dershowitz, the Felix Frankfurter Professor of Law, at Harvard Law School, a leading civil libertarian, and one of the top defense attorneys in the United States, has long been known as a reflexive defender of Israel's problematic human rights record and military adventurism. As soon as Finkelstein made clear his intention to release documentation demonstrating that Dershowitz's *The Case for Israel* was a "hoax plagiarized from another hoax" on *Democracy Now!* in September 2003, Dershowitz began a campaign to drive Finkelstein out of the academy (see Finkelstein n.d.; Goodman 2003). In 2004, Dershowitz contacted President Dennis Holtschneider, attaching a manuscript entitled "Literary McCarthyism," arguing that DePaul should fire Finkelstein because of his *ad hominem* attacks and unprofessionalism in leveling accusations of plagiarism against supporters of Israel. In addition, Dershowitz contacted the chair of DePaul's political science department, Professor Patrick Callahan as early as 2004, and again three months prior to the political science department's considering Finkelstein's tenure case (see Dershowitz 2006). There is also strong circumstantial evidence that Dershowitz sought to contact members of DePaul's Board of Trustees, specifically the chair of DePaul's Board of Trustees, Mr. John Simon, about Finkelstein, who Dershowitz labeled "a full-time, malicious defamer" (see Jenner and Block n.d., 2004).[9]

An unsettling pattern

Four months prior to Norman Finkelstein's tenure denial, in February of 2007, I sought to convene an academic freedom conference at DePaul, hoping to invite some of the top academics writing on academic freedom and the Middle East, for example Jonathan Cole, Akeel Bilgrami, John Mearsheimer, Robert Jensen, and Juan Cole. Aware of the circumstances surrounding Finkelstein's pending tenure case, I thought holding such a conference would highlight current threats to academic freedom, particularly with respect to the challenges critics of Israel face in the US academy in documenting the historical and diplomatic record on the conflict. I asked the Dean of the College of Liberal Arts and Sciences, Charles Suchar, if he would support bringing together such a distinguished group of scholars to talk about academic freedom at DePaul; fully aware that Alan Dershowitz was seeking to disrupt Finkelstein's tenure bid as it passed through the departmental and College levels (see Finkelstein 2007a).

In response to my request to hold such a conference at DePaul, Suchar told me that such an event would be unwarranted and a distraction from ongoing tenure and promotion processes. How could the convening of a conference on academic freedom be a distraction and disruption of the ongoing tenure and promotion process unless there was an ongoing effort among members of DePaul's administration to deny Finkelstein tenure in violation of academic freedom and due process protections? Would Suchar have deemed an academic freedom conference featuring Alan Dershowitz, Daniel Pipes, Martin Kramer, and Steven Plaut a distraction and disruption, particularly if these figures were arguing that denying Finkelstein tenure would protect academic freedom? The more perverse inference to be drawn is that it is part of the normal processes of the academy to deny tenure to someone who is an outspoken critic of Israel or that it is the institution's prerogative to reject the tenure bids of controversial scholars when the stakes are high. That is clearly what was happening: Suchar certainly did not want a group of the most respected progressive academics converging on DePaul to speak on current threats to academic freedom, particularly with respect to the curtailment of academic freedom for scholars working on the Israel-Palestine conflict just as Suchar was blocking Finkelstein's tenure bid by countermanding two faculty bodies in his role as the key point man in a rolling administrative coup assembled for the sole goal of denying Finkelstein tenure.

At that time, Suchar insisted that there were no threats to academic freedom emerging on campus, noting that Dershowitz's attempts to influence the process had been rebutted by DePaul's Faculty Governance Council while also arguing at the same time that an academic freedom conference would represent a disruption of, and distraction from, ongoing tenure and promotion processes. How an academic conference could be a disruption and distraction to ongoing tenure and promotion processes is anyone's guess. Three months after my exchange with Dean Suchar, DePaul found itself in the midst of one of the single biggest academic freedom controversies in the history of the US academy. In retrospect, it is quite clear that outside interference played an instrumental role in tainting Finkelstein's tenure process and that DePaul did not want any outside interference that might work in Finkelstein's favor entering the "process."

The primary and most visible outside interference against Finkelstein came in the form of Dershowitz's dossier about Finkelstein, which arrived in an email to many DePaul faculty members (see Menetrez 2007, 2008).[10] However, long before he sent this dossier, Dershowitz vowed to have some hand in monitoring, if not ultimately playing a role in the final decision about Finkelstein's tenure bid. As Dershowitz declared to the *Chicago Reader* in August 2005, a little over a year before Finkelstein would go up for tenure, "I will come at my own expense, and I will document the case against Finkelstein" and "I'll demonstrate that he doesn't meet the academic standards of the Association of American Universities" (Felshman 2005).

On 10 May 2007, the day before Finkelstein appeared before DePaul's University Board on Promotion and Tenure, Dershowitz spoke at Northwestern University on "Defending Israel," claiming in that context that Finkelstein had recently attended the Holocaust denial conference in Iran.[11] Whether or not Dershowitz met with a DePaul administrator or a member of its Board of Trustees on this date is unknown, but the timing was interesting. Dershowitz claimed that he was at Northwestern University because he was looking for a college for his daughter. A little less than a month later, on 8 June, DePaul's President Reverend Dennis Holtschneider officially denied Finkelstein tenure for his *ad hominem* attacks against those with whom he disagrees, affirming the University Board on Promotion and Tenure's 4–3 vote to deny tenure and promotion.

Holtschneider wrote in his 8 June 2007 letter to Finkelstein denying him tenure, "The UBPT has noted that your scholarship does not meet DePaul's tenure standards. Moreover, on the record before me, I cannot in good faith conclude that you honor the obligations to 'respect and defend the free inquiry of associates', 'show due respect for the opinions of others', and 'strive to be objective in their professional evaluation of colleagues.'" In essence, DePaul denied Finkelstein tenure along the very lines Dershowitz claimed disqualified Finkelstein for tenure nearly 3 years earlier. As Finkelstein noted, "He (Dershowitz) calculated that if I were denied tenure, it would delegitimize my exposure of him: how could a 'failed academic' (his phrase) be taken seriously?" (Finkelstein 2008–09). Ironically, President Dennis Holtschneider noted at the conclusion of his denial letter: "I am well aware of the outside interest in this decision, and the many ways in which the university community was 'lobbied' both to grant and deny tenure. . . . As much as some would like to create the impression that our process and decision have been influenced by outside interests, they are mistaken" (Holtschneider 2007). Paradoxically, DePaul's process and decision in the Finkelstein had clearly been influenced by outside interests.

The question of civility: Substantive concern or red herring?

Or Phyllis Chessler writes a book on the new Anti-Semitism and she wants to show what a dreadful phenomenon it is. So she writes there is "a thrilling permissibility in the air, the kind of electrically charged and altered reality that acid trippers or epileptics may experience just prior to seizure. Doctored footage of fake Israeli massacres has now entered the imagination of billions of people like pornography. These ideas can never be forgotten. It as if the political equivalent of the AIDS virus has been unleashed into the world. To be a Jew is to live dangerously on the margins, with an open, circumcised heart." So I think it was perfectly warranted to write, "Acid trippers, epileptics, pornography, AIDS, circumcised heart. One begins to wonder whether Chessler's magnum opus, *Women and Madness*, was autobiographical."

(NORMAN FINKELSTEIN, "In Defense of Academic Freedom" speech, 12 October 2007)

The first public evidence that Finkelstein's tenure case was in jeopardy emerged in a memorandum written by the College of Liberal Arts and Sciences Dean, Charles Suchar, in March 2007. This memorandum relied heavily upon arguments made in a minority report by three members of DePaul's political science department, as well as Alan Dershowitz's publicized views on Finkelstein's scholarship. By portraying Finkelstein as a difficult colleague, who would only become more difficult if granted tenure, the minority report authors were pivotal players in creating the necessary grounds upon which the tenure denial would be built. These senior professors in the department, one of whom was in regular contact with Dershowtiz at least 3 years before Finkelstein went up for tenure, held a distinct ideological agenda. This agenda took shape in various arguments within the minority report about Finkelstein's supposed shortcomings as a scholar and his lack of collegiality. Ultimately, these arguments emerged in and through the very language Suchar used to evaluate Finkelstein's scholarship. As Suchar reported in his 22 March 2007 memo:

> My reading of Dr. Finkelstein's work, especially the *Holocaust Industry*, where in one chapter alone Goldhagen, Morris, Wiesel, Kosinski and many others are collectively attacked as *"hoaxters and huxters,"* typifies his apparent penchant of reducing an argument and oppositional views to the inevitable personal and reputation damaging attack, demeaning those with whom he disagrees (emphasis added). (Suchar 2007)

The second chapter of Finkelstein's *The Holocaust Industry: The Exploitation of Jewish Suffering* is entitled "Hucksters, Hoaxers, and History." Neither "hoaxters and huxters" nor "hoaxers and hucksters" appear anywhere in the chapter's text. Since Suchar placed these words ("hoaxters and huxters") in quotation marks, he indicated that he was quoting directly from the text he was referencing. However, if neither "hoaxters and huxters" nor "hoaxers and hucksters" appear anywhere in the text of the second chapter of Finkelstein's *The Holocaust Industry*, where did Suchar find the phrase "hoaxters and huxters" around which he placed quotation marks, indicating that it appears in Chapter 2 of *The Holocaust Industry*? Coincidentally, Suchar misspelled these words just as Dershowitz misspelled them in his propaganda package that was sent to Professor Patrick Callahan of DePaul's political science department, one of the three professors who wrote a minority report against Finkelstein, in December 2006.[12] As Dershowitz noted in his 18 September e-mail to Callahan:

> Among the dozen or so writers whose careers Finkelstein has tried to destroy with the same accusations—"fraud," *"huxter,"* "shake-down artist," "plagiarist,"—he has only ever written a full book about one other: Daniel Goldhagen. Goldhagen did a wonderful job of going point-by-point on Finkelstein's many lies and distortions (emphasis added). (Dershowitz 2006: 5)

In addition, note that Suchar misspells "hoaxer" as "hoaxter," another curious misspelling. In the course of attacking a supposed "small but influential group of anti-Israel, anti-peace, and anti-truth zealots," Dershowitz spells "hoaxers" as "hoaxters" in Chapter 16 of his *The Case for Peace*:

> To date, the Chomsky-Finkelstein-Cockburn attack team has targeted at least the following writers who support Israel and seek justice for Holocaust survivors: Stuart Eizenstat, Martin Gilbert, Burt Neuborne, Yehuda Bauer, Gerald Feldman, Richard Overy, and Abba Eban. They have called these distinguished Jews "hucksters," "*hoaxters*," "thieves," "extortionists," and worse. The pattern of attack is always similar (emphasis added). (Dershowitz 2005: 178)

It should also be noted that Benny Morris, the Israeli New Historian, is not "attacked" in this chapter, as Suchar suggests. Indeed, the only reference to Morris in the entire chapter is in the following sentence: "Repudiating a book the museum originally endorsed because it included a chapter by Benny Morris, a prominent Israeli Historian critical of Israel, Miles Lerman, the museum's chairman avowed, 'To put this museum on the opposite side of Israel—it's inconceivable'" (Finkelstein 2003: 77–8). It is troubling that Suchar would interpret Finkelstein as painting Morris with the same brush as Goldhagen, Wiesel, and Kosinski, suggesting that the contents of Finkelstein's five books were quite unfamiliar to Suchar.

In retrospect, it seems clear that Suchar was well aware in March of that year that DePaul would, ultimately, deny tenure to Norman Finkelstein in June of 2007, for the very reasons Alan Dershowitz, Finkelstein's nemesis, claimed it should, that is, that Finkelstein was not a scholar, but a propagandist; that his tenure case was not about academic freedom, as the Left, claimed, but instead about academic standards; that the academic standards had been lowered by those who had hired Finkelstein because his politically motivated scholarship found a sympathetic hearing among certain DePaul faculty radicals (see Dershowitz 2007a, b; Plaut 2007a, b). Suchar played a key role in Finkelstein's tenure denial, withholding his support for Finkelstein's application because of the his "reputation-demeaning attacks" against Elie Wiesel, Alan Dershowitz, Daniel Goldhagen, and others found in Finkelstein's *The Holocaust Industry*. Suchar concluded that Finkelstein's tone was that of a mean-spirited polemicist and ideologue, stating that Finkelstein's conduct—which included threatening to sue the three members of DePaul's political science department who voted against Finkelstein's tenure bid and filed a minority report alleging there were inaccuracies or misrepresentations in his scholarship—did not bode well for the University and public discourse. In brief, Finkelstein could not expose the scholarly fabrications or hold accountable those seeking to deprive him of his professional livelihood without being characterized as polemical, difficult, and uncollegial.

Ultimately, Suchar could not support Finkelstein, who at the time of his tenure application was the author of five books, which have been translated into 46 different languages, because Finkelstein lacked what Suchar labeled "Vincentian personalism," which apparently necessitates respecting the God-given dignity of others and respecting a range of intellectual opinions. In other words, Suchar portrayed Finkelstein as an ideologue who was incapable of respecting the viewpoints of those with whom he disagreed. In agreement with the minority report, Suchar noted that Finkelstein's attacks against those with whom he disagreed bordered on character assassination. It should be noted, however, that DePaul's political science department in an exhaustive fourteen-page rebuttal of Dershowitz's specific allegations against Finkelstein of character assassination and academic misconduct concluded that Dershowitz's characterizations of Finkelstein's scholarship were baseless. In his memorandum withholding his support for Finkelstein's tenure bid, Suchar did not address this rebuttal, just as he overturned the Departmental and College Personnel Committee's recommendations.

That DePaul administrators would use the name and reputation of St. Vincent DePaul to justify the abrogation of basic academic due process to a dissenting intellectual, brought a level of irony and sadness to this case that merits analysis. To assert that someone defending Palestinian human rights in the context of an overwhelmingly pro-Israel discursive environment within the United States, at great professional cost to himself, lacks "Vincentian personalism" because of his style of engagement with those with whom he disagrees demonstrates the farcical level to which those seeking to block an open and critical debate on the Israel-Palestine conflict will stoop to defend themselves against exposure, as well as to avoid becoming the object of the Israel Lobby and its many adjuncts. As Finkelstein noted during his 12 October 2007 talk at the Academic Freedom Conference at the University of Chicago, the language of "thugs" and "hoodlums" in certain circumstances is more appropriate than the elegant and restrained language used by commissars seeking to justify state violence (Finkelstein 2007c). Specifically, "Certain circumstances warrant incivility." In the context of explaining why incivility is a necessary part of the give and take of intellectual life, Finkelstein explained:

Young people yearn for persons in authority to speak the unvarnished truth and give expression to the moral indignation warranted by the occasion. There are moments that require breaking out of the constraints of polite discourse to sound the alarm that innocent people are being butchered while we speak due to the actions of our government. Now these sorts of incivility shouldn't be a substitute for truth. . . . Such a cry of the heart is also within, in my opinion, the bounds of civil discourse. I have never really understood why polite incivility, the clever put down, which the British specialize in and is a staple of academic life, should be preferred over impolite incivility. . . . I, at any rate, see no virtue to polite civility, which can be more vicious and hurtful, and which in its cleverness and wittiness is often testament to the lack of moral seriousness. . . . There is the case of, in my opinion, the ridiculous, or deserving of ridicule. If an academic or a public figure is a charlatan, he or she deserves to be reduced to ridicule. If there is no scholarship, but simply theater and wind baggery (and you have demonstrated that there is no scholarship, but only theater and wind baggery), then there is a time honored tradition for shouting that the Emperor is naked. So if Professor Elie Wiesel comes to your university, charges a lecture fee in the tens of thousands of dollars and the subject of his lecture is that "The secret of Auschwitz truth lies in silence," and he goes on to say that, "Words are kind of a horizontal approach, while silence offers you a vertical approach. You plunge into it," I think it's perfectly reasonable to ask the question, "Does Elie Wiesel parachute into his lectures?" Because this is sheer nonsense. And why shouldn't we say it?[13]

Clearly, Finkelstein had his exposure of Alan Dershowitz's *The Case for Israel* in *Beyond Chutzpah: The Misuse of Anti-Semitism and the Abuse of History*, and Dershowitz's unrelenting campaign of defamation and deceit in response to that exposure (which resulted in Finkelstein's dismissal from DePaul) in mind when he delivered these remarks. Furthermore, DePaul's unwillingness (perhaps inability) to withstand Dershowitz's outside interference in Finkelstein's tenure case demonstrates that "theater and wind baggery" will be protected by the mainstream academic institutions if the stakes are high enough.

The real stakes

Since Finkelstein's compelling indictments of American Zionism in books such as *The Image and Reality of the Israel-Palestine Conflict*, *The Holocaust Industry: The Exploitation of Jewish Suffering*, and *Beyond Chutzpah: The Misuse of Anti-Semitism and the Abuse of History* could not be rebutted by serious counterarguments, his ideological nemeses resorted to attacking Finkelstein's tone, writing style, and personality, effectively shifting the terms of the debate from the Israel-Palestine conflict to issues of civility and behavior. One of the more bizarre claims offered in service of this effort was that a scholar could deter others from wanting to participate in a debate. As Suchar explained to me in the context of defining the "new" academic freedom, as well as defending DePaul's decision to deny tenure to Finkelstein, a scholar can create a situation where he freezes others out through his scholarship.[14] This argument was clearly fashioned to respond to Finkelstein's exposure of Dershowitz's *The Case for Israel*, as well as Finkelstein's critiques of other significant defenders of Israel, as part of DePaul's larger argument that denying Finkelstein tenure was in the best interest of protecting academic freedom and civil discourse. Academic freedom has never been constructed in this way to limit scholarly debate, prohibiting a thorough-going critique of one's ideological enemies' arguments because the critique itself might be wounding and hurt these ideological enemies' feelings. Ultimately, this new definition of academic freedom absolves Israel's defenders from having to respond to the critiques being offered, regardless of how justified, meritorious, and well-grounded these critiques might be.

By insisting that one's ideological opponents be treated or described in a certain way by drawing upon DePaul's Vincentian heritage, DePaul's administration ultimately played a key card in the cultural Right's assault on academic freedom by introducing a new surveillance mechanism into academic culture: one must treat Israel's US apologists with the proper amount of respect and deference, or stand accused of breaching the AAUP's statement on professional responsibility; "polariz[ing] and simplify[ing] conversations that deserve layered and subtle consideration" ("more for inflammatory effect than to critique or challenge certain assumptions"); engaging in reputation-demeaning attacks; and representing a serious threat to public discourse. Perhaps Finkelstein's tenure denial represented a successful test case, sending a warning to other untenured critics of Israel. As David Klein reminds us in his "Why is Norman Finkelstein Not Allowed to Teach?", "An unstated axiom for US universities is that criticism of Israel by untenured faculty members [and perhaps even tenured faculty members] is not allowed" (Klein 2008–09: 308). Regardless of the strength of a scholar's publication and teaching record, s/he will face the possible loss of his academic career if s/he critically interrogates Israel's grip over the US public sphere's understanding of the Question of Palestine. As DePaul Professor Bill Martin noted (citing a statement of support on the Norman Finkelstein Solidarity website) in his "Urgent Need to Right Wrong at DePaul University," "Keep the c.v., change the subject, and Norman Finkelstein has tenure" (Martin 2007).

Institutional politics

Given that the reasons DePaul offered for denying Finkelstein tenure were nearly nonsensical, despite the various disclaimers that outside interference had nothing to do with the eventual outcome, one must look at the institutional and cultural constraints governing how the case was ultimately decided by DePaul's decision makers, particularly at the level of the Board of Trustees.[15] While the Board of Trustees normally has nothing to do with personnel decisions at a university, particularly with respect to tenure and promotion, Finkelstein's case presented a highly unusual set of circumstances (see Williams 2007b). There were additional parties external to the university including the Anti-Defamation League, the American Jewish Committee, and the American-Israel Public Affairs Committee (AIPAC), which undoubtedly held a stake in the outcome of Finkelstein's tenure case. As a persistent and effective critic of Israel's policies in the occupied territories, Finkelstein challenged many of the myths AIPAC seeks to sustain as facts in the US public sphere. In addition, Finkelstein has over a 20-year period proven to be a serious adversary of the positions on Israel endorsed by AIPAC and other Zionist organizations. Given his unstinting criticism of how American Zionist organizations with strong ties to Israel have capitalized upon the Holocaust to immunize Israel from harsh international criticism, Finkelstein has been relentless in demonstrating how the memory of those who perished in the Holocaust has been for exploited for financial and political gain (e.g., Finkelstein 2003).

While DePaul worked strenuously to deny that third parties had anything to do with its decision to deny tenure to Finkelstein, the paper-thin rationales that it offered suggested precisely the opposite: that significant pressure, political and financial, were shaping the final decision.[16] DePaul's concern about Finkelstein's reputation was actually a concern about its own reputation among determined and powerful lobbies. Within the academic realm, external pressures (no matter how intense) are not supposed to influence academic decision-making. This is the *sine qua non* of academic freedom; without it the very basis for academic freedom is compromised and threatened. As Thomas Haskell (1996: 54) notes, "From my standpoint, no justification for academic freedom can succeed unless it provides ample resources for justifying the autonomy and self-governance of the community." While appreciating Haskell's insight, I would argue that the autonomy and self-governance of US academic institutions have been subverted by the protective discourse that envelops discussion of the Israel-Palestine conflict.

The cultural context

Attacks against the academic freedom of Israel's critics do not emerge out of nowhere. These attacks gain traction within a culture that refuses to recognize the plights of the Palestinians living under Israel occupation. This refusal to recognize the plight of the Palestinians emerges with a larger discourse of anti-Arab racism. According to Steven Salaita (2006: 13), "[Anti-Arab racism] engages in a constant dialectic with other types of racism (both American and European), as well as colonialism, capitalism, nationalism, exceptionalism, and religious fundamentalism." The discourse of Zionism obtains its own supremacy in concert with anti-Arab racism by positing the superiority of Jews in relation to all non-Jews, particularly Palestinian Arabs; this discursive supremacy has, by small accretions of authority, grown significantly over the last century.

In his *Israeli Exceptionalism: The Destabilizing Logic of Zionism*, M. Shahid Alam (2009) traces the historical roots of Zionism, arguing that a unique set of social-political conditions have enabled Israel a unique immunity in world affairs. If nothing else, DePaul's handling of Finkelstein's tenure case proved that the immunity Alam describes extends to the academic realm as well; Finkelstein's scathing critiques of Israel's apologists exposed how the ideology of philo-semitism protects those who defend Zionism against serious criticism. In his *The Holocaust Industry: The Exploitation of Jewish Suffering*, Finkelstein indicts those who would use the Holocaust to justify Israel's treatment of Palestinians living under occupation, as well as those who would use Jewish suffering to extort money from European countries such as Germany and Switzerland under the cover of Holocaust reparations. In brief, Finkelstein argued that a lucrative extortion racket was being carried out in the name of needy Holocaust survivors, while in fact the money being generated was actually going to Zionist-advocacy organizations such as the World Jewish Congress. Upon the publication of *The Holocaust Industry*, Finkelstein promptly vacated his long-term instructor position of political science at Hunter College, City University of New York. Despite possessing an outstanding teaching record and three internationally-recognized books to his credit at that time, he was forced out under the pretext of a budgetary cut within the political science department. Finkelstein chose not to return to the department after this injustice was inflicted upon him. The department's treatment of Finkelstein was part of a larger pattern, as scholars who write critically on the Israel-Palestine conflict are often pushed out of their academic positions through various underhanded means.[17] In explaining how parties external to the university can subtly exert pressure on departments to rid themselves of dissenting scholars, Finkelstein notes how

> [s]ometimes phone calls are made, no doubt about it, but I think things work through a crystallizing of a consensus—in the sense of "this guy is more trouble than he is worth, and so it is time to let him go." I think this is what happened at Hunter College, that yes I had an excellent teaching record, yes I had an excellent publication record, but it's also true that "a lot of people are complaining about him and we do get all these phone calls and there are faculty members who are very uncomfortable with him because he is just not professional" and so on and so forth. Finally, a consensus crystallizes that it is time to let him go. (Apatu 2001)

Of course, Finkelstein's first foray into the realm of public controversy and the Israel-Palestine conflict began with his exposure of Joan Peters' *From Time Immemorial* in 1984. Peters' book, published to rave reviews and endorsed by some of the leading lights in the world of American Arts and Letters, including Bernard Lewis and Saul Bellow, advanced an ideologically serviceable thesis for American Zionists, who were eager to absolve themselves of any culpability in producing the Palestinian refugee problem. In his "The Fate of an Honest Intellectual" (2002), Noam Chomsky tells the story of Finkelstein's unsuccessful attempts to publicize his findings about *From Time Immemorial* while he was a PhD. student in the Middle East

Studies Department at Princeton. According to Chomsky, "[Finkelstein's] professors—this is Princeton University, supposed to be a serious place— stopped talking to him: they wouldn't make appointments with him, they wouldn't read his papers, he basically had to quit the program."[18]

According to Avi Shlaim (qtd. in Ridgen and Rossier (film), 2009), "This was the book [*From Time Immemorial*] American Jews wanted to have," because it supposedly proved that the Palestinian population was not driven out of what would become Israel in May 1948. Indeed, according to Peters (2001), the Palestinians had duped the world about their status as a dispossessed people and in fact they immigrated to what would become Israel just a few years before 1948, attracted by its wealth and social services. Peters claimed to have located the key demographic data to prove her point, insisting that this previously unrecognized evidence demonstrated an "exchange of populations" between Israel and Arab countries such as Iran, Iraq, and Jordan. According to Peters, the number of Jews departing from Palestine for Middle Eastern countries matched the number of Arabs who in-migrated to Israel. This "exchange of populations" was corrected when these Palestinians were driven out of what would become Israel and when Jews from these Middle Eastern countries came back to Israel.

Finkelstein's exposure of Peters' *From Time Immemorial* was eventually published in a small journal called *In These Times*, but it was completely ignored in the mainstream press and journals of intellectual opinion. As Chomsky notes in his "The Fate of an Honest Intellectual" (2002: 246), there was a deliberate attempt to suppress Finkelstein's findings about *From Time Immemorial* and to encourage him to cease his inquiries: "Meanwhile, Finkelstein was being called in by big professors in the field who were telling him, 'Look, call off your crusade; you drop this and we'll take care of you, we'll make sure you get a job', all this kind of stuff." Twenty years later, in yet another ironic twist, Dershowitz would recycle some of Peters' arguments in his 2003 book, *The Case for Israel*, which would become a focal point of critique in Finkelstein's *Beyond Chutzpah: The Misuse of Anti-Semitism and the Abuse of History*. Dershowitz's efforts to prevent publication of *Beyond Chutzpah* have been well documented (see Finkelstein 2007b; Abraham 2005).[19]

The damage to academic freedom

It takes an enormous amount of academic courage to speak the truth when no one else is out there to support him. So I would say that his place in the whole history of writing history is assured, and that those who in the end are proven right triumph, and he will be among those who will have triumphed, albeit, it so seems, at great cost.

(RAUL HILBERG on *Democracy Now!*, 9 May 2007)

Scholars who write critically about the Israeli government's treatment of the Palestinians since 1948 face various pressures and obstacles as they broach sensitive issues about the US-Israel special relationship that many powerful interest groups have an interest in suppressing. Driving those interest groups is a fear that, if a public awareness about the plight of the Palestinians living under Israeli occupation were to emerge, it could lead to a reevaluation of US public support for Israel (Pappe 2010). As John Mearsheimer and Stephen Walt have convincingly argued, the Israel Lobby, a loose coalition of individuals and organizations, seeks to control public discussion of the Israel-Palestine conflict in the United States because of the key role US taxpayer support plays in supporting Israel's military domination of the Middle East, its continued settlement expansion in the West Bank, and the key role US support for Israel plays in fomenting anti-American resentment in the Arab world (Walt and Mearsheimer 2008). Because of the vital stakes in maintaining current levels of aid, those who argue that US support for Israel must end due to the persecution of the Palestinians must out of necessity be silenced as they are a direct threat to pro-Israel interests.

Because Israel's treatment of the Palestinians is so unjustifiable, the details cannot be allowed circulate in the public sphere, with the average citizen being prevented from understanding the relevant issues and concerns. The demonization of Muslim Arabs, as extremist and violent, solidifies Israel's image as a beleaguered European offshoot seeking to maintain its existence against rabid anti-Semites. Israel's leadership and its allies in the United States realize that key US aid is absolutely essential to Israel's expansionist plans in the region, its larger military goals, its ethnic cleansing of the Palestinians from *Eretz* Israel, and its overall domination of the Middle East. The United States appears to have no choice but to support Israel because of the Zionist Lobby, which refers to the formal and informal networks within the United States committed to promoting Israeli propaganda, silencing and smearing Israel's critics, and engaging in extensive fundraising efforts, grassroots activism, and the overall corruption of public discourse.

The story of Zionism's penetration of the academic institution has yet to be written, an indication perhaps of how difficult it is to document clearly identifiable instances in which either academic judgment or administrative decision-making was being directly influenced by the power of the Israel Lobby or by a university administration's concerns about how a faculty member's criticism of Israel could anger a particularly important external constituency. While faculty are generally left to their own discretion when deciding whether to research and write about controversial issues in the public sphere, with the implicit understanding that this extramural advocacy is protected by academic freedom and their rights as private citizens, those who decide to speak out publically and critically about Israel's occupation of the West Bank, or its general treatment of the Palestinians since 1948, do so at their own risk; they may face a number of different obstacles regardless of whether or not one is writing as a scholar within one's discipline or simply as a concerned citizen.

Given the contested nature of seemingly all factual claims about the conflict within the US public sphere, it becomes nearly impossible to make a confident assertion about Israel's occupation, its territorial borders, the violation of human rights, nationalism, military aggression, or the possible illegality of military action because there are a host of watchdogs that deliberately seek to sow confusion about factual matters around which there should be relatively little controversy. As Ian Bickerton writes in his *The Arab-Israeli Conflict: A Guide for the Perplexed*, "Virtually every aspect of the conflict is contested. Events are disputed on the ground and the accounts of those events and their history is contested. . . . The participants in the Israel-Palestine conflict have created their own narrative about themselves, their protagonists and the place that is being contested" (25). That seemingly all claims about the conflict are so controversial speaks to the amazing efficiency of pro-Israel advocacy within the United States, where organizations such as the Anti-Defamation League, the World Jewish Congress, American Jewish Committee, and the 51 member organizations of the Conference of Presidents of Major American Jewish Organizations exert an unbreakable control over all public discussion about the Israel-Palestine conflict. These organizations realize that the public must remain confused about the relevant issues, most especially the Palestinians' legitimate grievances against Israel.

Marginalizing dissenting scholars such as Norman Finkelstein has become increasingly difficult because Israel's critics have become more effective in highlighting Israel's indefensible behavior. Punishing those who take advantage of the cracking consensus around the diminishing sustainability of US support for Israel, either by summarily dismissing them or by denying them tenure, sends a strong message that the frequently invoked criteria of "fairness" and "due process" are constructed to serve those in power; these criteria will be violated in the academic space when Israel's image is in jeopardy.[20] The Question of Palestine, then, is out of bounds with respect to academic freedom protections—scholars who write critically of Israel, in fields ranging from political science to archeology, have faced defamation for conducting critical and comprehension examinations of Israeli treatment of the Palestinians in the last 67 years. This silencing is simply unacceptable to anyone committed to democratic deliberation and critical thinking. Those seeking a just resolution of the Question of Palestine must defend academic freedom as an individual right for the researcher at all costs against those who are determined to reserve it for themselves and their ideological allies.

CHAPTER FIVE

Edward Said in the American imagination after 9/11

No cause, no God, no abstract idea can justify the mass slaughter of innocents, most particularly when only a small group of people are in charge of such actions and feel themselves to represent the cause without having a real mandate to do so

(EDWARD SAID in "Islam and the West Are Inadequate Banners," *London Observer*, 16 September 2001).

In the summer of 2002, Stanley Fish reminded us of the scary times in which we are living, particularly with respect to controversial public speech about American foreign policy. In the journal *Responsive Community*, Fish—in an article entitled "Don't Blame Relativism"—spoke of the various threats that have been posed to academic freedom after 9/11.[1] Fish foresaw a time in which a US Senator might peer down from a raised dais, look into the eyes of a frightened English professor and ask, "Are you now or have you ever been a postmodernist?" Although neither Fish, nor any of us, have yet to hear US Senators asking academics this question, the current political climate on our college campuses suggests that such a time might not be that far in the future.

Of course, Fish was responding to the *NY Times'* Edward Rothstein who in two opinion pieces (22 September 2001 and 13 July 2002) expressed concern that rarefied forms of academic talk could be used to understand rather than condemn the terrorist attacks. Rothstein was at least generous enough to acknowledge in the second article that "[o]f course, po[st]mo[dernism] isn't directly or indirectly responsible for 9/11. But cannot po[st]mo[dernism] be

taken to task for its views and effects without Fish and others retreating into
McCarthy-era rhetoric posing as victims of Western absolutism? They are
acting as if they were not quite secure in their possession of the truth."[2] After
9/11, "possession of the truth" seems to be something to which members of
the cultural Right are especially privy.[3]

After Rothstein's first diatribe, Fish could have easily added to the list of
possible questions that might issue forth from the mouth of a US Senator
the following: "Are you now or have you ever been a postcolonial theorist[4]
or a follower of Edward Said?" Rothstein, in his 22 September 2001
article, entitled "Attacks on U.S. Challenge Postmodern True Believers,"
condescendingly labeled postmodernism "pomo" and postcolonial theory
"poco," alleging that poco goes further than pomo in doing away with
standards of judgment. He claimed that, "For while affirming most of the
pomo rejection of ideals and universals, poco establishes its own universal:
Western imperialism becomes a variety of Original Sin. The implication is
that any act against the West by a postcolonial power can be seen as a reaction
to an act by the West." Rothstein praises Said—whom he acknowledges as
one of the founders of postcolonial theory—for "point[ing] out that unlike
radical pomo advocates, [Said] accepts universal principles like 'human
rights.'" However, according to Rothstein,

> Said refers to "ideological confections": ideas like "the clash of civilizations"
> that, coincidentally, were invoked by many European and American
> leaders in condemning the terrorist attack. Such "false universals" Said
> says, are used to legitimize "corporate profit-taking and political power."
> Similar arguments have become commonplace in worldwide protests
> against "globalization."[5]

Said has expressed disdain for Samuel Huntington's "The Clash of Civilizations" thesis, continually emphasizing that we live in political world not
in a metaphysical one that can be neatly divided into Manichean categories
such as "East" and "West." Indeed, to divide the world by such divisions is
to engage in the "clash of ignorance."[6]

Nonetheless, Rothstein continues his attack:

> Following [Said's] logic to its extreme conclusions, and the rejections of
> universal values and ideals leave little room for unqualified condemnations
> of a terrorist attack, particularly one against the West. Such an attack,
> however inexcusable, can be seen as a horrifying airing of a legitimate
> cultural grievance. Military responses can seem no different. And so
> the conflict becomes a series of symmetrical confrontations, as is often
> asserted about battles in Israel.[7]

In Rothstein's opinion, Said's logic (and postcolonial theory more generally)
holds dire implications for intellectual culture and world politics: the issuing

of apologies for terrorism committed by individuals of previously colonized countries and presently occupied populations when that terrorism is directed against Western imperialism and the beneficiaries of Western imperialism.

For Rothstein, such a ledger sheet logic—that attempts to frame terrorist action according to a "tit for tat" analysis—allows for a form of nefarious argumentation that conceptualizes terrorism as an attempt to right historical wrongs that have taken place over several centuries. Such historical contextualization, it seems, might lead us to commiserate with terrorists and their aims, possibly legitimating the use of violence against civilians to advance a political agenda.

In his first op-ed piece Rothstein quoted—with seeming approval—Christopher Hitchens, who asked shortly after the 9/11 attacks, "Does anyone suppose that an Israeli withdrawal from Gaza would have forestalled the slaughter in Manhattan? It would take a moral cretin to suggest anything of the sort; the cadres of the new jihad make it very apparent that their quarrel is with Judaism and secularism on principle, not with (or just with) Zionism."[8] Hitchens' rhetorical question and his forthright answer clearly demonstrate that—for all but the Chomsky left—the 9/11 perpetrators should not be understood as fighters against political oppression (Palestinian, Afghani, or otherwise) but instead as nihilistic zealots bent on causing maximum death and destruction for Jew and non-Jew alike. While Hitchens refused to ascribe a specific political agenda to the 9/11 perpetrators, Rothstein—along with such equally problematic figures as Stanley Kurtz and Dinesh D'Souza—views just such an agenda as gaining a shape and motivation in postmodern and postcolonial theory.

The events of 9/11 automatically brought those objects that have been of critical concern for Said for over 30 years into sharp focus: the understanding and coverage of Islam,[9] religious fundamentalism, nationalism, the Question of Palestine, and the public sphere. Expert discussions on the "Arab mind" and the policy intellectual's attempts to talk about "Islamic resistance to modernity" have constantly occupied the center of Said's efforts[10] to educate Americans and citizens of the Arab world about the pitfalls of such attributions, warning that totalizing assumptions always get one into trouble, particularly in a world of radical heterogeneity. In this sense, 9/11 proves the importance of and reconfigures such Saidian works as *The Question of Palestine*, *Covering Islam*, *The Politics of Dispossession*, *After the Last Sky*, *Orientalism*, and *Culture and Imperialism*.

Providing critical commentary about Edward Said after 9/11 is difficult precisely because the process of describing his immense influence and various political and cultural interventions easily engages one in transferential relations, which presents one with the danger of becoming implicated in and repeating the very problems Said analyzes.[11] In discussing a figure such as Said in the context of the Israel-Palestine conflict within the American public sphere, one can easily succumb to the repetitive process of "acting out" against rather than "working through" a particular set of theoretical and historical problems. For Dominick LaCapra, "Acting out is a process but a repetitive one. It's a process whereby the past, or the experience of the other, is repeated as if it were fully enacted, fully literalized."[12] In the course of battling various interlocutors, commentators on 9/11—on both the Left and Right—have tended to repeat the very processes they are seeking to elucidate.

In his response to Rothstein and others, Fish claimed that two arguments about postmodernism were being made; often, both at the same time. One, that postmodernism caused the events of 9/11 and two, that postmodernism was proven wrong by 9/11.[13] Similarly, many commentators seemed to argue that

1   Postcolonial theory—as represented in the work of Edward Said— caused 9/11 and

2   Postcolonial theory—as represented in the work of Edward Said— was proven wrong by 9/11

Both ascriptions, with respect to postmodernism and postcolonialism, are preposterous and don't withstand even the most superficial analysis. The more interesting question, of course, is why anyone would connect seemingly rarefied forms of academic talk to a historic event on the world stage. A perhaps facile answer is that this is what happens when academic theories are "translated" into the language of public discourse and are "transported" into the public sphere.[14] However, members of the Cultural Right appear pretty confident that they have the central tenets of both theories down pat and are equally confident that no more explanation is needed—either for them or for the general public. How does one go about explaining this misplaced confidence in figures such as Rothstein, who never takes the time to examine a single supposedly postmodern or postcolonial text (equating Stanley Fish with pomo and equating Edward Said with poco) in the course of excoriating the supposed academic "Left"?[15] Cultural relativism has long been a favorite scapegoat of those wishing to rally a country around a cause while stifling dissent. I found this out firsthand.

On 24 April 2002, I took part in a roundtable entitled "The Courage to Refuse: Fighting Disinformation and Ignorance at the Academy," a forum that was devoted to analyzing the reductive media coverage of the Israel-Palestine Conflict within my campus community. As soon as the framework for the roundtable was established, I—along with my co-hosts—found myself face-to-face with a terrible predicament: advocacy on behalf of Palestinian human rights was perceived by some as advancing potentially anti-Semitic arguments. Because we wished to insert our own views and voices into this intractable international situation and sought to address the gross asymmetries between pro-Israeli and pro-Palestinian factions that affect the coverage of the conflict on campus, an immediate reaction followed whereby the "the voices of dissent" were attached to postmodernism and anti-Semitism. Interestingly enough, one of our ideological opponents on campus found us to be "influenced by postmodern relativism [which allowed us] to equate Israeli defensive action with Palestinian terrorism again civilians." As this person stated,

> Encouraged by the postmodernist tradition of relativizing the truth, denying reality, and priding oneself on the ability to get to any point from any other, one has to establish a moral equivalence between a small bunch of professional terrorists deliberately targeting Israeli and Palestinian civilians and their Israeli victims trying to defend themselves.

This person went on to claim that

> [t]he agenda is thus stacked, deliberately or ignorantly, against Israel, and the result is a foregone conclusion: the right to dissent (i.e., to condemn Israel against any factual and historical data) and to feel good about themselves (by equating the terrorists and their Israeli and Palestinian victims) will be easily confirmed by the absolute majority of participants. Your voices will be ignored and/or a permanent participant of such events will repeat his mantra that you are indoctrinated while his friends are talking from the heart. The mantra will be applauded by the open and covert terrorist sympathizers in the audience.

Finally, this person—who decided not to attend the discussion—stated

> . . . any voice of reason will be overrun at a meeting like the one called by the roundtable organizers. They will not be interested in listening to you. This is not what the meeting is about. Anybody interested in the truth or, for that matter, in the well-being of the Israelis and Palestinians alike, has no business to attend.[16]

In my brief talk at this roundtable, I drew heavily on the writings of Edward Said, attempting to capture the effects of Zionism from the standpoint of its Palestinian victims.[17] Although Edward Said has never called himself a postmodernist, he—in this post-9/11 logical economy where postmodernism can promote anti-Semitism—becomes as controversial a figure as ever because he embodies the Palestinian Question and, perhaps more importantly, because he serves as a persistent reminder of Palestinian nationalism and resistance.

Postmodernism and postcolonial theory, it would seem, problematize and interrogate the narratives of nationalism and views them as constructions.[18] If we are to draw upon Stanley Fish's definition of postmodernism, in his eloquent riposte to Edward Rothstein, "as a series of arguments," we understand that postmodernists don't deny that there are things like reality and objectivity or national narratives in the world but do doubt the possibility of ever being able to deploy a vocabulary that will convince our enemies of the rightness of our position and the wrongness of theirs.

The fact that no such vocabulary can be deployed, however, should not cause consternation. There are national aspirations, preferred values, and textual authorities from which we draw such vocabularies. However, our enemies have other national aspirations, have other preferred values, and have other textual authorities through which they make sense of reality. These enemies, perhaps, invest phrases like "minimum standard of living," "military-industrial complex," and "the War on Terrorism" with different types of meaning. It might be said that those attempting to understand the different connotations of these phrases for our supposed enemies might be doing postcolonial theory. In other words, postcolonial theorists are attempting to understand Third-World *schadenfreude* or the taking of joy in the misfortune of First World others.[19]

After 9/11, pomo and poco have been condemned as promoting anti-Semitism because both question the cohesiveness of the Zionist narrative and that questioning, according to some, inevitably leads to the latter, objective anti-Semitism. This of course raises the very sensitive issue concerning the uses of moral capital generated through the Holocaust, to rationalize the oppressive treatment of the Palestinians of the occupied territories.[20] Zionism, as the founding ideology of Jewish nationalism, posits the supreme rights of Jews to inhabit ancient Palestine. According to some, if you reject or critique that founding ideology or support or commiserate with the victims who have suffered because of that ideology, you are anti-Semitic.[21] If you are unable to condemn your enemies with a vocabulary of moral absolutes, you are a postmodernist.

In *Why We Fight: Moral Clarity and the War on Terrorism*, William Bennett claims that after 9/11 he was made angry by the seeming incapacity of some Americans, particularly academics in the humanities, to come to the nation's aid in what he saw as a crystal clear case of "good versus evil." His outrage, if you will, betrays the perspective of a disappointed "patriot" who expects a confirmation of his ideological leanings in a world largely out of step with him. When his ideological leanings are not confirmed, he scapegoats those who are the bearers of a long overdue message: there are plenty of people in the world who cannot condemn the events of 9/11 in the language of absolutes that Bennett finds so necessary. The academics for whom Bennett holds contempt are presenting alternative "narratives" or "perspectives" at a time when the narrative of American dominance is under attack.

While Stanley Fish tells us that postmodernism is just another name for serious thought, Bill Bennett and Edward Rothstein tell us that postmodernism and postcolonialism are forms of academic thinking that weaken moral resolve and patriotic commitment and are attempts to understand or perhaps sympathize with our enemies—the very enemies who wish to see our destruction. Bennett, in particular, in his book *Why We*

Fight, finds cultural relativism undermining not only patriotism but also US support for Israel. For Bennett, to be a US patriot is to be a supporter of Israel and its unfortunately repressive policies in the occupied territories. He even manages to imply that postmodernism or cultural relativism—with its commitment to placing oneself in an enemy's shoes (perhaps the shoes of a Palestinian)—possesses the potential to advance anti-Semitic arguments.

If postmodernism (Rothstein and Bennett never name any supposed "postmodern" thinkers, viewing Fish as postmodernism's provocateur) allows us to think about the subject positions of the weak and the dispossessed who are angry with a nation-state, it's Bennett's contention that such moves should be disallowed because they rationalize destructive action and commiseration with a people who harbor ill will for Americans and Israelis. After 9/11, under Bennett's logic, "We are all Israelis now."[22] According to Bennett, 9/11 paved the way for increased expressions of anti-Semitism. Is this the case? Or is it that the events of 9/11 led to an inventorying (self-questioning) of the various US-supported occupations/repressions around the world? Israel's occupation of the West Bank and Gaza has again and again been cited throughout the Arab world as a cause for great anger against the United States.

However, we really should help Bennett be more precise. Aspects of postmodern thinking and postcolonial theory advance not anti-Semitic arguments but post-Zionist arguments. Post-Zionism is the most recent and, to date, most effective effort within Israel to problematize Zionist discourse and the historical narratives it has produced, questioning its homogeneity and contradictions.

Zionism represents an ideology of exclusions, erasures, and repressions that must necessarily deny and ignore the Palestinians and their history. Zionism, in conjunction with Western liberalism, gains and maintains support through a whole vast array of symbols and archetypes secured through their promotion in US universities, foundations, political offices, and in American military interventions. As an ideological and religious vision, Zionism brings together the forces of nationalism and messianism.

The historical and political configurations that have made Zionism a very viable and coherent concept combine anxieties about anti-Semitism, the reality of the destruction of European Jewry, and the religious vision of Moses's leading the Jews out of Egypt into the promised land of *Eretz Yisrael* creating an easily manipulable and deployable device. Zionism operates as an Orientalist discourse that elides the history of non-European peoples, establishing a lived reality for the realization of a people's history and ontology through the creation of Israel and the effacement and destruction of another people who are directly deemed "inferior" and "incapable of civilization."

As a psychoexistential complex, Zionism solidifies the disparate elements of history and politics into a palpable, comprehensible, definable, and repeatable reality that can be passed down through generations. Zionism is a theory of detail, a disposition, a set of attitudes. As Said points out, three central factors inform the Question of Palestine:

1   the reality of Zionism as a systematic practice of Jews and against non-Jews;

2   the reality of Palestinian history, which is not a miscellaneous collection of haphazard occurrences but a coherent experience of dispossession by Zionism as well as an answering dialectic of fighting progress toward self-determination;

3   the real conflict between Zionism and the Palestinians, a conflict which is not a misunderstanding, but a real opposition between opposed forces, furthermore a conflict embedded in a specific region, having a concrete region, having a concrete history, and bringing into play a conjunction of many different regional, international, and cultural factors. There is an almost desperate irony in the contrast between the matted density of these three factors and the optimism expressed on occasion by well-intentioned policy makers.[23]

Zionism, of course, pivots on one main assumption—the cultural inferiority of non-Jewish Palestinians—and it is this assumption that gives warrant to the dispossession of territory in the spirit of *mission civilisatrice*. This view, of course, possesses various contradictions and slippages.

The Israeli-based journal *Theory and Criticism* has been using postmodern and postcolonial thinkers in advancing the post-Zionist debates for over 10 years. Drawing upon figures such as Said, Spivak, Bhabha, Derrida, Deleuze, and Lyotard, post-Zionist proponents such as Daniel Boyarin, Michael Gluzman, and Sara Chinski have dramatically exposed the inadequacies and harsh realities of Zionist categories for ethnic minorities (Palestinians, Mitzrahi and Sephardic Jews) and women within a rapidly and continually evolving Israeli society.

Other thinkers such as Baruch Kimmerling, Illan Pappe, Nev Gordon, Anton Shammas, and Emile Habiby also question such Zionist categories but do not draw upon the same postcolonial and postmodern figures. Postmodern and postcolonial theories are helping to loosen the grip of the Zionist hegemony in Israeli academic institutions. Kimmerling claims that ". . . the vast majority of contemporary academic historians and social scientists in Israel are not only Zionists, but also "proudly attached" to their Zionist convictions when producing their historiographic output, no less than the founding fathers of their vocation."[24]

All of these Post-Zionist writers "argue that the refusal to acknowledge the centrality of power relations occludes the actual conditions of Israeli life, particularly as they relate to Palestinian Arabs both inside and outside of

Israel" and "find unacceptable the taken-for-granted discursive framework within which Israeli public debates are carried out."[25] New Historians contribute to the elimination of this form of repression of historical fact, and therefore, their work may be regarded as therapeutic.

In some sense, William Bennett seems to suffer from the same anxieties that plague Zionist historians in Israel in their fight with post-Zionist revisionists. Bennett's and Rothstein's rhetoric sounds much like the angry musings of the Israeli writer, Aaharon Megged,[26] who "accuse[d] the New Historians of disseminating anti-Zionist propaganda and declare[d] that anyone who calls the Zionist movement and policies colonialist identified with the Palestinians—that is, Israel's threatening and destructive other."[27] Anita Shapira, the author of *Land and Power: The Zionist Resort to Force (1881-1948)*, wrote that "[s]ome of the "revisionists" have sought to give renewed legitimacy to the politicization of research, justifying this move by a vulgarized version of postmodernism: there is no reality but in the eyes of the beholder."[28] Shapira goes on to recite some *idée reçues* about deconstruction, claiming that—according to its internal logic—every narrative is equal in value to every other and that, by extension, the revisionist historians are claiming that an equivalence can been drawn between the Zionist and Palestinian narrative. Shapira's elaborate condescension and troubling misunderstandings of deconstruction suggest that she must find some way to put the newest generation of Israeli historians in their proper place,[29] claiming that "[h]istory has ceased to relate to what actually happened because even facts are an illusion."

> Thus, a depiction of what did not happen has equal weight: Why did Israel fail to reach a peace Agreement with its neighbors in the early 1950s? Why was the War of Independence not prevented? Why was a Palestinian state not established in 1948? Why did the Zionist leadership not save European Jewry? The very formulation of the question is accusatory: from the advantage of hindsight and from the standpoint of the present, the heroes of the past are forced to account for their deeds—not only for what they did but for what they did not do—before a self-righteous tribunal whose members have no doubt they would have acted more wisely and certainly more ethically.[30]

Shapira seems to be telling these "New Historians" to give up their revisionist historiography with its "dubious" methods, to acknowledge the generational gap that separates them from their Zionist counterparts, to understand that they did not fight the founding wars of the nation as these counterparts did, and to be thankful that their Israeli birthright was insured. Just as Bennett tells American academics in the humanities to tow the ideological line when it comes to waging the new War on Terror, Shapira and Megged admonished the "New Historians" to grow up before assessing the sins of their Zionist ancestors in their dealings with the Palestinians. Generational divides, as well as disciplinary methodological divides, are exacerbated in times of national and ideological crisis, inevitably making themselves the very subject of postcrisis analyses.

While Zionist historians use a positivist approach to the understanding of history, post-Zionists use a pluralistic/multiperspectival paradigm that might very well be deemed "postmodern" and "postcolonial" in its approach. The debates between Zionists and post-Zionists almost mirror the debates between the cultural Right and Left after 9/11 in the United States. Zionism—like the narrative of objectivity in the American culture wars after 9/11—has turned into an ideology, in the strict sense, an instrument employed by the established dominant groups to defend both their interests and the status quo.[31] In the instances of both the Israeli and American Right, representations of a nation's "collective memory" are at stake with post-Zionists wishing to write Israel's history from the standpoint of its Others and postmodernists and postcolonial theorists wishing to understand American imperialism from the standpoint of those it has most affected.[32]

The "post-Zionist" predicament, like the post-9/11 objectivity predicament, is thus one of pure anomie: a lack of clear and agreed value preferences and ideological injunctions, which could endow courageous and innovative decisions with general approval and legitimacy.[33] Edward Said, shortly after the 9/11 attacks, wrote:

> The intellectual's role is first to present alternative narratives and other perspectives on history than those provided by the combatants on behalf of official memory and national identity—who tend to work in terms of falsified unities, the manipulation of demonized or distorted representations or undesirable and/or excluded populations, and the propagation of heroic anthems sung in order to sweep all before them.[34]

Post-Zionist scholars in Israel and those who embrace the postmodern or postcolonial label in the United States are doing just what Said has done throughout his scholarly career: questioning cultural dogma and orthodoxy by deploying contrapuntal readings that examine "structures of attitude and reference."[35]

In a book filled with diatribes against postmodernism and the supposed provocateur of postmodernism, Stanley Fish—whom Bennett attempts to compare to Charles Manson, claiming that Manson simply took Fish's views on relativism to their extreme conclusion and asking "Why [under the logic of relativists] should Manson languish in a jail cell, while Fish is the Dean of Liberal Arts at a prestigious university?"—Bennett again and again finds postmodernism or cultural relativism incapable of making discriminations between Israeli defensive action and Palestinian terrorism or of paying close attention to moral and political messages. Compare Bennett's comment to Anita Shapira's:

> History as a chronicle of injustice and misery—that is the post-Zionist message. History becomes a sentimental description, in which we are

always supposed to identify with the vanquished and criticize the victors. Thus, the very fact that Zionism turned out to be a victorious movement makes it amoral.[36]

Shapira, like Bennett, views postmodernism and postcolonialism—as it is deployed by the post-Zionists—as issuing an indictment against strength, stability, conquerors, and state founders. Of course, it's not as if one needed postmodernism, postcolonialism or post-Zionism to understand that in this conflict where one stands determines what one sees.

These tendencies to connect postmodernism's and postcolonial theory's supposed "softness" on moral and political problems to an incapacity to see the enemy in our midst are discursive attempts to attain cognitive stabilization, that is, rhetorical moves that ground the contingency of events and preferences that shape our world within a framework that is consistent and recognizable. Clichés about and easily drawn equations between expressions of Third-World nationalism, particularly Palestinian nationalism,[37] and terrorism help us to avoid psychomachia—the internal division and conflict that produces the conditions of possibility so very necessary for the stabilization and legitimation of beliefs and discursive acts—and, more importantly, self-blame and self-interrogation. It is somewhat disingenuous, but perhaps human, to automatically impugn the motives of suicide bombers without trying to assess the grievances they bring with them. The language of moral condemnation inevitably uses an axiological system that allows for epistemic self-privileging and its concomitant, epistemic scapegoating. Barbara Herrnstein Smith, in her *Contingencies of Values: Alternative Perspectives for Critical Theory* persuasively demonstrated that axiological systems require an unexplained privileging of value that is circular and ultimately this privileging if critically examined always fails—as it always must.[38]

In his influential book, *That Noble Dream: The Objectivity Question and the American Historical Profession*, Peter Novick states that "[a] central problem for any new cognitive structure is to legitimize its epistemological foundation. This may involve a myth of an individual genius or hero whose personal qualities exemplify the way in which the new knowledge is acquired. . . . Without some such myth, cognitive structures lack grounding and authority."[39] Although Novick was referring to the concept of "objectivity" within the disciplinary history of the historical profession,[40] I think some useful lessons can be gathered from his insights. After 9/11, terrorism—as the weapon of our enemies—becomes this myth that will surprise us at any moment within the cognitive structure of "objectivity" whereby states act justly and those resisting racist occupations act illegitimately. Objectivity demands that this must be so.[41] Barraged with idée reçues about al-Qaeda, Hezbollah, Islamic Jihad, the al-Aqsa Martyr's Brigade and Hamas, this myth and cognitive structure stabilize the aspirations, textual authorities, and heroes that a nation falls back upon in times of crisis.[42] Forms of thought that question the centrality of these aspirations, textual authorities, and heroes will be ripe for attack in times of national crisis. The movement of previously neglected perspectives into the public sphere creates a clash of perspectives between dominant and marginalized groups that generates intellectual controversy all along the political spectrum. This observation has proven especially true in Said's advocacy for Palestinian self-determination in the American imagination.

Media coverage of the Israel-Palestine conflict in the American public sphere comprises one of the most scandalous chapters in the history of journalism (See Said's Introduction to *Blaming the Victims: Spurious Scholarship and the Question of Palestine*).[43] Although this might appear to be a hyperbolic statement, it does—at the very least—warrant examination. The framing of the gross asymmetries that exist between the Israelis and the Palestinians by American journalists often completely erases the very complicated history of 1947–48 that stands at the background of Israel's birth. For example, one might easily lose sight of the fact that Israel is engaged in a military occupation that violates the Fourth Geneva Convention and UN Resolution 242. The laudatory chorus of voices on the US journalistic scene (Thomas Friedman, Fouad Ajami, and Judith Miller being among them) have so readily effaced the basic facts of the conflict that "condemnations of Palestinian terrorism" and "calls for the defeat of threats against Israel's existence" have become just so many easily formulated assertions that pass with facile piety and craven hypocrisy.

The Palestinian cause has very few defenders in the American public sphere and even fewer outspoken defenders in comparison with the institutions and ideologies that promote the cause of Israel.[44] Drawing upon the example of the destruction of European Jewry at the hands of the Nazi killing machine during the Holocaust, these institutions and ideologies sometimes misuse moral capital to justify Israeli atrocities, claiming that the Palestinians wish to kill Jews because they are Jews, confirming the Zionist thesis that metahistorical anti-Semitism necessitates the existence of a state of the Jewish people and not an Israeli nation of its citizens. Indeed, both pro-Israel and pro-Palestinian partisans have capitalized upon Holocaust imagery, invoking the phrase "genocide" to describe one side's action against the other. Approaching this aspect of the conflict is naturally very sensitive because it inevitably ends up drawing comparisons between Jewish suffering and other types of group suffering.[45] In fact, espousing the plight of the Palestinian people in the American public sphere can cost you your career.[46]

Despite all the vilification and slander Said's name has endured throughout his remarkable career, it still remains as a remnant of the most intransigent resistance movement of the twentieth century: Palestinian nationalism. To use the word "Palestine," as Said has pointed out, is to commit an immediate act of resistance and political assertion.[47] The attempts to erase the history and memory of the Palestinian people are met by the indefatigable efforts of individuals such as Said, Rashid Khalidi, Noam Chomsky, Ibrahim and Janet Abu-Lughod and Norman G. Finkelstein. The asymmetries that exist between Israeli and Palestinian power are often overlooked or forgotten in the American public sphere because of various cultural and political forces.[48]

While it's perhaps impossible to provide a counterweight to the influence of these forces, one can safely view Said as a sign of Palestinian resistance in the public sphere in that his scholarship and activism seem to always return to the plight of the Palestinian people and their quest for self-determination. The bloody events of 1947–49 and the creation of what Benny Morris has called the "Palestinian refugee problem" are rarely discussed—if even known—in the American public sphere in all the media coverage of the Israeli-Palestinian conflict that presents decontextualized and de-historicized images that blame the victims and labels them as terrorists.[49]

Said has never attempted to rationalize or explain away terrorism. He has always argued that peaceful coexistence remains the answer to the conflict with the Palestinians being embraced as "equals" by the Israelis. Recently declassified Israeli documents have allowed for the re-telling of Israeli history by the "new historians." For example, Benny Morris and Tom Segev reveal how the tragic dispossession of the Palestinians was the price of Israel's birth.[50] Benny Morris claims that

> The new history is one of the signs of a maturing Israel (though, no doubt, there are those who say it is a symptom of decay and degeneration). What is now being written about Israel's past seems to offer us a more balanced and more "truthful" view of that country's history than what has been offered hitherto. It may also in some obscure way serve the purposes of peace and reconciliation between the warring tribes of that land.[51]

In *After the Last Sky*, Said states "There has been no misfortune worse for us than that we are ineluctably viewed as the enemies of the Jews. No moral and political fate worse, none at all, I think: no worse, there is none."[52] While always recognizing the horrific plight of twentieth-century European Jewry and never questioning the right of the existence of a Jewish homeland, Said has accepted his moral and political fate with great dignity because the burden of history required him to do so.

By challenging the dominant Zionist myths that create the reality that is the Israel-Palestine conflict in the American Public Sphere, Said challenged one of the most powerful ideological hegemonies in the United States: pro-Zionist institutions and organizations.[53] He called the exposure of pro-Zionist forces (organizations, institutions, and interests) in the United State as engaging in the last American taboo: speaking out against the hegemony of Zionist American Jews. The very fact that the discourse parameters that govern the Israel-Palestine conflict are more open in Israel in than in the United States indicates a fundamental psychological resistance to the facts of the conflict. In his *The Fateful Triangle: The United States, Israel, and the Palestinians*, Noam Chomsky writes that this conflict has proven to be one in which no one has shown themselves capable of telling or facing the truth.

Pro-Zionist American Jewish and Christian support for Israel, particularly as this this support manifests itself in the wide-ranging impact of the American-Israel Public Affairs Committee and the Anti-Defamation League in the policy arena, is well known. These organizations seemingly condemn any characterization of the conflict not favorable to Israel as "anti-Semitic," making American politicians extremely reluctant to criticize Israel's occupation of the West Bank, its military adventurism, and its poor treatment of its Arab Palestinian citizens. Indeed, a common wisdom has emerged dictating that dissenting from the "support-Israeli-aggression-at-any-and-all-costs" position will result in such a massive political backlash that it is better to remain silent than to stand in the way of an interest that has become a part of the American political establishment.

As Christopher Hitchens has indicated, one does not and perhaps should not make references to the influence of the Israel lobby in the United States while in polite company.[54] The influence of the American-Israel Public Affairs Committee has come under increasing scrutiny in the last several months as AIPAC has taken an interest in seemingly obscure political races. Cynthia Mckinney, a critic of US policies in the Middle East, was defeated by an unknown candidate through AIPAC money and support. As Alexander Cockburn has recently written, "AIPAC dares American politicians to place their head over the Israel-Palestine parapet, saying 'If you take the anti-Israel stand, we'll blow you away!'"[55] This message has been learned by American politicians at all levels of government.

As a Palestinian within a culture that wishes to erase and forget that there are Palestinians, Said never allowed us to forget the pangs of dispossession, anguish, and migration that are endured by those living under occupation. While it's important not to engage in gratuitous symbolization with respect to Said's biography and example, one is inevitably led to connect his life to a population that he made such a personal cause and abiding concern.

Those who were threatened by Edward W. Said's presence on the critical scene for nearly 40 years were perhaps most frightened by his explorations of, and theorizations about, the role of the intellectual in society. Those who felt threatened were not simply political enemies, who disagreed with his positions on the Israel-Palestine conflict, but were also professional enemies disturbed by the political turn in his work, announced most prominently in *Orientalism* and continuing through to *The Question of Palestine, The World, the Text, and the Critic, Covering Islam, Culture and Imperialism,* and *Humanism and Democratic Criticism*.[56] From his extensive writings on the Question of Palestine to his frequent reminders about the pitfalls of professionalization and hyper-specialization and how these (perhaps purposively) tame the most persistent of critics, Said kept us alert and just a little uneasy about our possibly complicity in discursive formations (literary canons, professional norms, and structures of attitude and reference) that contribute to the subjugation of the Other.

Since Said's passing in September of 2003, we are left to contemplate how his very large body of work can be brought to bear on the very social and political problems he devoted his life to studying. Foremost in Said's mind at the time of his passing was the role of the intellectual in society, a theme he explored in his Reith Lectures from 1993 which became *Representations of the Intellectual*. In these lectures, Said looked at the intellectual as an agitating force in society, a presence that could—in the service of justice and speaking truth to power—disturb orthodoxies and taken-for-granted habits of thought and action. Said found these intellectual representations in James Baldwin, Malcolm X, Virginia Woolf, Simone de Beauvoir, Mary McCarthy, Jean-Paul Sartre, Hannah Arendt, and Noam Chomsky, whose pictures appear on the front cover of *Representations of the Intellectual*. Beyond these figures, however, Said also found inspiration in the intellectual representations of C. L. R James, Frantz Fanon, Theodor Adorno, Julian Benda, and Antonio Gramsci, who are also discussed in the book. For Said, the intellectual's primary task is to tell the truth, the consequences be damned, and these intellectuals did so in the context of anti-colonial and anti-fascist struggles throughout the twentieth century.

In the Reith Lectures, Said aptly described the pitfalls of professionalization and how the professional reward system can tame the fiercest of critics, trapping her in a guessing game about whether her pronouncements against the status quo might put her on the wrong side of the powers that be. To succumb to this professional reward system is the modern *trahison des clercs*, as there will always be excuses and rationalizations available to justify walking away from a controversial position or divisive pronouncement that might cause you to lose friends and allies. If one is looking for that next prize, major grant, or much sought after speaking engagement, the natural tendency is to hide one's political passions and to go with the flow for fear of offending some powerful interest or wealthy patron. This tendency reduces most intellectuals to the status of functionaries who are willing to serve the interests of power and most hesitant to upset the reigning political configuration for fear of having to stand against a powerful constituency. Said, of course, saw this predicament play itself out again and again with respect to the Question of Palestine, as intellectuals and politicians have found every possible excuse to avoid confronting the powerful Israel Lobby in the United States, as Israel's occupation of the Palestinians continues to create oppressive conditions in Gaza and the West Bank. Looming in the background, of course, are the prospects of a wider regional war in the Middle East involving the United States, Israel, and Iran, and the possibility of a nuclear war. All too frequently, intellectuals cite their relative lack of expertise to speak out on issues of public concern, noting the importance of possessing the right credentials before speaking truth to power. Said viewed this emphasis upon credentials and expertise as a smokescreen designed to exclude the average citizen from the arena of debate, with the arcane mysticism surrounding the technical terminology of the guild seemingly designed to intimidate the un-initiated and the unconnected.

Said's intellectual legacy

Said sought to develop a model of the public intellectual that would enable academic workers to pursue a state of being he labeled "amateurism," a willingness to speak on issues of public concern outside of the their areas of scholarly expertise, demonstrating that such issues would not be ceded to the cult of expertise dominating so many debates in the public sphere.[57] Although he held no formal training in Middle East Studies, Said established himself as a reputable commentator on the Middle East.[58] He experienced "the punishing destiny of a Palestinian living in the West" and used that experience to write movingly about the pain of Palestinian dispossession at the hands of the imperial powers. In a response to the Gramscian call to trace the cultural influences upon the construction of his subjectivity, Said brought an autobiographical component to his public intellectualism as he sought to understand his unique condition as an "Oriental" writing back, so to speak, against the Western discursive mechanisms that reduce Middle Eastern peoples to caricatures and stereotypes.

Whether writing about the insidious ways Orientalism and Zionism accrete discursive authority for their political goals through a slow process of negating the remnants of the Palestinian presence, or denouncing intellectuals in the Arab world for continually blaming the West for the region's many problems (petty dictators, lack of economic development, lack of religious toleration, abuse of human rights, restriction of the women's movement, etc.), Said sought to arrest the tendency among humanists to leave the field of political battle to pundits and media personalities intent upon reducing human experience to the binary of "us and them," seeking instead to highlight the discrepant experiences that bind human beings to one another.

Said's constant prodding, one might even say goading, of literature professors was disturbing to many because it was a persistent reminder that academic professionals could be so much more than academic professionals in the context of the public sphere—if they would only push themselves to leave their petty fiefdoms of professional concern and venture into the realm of the political. For those who chose not to develop their professional life in this way, Said's ruminations about "speaking truth to power" may have created a cognitive dissonance of sorts. What is the proper way for an English Professor, for example, to become engaged with issues of international significance when her professional training has equipped her to interpret poetry? Said's point was that such interpretive training enabled radical intellectual engagement with ideas, communities, and constituencies in the world.

There was also a less-than-hidden indictment in texts such as *The World, the Text, and the Critic*, as Said seemed to heap scorn upon his fellow literary theorists, suggesting that they had essentially given up in the wake of the "Rise of Reaganism," with its emphasis on free markets, *laissez faire* capitalism and deregulation.[59] Critics were content to pursue arcane hermeneutics and irrelevant invocations of the post-human.[60] As Said suggests, the 1980s represented the time of the literary critic's departure from the political scene, as the critic gave up the field of struggle to politicians, generals, and policy intellectuals; realizing perhaps that she was no longer really relevant to the burning debates about culture, imperialism, and resistance politics. Said's great refusal to accept this predicament positioned him against the reigning sentiments within the Modern Language Association, which seemed to subscribe to a politically correct version of public intellectualism, while avoiding stands on difficult issues such as Zionist colonization of Palestine.

Said's constant reminders about the importance of affirming human agency seemed to irritate those who counted themselves among the post-structuralists, who argued that human agency and subjectivity were limited and conditioned by institutions, language, as well as one's race, sex, and class, and that the belief in the prospect of meaningful human action was naïve. His seeming dismissal of Derrida and Foucault created a minor scandal within the profession, with allegations that Said had misunderstood both thinkers.[61] Said had to hold on to the prospect of human beings exerting their agency in the world to transform it; otherwise, he was would have been left with the prospect that oppression was somehow natural, perhaps metaphysical, a simple part of the world humans inhabit. That was a sure route to despair.

As part of this insistence that social change can be initiated by human beings working with one another in the world, Said sought to establish with master conductor Daniel Barenboim a collective effort between Palestinian and Israeli youth to create a traveling orchestra called the "West-Eastern Divan Orchestra," which performs throughout Europe and the Middle East. This effort captures how Said viewed the field of cultural production, as a space for bringing people—who are alienated from one another because of differences produced by geography, religion, political affiliation, and language—together through art. That musical performance enables cross-cultural exchange among a group of young people separated by walls, borders, checkpoints, the ethnic exclusivism of Zionism, and the aspirations of the Palestinian people searching for a state of their own, speaks to the capacity of people to transcend the limitations of their filiative origins and to embrace affiliative beginnings. If it is the case that anti-Semitism and Orientalism spring from the same discursive well, we must, then, recognize the Palestinian Arab as the new Jew. Orientalism, as anti-Semitism's "secret sharer," configures the Palestinian Arab as the new vulnerable whose liquidation and removal is at the heart of the Zionist project. Comparing the discrepant experiences of Palestinian Arabs living under Israeli occupation to those of Jewish displaced persons at the end of World War II can promote an understanding of the commonality of human suffering.

Now that Said is no longer with us, we are left to assess the gravity of Said's explorations and theorizations about the role of the critical intellectual, while also deciding upon how Said's legacy must become a part of that exploration and theorization. Indeed, we must evaluate how Said created new conceptualizations of what it means to be an intellectual in a basically depoliticized society. Some recent books and edited collections have attempted to do just that by situating Said's critical legacy within a number of different disciplinary domains and by extending that legacy to a variety of social concerns that will undoubtedly trouble us for some time to come.[62]

The complexity of Said's thought can be measured in several ways. First, Said's *Beginnings*—written in the 1960s—seemed to sketch out the full dimensions of Said's critical program, which he enacted through the 1970s, 1980s, and 1990s. Said wished to bring a diverse group of thinkers—such as Barthes, Levi-Strauss, Foucault, and Derrida—around to questions of how human agency could be obtained and enacted in oppressive social circumstances, although each of these thinkers was considered anti-humanistic and skeptical about human agency. Second, the problem of human agency became, in the midst of immensely important world events of the 1960s, central to Said's projects. Although Said's political transformation took place early in his academic career, it was during the 1967 Israeli-Arab Six-Day War in fact when he came to consciousness as an Arab-American. One can trace a political urgency in Said's *Orientalism*, *The Question of Palestine*, and *Covering Islam*, in which he seemingly predicted the current situation in the Middle East. The demonization of Palestinians, and Arabs more generally, in the intellectual and media discourses of the 1970s clearly played a role in mobilizing the general public's sentiments against the Palestinian liberation movement and the PLO as the movement's representative. Increasing gas prices, an oil embargo, the Iran hostage crisis, and the killing of Israeli athletes by Palestinian fighters at the 1972 Munich Olympics contributed to the Western belief that Arabs—particularly Palestinian Arabs—were inscrutable, uncivilized, irrational, and committed to the use of violence in the service of extremism.

As Jack Shaheen documents in his book *Reel Bad Arabs*, the hundreds of movies that Hollywood produced in the 1970s, 1980s, and 1990s depicting Arabs as the epitome of evil made Washington's task of portraying the Arab world as a bastion of corruption and villainy, where US intervention was necessary, that much easier. Said viewed with increasing skepticism the United States' involvement in the Middle East, sensing and expressing his concerns about the prospects of an impending catastrophe in the region with the escalating arms race between Israel and its Arab neighbors.[63] Third, Said realized that any attempt to represent a people, a territory, or a conquest within a discourse involved an immense metaphysical machinery—bringing together power, knowledge, and truth—to simplify what is a complex human reality. For all these reasons, Said was ahead of his time.

A recent collection of essays, entitled *Waiting for the Barbarians: A Tribute to Edward Said*, attempts to make sense of Said's career as a professor of literature, a prominent public intellectual, and, perhaps most memorably, as an activist in the context of the Israel-Palestine conflict. The contributions by Rashid Khalidi and Saree Makdisi assess Said's fashioning of a distinctive intellectual style in his advocacy for the Palestinian narrative in the United States, bringing his commitment to humanism to this effort. Khalidi notes that, "When he spoke about Palestine, [Said's] focus was essentially humanist: this was a problem, he argued, that could not be solved in an annihilationist manner, a problem that admitted of no zero-sum solution, a problem that finally had to be resolved by both peoples accepting the humanity of the other" (49). Consistent with this humanist outlook, as Makdisi argues, ". . . Said's work offered us the very antidote to which he was referring: interference, transgression, a breaking out of the confines of specialized disciplinary audiences, and speaking to a broader public" (60). Said brought together an enlightened humanist outlook and a committed public intellectualism that disturbed the conventional location of the English Professor in the research university. How else could he have addressed the Question of Palestine so effectively and in front of so many different audiences? Humanism, as he reminded us during his March 2003 address before the Arab-American Anti-Discrimination League, is "the last remaining resistance we have against the inhuman practices and injustices that have disfigured human history."[64] As Makdisi claims, "Thus the idea of Palestine was always, in Said's work, inseparable from the larger humanist project on which he had embarked, a humanist project that sought to rescue humanism itself from the larger claims of European imperialism with which it had come into the world."[65] This project has found an application within contemporary academic debates about the Middle East.

The intense attacks that have been waged against academic freedom in the wake of 9/11, with Said's *Orientalism* being blamed for the supposed anti-Americanism in Middle East Studies, anthropology, area studies, and other related disciplines, signal that it is more important than ever to defend the university as a place of critical intellectualism and as a site devoted to the open exchange of ideas and positions. In their *Uncivil University: Politics & Propaganda in American Higher Education*, Tobin, Weinberg, and Ferer claim that, "What could possibly be more horrific in terms of perverting the purpose of multiculturalism than the notion that scholarship has to be based on one's race, ethnicity, or gender in order to be legitimate? This is partially due to the sad legacy of Saidism, the paradigm put forward by Edward Said, that [sic] led to the ideological poisoning of Middle East Study centers and departments all over academe."[66] This crudely reductive rendering of Said's intellectual legacy is unfortunately representative of the kind of caricatures that have gained wide circulation in the public sphere, where the construction of a strawperson—assembled from the arguments of a serious intellectual critic—serves to render serious intellectual debate moot.

As a Palestinian educated in the Ivy League, Said became a professor of literature at Columbia in 1966 and used his privileged position to question the very knowledge traditions of which he was a beneficiary. He recognized the uniqueness of his predicament, realizing that the humanistic traditions he had mastered were responsible for subjugating people who looked just like him. The works of the great humanistic tradition, Dante's *Inferno*, Pope's *Epistles*, or Auerbach's *Mimesis*, spoke to the condition of the European subject and did not consider the specificities of the minority positions Said was interested in examining. Herein resides a paradox—Said became the native informant, translating for his Western interlocutors the secrets of the East, demanding that knowledge and power be held responsible for the human catastrophes they have produced, whether in the context of Indian resistance to British rule or Palestinian resistance to Israeli colonization. However, such an observation rubs against the grain of Said's own thought, as he called for intellectual workers to transcend the markers of class, race, ethnicity, and religion and to recognize the lines of solidarity that bind them. However, he always sought "criticism before solidarity," a call to reject the easygoingness of belonging to a group, club, party, or organization.

Edward Said deeply believed in the power of human beings to shape the world around them. His continual emphasis upon how agency is created in concert with traditions or through the making of counter-traditions belied his absolute belief in how people can change oppressive circumstances through their efforts. Of course, the one situation that was most on his mind, the Question of Palestine is the one situation that no one has been able to change. Said, the Palestinian intellectual, steeped in the learning of the American academy, dismantled the imperialism of the West and exposed its effects upon literature, art, and our very perceptions of the world. How do humans come to perceive the world around them in the multitude of ways that they do? Is it merely happenstance that some perceptions predominate over others? I think Edward Said's work gives us intelligent ways to think about these questions.

Said and the contemporary public sphere

The declining role of the public intellectual was of concern to Said, particularly as this decline coincided with the rise of the policy intellectual who was certified to speak on certain questions within narrowly defined knowledge configurations, but unprepared to address larger themes of justice, universal human rights, and speaking truth to power. By the mid-1970s, the disappearance of figures with the stature of Bertrand Russell, Jean-Paul Sartre, and Hannah Arendt from the public stage created a serious crisis for the concept of the public intellectual itself, as the number of individuals capable of speaking to a wide range of concerns and issues seemingly disappeared. In his *The World, the Text, and the Critic*, Said notes that "the rise of Reaganism" brought with it a change in critical practice within the field of English Studies, as once renegade professors found themselves tamed by the poststructural turn, which dictated that expressions of insurgency could be confined to textual investigations without participating in risky, and potentially costly, radical politics. In other words, instead of speaking truth to power, the public intellectual could become immersed in the intricacies of textual analysis, almost to the point of avoiding the reality before her.

As Timothy Brennan explains in his *Wars of Position: The Cultural Politics of Left and Right*, intellectuals stopped making claims upon the state by the 1980s, preferring instead to nurture radical states of being without risking the prospect of announcing one's political allegiances in scholarship (9–10). Said worried that the emphasis upon textuality and discourse, announced most prominently in the critical programs of Derrida in *Of Grammatology* and Foucault in *The Order of Discourse*, sought to actually restrain intellectual intervention and question whether stable representations of the world are possible, suggesting that reality itself was more complex than human perception itself could appreciate. Derrida's "there's nothing outside the text" and Foucault's conception of the archeology of discourse complicates the concepts of power, resistance, and intellectual intervention to such a degree that human agency becomes constrained; so much so that those who are naïve enough to believe that people are free actors in the world are belittled as "volunteerists." It is this dismissal of human action in the world that so disturbed Said, as he condemned these invocations of complexity and textuality as a modern version of the treason of the intellectual.

Within the context of the Question of Palestine, Said confronted the treason of his fellow professional intellectuals on a regular basis, condemning the unwillingness of those who were ideally situated to question the US-Israel special relationship and its implications for the dispossessed and powerless Palestinian population living under an occupation that seemingly went unreported and unacknowledged in the West. The power of the Israel Lobby intimidated supposedly progressive intellectuals from speaking out against Israel's growing hegemony in determining the shape of US foreign policy in the Middle East.[67] This power of such an immense lobby to limit free expression and dissent about such an important policy issue signaled to Said that special interests were coming to dominate the American public sphere in a harmful way. If the silence of the intellectual classes could be obtained through intimidation tactics and smear campaigns, which have come to characterize debate about the Israel-Palestine conflict, particularly as these attacks have been directed against those challenging the ability of the Israel Lobby to control the parameters of speech about the Middle East, Said feared that public debate about the crucial and relevant issues would end. That he would not cede the field of debate to the cult of expertise represented by the likes of Paula Zahn, Bernard Lewis, and Fouad Ajami spoke to his passion for dismantling knowledge systems that accrete false authority for themselves in the process of colonizing large swathes of intellectual territory, neutralizing challengers along the way.

The trappings of power are seductive, easily reducing the most alert intellectual to a state of apathy and subservience to the status quo. This tendency to gravitate toward and serve concentrated power is perhaps a recognition of human finitude. As mortal beings, humans come to quickly recognize their limits and as these are created between culture and system. This famous phrase, "between culture and system," is a condition Said elaborates upon in his *The World, the Text, and the Critic*. With this phrase, Said is attempting to pinpoint the specific limitations that are placed on human agency and freedom by the filiative and affiliative relationships one develops throughout one's life. Human beings, then, are caught between cultural norms and discursive constructions—literally systems of discourse created by institutions—that create the very grids of intelligibility for human possibility. Filiative relationships refer to the connections human beings form with one another based on blood and common ancestry, whereas affiliative relationships arise in the context of professions, organizations, and movements; they are relationships that are chosen rather than determined. In choosing to affiliate with a group, an organization, or an institution, one exercises agency in deciding with whom one will associate, work, and develop programmatic goals.

This freedom of choice in the affiliative relationship held all sorts of creative possibilities for resisting injustice in the world, as men and women— regardless of race, religion, or creed—could join with like-minded people to challenge and transform troubling cultural hegemonies. The possibility of affiliation provides the conditions of possibility for intellectual kinship, resistance politics, and organizational mobilizations and movements. These are relationships that depend upon people being inspired by ideals and long-term goals, rather than tribal solidarities for the promotion of an identity politics. For example, people from a variety of religious faiths and political locations affirm the fundamental importance of protecting human rights within the context of the Palestinian struggle against occupation, believing that it is important to show solidarity with those populations experiencing oppression and dispossession.

It is the possibility of creating affiliative relationships, in the face of the crippling effects that filiations have left in their wake throughout human history, that interests the public intellectual, who seeks to address issues of human concern that appear to be intractable and irresolvable. As a public intellectual, Said sought to address the Question of Palestine in the American public sphere by identifying the political forces preventing an open discussion about Zionism's treatment of the Palestinians, whose plight as a colonized people hangs in the balance.

That the Palestinian liberation movement has come to represent an instance of the last resistance against colonial occupation, catalogued with the Algerian War for Independence as a classic case of indigenous resistance facing down imperial expansion, motivated Said to explain the Palestinian perspective to Western audiences.[68] That Said's intellectual resistance against the accommodation of most academic intellectuals took its inspiration from Palestinian resistance against Israeli occupation naturally produced controversy and suspicion about Said's political motives. Condemned as an enemy of Israel, reduced to the caricature of "The Professor of Terror," Said fought against the American corporate media's tendency to traffic in the Orientalist discourses he devoted his life to exposing in such works as *Orientalism, The Question of Palestine,* and *Covering Islam.*

It is the cult of expertise informing the supposed War on Terror that Said was prescient in exposing and deconstructing in this famous trilogy (*Orientalism, The Questions of Palestine,* and *Covering Islam*). As Said notes in *Humanism and Democratic Criticism,* "The cult of expertise has never ruled the world of discourse as it now does in the United States, where the policy intellectual can feel that he or she surveys the entire world."[69] Figures such as Steve Emerson, Daniel Pipes, Martin Kramer, and Fouad Ajami make the Arab world understandable to Western psychologies sympathetic to Zionism's aims in the Middle East. That there has been such a relative dearth of effective public intellectuals speaking and writing on the Israel-Palestine conflict confirmed Said's fear about American Zionism: that an open discussion and examination of this social-political hegemony is one of the last remaining taboos in the US public sphere—where asking probing questions about the US-Israel special relationship is ruled out of bounds within intellectual and journalistic circles.

With the exception of a handful of dissenting intellectuals, including Alexander Cockburn, Noam Chomsky, Jeffrey St Clair, Ali Abunimah, Rashid Khalidi, and Said himself before his passing, the number of effective and well-known advocates on the Question of Palestine can be counted on two hands. This flight from critical thought within American civil society represents a clear triumph of the corporate state, which teaches the citizen how and what to think on the critical issues. This tendency to adopt what is offered up by the corporate media as sacrosanct is a theme that Said picked up on in his *Humanism and Democratic Criticism,* where he writes in a chapter entitled "The Public Role of Intellectuals and Writers" that "True, it is a considerable disadvantage to get asked on to PBS's *NewsHour* or ABC's *Nightline* or, if one is in fact asked, only an isolated fugitive minute will be offered" (132–3). Despite the slim prospects of critical discussion emerging in such constrained formats, Said is hopeful that creative intellects will be in a position to "tak[e] advantage of what is available in the form of numerous platforms (or stages-itinerant, another Swiftian term) and an alert and creative willingness to exploit them by an intellectual (that is, platforms that either aren't available to or are shunned by the television personality, expert, or political candidate), it is possible to initiate a wider discussion" (*Humanism and Democratic Criticism* 133).

Said's disillusionment with the erosion of the public's faith in the public intellectual was most prominently announced in his *Representations of the Intellectual*, where he provided a historical analysis of the intellectual's diminishing role in society beginning with Julian Benda's *The Treason of the Intellectuals* and ending with Richard Crossman's *The God That Failed*. Whereas Benda documented how nineteenth-century intellectuals succumbed to the temptation to become apologists for nationalism, Crossman examined how communism failed as an appropriate political program in the twentieth century for intellectuals such as Ignazio Silone, André Gide, Arthur Koestler, and Stephen Spender, as each experienced increasing disappointment with "his experiences to the road to Moscow, the inevitable disenchantment that followed, [and] the subsequent re-embrace of noncommunist faith" (*Representations of the Intellectual* 111).

This god-that-failed-syndrome, for Said, continued well into the last years of the twentieth century, as far too many intellectuals in the Arab world could not bring themselves to denounce US policy in the Middle East, particularly in the context of the Israel-Palestine conflict, while issuing facile condemnations of other Arab intellectuals who took dissenting positions with respect to US support for Israel and other US-supported regimes in the region.[70] It is this willingness to stand alone and to draw energy from one's isolation and principled positions that distinguishes the intellectual from a policy analyst or the media pundit.

A way forward

The Saidian intellectual transgresses the usual modes of expression and the normal ways of doing, risking the possible loss of friends and patrons in the spirit of radical interrogation and human emancipation. As Said reminds us, "Part of what we do as intellectuals is not only to define the situation, but also to discern the possibilities of active intervention, whether we then perform them ourselves or acknowledge them in others who have either gone before or are already at work, the intellectual as lookout" (*Humanism and Democratic Criticism* 140). Said's call to intellectuals to locate possibilities and entry points for interventions into difficult debates and conflicts confirmed his humanistic outlook, demonstrating a commitment to what he long believed—that humans are capable of changing the world around them by working toward universal ideals of truth, justice, and human liberation Intellectual resistance within the context of the Question of Palestine was clearly uppermost in Said's mind.

Despite what he believed to be the deliberate mystification of these ideals in the service of self-serving political agendas, Said held on to the prospect of human action making a difference in resisting occupation, injustice, and tyranny. As he noted, "[O]ne needn't always present an abstruse and detailed theory of justice to go to war intellectually against injustice, since there is now a well-stocked internationalist storehouse of conventions, protocols, resolutions, and charters for national authorities to comply with, if they are so inclined" (*Humanism and Democratic Criticism* 136). Said's seemingly complete rejection of the notion that reality is socially constructed or that it is merely a linguistic construction captures quite perfectly, I think, his attitude toward the task of the contemporary intellectual. In the face of so much intellectual fashion and posturing, Said forcefully asserted that if intellectuals are to remain true to their mission, they must risk the possibility of being burned at the stake in the course of speaking truth to power. Said's stance confirms the relevance of his example for our current historical moment.

CHAPTER SIX

Noam Chomsky, intellectual labor, and the Question of Palestine

Adherence to doctrinal truth confers substantial award, not only acceptance within the system of power and a ready path to privilege, but also the inestimable advantage of freedom from the onerous demands of thought, inquiry and argument. Conformity frees one from the burden evidence, and rational argument is superfluous while one is marching in an approved parade.

(NOAM CHOMSKY, *The Culture of Terrorism*)

As I have attempted to explain through several different examples, which I have elaborated upon thus far in this book, an intellectual's assertion that the Question of Palestine exists also entails acknowledging the legitimate grievances of the Palestinian population dispossessed as a result of Israel's creation. This assertion is an act of intellectual resistance—whether it takes places in the US academy or in the public sphere more generally—that is of great symbolic and political importance. At the beginning of his *The Question of Palestine*, Edward Said writes the following about the Palestinians and the Question of Palestine: "For we have been outside history, and certainly outside discussion; in its own modest way this book attempts to make the Question of Palestine a subject for discussion and political understanding" (xlii). Furthermore, as Said notes in the book's conclusion, "Although the struggle over Palestine is grounded in the land itself, its astonishing international resonance—especially in the hearts and minds of Western, and particularly American citizens—remains crucial" and that "Palestine is the last great cause of the twentieth century with roots going back to the period of classical imperialism" (243). It has been with these statements from Said in mind that I have sought to bring the Question of Palestine into various professional spaces over the last 10 years. In this chapter and the next one, I describe these efforts through various theoretical prisms.

Perhaps no one individual has done as much as Noam Chomsky to explore the role intellectuals play within society, examining their purpose and ideological serviceability to concentrated power while also documenting in minute detail their usefulness to US elites over nearly a 50-year period of US global supremacy as a military and economic superpower. In his *For Reasons of State*, Chomsky laid out the intellectual program that has informed his analyses of intellectuals in society:

> [These essays] are concerned with certain problems of law and justice and the responsibility of the citizen in the face of state crimes; with the universities; the main center of intellectual life in the current phase of industrial society; with the contributions of academic fraud to the ideology of control, and more interesting, with the justification of injustice produced by scientists who cannot perceive that the force of their arguments derives from tacit acceptance of the most vulgar principles of the prevailing ideology.[1]

The intellectual's predilections for supporting national power are conditioned by a system of awards and incentives that make serious dissent quite difficult in contemporary American society. These awards and incentives include professional status, a relatively comfortable income, the ability to exercise influence within one's circles, a chance to receive recognition for one's work, and all the accolades that accompany when one conforms to cultural and institutional pressures. One goes to graduate school, plans for a career, and seeks out an academic position for the purpose of becoming part of professional and institutional networks, not to undermine and expose these networks as working coextensively with the state or the military-industrial complex.

Nonetheless, it is difficult to escape the fact that academic workers do play a specific role in the discursive machinery of the state and its violence-producing goals.[2] While it is certainly true that academic workers reflect upon the conditions of possibility informing their institutional locations and the scholarship produced within them, academic critiques of the role that intellectuals play in legitimating state violence remain within very narrow bounds. For example, consider Chomsky's powerful reflections in *Toward a New Cold War*:

> To put it in the simplest terms, a talented young journalist or a student aiming for a scholarly career can choose to play the game by the rules,

with the prospect of advancement to a position of prestige and privilege and sometimes even a degree of power; or to pursue an independent path, with the likelihood of a minor post as a police reporter or in a community college, exclusion from major journals, vilification and abuse, or driving a taxi cab. Given such choices, the end result is not very surprising. Few options are open to isolated individuals in a basically depoliticized society lacking popular organizations that question the legitimacy of existing structures of domination and control, state or private.[3]

In this brief passage, Chomsky sketches a political economy of intellectual life in the United States while also noting the limited options available to those who chose intellectual dissidence—particularly within the academy. Such dissidence can pose a distinct threat to the bureaucracy of the university and the concentrated power it represents, and will be dealt with severely if the stakes are high enough.[4]

Historically, there has been collaboration between the university system and the US government to pursue military research drawing upon the specific scientific expertise of academics in the pure sciences. In addition, the university has proven to be a productive center for recruiting undergraduate and graduate students into intelligence agencies such as the Federal Bureau of Investigation, the National Security Agency, and the Central Intelligence Agency. These possibilities for extensive collaboration between the university system and the government, then, pose interesting questions for the parameters of academic freedom for dissenting scholarship.[5] Scholarship that seriously interrogates US military policy in particular international hot spots is often placed beyond the pale, for the simple reason that it interferes with the functioning of the ideological institutions, as well as raising uncomfortable questions about the ends to which taxpayer money is being used, whether this money is being used to fund the US occupation of Iraq or the Israeli occupation of the West Bank. Contrary to popular illusions, democratic states must inundate their populations with a continuous stream of propaganda about how noble intentions drive the push to war.[6] It is this continual stream of propaganda that prevents US citizens from gaining a coherent picture of how foreign policy is formulated and an understanding of the specific interests that drive it, which is precisely why dissident intellectuals are denied academic freedom protections because their intellectual labor poses a threat to the propaganda system.

Controlling dissidence

In his *On Active Service in War and Peace: Politics and Ideology in the American Historical Profession*, Jess Lemisch traces the active efforts that have been employed to repress dissident scholarship in the American historical profession, documenting the extreme measures the profession has used to marginalize scholars who problematized how historical scholarship contributed to wartime propaganda efforts in the context of the Vietnam War.[7] These scholars, who were either denied tenure or were unable to get jobs during this period of intellectual repression, were often blacklisted as being incapable of separating their convictions from their scholarship. In this context, "convictions" included opposing US military intervention in Indo-China, expressing regret about the thousands of deaths such invasions produced, and questioning the judgment and morality of American leaders.[8] The suppression of such convictions in historical scholarship protects key national mythologies, marginalizing those who manage to reveal how the American public has been manipulated to support unnecessary and costly military interventions, with the US invasion of South Vietnam representing the most extreme example.[9] For a scholar to speak out against these interventions in her scholarship, at the time these interventions are ongoing, brings with it extreme professional risk.[10]

If the kind of intellectual independence described above is so threatening to various state and institutional formations and is inevitably going to lead to perpetual underemployment, then what incentive—if any—exists to challenge favored intellectual pieties?[11] The price one can potentially pay for challenging favored truths can be quite heavy. Controversial speech is a form of immaterial labor that can undermine the possibility of an academic advancing within an institutional hierarchy, particularly if that speech challenges or exposes certain state formations that must remain hidden. The "rules" Chomsky mentions above are never articulated out loud, but can be surmised by observing the behaviors of intellectuals at conferences, in department meetings, and within highbrow journals, where following proper etiquette is paramount—which often means not asking disturbing questions about the direct role American university intellectuals play in suppressing the United States' imperial history.[12] The maintenance of this etiquette, the surveillance of professional venues, the hyper-scrutiny of scholarship, and the creation of an institutional cult of personality that makes intellectual work routine lead to the view that this work has no direct connection to the outside world, controlling the independent critic and any possible predilection for her independence.

While the mechanism informing this tendency among intellectuals to conform to a version of the nation's history that is conducive to the needs of concentrated power structures is difficult to specify and articulate, one need to only look at how closely the university itself has come to mirror the structure of a transnational corporation in its most basic form. If one accepts that the university has adopted the form of a transnational corporation, one can come to see the very real demands placed upon university workers as they are forced to comply with the institutional pressures produced by late capitalism, leading to intellectual subservience and conformity. Chomsky's political corpus, however, challenges and questions the maintenance of professional etiquette, the motivations that lie behind the surveillance of various professional venues, and the destructive effects of institutionalized boredom in service to apologetics for state violence.

Toward a political economy of dissidence

What has Noam Chomsky's examinations of the American intellectual guild structure, in his numerous books about American domestic and international policy, meant for our understandings of intellectual labor? Does his political work radically reconfigure conceptions of intellectual labor by increasing our awareness of how dissident thought is contained and tamed when it makes claims upon—and challenges—the state? As theory within the humanities drifts toward embracing increasingly complex thinking, what points of connections—if any—exist between these theoretical projects and Chomsky's deeply unpopular observations about American intellectuals as outlined in his political corpus? These are important questions that explore the levels of dissidence that are sustainable in contemporary American life. The kind of dissidence that leads to the material penalties Chomsky describes in his *American Power and the New Mandarins, For Reasons of State*, and *Toward a New Cold War* is neither promoted nor protected within the academy or within US culture because it is dysfunctional to the operations of the mainstream institutions; it questions central national mythologies.[13] Scholarship that does question these key national mythologies is frequently classified as "simplistic" and "trafficking in binaries."[14]

For example, the binary thinking in Chomsky's political work—which many have dismissed as "simple minded"—makes truer and better connections to the world than the complex thinking represented in much theory within the humanities today.[15] Many globalization and cosmopolitan theories seek, for example, to justify and celebrate US neo-imperialism while ostensibly touting tolerance, global cultures, and globalization. As Timothy Brennan and others have argued, it has to be more than a mere coincidence that, as theory comes to increasingly celebrate complexity and complex thinking, it has often worked hand-in-hand with the extension of American imperial dominance.[16] That theory, as an intellectual project, would serve to make the simple "more complex" and the understandable "consonant with the realities of networked culture" should give us pause, particularly in the context of examining the effects of US foreign policy in a region such as the Middle East. This "will to complexity" should be questioned as promoting an intellectual complicity in concealing projections of American military power beneath what should properly be categorized an apologetics for neoliberalism's expansion, a refashioning of the very concept of intellectual responsibility tailored to avoid facing the harsh realities attending the expanse of the US Empire.[17]

Without placing the Real in quotation marks, Chomsky in his political work presents a truer and more accurate accounting of how and why events in the world play out in the ways they do than contemporary theoretical frameworks can. He does this without resorting to mystificatory devices such as "Empire," "the grammar of the Multitude," "biopower," and "the political" while also establishing a coherent theory of how power works that is capable of measuring competing interests and concerns. Those who dismiss Chomsky's political work as "simpleminded" or "simplistic" refuse to come to terms with the actual coherence of the explanatory frameworks that he offers, along with the significant empirical evidence he adduces to support his conclusions.[18]

Chomsky's arguments, as plainly understood as they may be in form, nevertheless have about them the complexity of reality, filled as it is with contingent events and the unpredictable actions of human agents. The denunciations of Chomsky's arguments arise out of a recognition that large and totalizing theoretical concepts such as "Empire" and "the Multitude" do not have the predictive power and analytic rigor that Chomsky's empirical testing and analyses do.[19] An uncomfortable inference can be drawn from these denunciations: Chomsky's refusal to provide ideological cover for the expansion of American Empire poses a threat to the maintenance of a certain intellectual pseudosophistication, which often functions to foreclose certain types of inquiry in advance as "radical," "out of bounds," and "infantile." The fact that lines of inquiry, which bring into focus the country's imperial past, can be closed off in advance of a possibly rigorous critique, and before the presentation of empirical evidence to justify it, signals a form of untenable, intellectual self-protection.

"It is frightening to observe the comparative indifference of American intellectuals to the immediate actions of their government and its long-range policies, and their frequent willingness—often eagerness—to play a role in implementing these policies," Chomsky writes in his "Some Thoughts on Intellectuals and the Schools" from his *American Power and the New Mandarins*. This comparative indifference among American intellectuals toward the immediate actions of their government and its long-range policies can find ideological cover in theories of complexity that refuse to assign blame or identify guilty agents. This problem is particularly acute, at this historical moment, for US intellectuals, as I will try to illustrate.

Chomsky's challenge

In September of 2004, I moderated an online discussion for the journal *Pretext* on Noam Chomsky's *Hegemony or Survival: America's Quest for Global Dominance*, which argues that United States' quest for global supremacy poses a distinct threat to the survival of the human species.[20] *Pretext*'s list-owner believed that *Hegemony or Survival*, while not the standard fare for *Pretext*, would provoke heated discussion among participants about issues ranging from intellectual responsibility within the context of crimes of state to the futility of the United States fighting Bush's War on Terror. When the *Pretext* moderator agreed to have Chomsky and Finkelstein on the list for a few months back in 2004, and announced to the list's subscribers that Chomsky and Finkelstein would be participating in an online interview, he received a storm of email about how irresponsible he was for providing a platform to these two critics of Israel and US policy in the Middle East to disseminate their views. While Chomsky and Finkelstein are controversial figures, and frequently generate strong reactions in response to their political views, it is difficult to seriously label their work and critiques as "unscholarly" or "unworthy of debate." With this fact in mind, the moderator agreed to go forward with the discussion.

Many of the messages the moderator received in response to his decision to bring Finkelstein and Chomsky onto the *Pretext* list were quite vitriolic, much of the heat generated in response to Chomsky and Finkelstein's long-time criticism of Israel's human rights abuses of the Palestinians living in the occupied territories. As I explained to the moderator, it was only predictable that he would be denounced as "irresponsible" by the theorists on the list for giving Chomsky and Finkelstein a forum to challenge the right to lie in service of crimes of state. That "responsibility" within the current intellectual culture requires barring dissident intellectuals from an electronic forum to discuss their work is really quite indicative of the kind of silliness that passes as "sober analysis" within the US academy, particularly when these crimes of state are ongoing.

The mechanism informing this subtle conformity with the policies of the present administration cannot be explained simply as arising out of a fear of professional repercussion or an institutional surveillance that produces a strong tendency toward denouncing prominent dissidents as "un-American" or "anti-Israeli," even though their analyses might be absolutely accurate. Instead, one must look at the rules of professional etiquette and taste that make Chomsky and Finkelstein appear as bizarre choices to include on this list in the first place, the *pretexts* that exist to exclude those perspectives that do not fit with conventional thinking, rules of conduct that are essentially drawn up in advance of any critical discussion's proper beginning.

As a relative handmaiden of neoliberalism, globalization theory contains within it the constraints of a professional decorum that puts distance between supposedly critical intellectuals and the actual field of battle where people die and blood is shed, allowing for evasive maneuvers and changes of course that accommodate the movement of capital. Such accommodations are part and parcel of the modern intellectual priesthood's role in advancing the aims of the nation-state.[21] Although critical intellectuals abjure this kind of censorship, believing themselves to be radical and opposed to any and all apologies for unjust regimes that advance the interests of transnational corporations, the intense pressures that accompany the demands to comply with the dictates of concentrated power are overwhelming, producing the kinds of intellectual surveillance I described earlier.

The central role that axiology, the system of logic underpinning subjective value systems, legitimating the exclusion of some ways of knowing while embracing others, plays in justifying what can be thought and written about in academic scholarship cannot be underestimated or ignored. When central tenets of an axiological system are challenged, as dissenting scholarship often does, the system must remove the offending presence—even by illegitimate force if necessary, as several recent tenure battles have demonstrated.[22] The productive ambiguity of cosmo theory's language protects intellectuals from confronting their complicity in supporting crimes of state by providing them with safe havens such as "complexity," "undecidability," and "distributed networks." Indeed, these "critical terms" have allowed for a sort of arcane mysticism to creep into academic theorizing, legitimizing the avoidance of direct confrontations with power as unnecessarily polemical, reactionary, and provocative.

Assessing the current historical moment

In September of 2004, insurgent attacks against US troops in Iraq were beginning to peak; American citizens were coming to understand the full gravity of Bush's fateful decision to invade a relatively helpless country while beginning to question the real motives for the invasion. Iraq's descent into chaos, as a result of the US invasion in March of 2003 and the seemingly interminable occupation, created an exigency for examining the politics propelling the Bush administration's decision-making in the Middle East, opening up an opportunity to interrogate in this context previously forbidden topics pertaining to US Middle East policy, Israel's quest for regional supremacy, and the key role US intellectuals and journalists play in shaping public perceptions about US and Israeli militarism. Indeed, how could the *Pretext* list avoid these issues any longer, while the Middle East continued to be rocked by cataclysmic violence seemingly generated by illegal occupations, religious division, and territorial disputes? Any genuine commitment to intellectual responsibility seemed to recommend serious engagement with issues around the Middle East conflict.

Furthermore, it seemed to me—at that time—that scholars of rhetoric and critical theory desperately needed to engage the relevant issues with one another around how the Bush administration misled the country into invading Iraq and the key roles US and Israeli policy have played in the region with respect to creating reservoirs of resentment against the United States. While US support for Israel's occupation of the West Bank—and until recently Gaza—is frequently cited in the Arab world as the most proximate cause for widespread anger against the United States, one cannot lose sight of how effective US counterinsurgency has been in breaking indigenous movements from Egypt to Saudi Arabia to Iraq since Israel's defeat of Nasser in the Six-Day War. In addition, the circumstances surrounding the CIA's toppling of Mossadeq in 1953, which led to the installation of the Shah of Iran, who became a regional gendarme for the United States, remain relatively unknown. Indeed, the United States' unwillingness to recognize the grievances of the indigenous populations throughout the region, and the resentment this has produced, remains unfathomable to much of the US population. Increasing the public's comprehension of the vital issues remains tantamount.

Unfortunately, this historical amnesia plagues the academic intelligentsia as well, since there appears to be a commitment to forgetting the facts of history when they are no longer convenient for the aims of American Empire. Examining the ways in which certain forms of intellectual labor are constructed and valued seems necessary to understanding how academics select the lines of inquiry they do in their scholarship. If there is an emphasis on reflecting on states of being (desire, affect, etc.), rather than on states of affairs within the world (uses of power, intellectual deceit, etc.), how can a theory of intellectual activity be generated to help us understand intellectual production?[23] That so many academic intellectuals avoid being designated as occupying a specific and identifiable political position by invoking complex articulations, as these are supposedly staked out by the term "theory," should lead one to question what political work takes place by avoiding the establishment of positions that are tied to political commitments. Indeed, to establish a strong political position is to be considered simplistic, lacking nuance, engaging in binary thinking, or advancing a politically motivated critique. These denunciations of position-taking are troubling because they sanction an easygoing complicity in obscuring operations of power, even when those operations are quite transparent, while avoiding the unpleasantness that often accompanies exposing intellectual mendacity. As I learned during the *Pretext* discussion, evasion of substantive issues is characteristic of those who wish to avoid confronting the evidentiary burden Chomsky delivers when he analyzes the factors influencing US foreign policy in the Middle East.

Pretext of avoidance

Generally speaking, while the *Pretext* list is devoted to examining writers of, and issues pertaining to, critical and rhetorical theory, it occasionally takes up more overtly political issues such as those covered in *Hegemony or Survival*. Chomsky's *Hegemony or Survival* frames a decision that will eventually have be made by human beings—"Will it be hegemony or survival? You decide." In other words, will the United States' quest for global supremacy drive the human species to extinction, or will sober realism prevent this impending disaster?[24]

The survival of the human species is by no means a sure thing since environmental destruction, terminal nuclear war, and the pursuit and ongoing depletion of vital resources such as oil and water could very well end human life on the planet. As the United States has made clear in documents such as The Project for the New American Century's "Rebuilding America's Defenses" and the Institute for Advanced Strategic and Political Studies' "A Strategy for Securing the Realm," it will dominate the world by force and will tolerate no competitors. What are the consequences of this commitment to hegemony for human survival? According to Chomsky, quests for hegemony are obviously interrelated with human survival; decisions about global domination are not irrational (profit motive, expanding global markets, etc.) with respect to the institutional frameworks within which they are made; however, they are extremely hazardous and irrational from the standpoint of human life. The increasing world tensions because of the continued prospect of nuclear proliferation, terrorism, and environmental collapse are certainly matters of concern. The United States is alone in the world in trying to move toward the militarization of space; these policies are in place to assure US dominance over capital investment, an extreme threat to survival. Across the board, the decision to be a hegemon and, in turn, whether this poses a threat to the survival of the human species is something we must face if we want to have a future.

Chomsky fielded questions from *Pretext* subscribers, many of whom are leading theorists in English and related fields, for over one month. Although Chomsky has been recognized as one of the veritable geniuses of the twentieth century, a touchstone of the Left, subscribers had a very difficult time in interacting and communicating with him about his book and his many reflections about the state of intellectual culture and the distinct role US intellectuals play—within the academy and middle-brow journalism—to justify US military adventurism, all of which Chomsky has repeatedly described with contempt and derision. While Chomsky made frequent reference to "facts," "the historical record," and within the context of discussing contentious issues such as the Israel-Palestine conflict, "the uncontroversial claim" that Israel's persecution of the Palestinians in the occupied territories far surpassed any potential claims of victimhood Jews could lay claim to against Palestinians, list participants—perhaps having grown up on a good dose of postmodern theory—sought to check Chomsky by informing him that truth, facts, and the historical record are socially constructed and that it is foolhardy to believe that one could act as if one were an observer on the world stage reporting events as they actually happened. Chomsky found himself confused by these objections to his use of phrases such as "the uncontroversial record," "facts," and "well-documented atrocities," wondering why participants sought to avoid serious discussion about substantive issues while concocting tales about his "tone, hauteur, rage, and curt answers."

Given Chomsky's stature as a scientist in the field of linguistics, it was truly ironic that he found himself chided in this way. After all, the Chomskyian revolution in linguistics transformed the entire field, creating a new approach to understanding the underlying structure of human language. If Chomsky's stature in linguistics can be viewed as impeccable and unquestionable, why would anyone assume he would be less conscientious and scrupulous in studying US foreign policy? The answer to this question contains within it a cautionary tale about the particular hazards attending taking dissident political positions in the United States and the particular dangers associated with refusing to engage in the willful obfuscation of painful realities informing much contemporary theory.[25]

Communicative impasse

What many viewed as a misfit between Chomsky—the octogenarian who has transformed the field of linguistics and established a reputation as the most persistent critic of US foreign policy—and the audience comprising the *Pretext* list may in fact be a commentary on the state of theory in the humanities, that is, an important moment reflecting how intellectual labor has been radically reconfigured within the academy since the late seventies and early eighties.[26] The reasons for this reconfiguration warrant extended analysis.

The fact that I was accused of politicizing the *Pretext* list by having Chomsky on it to discuss his *Hegemony or Survival*, particularly when discussion turned to specific aspects of the Israel-Palestine conflict, such as the circumstances leading up to the '82 Lebanon War and Israel's specific desire to subvert a PLO peace offensive, reveals the extent to which the humanities have been depoliticized when it comes to examining intellectual silence and evasion around key US foreign policy issues. As experts have indicated in reference to Israel's attack upon Southern Lebanon on 6 June 1982, "Operation Peace for Galilee" is a misnomer; the operation should have been called "The Operation to Safeguard the Occupation of the West Bank,"[27] as Israel sought to create a Christian-Maronite broker state in Lebanon, while breaking any remaining vestiges of Palestinian nationalism by crushing the PLO. Within the context of the *Pretext* discussion, there was not even disagreement with Chomsky about the circumstances surrounding Israel's '82 invasion because no one seemed to be even remotely aware of what had occurred between 6 June and October of that year; although events within this time period—from the Israeli invasion to the Sabra-Shatila massacres—were all preludes to the bombing of the US Marine barracks on 23 October 1983.

Just as the specific circumstances surrounding the '82 Israeli invasion of Lebanon became an object of debate on the *Pretext* list, all participation stopped. Not only did participation stop, it ground to a complete halt as the discussion could not be framed through any of the theoretical frameworks available to the participants, who were eager to condemn Chomsky for not recognizing the force of his unconscious "anti-Semitism" behind his criticisms of Israel's '82 invasion. If only Chomsky would read more Žižek, as one participant argued, he would understand the latent anti-Semitism behind his responses: Never mind that fact that Israel had long planned, sought to create a pretext for, and carried out the invasion. It was easier to talk about an all-pervasive anti-Semitism, unconscious forces, and what Žižek had written about "the figure of the Jew" in *Welcome to the Desert of the Real.*[28]

The person who most objected to my questions and Chomsky's responses was a former Israeli Defense Forces Officer who believed he could intimidate list members into believing his recounting of Israel's June '82 invasion, that is, that Israel launched the invasion in response to Palestinian attacks on Israel's Northern border. These symbolic attacks, in response to Israeli shelling, were used as pretext for the Israeli invasion. As Chomsky calmly recited the facts, the former IDF officer had nowhere to hide, withdrawing from the discussion a few messages later while demonstrating that he lacked the very knowledge about Israel's invasion that he accused me of not possessing.[29] Of even more interest is the fact that no one seemed to be aware of the circumstances surrounding Israel's invasion of Lebanon, perhaps not realizing these events are pivotal to understanding much of what is happening at this moment in the Middle East. Indeed, Osama Bin Laden referenced Israel's massive air strikes in Beirut in June '82 when explaining why Al-Qaeda selected Manhattan's skyline for the 11 September 2001 attacks: Beirut's skyline matches Manhattan's quite closely. None of this registers within the reigning intellectual culture.

Analyzing the impasse

So, what does it mean that a list of nearly two hundred theorists had nothing to say about these topics of serious concern? While one can only make limited conclusions based on this one discussion, some possibly disturbing inferences can be drawn. First, theory—or at least a certain brand of theory—seems to sustain an interest in claiming that history, since it is constructed, cannot be subject to a factual inventorying—historical facts can be dismissed as passé; perspectives and experiences, according to the dictates of postmodern theory, are all that is relevant. Since perspectives are multiple, and factual pronouncements about history are unitary and in turn dismiss other possible perspectives, requiring a foreclosure of possibility, it is unsurprising that Chomsky's attempts to document "the historical record," "the uncontroversial facts," and "state apologetics" seem bizarre and somehow incorrect, although Chomsky in books such as his *The Fateful Triangle: The United State, Israel, and the Palestinians* demonstrates a commitment to rigorous analysis through in-depth empirical testing, revealing that he has scoured all available media and government sources before asserting that the US media—despite being accused of being hypercritical of Israeli military actions in the summer of 1982—was in fact highly protective of them. Indeed, it is the extensiveness of the documentation supporting his assertions about US and Israeli policy in the Middle East within his political work that accounts for the bitter condemnations lodged against his deeply unpopular conclusions.

Chomsky's accounting of the months leading up to the '82 invasion, as he develops it in his *The Fateful Triangle*, is considered as the definitive albeit an iconoclastic version of this crucial historical period. The specific details surrounding Israel's invasion of Lebanon in 1982 still remain relatively unknown, or seemingly so, in left-liberal intellectual circles in the United States. It's not so much that the details are unknown as they have been completely ignored, distorted, and covered up with highly useful and ideologically serviceable hasbara. Hasbara, a Hebrew word for "explanation," "propaganda," or "facts for the outside world," refers to Zionist efforts to present Israel's attempts to ethnically cleanse the Palestinians in the language of "security needs," "terrorism prevention," and "Just Wars."[30] These efforts continue into the present.

The current administration's war on terror cannot be understood without confronting the specific facts surrounding the summer of 1982 in Lebanon. Popular understandings of the Israel invasion of Lebanon revolve around the readily disputable myth that Israel was facing daunting attacks from its northern borders, along with the fear that the PLO would establish a permanent base in Lebanon from which to launch further invasions against Israel. Hasbara efforts point to Palestinian attacks at Metulla and Ma'lot as providing an adequate pretext for the Israeli invasion.[31] Such efforts illustrate how in this conflict—as Norman G. Finkelstein points out—illusory images stand in for reality within the American media and scholarship; these images would quickly implode if subjected to critical investigation.[32]

Throughout early 1982, the PLO repeatedly offered serious proposals for peace to Israel in accordance with the international consensus. Serious analysts of Israel's "Peace for Galilee" Operation have called the invasion the "Operation to Safeguard the West Bank." Israeli peace proposals have never been serious, and in essence, Israel has never really made a "peace" proposal other than the ones that have continued colonization of Palestinian land, with US diplomatic cover.[33] Israel fought the '82 Lebanon War to prevent the realization of a comprehensive diplomatic settlement in the region, a veritable catastrophe for Israeli hawks at the time. The invasion that started the war had been discussed openly within Israeli military circles for several months, as the late Israel Shahak points out in his *Open Secrets: Israeli Foreign and Nuclear Policy.*[34] Despite these uncontroversial facts, Israel's invasion is often referred to as "Operation Peace for Galilee," suggesting that Israel's invasion had as its purpose to create peace in the region; in actuality, the invasion was aimed at ensuring that the Palestinian Liberation Organization's efforts at forging a comprehensive peace plan would be interrupted.

Israel's inability to create a pretext for the invasion of Lebanon led to a desperate attempt to link Abu Nidal's assassination of Israeli Prime Minister Shlomo Argov in London to the PLO. In the summer of 1982, Abu Nidal was at war with the PLO; Israel was well aware of this. For nearly 3 months, despite a US-brokered truce, Israel had been attempting to establish a pretext for the invasion of Lebanon by inciting the PLO along its northern border. Beyond symbolic retaliations, an adequate pretext for Israel's invasion was not established. When Abu Nidal assassinated Israel's ambassador Argov, Israel invaded Lebanon in response, despite knowing that Nidal had no connection to the PLO. Israeli Defense Forces surrounded Beirut and killed 20,000 civilians over 3 months, with the Sabra and Shatila refugee camps being the worst of the atrocities as Maronite-Christian Phalangists performed the executions as Israeli soldiers looked on with binoculars. The Kahan commission, due to the insistence of Israeli citizens, found defense minister Ariel Sharon personally but not criminally responsible for Sabra and Shatila.

Chomsky's concerns about the survival of the human species in the wake of the disastrous US invasion of Iraq were, as articulated in *Hegemony or Survival*, not of real interest to *Pretext*'s theorists who were well versed and invested in contemporary discussions about affect, complexity, chaos, and trauma. These theoretical concepts were incapable of engaging Chomsky's objects of concern: human rights, "crimes of states," the historical record, the doctrinal system, intellectual deceit, and the evasions of the intellectual priesthood in justifying its silence about unworthy victims of US aggression (Timorese, Nicaraguans, Palestinians, etc.). What is one to make of this seeming communicative impasse between a leading guru of the Left, who has dedicated much of his life to addressing issues typically swept under the rug by the academic intelligentsia, and these theorists—who are capable of quoting Derrida, Agamben, and Kristeva at length—but have no time or interest in engaging Chomsky? In his *At Home in the World*, Timothy Brennan writes:

> Assessments of the present always lead to a kind of future. Thus, postnational theorizing, prognoses of an emergent globalism, the insistence that the transnational corporations have relegated state decision-making to subsidiary issues, although extreme and inaccurate, do encourage these outcomes. At the very moment that the ethnographers of metropolitan masscult, the students of professionalism, or the theorists of the intellectual have made a convincing case for the role the imaginative and ideological forms play in the exercise of power, they have stopped short of casting the glance homeward by neglecting to look at how their cultural and aesthetic work dovetails with more explicitly governmental analysts arguing, and celebrating, an "inevitable" globality.[35]

While it may be true that academic specialization has increasingly created niche interests within the broad endeavor known as "theory," one would hope that questions about important events within the world would not—in the theorist's estimation—become passé and boring, particularly when intellectual silence on such issues is an unarticulated expectation of those wishing to advance within the secular priesthood. That Chomsky repeatedly articulates these embarrassing intellectual silences and evasions perhaps explains why he is so hated within academic quarters. After all, who wishes to be reminded of the price of the academic wager while being forced to acknowledge the unfortunate gap between theory and practice and between words and actions:

> The "left intellectuals" (or whatever the right word is) are either involved in unintelligible varieties of postmodernism (mostly nonsense, in my opinion), or otherwise talking to one another. Most of the "intellectual community" is, as usual, serving power in one or another way. It leaves a huge gap, a matter of huge importance these days, I think.[36]

This huge gap in the academic viewpoint, this unwillingness to tackle pressing and important issues about US human rights violations throughout the Middle East at this time when US troops are stationed throughout North Africa and West Asia, and the seemingly lack of interest in even pursuing certain lines of scholarly investigation cannot be a simple accident or oversight.

Containing Chomsky

Chomsky's insistence upon highlighting and exposing this corruption of intellectual culture naturally brings with it strong reactions from the very individuals he is in some sense criticizing. In an article entitled "Symbolic Terror," which was published in *Critical Inquiry* shortly after 9/11, Geoffrey Harpam writes:

> It is Chomsky's refusal to be terrorized, his insistence that the terror really makes sense, that it has a germ of rational motivation, that this germ can and should be incorporated into our national self-description, included among the narratives that we tell ourselves, that is the most terrifying, and terroristic, aspect of his thought.[37]

Harpam's observation is yet another sign of the reigning code of conduct within elite intellectual circles. Can one actually locate a single specialist on terrorism, or a single intelligence agency, that does not have the same "insistence" as Chomsky. Are they all "terrifying and terroristic"?

Surely, those who seek to explain why terrorism might be consistent with the long-term goals of certain organizations, which hold legitimate grievances against the United States and huge reservoirs of sympathy and support for violent acts, cannot justly be accused of refusing to be terrorized.

Chomsky's consistent post-9/11 message has been: "If we want to reduce terror, we should stop participating in it."[38] "We" meaning the United States and its client states. Keeping this message in mind, is it accurate, then, as Harpham seems to suggest, to assert that Chomsky's thought has terrifying and terroristic aspects? Chomsky seems to be taking the concept of universality (we apply the same or higher standards to ourselves as we do to others in evaluating the consequences of our state's actions) seriously. Is such a "rhetoric" glib and self-righteous? Chomsky has also written constantly about how to deal with terror that passes though the doctrinal filters: others terror against us. It is true that while he does not state anything original, repeating the standard conclusions of specialists and intelligence agencies (often quoting them, particularly Israeli intelligence)—the conclusions are unacceptable and hence "terrifying and terroristic."

As for the oft-cited charge that Chomsky engages in *ad hominem* attacks in dealing with political opponents in debate and employs hyperbolic language in describing US-created atrocities, I think it is important to recognize that he has written extremely careful studies on many different topics relating to terrorism and counterinsurgency; one of them, *Hegemony or Survival*, was heralded as a must-read for US citizens by Hugo Chavez when he spoke before the United Nations in September of 2006. "The hegemonistic pretensions of the American empire are placing at risk the very existence of the human species," Chavez said and he "appealed to the people of the United States and the world to halt this threat, which is like a sword hanging over our head."[39]

Those who charge Chomsky with employing *ad hominem* attacks have the responsibility to cite the supposed *ad hominem* attack and its attendant hyperbolic use of language, with the source, so readers can check. In the absence of such documentation, the charges should be dismissed. Chomsky's "incivil discourse," if that's what it is, suggests that the problems he tackles are immediate, and, in his estimation, demand immediate attention. For example, in the context of wrapping up his description of his attempts to get the US press to cover the Clinton administration's $500 million helicopter sale to Israel in late 2000 and early 2001, right at the time of the beginning of the second Palestinian Intifada (as the US press was reporting that Palestinian civilians were being killed in apartment complexes, but not reporting where the helicopters had come from) Chomsky wrote: "There are examples of vastly greater scale and horror, right now. The lesson is to try harder."[40]

In October of 2000, the Clinton administration sold nearly 500 million dollars of attack helicopters to Israel, something unreported in the US press, while the US government called on both Israel and the Palestinians to cease hostilities against one another. Israel used these attack helicopters for "civilian population control" in the occupied territories shortly after the outbreak of the Second Intifada, something which was reported in the US press. Shortly after the helicopter sales were reported in the European press, Chomsky joined a delegation of journalists and others political activists in Boston who were attempting to get mainstream newspapers—such as the *Boston Globe*—to report the unprecedented helicopter sale to Israel for "civilian population control." These efforts, regrettably, were to no avail. What is important to note here is that the US government was calling on both sides to cease hostilities, while it provided crucial support to one side—Israel. When Palestinians civilians are murdered, with crucial US taxpayer support, it is not considered murder. This example is instructive with plenty of evidence in the historical record—for those who care to look.[41] This is just one of many instances of Chomsky seeking to expose the intellectual mendacity of government and media officials in the public sphere, particularly when this exposure allows the US public to learn the truth about how taxpayer dollars are being spent to commit atrocities against helpless civilian populations.

Chomsky's unpopular example

While Chomsky has long been unpopular among a certain segment of the academic establishment, what is much less recognized is how his work is often dismissed by those who have not taken the time to read it. Chomsky's persistent reminders about the dangers attending intellectual subservience to the state, and the transnational corporations that dominate it, can become annoying, leading perhaps to a passive acceptance of intellectual conformity and corruption within the mainstream institutions as a natural state of affairs, and certainly not something to be resisted. Arundathi Roy reflects on Chomsky's Herculean Task in the following:

> Being in America, working in America, writing to convince Americans of his point of view must really be like having to tunnel through hard wood. Chomsky is one of a small band of individuals fighting a whole industry. And that makes him not only brilliant, but heroic.[42]

While he has expressed continual contempt for the North American intellectual's seeming refusal to use the power and privilege accorded her in the service of meaningful social change, Chomsky continues to believe that dissident intellectuals will continue the necessary ongoing struggles for social change on behalf of those Third-World populations that rely upon it just to scrounge together an existence. So what are we to make of Chomsky's "banal" approach to understanding the world and its implications for his hard-hitting critiques of intellectuals and American foreign policy at this historical moment? Can it be easily dismissed as hopelessly naïve and unrealistic—completely out of touch with the current intellectual current?

A specific rhetoric of evasion has attended intellectual discourse on Chomsky's political work that signals a larger problem with the intellectual class in service to a domestic power structure. Chomsky raises troubling questions about the viability of sustained critiques against state power and whether or not Western intellectuals are even capable of making them. The rewards that flow power and influence, after all, are quite immense. The extreme indoctrination of the educated classes prevents a telling of this history, which should be at the center of contemporary understandings about the current perils of US foreign policy in the Middle East. A sustained engagement by serious intellectuals with Chomsky's political corpus will prove useful to identifying and dismantling aspects of the current academic guild structure that so seriously plague contemporary intellectual discourse while also preventing intellectuals from asking the most searching and important questions of the modern era. Most surprisingly, academic intellectuals are often the people most ignorant of Chomsky's political writing; proudly so, in fact.[43]

When Chomsky tells us that "the facts are readily available for those who care look" or that "anyone can read human rights reports," he seems to assume that we, and our colleagues, know where to look for these human rights reports or the alternative news source that would tell us that "The United States is the only country in history to be found guilty of international terrorism" (in this case against Nicaragua) or that "The United States invaded South Vietnam and supported terrible atrocities in East Timor." This certainty about facts and history, when coupled with Chomsky's rejection of postmodern theory, for example, reflects his deep belief in a no-nonsense approach to intellectual affairs: how many intellectuals and writers set out stating they do not wish to persuade anyone of anything, just to present the facts and to let listeners or readers decide for themselves what is true?

> I don't have any theory of rhetoric, but what I have in the back of my mind is that one should not try to persuade; rather, you should try to lay out the territory as best you can so that other people can use their own intellectual powers to work out for themselves what they think is right or wrong. For example, I try particularly in political writing, to make it extremely clear in advance exactly where I stand. In my view, the idea of neutral objectivity is largely fraudulent. It's not that I take the realistic view with regard to fact, but the fact is that everyone approaches complex and controversial questions—especially those of human significance— with an ax to grind, and I like that ax to be apparent right up front so that people can compensate for it. But to the extent that I can monitor my own rhetorical activities, which is probably not a lot, I try to refrain from efforts to bring people to reach my conclusions.[44]

Chomsky's unwillingness to be persuasive and his reluctance to employ a style that might be more convincing is disarming and threatening at the same time. For one to be so invested in "the facts" and "truth" is contrary to academic conceptions of how reality is more complex than it seems, suggesting that the search for more complex explanations might in fact be convenient pretexts for avoiding the obvious. However, Chomsky's political writings do allow for an inventorying and calculating of material interests, maintaining a consistency across time, and possessing a predicative capacity that is better than supposedly more complex theories. Apropos of this, consider the following reflection from Norman Finkelstein about Chomsky's intellectual attributes: "Basically to free yourself from ideological controls and go where reasoning and the facts take you, which is easy to say but difficult to practice. Another interesting aspect of Professor Chomsky is that his writing rises above the jargon of the times. Books which were written in the 1960s read like they were written yesterday."[45] It is the continued relevance of Chomsky's political work, its capacity to remain relevant despite the passage of time while other intellectual fashions fade into the background, suggesting that he is writing about politics in a way that helps average citizens to make sense of the world around them. Chomsky's capacity to speak to a wide range of audiences demonstrates how one can be brilliant, antinomian, radical, accessible, analytically scrupulous, and internationally renowned as a scientist all at the same time. This example poses a major challenge to the modernist common sense of the academy, which often posits that academic specialization requires the production of hyper-specialized vocabularies that can only be understood within small circles of similarly situated specialists.

Chomsky's continued relevance

After 9/11, Americans more eagerly sought to understand the forces that currently shape the world and the US role in it. Some of Chomsky's books, such as *American Power and the New Mandarins* and *For Reasons of State* were reissued because of an overwhelming need for alternative sources of information, as the rationalizations of the Washington commissars became patently transparent. His 9/11 became a "surprise bestseller" in the words of the *New York Times*. The end of the cold war, according to Chomsky, necessitated the creation of new wars. The technological sophistication of Third-World nationalists (Khomeni, bin Laden, Qadafi, Hussein, etc.) were fashioned as a new and "productive" threat to US hegemony since the blame could "no longer be laid at the Kremlin's door."

During the 1980s and 1990s, Chomsky had been all but shut out of the mainstream media. 9/11 changed that as Chomsky appeared on *Booknotes* and in other mainstream news outlets, as US citizens yearned for accurate information about the Middle East. Although Chomsky has long had a following, consisting largely of intellectual dissidents and academics, 9/11 seemed to increase that audience and decrease Chomsky's isolation as he appeared before the World Bank and on C-SPAN. His isolation, that many claim resulted from his "radical" and "extreme" views, can be attributed to a single source: his criticisms of US foreign policy; his criticism of Israel's treatment of the Palestinians in the West Bank and Gaza; and his continual attacks on "the subservience of the intelligentsia." 9/11, however, brought many to the conclusion that Chomsky was quite correct in his analysis of US foreign policies in the Middle East, confirming that the terrorist attacks were an inevitable consequence of those policies.

In addition to the broadening of his audience, Chomsky witnessed one-time disciples such as Christopher Hitchens and one-time admirers such as Todd Gitlin, Michael Berube,[46] and Geoffrey Harpham turning on him, rejecting the mentor because he had taken a view that results in "nothingness, at the very best," in drawing a parallel between terrorist actions (9/11) and US interventions in Nicaragua, Sudan, and Afghanistan.[47] Each of these intellectuals objected to Chomsky's use of projected death figures, provided by Human Aid organizations, and his chiding of US foreign policy for deaths that never occurred in Sudan and Afghanistan; all in an apparent attempt to draw symmetry between US military actions against supposedly hostile military targets and Islamic terrorist actions directed against civilian targets.[48] Hitchens, Berube, and Harpham seemingly parted company with Chomsky because they saw the nihilist behind the one-time idealist, as Chomsky highlighted the supposed racist contempt of these figures for the victims of US military errors. This phenomenon of Chomsky repelling his one-time allies while attracting more people among the general public to his point of view, is an extremely interesting commentary on the state of intellectual labor in the academy.

Ironically, Chomsky's popular base seems to have expanded while his academic base has contracted. How can we account for these opposed tendencies? Is it that Chomsky has exposed the commitments guiding "elite educated opinion" in a way that some can no longer tolerate? In their "Crude Wars," Timothy Brennan and Keya Ganguly write that "[i]t has become fashionable for cultural critics to reject supposedly outmoded theories of political economy, to disdain the simple exposure of hidden agendas, to scoff at the likes of Noam Chomsky or Armand Mattelart on the grounds that their notions have been superceded by the ever-inventive strategies of the market."[49] To what within current conceptions of intellectual labor can we really attribute this tendency to scoff at the likes of Noam Chomsky and Armand Mattelart? Why should these critics of transnational corporations and neoliberal capitalism be so easily ignored? These questions are significant and should be at the center of writing an accurate intellectual history for the current historical moment.

Confronting history

In the wake of the re-declaration of the War on Terror in "response" to the events of 9/11, US citizens have been forced to take stock of recent history and our countries use of massive violence, particularly as it has been directed at indigenous populations, as we attempt to understand our place in the world, as what some have called a "global hegemon," at this particular historical moment. While on the one hand President Bush mouths popular pieties that the United States is a freedom-loving and law-abiding country, the historical record demonstrates that sticking to the letter of the law has not been one of the country's strong suits. In fact, with respect to the current situation in the Middle East and the invasion and occupation of Iraq, the flouting of international law and consensus has been at the forefront of US foreign policy for the last 50 years.[50]

The United States' overwhelming monopoly over the instruments of violence and mass death, perhaps unsurprisingly, leads to the sweeping of these facts out of the way, vetoing them out of history, proving that the state and the educated classes can rise to the demands of the doctrinal system and its propaganda apparatus. No contradiction, no matter how stark or upsetting, cannot be resolved or explained away when there are brilliant minds at work. How, then, one may ask, have US citizens been able to avoid addressing their direct complicity in the US government's criminal behavior as this has manifested itself in the Bush administration's continued criminal occupation of Iraq, which was of course preceded by an illegal invasion that was condemned by an international consensus? This state of affairs, in conjunction with the US government's continued support of Israel's 40-year occupation of the West Bank and Gaza, continues to create strong resentment against the United States government.

The US press has been effective in shielding the public from the images of destruction in Iraq and Afghanistan, the images that would move even the hardest heart to reflect upon the very foreign policy plan—in service to a domestic lobby that seeks to control the resources of the entire region—sanctioning the effective murder of nearly a hundred thousand civilians, who cannot be considered terrorists or those who abetted either Osama bin Laden or Saddam Hussein, two former US clients. The profound criminality, of what Tariq Ali has frequently called "the Anglo-American invasion of Iraq," has been easily been ignored by Western audiences because the United States invaded a defenseless and non-white nation, which possessing the second largest oil reserves in the world, in addition to being a geopolitical strategic asset.[51]

While the stated reasons for the invasion (Iraq's weapons of mass destruction, the necessity of overthrowing Saddam Hussein's regime, bringing democracy to the oppressed Iraqi people, etc.) have all been exhausted and proven to be quite ridiculous, US citizens are left to ponder the real reasons for the invasion: the United States' continued need to dominate the world's petroleum reserves; its desire to build three major military bases in Iraq— along with three in Afghanistan—which will give the United States complete control—along with its Israeli "cop on the beat"—of the entire Middle East region; the United States' desire to show the rest of the world the power of the US military, registering how massive an assault the United States could wage against similar regimes in the Middle East and elsewhere. The message was clear: any challenge to US military hegemony and US dominance of world markets will be met with an invasion. North Korea, smart enough to understand that arming itself with nuclear weapons would make the commissars in Washington think twice about invading, challenged the United States to make the first move; since North Korea wasn't defenseless—one of the primary prerequisites of the Bush doctrine—it stood out as a worthy opponent and hence not a target of interest.

Turning to another relatively uncontroversial and well-documented instance of how the United States' disregard for international law impacts world politics, consider the 1987 World Court ruling against the United States for international terrorism in Nicaragua. The judgment itself was dismissed with contempt by leaders in the Reagan administration, with the jurisdiction of the court itself being ridiculed. Nicaragua, instead of dropping bombs on Boston, turned to the World Court for relief against the mining of its harbors, as well as the continued onslaught against its civilian population and democratically elected government. The Reagan administration's funding of the Contras, through weapon sales to Iran through Israel in direct contravention of the Boland Amendment, suggested that since the American taxpayer cannot be relied upon to understand the gravity of communist fighters only "three days driving distance from Harlingen, Texas," or the significance of purported sales of MIG jets to El Salvador, covert operations have to be put in place to spare the paymasters the pain of confronting the inevitably "complex" aspects of foreign policy in Central America. Simpler minds, however, are able to deduce that what happened in Central America throughout the eighties conforms to the merest of truisms: state violence works, irrespective of laws, courts, and niceties that the United States expects other weaker countries to abide by. That the United States, as the only country ever to be found guilty of international terrorism, could twice declare a war on terror demonstrates just how elastic the doctrinal system can be when it comes to rising to the needs of the powerful. In this case, "the powerful" consist of transnational corporations, overwhelmingly US dominated, that seek to control the world's expanding economic markets in conjunction with US military planners.

Naturally, there is a strong resistance to facing the United States' external behavior, its continual flouting of the diplomatic record and international law, and the overall reliance on massive violence to ensure the flourishing of "democracy," "free markets," etc., rhetorical devices that are really calls to violence against weak Third-World countries that might be ripe for expanding markets of US corporations. Scholars who bring up the United States' or its favorite client states' numerous violations of international law, in exactly the language with which we would condemn a hated enemy, face a hysterical stream of abuse and vilification. Once we understand the bounds and demands of educated discourse, all becomes clear. As Chomsky points out, "A person who has not internalized these conventions ['the team', by definition, is the United States and 'the mainstream' is the position occupied by 'the team', however much the world may be out of step] can scarcely be taken seriously; accordingly, such commentary, which abounds, does not even evoke an amused smile in cultivated circles."[52]

The inability of articulate audiences to comprehend Chomsky's political writings results from their own corruption and indoctrination; average people completely understand Chomsky's insights with respect to the operation of power whereas elites exhibit only blank looks of incomprehension. If these writings were to gain some salience within the mainstream, they would pose a distinct threat to the doctrinal system, the reconstruction of American imperial history, and the academic guild structure, while also charting a path for young scholars who wish to escape the trap of commissar politics.

Screening out those who might try to rise to the challenge of the responsible intellectual that Chomsky sets out within his political writing has been an unarticulated imperative of elite, intellectual culture within academe, particularly since the 1960s. The imperial history Chomsky has been so persistent in documenting demonstrates how ideologically serviceable this scholarship has been for the promotion of US power, particularly in its avoidance in addressing the direct complicity of the intellectual classes in promoting a scholarly discourse that masquerades as being vigilant and antagonistic to collusive intellectuals while serving a vital propaganda function for the economic philosophy of neoliberalism. In fact, Chomsky convincingly demonstrates that collusive intellectuals are crucial to sustaining the triumphs of the propaganda system, which places the merest truisms out of reach of the general population that often pays the heavy costs to the Pentagon system and high-tech industry.

Beyond his relentless documentation of "the facts," the most fascinating and, at the same time, most troubling feature of Chomsky's political writings is its seemingly repeated insistence that history, the history we read in schools and come to perhaps understand as "official," has been written quite willfully and deceptively to serve the interests of US power—particularly the relatively recent history of US military intervention and overseas imperialism from the time of the Vietnam war to the present—as well as to protect ordinary citizens from the basic and well-established facts about the severe human cost paid by designated enemies, "unworthy victims," who are not white and remain faceless to us, those who essentially occupy the role of paymasters. Managing this history, and silencing or marginalizing dissenting revisionist histories, requires constant ideological management—a task the propaganda system has been quite effective in serving. That this history has been subject to a careful reconstruction and that it must be protected from critical interrogation and inspection has been repeatedly demonstrated by Chomsky over the years:

> Not surprisingly, inquiry reveals a highly selective culling of facts and much outright lying. Some areas of the world are almost entirely blacked out, where disclosure of major abuses would disturb both pliable clients and the U.S. economic, military, and political interests that find this pliability advantageous. As we have described throughout the two volumes [*The Political Economy of Human Rights*], the first principle of the Free Press is the averting of eyes from benign or constructive terror, along with a general avoidance of invidious language and a sympathetic understanding for the difficult problems faced by the terrorizing elites backed by the United States.[53]

The treatment his work has received suggests that if he were to gain a mainstream salience, serious questions would be asked about how what Chomsky calls "articulate elites" control the state and maintain a monopoly of violence.

The simplicity and straightforwardness of Chomsky's prose, his relentless marshaling of information, the devastating clarity, and the distinct moral sense guiding his critical writings have buoyed the spirits of non-intellectuals against the corruptions of an age. He continues to believe in fundamental human goodness, within an intellectual era that has seen the concept of post humanism attack the whole concept of "the human." His refusal to accept the logic of neoliberalism, and the vast devastation it has wreaked upon the Third World, bespeaks a rhetoric of great refusal—the ruling order is based upon a history of bloodshed and violence, which if accurately documented, would radically alter basic understandings of how we measure history. Chomsky's moving and continual passion for the oppressed (a virtue supposedly guiding much academic work, but rarely actually demonstrated) guides him through a relentless schedule of talking, writing, and corresponding with ordinary people who are far away from centers of concentrated power.

Chomsky's political work has not been given the careful treatment it merits; instead, we are handed idée rescues about his "defense" of Faurisson's findings (Werner Cohen), his "apologies for Pol Pot," (Keith Windschuttle), his predilection for conspiracy theories, and that he is "a fanatical defender of the PLO" (Elliot Abrams).[54] One might very well predict, if she were a careful watcher of the doctrinal filters, that this very situation would obtain: Chomsky's work does not meet the requirement of concision—a requirement that has crept into academic scholarship—in that he does not provide any of the usual guideposts that might constrain his thought within a particular economy of well recognized academic terms, tropes, figures, etc. (postmodernism, post humanism, social constructionism, etc.). That he has resisted the general tendency to write preening academic prose and has instead continually delivered up "just the facts" bespeaks either a tremendous narcissism or a heroic effort that will stand the tests of verification and time. Chomsky's political scholarship directly threatens the academic guild structure, forcing it to deal with its own complicity in the promotion of US aims of state, and the studied ignorance of this work is not an accident or due to error. Instead, a whole effort has arisen to "contain Chomsky" and the effects of his work.

Condemnations of Chomsky seemingly never attempt to deal with the massive documentation he provides or the numerous invitations he has issued to his interlocutors to show him where he's wrong or misguided. Inevitably, he's called anti-American, anti-Israeli, anti-Semitic, a Holocaust denier, a tireless enemy, the greatest mind of the twentieth century contaminated by radical politics, someone who took his political commitments too far, etc. He's not postmodern enough, sophisticated enough, hip enough, etc. Bashing Chomsky, as Norman G. Finkelstein points out in a recent essay, has become ritualized among apostates seeking a grand exit from the political left:

> A rite of passage for apostates peculiar to U.S. political culture is bashing Noam Chomsky. It's the political equivalent of a bar mitzvah, a ritual signaling that one has "grown up"—i.e., grown out of one's "childish" past. It's hard to pick up an article or book by ex-radicals—Gitlin's *Letters to a Young Activist*, Paul *Berman's Terror and Liberalism* . . . that doesn't include a hysterical attack on him. Behind this venom there's also a transparent psychological factor at play. Chomsky mirrors their idealistic past as well as sordid present, an obstinate reminder that they once had principles but no longer do, that they sold out but he didn't. Hating to be reminded, they keep trying to shatter the glass. He's the demon from the past that, after recantation, no amount of incantation can exorcise.[55]

This obligation to take a cheap shot at Chomsky before announcing that one has reached political maturity has, indeed, become a rite of passage, a departure from the realm of commitment into the realm of the comical, where arguments no longer really matter. As Finkelstein concludes:

> Two altogether opposed political stances can each draw an audience's attention. One is to be politically consistent, but nonetheless original in one's insights; the other, an inchoate form of apostasy, is to bank on the shock value of an occasional, wildly inconsistent outburst. The former approach, which Chomsky exemplifies, requires hard work, whereas the latter is a lazy substitute for it.[56]

Chomsky brings academics up against an uncomfortable conclusion: some academic scholarship actively contributes to a system of apologetics for state violence; and, if this scholarship were pursued with an iota of concern for objectivity rather than in subservience to the state, a great deal could be done to alleviate human suffering in the world. It is this recognition of the challenge contained within Chomsky's political corpus that is particularly unpalatable to academics in the social sciences and the humanities.

Chomsky's relentless pursuit of rescuing the historical record from the mendacity of the intellectual guild structure is dramatic, necessary, and naturally upsetting to those most invested in its preservation. Although he sought to engage those contributing to the *Pretext* discussion in some serious intellectual inquiry, he was frustrated by the complete lack of interest in examining the facts surrounding Israel's invasion of Lebanon in June 1982. As he wrote:

> I've always been intrigued by intellectual history, as you know, and in particular by the way intellectuals protect themselves from finding out the truth about themselves—which, rather typically throughout history, is support and apologetics for the crimes of the power system they serve. In this field, the method seems to be to evade facts entirely, and to concoct tales about rage, hauteur, style, curt answers, etc. I don't recall having seen one substantive comment, except for the efforts of the ex-Israeli who quickly withdrew when his claims were shown to be false. It's also interesting that there seems to be no need to substantiate even the tales, irrelevant as they are, apart from serving as a useful device of self-protection.[57]

That there could be no serious intellectual exchange with Chomsky on the *Pretext* list merits our reflection. One the one hand, Chomsky was accused of offering up truisms about intellectuals, things people know about how the intellectual world operates but did not feel required to articulate, while on the other hand being condemned for rejecting complex explanations about politics and serious world events. These complex explanations, as the examples I have examined indicate, provide untenable connections to reality, obfuscating the crimes of Holy States and protecting various dimensions of state worship among supposedly critical intellectuals from scrutiny. Chomsky's insistence that political events and the atrocities that often arise within them can be documented precisely, and that body counts and dates do matter, has an unsettling effect upon those who have invested in the critical language of postmodernism and its related idioms.

By insisting on identifying the guilty parties, and the intellectuals that often support them, Chomsky demands that we be honest about the practices that guide our conceptions of political responsibility, risking the ostracism that public exposures of inconvenient truths often bring with them. As he writes in the context of describing the immense destruction that was being visited upon Vietnam in *For Reasons of State*: "The cultural and institutional barriers that block the way to a more just and humane society are immense. There are, nevertheless, long-term tendencies that threaten the hegemony of coercive institutions and ideologies."[58] Sustaining and nurturing these long-term tendencies that threaten the hegemony of coercive institutions and ideologies is crucial to creating a culture committed to seriously dealing with the country's imperial history.

Noam Chomsky's political corpus forces a fundamental reassessment of how intellectual labor attains value and functions within the American academy and beyond while also raising troubling questions about the irrelevance of so much contemporary academic inquiry and theorization, which has historically functioned to obfuscate and obscure the truth about the United States' imperial behavior. A new conception of intellectual labor will have to confront Chomsky's critiques of the intellectual class, noting the distinct tendency that intellectuals have in gravitating toward centers of concentrated power and engaging in a perverse form of state worship, while ignoring or suppressing uncomfortable truths about themselves.

CHAPTER SEVEN

Recognizing the effects of the past in the present: Theorizing a way forward on the Israel-Palestine conflict

A harsh reality needs harsh words to describe it, live, and survive it. Laundered words allow us to perceive soiled realities as clean. We did not invent this method, but we improved it, as if we learned nothing from the evil ones who laundered words before us.

(AVRAHAM BURG, *The Holocaust Is Over We Must Rise From Its Ashes*)

Reflecting on the impasse

In assessing the many different efforts I have undertaken over the years to raise awareness about the hidden assumptions shaping the US citizen's understanding of the Israel-Palestine conflict, I have been continually struck by how little headway has been made to address the argumentative dynamics informing how people talk about and debate competing claims informing the conflict.[1] These argumentative dynamics are clearly driven by the demands and claims of history, cultural and religious identifications, the affective attachments accompanying competing positions, as well as the embodied states of the participants. While it is impossible for these participants to divorce themselves from their embodiments and affective attachments, it is possible for participants to develop a more nuanced understanding of why they react to certain knowledge claims about the Israel-Palestine conflict in the ways that they do, seeking to contextualize these reactions in the context of the present historical moment instead of through the reverberations of the past that so often distort perceptions. As Lynn Worsham notes in her "Going Postal: Pedagogic Violence and the Schooling of Emotion," "Without a fundamental revision in our conception of subjectivity and of our affective relationship to the world, the radical potential of recent pedagogy to reconstitute our emotional lives may be re-contained, in spite of its best intentions and the euphoria of its claims, as a strategy of condescension" (240). Worsham invites us to consider how our subjectivity and affective relationships are constructed and maintained over time, cautioning that— without a fundamental revision to our conceptions of both—the prospects of radical pedagogy will be channeled into strategies of condescension. For the purpose of this chapter, I think it is important to keep Worsham's cautionary note in mind as it reminds us how easily claims to liberation and transgression within current pedagogies can slide into simply telling others what to think or believe, or how to act, if they are to be considered ethical subjects. This tendency to insist that one is being ethical, while others are unethical or completely blind to the demands within an ethical system, is particularly pronounced in discussions about the Israel-Palestine conflict.

Burkean and postmodern conceptions of identification teach us that just as we inhabit history as situated subjects, history (with all its hauntings) inhabits us. To speak of an "I" is to simultaneously also to speak of a "We." If as Diana Fuss reminds us identification is the name of the psychical mechanism through which one achieves self-recognition by detouring through the Other, position-taking cannot be simply viewed as an individual "act," but emerges in negotiating the border between the inside and the outside, the border between the self and one's environment (49). To identify where one stands is to simultaneously also identify where one stands in relation to a community of other voices, a community characterized by identification and division. As Burke teaches us, "put identification and division ambiguously together, so that you cannot know for certain just where one ends and the other begins, and you have the characteristic invitation to rhetoric" (25). How we answer this "characteristic invitation" determines the conditions of possibility for achieving community.

As committed public intellectuals, we have a great deal to contribute in elucidating how history, conscious and unconscious identifications, affective attachments, and the "embodied" shape one's understanding of—and the ability to make claims about—the Israel-Palestine conflict; including identifying how history and language, all too frequently, serve or obscure a particular politics. However, these uses (and possible abuses) of history and language to advance a particular viewpoint are not always in our conscious control, as I will try to elaborate. Indeed, history often "returns" to us like a boomerang with sometimes unexpected and startling effects.[2] By virtue of its returning to us in a different form, and within a potentially deformed context, this history necessarily becomes ripe for misrecognition and possibly illegitimate activation and deployment as part of (and within) a hegemonic politics.

Perhaps the reason so little substantive discussion about the Israel-Palestine conflict takes place is that participants within these debates rarely seem to have an interest in exchanging information; instead, interlocutors seem intent upon silencing or damaging the Other.[3] While this might seem like a provocative and far too sweeping claim about scholarship and debate within our field, I have witnessed how gingerly journal and press editors approach the topic of Israel-Palestine when it comes to determining whether a manuscript will see its way into print, suggesting that certain sensitivities around the conflict should not be explored for fear of offending the readership. These journal and press editors seem to prefer hewing to a very protective discourse around the Israel-Palestine conflict than to deal with some relatively straightforward dimensions of it that support the Palestinian narrative about the oppressive effects of Israeli colonization and militarism on the indigenous inhabitants. Among these relatively straightforward dimensions of the conflict are the international consensus on the Question of Palestine and the relevant international law, including UN 242, which requires Israel to withdraw to its pre-June-1967 borders and immediately evacuate the settlements in the West Bank.

Even establishment politicians such as Barack Obama and Jimmy Carter have insisted that Israel must comply with this aspect of international law if the Israel-Palestine conflict is to be resolved.[4] In this context, the ridiculous charges of anti-Semitism and bigotry that have been leveled against Carter and the silly attempts to portray Obama as harboring anti-Israel sentiments create an interesting discursive predicament. The rise of the so-called New Anti-Semitism has also imposed an unhealthy and stifling form of political correctness on the field, which has resulted in the censorship of hard-hitting scholarly criticisms of Israel's occupation and its effects on the Middle East peace process. To work past this predicament, we must reframe our identifications with respect to Israeli and Palestinian nationalism if rhetoricians are to find a way out of the discursive impasse that currently hampers discussion about the historical and diplomatic record.

When debates about the conflict end with facile invocations of anti-Semitism, as they did in the list-serv exchange I will describe below, with participants angrily withdrawing because the Other is either hopelessly racist or uninformed, it is small wonder that serious discussion about the historical and diplomatic record around the Israel-Palestine never takes place. Debate, or an exchange of views, seems not to be the point. Instead, the rhetorical situation enables participants to unleash aggression and to employ a particular affective stance against those with whom they disagree. The position one may have held at the beginning of the debate is simply reaffirmed. I would like to examine some ways out of this troubling discursive impasse, exploring why the Israel-Palestine conflict is particularly susceptible to this sort of dynamic. Let me begin by examining the debate that touched upon our professional community.

Disavowals

In Chapter 5, I examined how the life and legacy of Edward Said tend to become objects of transference within debates about Middle East politics. I would like to extend the analysis I developed in that article to assess how the memory of the late Rachel Corrie, for whom the Rachel Corrie Courage in the Teaching of Writing Award is named, took on a similar transferential role when a call for nominations for the award was posted to the Writing Program Administrators list in May 2006.

How could the circumstances surrounding the death of an American college student in Gaza become the object of intense discussion on a list-serv for writing program administrators? How could the politics surrounding the Israel-Palestine conflict and the Middle East, as the controversy over this college student's act of seeming martyrdom, come to ever so briefly grip the attention of our field? What seemed like a relatively straightforward decision to post a call for nominations for the Rachel Corrie Courage in the Teaching of Writing to the Writing Program Administrators list in May of 2006 quite unexpectedly led to an interrogation of the values informing our professional organization and its supposed politics. What narrative, if any, was the umbrella organization for writing instruction, the College Composition and Communication, forwarding about Rachel Corrie's death and Middle East politics, some asked, by allowing the Progressive Special Interest Caucuses and Coalitions (PSCC) to promote the Rachel Corrie Courage in the Teaching of Writing Award—an award seeking to recognize courage and risk-taking in the academy—and to present the award at the national conference (the CCCCs)? According to the award organizers, the Rachel Corrie Courage in the Teaching of Writing Award seeks to honor "a teacher in the CCCC who has taken professional risks in order to promote social justice through the teaching of writing" (Abraham, "Nomination Call"). In response, one list-serv member pointed out that the call for nominations was filled with "very disturbing loaded language," noting that the award was a polarizing and offensive way to pursue peace and justice: "I'm uncomfortable with an announcement that asserts its interest in peace while also subtly (or perhaps not so subtly) repeating some of the anti-Israel rhetoric that has become so common among us liberals lately" (Writing Program Administrators Archive). Another member stated that he felt the award to be problematic because it takes the tragedy that befell Rachel Corrie and raises it above "the thousands of other tragedies that have been going on in that region for decades." This person asked, "Where is the award for the busload of Israeli school children which was stopped so that children could be shot, execution style, at close range, for example?" This award, then, in this person's estimation, is a not-so-subtle way of expressing solidarity with the Palestinian people—and as a consequence—demonizing Israel.

According to other critics of the award, to make a value judgment about Corrie's actions—that they were in fact courageous—and to accept a specific reading of these actions as consistent with anti-colonial and liberationist struggle improperly politicized an organization committed to writing and rhetorical studies. To endorse a tendentious reading of Corrie's actions, according to some, was to uncritically accept a pro-Palestinian politics, essentially confirming that Corrie had been deliberately killed by the Israeli Defense Forces in March of 2003 when she was supposedly defending a Palestinian home in Rafah, Gaza against demolition. Could Rachel Corrie necessarily be framed as a victim, some asked, implying that she may have been responsible for own death. One participant, who was hesitant to get involved in the discussion because he was still a graduate student, felt obligated to point out that there is a tendency to align Jews, who ask legitimate questions about how Rachel Corrie died, with the repressive policies of the Israeli government. In other words, when Jews question whether Rachel Corrie was actually murdered, they are inevitably assumed to be automatic supporters of Israel and its policies, which is precisely the type of anti-Semitism that is at the heart of Zionism—an anti-Semitism that must be vigilantly guarded against. According to this logic, to even question the appropriateness of the Rachel Corrie Courage in the Teaching of Writing Award leads to accusations of siding with murder and occupation. As this participant wrote, "... a person who raises concerns about the naming of the award suddenly finds him or herself directly, or by implication, identified with murder, violence and injustice." Furthermore, this interlocutor suggests that when Jewish supporters of Israel raise legitimate questions about the appropriateness of the Rachel Corrie Courage in the Teaching of Writing Award, as well as the circumstances surrounding Corrie's death, they often become stand-ins for the Israeli government.

Another discussion participant brought up the example of Alyssa Flatow, a young Jewish student who went to study in Israel in 1995 and was killed by a suicide bomber. According to him, "The courage of her convictions led her to study in Israel, despite the risk of suicide attack, and she died in the pursuit of learning." He expressed the opinion that the Corrie award represents "a skillful rhetorical move designed to draw attention to a particular perspective on the Israel-Palestine conflict." He then encouraged list participants to think about how we would go about talking about an award meant to honor Alyssa Flatow. Would this award be any more or less appropriate than the Rachel Corrie award? To ask this question, according to this participant, would "get into a battle over the relative values of injustices, the moral status of different peoples, the tortured history of the region—and suddenly we are taking sides on the Israel/Palestinian conflict—a conversation I don't think is appropriate for the list." Despite the calls for list-serv propriety, the debate continued, with several participants insisting that the conversation about the Rachel Corrie Courage in the Teaching of Writing Award was appropriate for the

WPA list precisely because it involved questions about the CCC's values and its advocacy of social justice for disadvantaged populations.

Furthermore, disagreement revolved around the clear incommensurability between the courage Corrie displayed—in supposedly facing down an Israeli Defense Forces Bulldozer—and the risks adjuncts and the untenured take in confronting the political economy of the academy, as they cope with the unstable labor conditions that make their employment situation tenuous at best. In the context of this labor uncertainty, the untenured do in fact demonstrate courage when they challenge the labor conditions within their universities by asking administrators hard questions about the institution. In addition, for these untenured faculty to pursue controversial lines of inquiry within their scholarship and teaching could also possibly jeopardize their ability to later obtain a contract renewal or a tenure-track position. Labor uncertainty often produces conformity within institutional and cultural domains, whereby pleasing authority figures ensures one's economic survival. While there is a clear lack of parity between Rachel Corrie losing her life by standing in front of an Israeli Defense Forces bulldozer—as an act of resistance against Israeli colonization and in solidarity with Palestinian dispossession—and the brave adjunct who places her employment prospects in jeopardy by questioning her Dean or department chair about the casualization of labor within her college and department, both actions seek to disrupt the status quo.

As the award creator noted, the Rachel Corrie Courage in the Teaching of Writing Award is designed to recognize work that often goes unrecognized, work that advances social justice, grassroots, maverick opinions that are threatening to stalwarts in the CCCs. The award positions the CCCs leadership as the status quo (seemingly with respect to Middle East politics and academic institutional politics), and unresponsive to the demands of colonized populations, placing the CCC's leadership on the defensive and representing it as quiescent, disengaged, and uninterested in political struggle that might lead the organization to clash with political forces bigger than itself. As the nomination announcement makes clear, the award seeks to recognize an untenured scholar who "has taken professional risks in order to promote social justice through the teaching of writing." Furthermore, the nomination announcement advances the following claim: "It is well known that the politics of hiring, tenure, and promotion often motivate graduate students and junior faculty to write, teach, and serve in 'safe' subject and project areas; many are encouraged by mentors to shy away from genuinely 'controversial' or 'risky' subjects until they are tenured."

While many may disagree with this characterization of the CCC's leadership and the politics of the profession, it is clear that the Rachel Corrie Courage in the Teaching of Writing Award challenges academics to think about and through their location within the US academy and this location's relationship to other parts and populations of the world. The purpose of the award, then, is to ". . . encourage writing teachers early in their careers to take on research, pedagogy, and service projects that promote commitment to peace, justice, and human dignity—even when hazarding the ire of deans, chairs, editors, and hiring and review committees." While I do not think that deans, chairs, editors, and hiring and review committees are necessarily opposed to research, pedagogy, and service projects that promote commitments to peace, justice, and human dignity, they might be reluctant to endorse work that is perceived as engaging in advocacy for a despised population such as the Palestinians living under Israeli occupation.[5] If a young American citizen dies in the course of defending such a population, it only stands to reason that there might be attempts to smear this citizen's motives and actions.

Attempts to undercut the memory of Rachel Corrie take the form of questions about the circumstances around Corrie's deaths well as questions about those seeking to memorialize Corrie as a martyr who died at the hands of the Israeli government: Did the driver of the IDF bulldozer deliberately run over Rachel Corrie? Was the IDF bulldozer driver being unjustly blamed for causing Corrie's death in what was in fact an accident? Did the driver actually see Rachel Corrie in her orange vest, standing on top of a pile of dirt with the bulldozer in front of the soon-to-be demolished home? Had anti-Semites and anti-Israel activists in their zeal to condemn Israel seized upon Rachel Corrie's death, memorializing her to unfairly highlight and condemn the Israeli occupation? If one were to suggest that the circumstances around Corrie's death—and her parents efforts to involve the US and Israeli governments in an investigation of those circumstances—had been underreported or purposely embargoed in the United States, would one then be engaging in the classic anti-Semitic canard that "Jews control the media"? These were just a few of the questions encircling this debate one May morning in 2006 on the Writing Program Administrators list-serv.[6]

As a white, privileged American woman, and a member of the International Solidarity Movement who was allegedly murdered by the Israeli Defense Forces (IDF), Corrie served as a tragic reminder of how US support for (and defense of) Israel's occupation seemingly knows no bounds, even when an American citizen is killed under troubling circumstances. According to the nomination announcement, "Rachel was attempting to block an Israeli military bulldozer from demolishing the house of a pharmacist and his family when the driver of the bulldozer ran over her, then backed up and ran over her again." Furthermore, "Wearing a bright orange jacket and using a bullhorn, Rachel was, by all eyewitness accounts and in horrifying photographs published on the Internet, exceptionally visible." For many participants on the WPA list, both of these claims were far from factual. For some, claims that were being reported as factual by the award creators were tendentious and partisan, deliberately slanted against the Israeli government. Perhaps equally controversial was the claim within the nomination announcement that Corrie's "parents, some members of Congress, and grassroots organizations including several Jewish peace groups have called for an independent US investigation into her death. Such an investigation has yet to happen, and the US media virtually buried the story—though it was featured prominently in the United Kingdom and in many other countries." As I explain below, the lack of US media coverage about the circumstances around Corrie's death became a focal point of controversy among participants on the WPA list, with some insisting that to merely suggest that there was a dearth of coverage about Corrie's death is to traffic in the anti-Semitic canard that "Jews control the media."

While Corrie's actions have been praised by certain members of the progressive community, others have described her as a naïve idealistic young woman who took her ideals too far, someone who had been duped by "left-wing propaganda" on the conflict. For many participants, what justice looks like in the Middle East is far from clear; therefore, the Rachel Corrie award is inappropriate because it presents the Palestinians as the only group with a legitimate grievance in a war-torn region, portraying a complex situation in a simplistic binary of right and wrong. As one participant complained, the award supporters "treat extremely complex situations in [a] simplistic manner and the price for doing so is continued conflict and lack of resolution." This same participant insisted that I had opened the way for expressions of racism against Jews because of my attempts to bring discussions of the Israel-Palestine conflict into the field, suggesting that criticism of Israel—or critical discussion about the conflict—is tantamount to anti-Semitism. This person insisted that the Rachel Corrie Courage in the Teaching of Writing Award, based on the same martyrdom that was behind Palestinian extremism, represented a denial of one group's nationalism (Jewish nationalism apparently), and sought to portray what justice might look like in the Middle East without taking into account the various complexities of the situation. According to this person, the award creators sought to carry on as "almighty" by portraying a clear "right" and "wrong" in the Middle East.

Some critics of the award questioned whether Corrie's motives as an activist for peace were as pure as her supporters believed, stating that they had read news accounts that described Corrie as protecting terrorist tunnels in Gaza, and as a member of the International Solidarity Movement (ISM), harboring and providing comfort to known terrorist organizations.[7] What some viewed as an altruistic act of sacrifice, Corrie's decision to stand in front of an Israeli Defense Force's bulldozer to protect a Palestinian pharmacist's home, others viewed as anti-Israel activism, which had been capitalized upon by the award creators to promote a political agenda. While there can be little dispute that the politically charged circumstances surrounding Rachel Corrie's death make it difficult to separate Corrie's sentiments toward Israel and the United States from those of the award creators and winners, it is important to remember that the purpose of the Rachel Corrie Courage in the Teaching of Writing Award is to recognize pedagogical courage and risk-taking. Such courage and risk-taking may very well have nothing to do with the Middle East. Indeed, most of the winners of the award have not focused on the Middle East in either their teaching or scholarship.

One critic of the award stated, "Imagine putting this award down on your c.v.," suggesting that no reasonable person would consider doing so. This participant implied that applying for and winning the award were demonstrations in themselves of one's bias and bigotry, apparently against Israel, and that no one in their right mind would list the award as a legitimate professional accomplishment—apparently the award is something to be hidden rather than advertised. Furthermore, according to this person, the creators of the award designed it to "push buttons politically (propaganda), not pedagogically." These are somewhat curious claims that were generated when the award announcement was sent out through the WPA list. One might be left to wonder, "Who is afraid of Rachel Corrie?" Clearly, the memorialization of Corrie's actions in Gaza touches upon some sensitive issues, issues that are disturbing to some members of our professional community. The attempts that were made to frame the award as "inappropriate," "unprofessional," and "as propaganda" sought to blame Rachel Corrie for her death, to deprive the moral, legal, and historical basis for the justice of the Palestinian national movement and to smear those associated with advancing criticisms of Israel. Instead of recognizing these dimensions of the debate, it was far easier to frame the disagreement about the award as a matter of professional decorum and propriety.[8]

In his "Dignity and Solidarity," a speech delivered on 15 June 2003 before the American-Arab Anti-Discrimination League, Edward Said described Rachel Corrie's actions as "heroic and dignified at the same time," a recognition of Corrie's sacrifice for something larger than herself. Said discussed the circumstances around the US government's decision not to investigate Corrie's death: "An American citizen willfully murdered by the soldiers of a client state of the US without so much as an official peep or even the *de rigeur* investigation that had been promised her family." According to Said, Corrie had traveled to Gaza "to stand with suffering human beings with whom she had never had any contact before." Finally, Said noted the significance of Corrie's actions:

What Rachel Corrie's work in Gaza recognized, however, was precisely the gravity and the density of the living history of the Palestinian people as a national community, and not merely as a collection of deprived refugees. That is what she was in solidarity with. And we need to remember that that kind of solidarity is no longer confined to a small number of intrepid souls here and there, but is recognized the world over. ("Dignity and Solidarity")

Despite Said's solemn remembrance, other accounts of Corrie's death (and its significance) have been less than respectful. According to Joshua Hammer,

If Corrie thought that a white, American, female college student putting her life on the line could somehow change hearts and minds, she would, in death, be little more than a news blip, convincing people of nothing more than what they already believed. What remained unclear were the precise circumstances of her death—and why a 23-year-old woman from Olympia, Washington, would have placed her body in front of Israeli military bulldozers in the first place.

Given these disparate accounts of how Rachel Corrie died and what she represented, it is perhaps unsurprising that heated discussion ensued when a call for nominations for an award created in her memory came across a major list-serv. The dynamics of this discussion in our field, among our colleagues, did surprise me, however. As Barbara Herrnstein Smith reminds us, "The dynamics of intellectual controversy often mirror, shadow, and predict quite closely the dynamics of larger human conflict."[9] Smith's statement certainly seems to ring true as I turn to an examination of some of the specific exchanges between participants on the WPA list about the Rachel Corrie Courage in the Teaching of Writing Award.

The memory of Rachel Corrie in the present

Consider the following response to me from an interlocutor on the WPA list in May of 2006, when the controversy about the Rachel Corrie Courage in the Teaching of Writing Award developed[10]: "Abraham, you know damn well that what Luisa said had heavy racist overtones in it: JEWS CONTROL THE MEDIA. If you don't admit that, you are lying or believe it." In this context, the person identified as "Luisa" had alleged that "we are all under the influence of a group that can readily draw sympathies from the horrible crimes against them during WWII." As one might expect, several list-serv participants found this assertion, or at least the assertion they believed Luisa had made, offensive and beyond the pale. One person noted that

> [t]o assign Jews some kind of mystical influence over the thoughts of Americans, that's beyond the pale. And to treat Jewish memory of the Shoah and the loss of a third of the Jewish population of the world, along with entire cultures of Jews—Yiddish speaking Jews of Eastern Europe, the Jews of Salonika—as merely an industry run by a highly influential cabal of Jews who want to play on the sympathies of the world, well, it's a willful caricature of Jewish history and community and shows a lack of familiarity with the role of history and memory in Judaism.

As I quickly pointed out, one must draw the crucial distinction between "Jews" and "Zionists" before alleging that someone has engaged in anti-Semitic rhetoric. To criticize Zionism, which is an ideology derived from European romantic nationalism, is not to criticize Judaism, Jews, Holocaust survivors, or the use of the Holocaust. As Marc Ellis insists through the title of his recent book (*Israel ≠ Judaism*), Judaism and Israel are not equivalent, although Zionism as a nationalist ideology seeks to promote Israeli actions as Jewish actions. Furthermore, one might also insist that to take issue with the Rachel Corrie Courage in the Teaching of Writing Award is to be blind to the history of Palestinian suffering?

I defended Luisa, insisting that she was referencing "Zionists," not Jews, suggesting that Zionism itself has historically engaged in anti-Semitic caricatures in its attempts to position Israel as the Jewish state, even though many Jews refuse to allow Israel to speak for them. My interlocutor, however, insisted that I was either being willfully ignorant in asserting that Luisa meant Zionists, not Jews, or that I really did believe that "Jews control the media." In other words, if I did not agree with my interlocutor I was either turning a blind eye to racism or lying. To some, Luisa appeared to suggest that Jewish "influence" has successfully manipulated the Holocaust for political purposes in the context of diminishing Israel's culpability in its treatment of the Palestinians. Any suggestion that the Holocaust has somehow been misused by Israel's defenders to justify Israel's occupation of the Palestinians immediately creates controversy, including the allegations that one is suggesting that "Jews control the media." As the award creator noted, the fact that "Jewish media control" even came up in a debate about whether or not this award is appropriate "utterly trivializes the reality of anti-Semitism by claiming that just about anything under the sun that strikes the imagination of a speaker rightfully fits that category."

That Corrie's actions were of historical significance, providing an exemplar through which to recognize a courageous teacher advancing vital issues through teaching and scholarship, was too much for some list-serv participants who believed that Corrie's death had been misused within the professional organization of the Conference of College Composition and Communication to advance a distinctly pro-Palestinian politics. As another participant noted, "Being a Palestinian sympathizer hardly aligns a person with violence and injustice. To say that there is no clear side of justice in the Middle East is to ignore a lot of history and to succumb to the propaganda campaign that has allowed so much unnecessary death to continue." Assigning blame and responsibility to parties in the Middle East conflict, particularly in the context of Israel-Palestine, creates immediate controversy, allowing for the invocation of the "cosmic struggle" argument, that is, no side can be blamed for what is happening because the conflict has been going on since time immemorial for reasons that are beyond human comprehension. Instead of assigning blame, the most common retort is that the conflict is too complex for comprehension, or that so much propaganda swirls around the conflict due to excessive partisanship that it is impossible to know the truth about where justice resides in the conflict. In response to the participant who claimed that to assert that there is no clear justice in the Middle East is to succumb to the propaganda campaign that is responsible for so much bloodshed, another participant stated, "One can easily go after the rhetorical stance taken up by this award and show how it IGNORES history and how this award is a very specific case of PROPAGANDA" (emphasis in original). As to who was being propagandized by whom was not at all clear, as those supporting the award accused the award's critics of having succumbed to propaganda and vice versa. As one critic insisted, "I don't believe I ignore history or have succumbed to a propaganda campaign by feeling that there are legitimate competing interests at play in the Middle East, even for the very liberal, sensible, non-religious-fanatics among us."

The circumstances around Corrie's death came to represent a more general debate about the politics informing the Israel-Palestine conflict. In other words, Corrie became an object of transference in this controversy, representing a conduit through which the controversy could develop and play out.[11] Participants seemingly either strongly identified with Corrie and her actions or completely disavowed that she could possibly stand for what the award named after her claimed she did. Corrie's actions in Gaza and their significance were also taken up in discussants' affective transmissions, with each message to the list seemingly escalating the political and professional stakes of the exchange. Furthermore, participants who agreed with one another solidified their identifications by situating themselves as reasonable and compassionate while seemingly characterizing those who supported or criticized the award as somehow biased or uninformed. In this debate, Corrie was either a victim of IDF aggression or a terrorist (Hamas, Hezbollah, etc.) sympathizer. In other words, she was either defending an innocent Palestinian's home or protecting a terrorist's stash. Establishing whether Corrie was to be remembered as the victim of a tragedy, and by inference a victim of Israel's colonization project, or as a naïve college student who had been manipulated by the International Solidarity Movement to stand in front of an IDF bulldozer as part of a publicity stunt gone terribly wrong, became the very object of debate.

When a contested figure such as Corrie becomes an object of transference, through which participants debating her legacy have a tendency to repeat the very problems they are supposedly subjecting to critique and analysis (the use and seeming repetition of violent metaphors to examine violence or the recycling of anti-Semitic tropes in a discussion about the Holocaust and Israel, for example), the debate itself becomes susceptible to resuscitating echoes (or "uptakes") of the past. These uptakes tend to seize upon a particularly affective-laden event or meaningful signifier from the past, re-deploying it in the present for the purpose of maintaining a unified meaning and coherence. When one speaks of Jewish History, the Jewish People, or Jewish suffering, there is a tendency to lump a good bit of history together, say, from 70 A.D. (the destruction of the Second Temple) to 1948 (the founding of the state of Israel), for example. While this strategy contributes to the circulation of a lachrymose narrative about Jewish suffering, it simultaneously enables a conflation of memory, whereby supposed threats to Jewish memory in the present seemingly enable one to reach for events from the past, as part of an effort to suture together—what is in fact—a rather fragmented history.[12] That the controversy about the Rachel Corrie Courage in the Teaching of Writing Award became an occasion to express concerns about anti-Semitism while also affirming a lachrymose narrative about historical Jewish suffering, should hardly be surprising. Add to this the communal response that was seemingly demanded in the wake of the "We are all under the control of a group" comment, one is left to wonder if we are fully aware of the forces shaping our perceptions of conflict in the Middle East.

According to some WPA list-serv participants, since the evidence was far from clear as to how Corrie was killed, or in what capacity Corrie was acting when was she killed, the CCCCs should stay far away from endorsing Rachel Corrie's memory or the award meant to recognize an untenured faculty member taking risks in teaching and scholarship to advance peace and social justice. The PSCC (Progressive Special Interest Caucuses and Coalitions), not the CCCCs, sponsored the award. According to some, embracing Corrie as the epitome of courage was neither professionally responsible nor neutral; to embrace Corrie's memory as a victim of Israeli violence was to be partisan, unprofessional, and un-objective. This is an interesting discursive move: suggesting that those who were convinced that Corrie had, in fact, been deliberately killed by the IDF—instead of simply being the victim of an accident—were simple minded, seeing clear justice in the Middle East conflict, while also promulgating propaganda as part of that vision. It is not that those making this accusation had done the research to conclusively determine that Corrie was the victim of an accident, but that Corrie's death had not been reported as a deliberate killing in the US mainstream media.[13] In brief, according to many, Corrie had been taken up as part of a propaganda campaign to defame and delegitimize Israel, at a time of supposed increasing anti-Semitism through the world. To name an award seeking to recognize courageous teaching and scholarship after Corrie was a controversial idea because some did not think that Corrie's actions were in themselves courageous, particularly if her memorialization was being employed to criticize Israel. As one astute observer insisted, political choices are made all the time in the course of memorialization, such as when a museum, airport, or in this case, an award is named after a person—controversial or not. How many objected to the naming of Reagan National Airport in Washington D.C. out of principled objections to the Reagan administration's involvement in the mining of the Nicaraguan harbors throughout the 1980s, which was condemned as international terrorism? According to this person, objecting to the Rachel Corrie Award, without objecting to the naming of Reagan National Airport, was hypocritical. Perhaps some found Corrie's actions, or at least the way in which they have been memorialized, potentially anti-Semitic because they frame Israel—as the Jewish state—in a bad light. In brief, the debate seemed to revolve around several questions.

First, what were the exact circumstances around Rachel Corrie's death in Gaza? And could these circumstances be objectively verified to satisfy all interested parties? For example, could Corrie's death been the result of negligence or even a willful disregard for her life by the IDF? Furthermore, what was Corrie doing when she died? Yes, she was seeking to block an IDF bulldozer as it attempted to demolish a Palestinian pharmacist's home, but she must have realized such an action was pointless. Perhaps she was trying to reach the bulldozer driver on some human level, appealing to him to stop acting as an extension of Israel's state policy. Furthermore, we might ask what Corrie believed herself to be doing when she stood in front of the six-ton D9 Caterpillar bulldozer, specially built to demolish homes. Was she doing more than reminding the bulldozer driver of the illegality of his actions according to international law? Those who were standing with Corrie watched as she was run over.[14] Do they share any culpability in Corrie's death? They claimed to have tried to warn the bulldozer driver that Corrie had fallen down and was struggling to climb up the mound of earth that was accumulating in front of her.[15] The driver maintained that he could not see Corrie. However, as one participant pointed out, "... the pictures that the International Solidarity Movement presented in an effort to prove that he [the bulldozer driver] could not have missed seeing her were later revealed to have been presented out of sequence." Furthermore, "While they seem to suggest that Corrie was easily visible and that the driver would have had to go out of his way to hit her, the photos were not taken in quick succession but several hours apart." As another participant aptly put it, "Readers [of the call for nominations] are urged to view the pictures of her [Corrie], as if this absolved the situation of its complexity."

If, as some critics of the award alleged, that Corrie was anti-Israel and anti-American because she was critical of Israeli and US policies in the Middle East, does this present a problem for the CCCCs if the PSCC sponsors an award named after her? What does it mean to be anti-Israel or anti-American after all? Answers to these questions are complex, particularly as these questions are debated in a discursive space where criticisms of Israel appear strange and are easily classified as anti-Semitic. There are some theoretical concepts that can help us move beyond this discursive impasse, radically reconfiguring our understanding of how to discuss the Israel-Palestine conflict within the profession and beyond: affect, belatedness, and transference.

These three concepts are applicable to understanding the hidden energies and psychological forces at work in our argumentative dynamics about the Israel-Palestine conflict. These psychological forces are so powerful because of the history of anti-Semitism, the discursive dimensions of the Holocaust, and what Michael Rothberg calls "multidirectional memory," the ways in which a particular memory can flow in different directions based upon one's experience, history, and positionality.[16] Multidirectional memory is particularly relevant in the context of examining what happens when the discourses around the Holocaust clash with discourses around anti-colonial struggle, including the Palestinian struggle for national liberation.

The affective component

In describing the affective dimension of the conflict, I am drawing upon the work of Teresa Brennan, who in her *The Transmission of Affect* defines affect as "the physiological shifts that accompanies a judgment" and "the energy transfer or exchange between aggressor and passive recipient" (49). Far too often, interlocutors debating the Israel-Palestine conflict become enmeshed within affective environments within which it becomes extremely difficult to separate position-taking from assignments of moral culpability. As one WPA participant astutely pointed out in the discussion of the Rachel Corrie Courage in the Teaching of Writing Award:

> Not much interest in *inter*locution going down here among us-rhetoricians . . . but lots of interest in ranting in the name of justice against the other on the list who is classically and hopelessly stupid or biased or prejudice or uninformed or insert-your-slam-here. In fact, it seems that the other is so morally or intellectually out of it that engaging with him or her in honest-to-the-gods deliberation would be like shooting fish in a barrel. This thread—on a Writing Program Administrators list, no less—seems to operate as a microcosm of the broader realm of "civic discourse," which makes sense but which also sure does deflate any

self-important claims rhetoricians make about the need for the sorry-ass political body to study rhetoric. And it reminds me of why I have no faith in "argumentation" or the "civic" model of operative rhetoric.

The affective dimensions around this conflict, which include libidinal energies and investments, cannot be accounted for by the "'civic' model of operational rhetoric."[17] The reason for this is quite simple: the energy exchanges suffusing any affective environment are not even recognized, much less accounted for, in this model because bodies are treated in isolation instead of in context and in concert. In other words, the notion that my affective energy in the heat of debate would interact with and change someone else's physiological responses is not something traditional theories of argumentation consider. In other words, the debate ensures its own polarization because of the overdetermined affective environments within which it occurs. Each point meets a counterpoint, leading to a sure escalation of heated rhetoric and an increased affective energy pitched at higher and higher intensities.

How does one achieve the necessary intellectual and affective distance from the complex issues surrounding the Israel-Palestine conflict before entering into an informed and good-faith discussion about them? Appropriate "distance" in this instance refers to the achievement of a certain ability to recognize and avoid the polarizing influences and affective transmissions that often infuse analyses of issues such as nationalism, occupation, ethnic exclusion, and the historical grievances accompanying dispossession. These influences and transmissions, which often infuse defenses of nationalistic commitments, are often intense and irrational, verging on a type of fundamentalism. Indeed, these transmissions have a contagious quality to them, ensuring controversy once they are unleashed.

In her *Toward a Civil Discourse*, Sharon Crowley describes how fundamentalist ideologies develop, noting how "densely articulated belief systems" that preclude the kind of inventiveness that makes for flexible and contingent thinking take root. Fundamentalism interferes with one's capacity to process new information and to notice evidence that does not confirm one's strongly held perspective. A fundamentalist ideology literally gives one tunnel vision with respect to how one views the world and processes events within it. Drawing on Clore and Gasper, Crowley argues that "densely articulated ideologies construct bad affective grammarians who pay intense notice to objects and events that can be threaded into the intricate tapestries of their belief system(s)." As Crowley notes, "They notice because almost everything that is made legible by their belief system(s) is weighty with affect for them" (85).

When someone interprets an event through an interpretive framework weighty with affect, one can only view that event as either contributing to or undermining one's worldview because of how the structure of feeling informing the event shapes one's very understanding of—and relationship to—it. In other words, as the fundamentalist subject encounters an event within the social field, she processes this event as consistent with what she already believes, even if the event itself has no relation to the belief in question. In this sense, the fundamentalist maintains her tunnel vision. If she were to lose it, she would lose her very identity. Finally, Crowley draws this conclusion: "If this account is correct, extremists have difficulty taking notice of events or objects that neither support nor attack their beliefs. That is to say, whatever is new and neutral in relation to their system of beliefs is unlikely to pass unremarked" (35). Crowley works, then, to build a rhetoric of fundamentalism by noting just how resilient and impervious to change some belief systems can become. We see such impervious belief systems at work within debates about the Israel-Palestine conflict.

Belatedness

It is a commonplace of psychoanalysis that the past frequently intrudes upon the present, often in unexpected and novel ways.[18] A bad romantic relationship, for example, can return and influence all future relationships, persistently exercising control over us and shaping how we view others, while all the while not announcing itself in any definable or visible way. Similarly, a bad educational experience in high school or early in college can reappear in terms of a confidence problem in graduate school or in a first job. The reason such experiences exercise such a hold on our attention, seemingly reappearing in other contexts, is because they have played a formative role in shaping our identities, establishing an important place in the solidification of our self-esteem and our ability to understand our positionality in the world. Jean Laplanche reminds us, "It takes two traumas to make a trauma," by which he means that the first trauma instills in us the fear that that we will re-experience the absence and loss of the original traumatic event.[19] When the second trauma overtakes us, it has so much resonance because we experience and feel the second trauma through the framework created by the first.[20]

When certain traumatic experiences are reawakened in us because of a particularly painful memory, we tend to react quite defensively, insisting upon removing the conditions that have led us to revisit the past, or more precisely, that has led the past to revisit us. Certain triggers can quickly and quite unexpectedly bring the past "back" into the present, surprising even the most astute and critical observer of a particular social scene. That there is a degree of uncontrollability to these intrusions is consistent with the notion that the unconscious exercises its influence upon the conscious mind in slightly detectable ways, from a slip of the tongue to a particularly realistic dream that corresponds to—or embellishes—upon the events of the previous day or a particularly memorable moment. How the past will "return" to us is enigmatic, defying any easy explanation.

The past continually seeks to catch up with and exercise its hold on the present, erupting into the contemporary scene, even as we work diligently to keep this past at bay. As the past makes its way into the present through either unconscious language choices or conscious manipulation of certain tropes, we are often surprised at how quickly the past can literally dictate the unfolding of the present. This phenomenon, which Freud labeled "belatedness," or deferred action (*nachträglichkeit*), reminds us that past events take on more and more significance and often become more and more meaningful (affect-laden) in our conscious minds because it takes time for the memory—particularly a memory about a traumatic event—to develop or catch up with the present.[21] These belated memories seem to have a boomerang effect upon the psyche of the subject, "returning" the full force of the prior event with particular energy. When these forces are unleashed, there is a tendency for subjects to seek narrative dominance.

Belatedness is certainly operative with respect to contemporary discussions of the Israel-Palestine conflict, as day-to-day events in the Middle East seem to inevitably become refracted through the prism of Jewish suffering leading up to and during the Holocaust. Perhaps it is only to be expected that this history of Jewish suffering should be invoked to contextualize and explain the violence and religious hatred that drives the "clash of civilizations" mentality of the disputants and partisans in the conflict. Israel, as a Jewish state, is often described as being under siege and in a battle for its very survival against the various Islamic organizations who seek to advance the nationalist aspirations of the Palestinian people.[22] These organizations are described as anti-Semitic because they seek the physical destruction of Israel, in its form as a state dedicated to the preservation of a Jewish majority, and the return of the Palestinian refugees who supposedly lost their homes to invading Zionist forces in 1947 prior to Israel's creation. Writing in his *My People* in 1968, the renowned Israeli statesman Abba Eban claimed, "There is not a single image, phrase, or adjective in the Nazi vocabulary which Arab propaganda, directed from Cairo, has not adopted and diffused in the political warfare against Israel. . . . The murder of six million Jews by Nazis was alternately denied and applauded . . . Israel's very existence was portrayed in Arab writings and politics as a crime for which the only expiation lay in Israel's disappearance" (quoted in Isacoff 52). This transposition of Nazi rhetoric into the Arab's struggle with Israel after 1967, particularly with respect to the demands of dispossessed Palestinian refugees, only contributes to the conflations of historical moments identified above.

Since the claims these Palestinian refugees make upon Israel involve providing redress for dispossession and ultimately a return to Israel, which would disturb Israel's demography as a Jewish state, these claims are often characterized as threatening Israel's existence. In other words, any political action or statement that makes a gesture toward disturbing Israel's Jewish character seems to become configured—by definition—as anti-Semitic. These actions and statements create an affective energy, drawing participants into an endless labyrinth of accusations and counter-accusations about ideological purity, victimization, and the authority of cited sources.

This configuration becomes operable because Zionism posits that criticisms of Israel, as a Jewish state, are anti-Semitic because Israel is the state of all Jewish people, both prior to Israel's creation and into perpetuity, and because the history of anti-Semitism is understood to have reached its zenith in the Holocaust, a culmination of centuries of gentile hatred against Jews. This positioning of Israel within Zionist ideology as a Jewish homeland, even before Israel officially existed as a nation, allows for an easy transposition of historical events, enabling the anti-Semitism of one age to become identified with the words and actions directed against Israel in the context of the contemporary crisis in the Middle East. Often, these transpositions are inappropriate and lead to incorrect conclusions about people's motives as they participate in furthering discussion and understanding about the Israel-Palestine conflict.[23]

As rhetoricians, we should be concerned by this possible misuse of history in these debates; indeed, the charge of anti-Semitism, if it is to be taken seriously, must be leveled with precision and not as a scatter-shot propaganda device for scoring cheap political points.[24] In this discursive environment, every statement introduced into the debate contains a hidden motive, or at least a hidden rhetorical or historical resonance whereby nothing can be interpreted as being offered in good faith: "You claim that the Rachel Corrie Courage in the Teaching of Writing Award is about X (rewarding courage, risk-taking, innovation, etc.) but it is really about Y (anti-Israelism, pro-Palestinian politics, and anti-Semitism)." It is this displacement of a particular conception of anti-Semitism, a conception that had a particular meaning and resonance at a particular point in history, which tends to confuse participants in contemporary debates about the Middle East. As rhetoricians, we should be much more vigilant about the prospects of importing this flawed conception of anti-Semitism into the field of rhetorical studies, particularly when doing so has the potential to hurt possibilities for dialogue and understanding.

Perhaps no caricature of Jews provokes as strong and quick a response as the suggestion that American Jews exercise undue "influence" over the media, particularly in the context of discussing media coverage of the Israel-Palestine conflict, or US Middle East policy. Of course, many Jews do not agree with Israel's policies and refuse to believe that Israel is *the* Jewish state since its actions do not speak for them. If a Jew condemns Israel given this ideological economy, does she then renounce her Judaism? Or has Zionism through Israel illegitimately usurped Judaism for its purposes, engaging in anti-Semitic caricatures ("All Jews think alike" or "All Jews are capable of having Israel represent them") to silence dissent against its policies? This is the most prevalent form of anti-Semitism animating our contemporary historical moment, as Zionism and Israel seek to speak for Jews throughout the world.

The presentation of Israel as a Western rampart in the Middle East, an offshoot of Europe posed as a defender of Western values that holds nothing in common with its Arab neighbors, provides a comforting narrative to those seeking to use Huntington's clash of civilizations model to provide tacit endorsement to Israel's increased militarization within the Middle East and colonization of Palestine. In this context, resisting Israel's colonization project either through physical actions or in written and spoken words is configured as anti-Semitism, the same anti-Semitism that created the environment within which the Holocaust was conducted. Surely, every critic of Israel is not being critical of what Israel (as the Jewish state) does because she is anti-Semitic.[25] The usual refrain to this observation is that mere criticism of Israel is not anti-Semitic, but when criticism becomes intemperate and is continually generated without proper context and proportion—singling out Israeli actions without comparing them to the actions of other countries facing similar threats—then such criticism crosses into anti-Semitism.[26]

Transference

Related to the phenomenon of *nachträglichkeit* (belatedness) and affect is the psychoanalytical concept of transference, which as I mentioned earlier, is the tendency to repeat the very problems one sets out to study and identify, for example, using anti-Semitic tropes in the course of studying anti-Semitism or employing sexually violent rhetoric in the course of discussing sexual violence. Or more directly related to the concerns of this article: the tendency to repeat the use of warlike metaphors in discussing various positions within the Israel-Palestine conflict. There indeed seems to be a tendency for interlocutors to adopt the same rhetorical stances as the actual disputants in the conflict, unwittingly repeating the very same problems they set out to discuss and solve. According to Dominick LaCapra, one can cope with the problem of transference either by engaging in greater empathic identification or by working through the very tendency one seeks to analyze and study.[27]

The potential for transference exists in the relationships professors develop with their graduate students and in the relationships psychoanalysts develop with their patients; these are situations within which a sufficient power differential exists, leading to the introduction of inappropriate feelings from the past into the present. In other words, we tend to repeatedly seek out the same kinds of relational dynamics in our personal and professional lives without realizing that we are inappropriately transporting the feelings and desires from another time and place into the present. So, we may transfer a libidinal investment or aggressive drive in a relationship from the past into the present, recognizing something in the formation of an opposing point of view that reminds us of that past relationship. So, a bad relationship with my father may emerge later in my life if I recognize a behavior of my father in someone else. This tendency to repeat my feelings of anger or resentment existing in the relationship with my father in a completely different context is a function of my not recognizing the source of my psychological pain.

The return of the past through the mention of a name or an event and the different memories that are evoked in the process of remembering those names and events represents a complex process of reconciling personal histories with events in the world. In other words, our libidinal investments (the ways our narcissistic identifications and attachments become mobilized) manifest themselves in the social field when we remember a controversial event or an individual associated with a controversial event. An analysis of libidinal attachments, then, requires us to suspend conceptions of justice and "right and wrong" and to concentrate on how individuals approach social antagonisms in the ways they do, noting how they create identifications with respect to social conflicts based on race, gender, ethnicity, religion, and class.

For example, I must continually interrogate why I find the Palestinian claims to justice in the conflict so compelling. Is it because I am, as an Indian-American man, a postcolonial subject? By this logic, I am committed to Palestinian liberation because of the history of European colonialism, which directly touched my ancestral heritage, although I am unaware that my commitment springs from this aspect of my identity. Naturally, there are limitations to this sort of identity-based psychoanalysis. Perhaps the sources I find compelling are written by people with my politics and are written within an intertextual chain that I understand. In other words, I agree with the conclusions of Israel's New Historians because they write about the conflict in ways that I have come to understand based on my anti-colonist perspective and politics. So, if the scholarship of Illan Pappe, Neve Gordon, Tom Segev, Avi Shlaim, and others is attractive to me, it is because these scholars' once-considered radical opinions, which have rendered a more accurate accounting of the historical events surrounding Israel's creation than previous historians, conform to international law and the international consensus for a just resolution of the Question of Palestine. This body of scholarship largely refutes the long-held belief that Israel fought a war for independence in 1948, prior to it being granted statehood by the UN, and that it is a weak, beleaguered nation fighting for its survival.

A wider view

One of the reasons the WPA discussion about the Rachel Corrie Courage in the Teaching of Writing Award went so awry is many participants seemed to have a fundamental misunderstanding of the balance of forces within the conflict. In addition to positioning Corrie as a martyr who had been seized upon by those seeking to score cheap political points against Israel, some participants seemed to genuinely believe that Israel is the weaker party in its struggle with the Palestinians, seemingly vulnerable because it is surrounded by Arab countries supposedly eager to see its destruction. If to memorialize Rachel Corrie as an example of the kind of courage worthy of emulation within the profession is to advance an anti-Israel politics, then Corrie is standing in as a sort of metonymic replacement for something called "anti-Israel activism," which is really tantamount to advancing Palestinian human rights. When Palestinians living under Israeli occupation exert agency, in framing and advancing their rights as part of an anti-colonial struggle under international law, Holocaust discourses often construct them as seeking to contest Israel's "right to exist," an abbreviated reference to Israel's "right" to exist as a state dedicated to preserving a Jewish majority, with the "as a state dedicated to preserving a Jewish majority" portion of this discursive construction almost always absent in the context of popular representations of the conflict.[28] However, for many, the preservation of a Jewish majority in Israel is particularly important in the wake of the Holocaust, even as Israel refuses to truly become a part of the Middle East, acting instead as an offshoot of Europe, "the portion of the rampart of Europe against, an outpost of civilization as opposed to barbarism."[29]

Israel, as the Jewish state, is a modern nation with one of the best militaries in the world, reserving the right to use its nuclear arsenal if threatened. Israel's determination to rid Iran of its nuclear arsenal, for example, is often framed by media pundits as a struggle to defend civilization against the maniacal aspirations of Mahmoud Ahmadinejad, who supposedly seeks to wipe Israel off the map of time. In fact, Israel has long feared Iran as a competitor because of its pretensions toward modernization and because of the challenge it might pose to Israeli regional hegemony. If one suggests that Israel has engaged in immoral or illegal conduct in its dealings with the Palestinians, due this affective dimension whereby to criticize Israel is to somehow criticize the Jewish people, one is likely to be constructed as issuing an indictment of Jews, even if one goes to great lengths to insist that this is not what one is doing.

Inevitably, interlocutors seem to draw comparisons between Jewish and Palestinian suffering, without realizing that these comparisons are not only inappropriate, but quite unnecessary. Herein resides the dilemma: the Israel-Palestine conflict brings together two distinct histories of oppression and suffering that are simply incompatible and incomparable, leading to easy conflations of memory—where both Hamas and Israeli settlers in the West Bank can be compared to either Nazis or freedom fighters, depending upon the point to be made. Hamas can be compared to the Nazis because as an organization it is dedicated to the destruction of Israel as a Jewish state; however, one cannot simply state that Hamas is driven to destroy Israel because of anti-Semitism. Instead, one must recognize that Hamas seeks

Israel's destruction because Israel is viewed as occupying and colonizing Palestinian land. The reason Palestinian resistance against Israeli occupation is often configured as anti-Semitic is that the occupiers of Palestinian land are Jewish. Just as American Indian resistance against European settlers in the New World could not be credibly framed as arising from "anti-Europeanism" or "anti-Whiteism," we should be equally skeptical of framing Palestinian resistance to Israeli domination as arising from anti-Semitism.[30] What allows for these easy conflations and transpositions?

A theme that consistently animates discussions of the Israel-Palestine conflict is that Israel is fighting a war for its very survival and that its fight against various Islamic enemies is simply a continuation of the Jewish fight against the Nazis, which if lost, will result in another holocaust against the Jewish people. Leaders as diverse as Yasser Arafat, Saddam Hussein, and Mahmoud Amadinejad have been compared to Hitler because of the supposed threat they pose(d) to Israel's existence.[31]

Israeli exceptionalism enables an abuse of history and historical memory and a general confusion about what constitutes a legitimate threat to Israel's existence.[32] What allows for this transfer between historical moments? Is it simply a matter of politics whereby Israel's defenders are trying to win a propaganda war, or is it a conflation of memory where the modern day "war on terrorism" is a continuation of the war for Jewish survival that was part of the Holocaust, the creation of Israel, etc.? With such an expansive sense of history and Jewish memory, which allows for the threat against Jewish survival to take the same general motivation in different forms across history, it only stands to reason that what will trigger a conflation of memory may be something as innocuous as raising the issue of Palestinian victimhood, or preserving the memory of a young college student who was attempting to defend a Palestinian home against demolition by an IDF bulldozer.[33] The faces of these victims are threats to the historical narrative about Jewish suffering, as they refute conceptions of Jewish victimization, while simultaneously suggesting that Jews can also be victimizers.

If to embrace Rachel Corrie as a heroine is to embrace a Palestinian politics, what does that politics look like exactly? Is it pro-terrorism and anti-Israel? The Exodus narrative about the creation of a Jewish state in the midst of a hostile Middle East has created an affective environment within which it difficult to be critical of Israeli military actions because of the victim status Jews have been assigned historically. Although this victim status disappeared long ago, it still plays a powerful affective role in shaping contemporary discussions about conflict in the Middle East. In insisting that that the victim status of Jews disappeared long ago, I am referencing the fact that Jewish prosperity and success in the Western world since World War II have been unmatched by any other ethno-religious group.[34]

As Marc Ellis explains in his *Judaism* ≠ Israel, "When Jews see themselves as cosmic actors on a universal stage, those who critique aspects of Jewish power find themselves in the Jewish existential drama" (19). Edward Said notes in his *After the Last Sky*, "There has been no misfortune worse for us than that we are ineluctably viewed as the enemies of the Jews. No moral and political fate worse, none at all, I think: no worse, there is none" (134). That the Palestinians have been necessarily positioned as somehow metaphysically opposed to Jews because of the Israel-Palestine conflict, instead of being viewed as engaging in a resistance struggle within a particular historical context, does serious damage to any deep understanding of the roots of the conflict. As scholars committed to understanding the specific circumstances informing rhetorical situations, we must be diligent in understanding how the easy conflation and transposition of the highly charged language from events in the past with/into the present can greatly hamper efforts to create the conditions of possibility for reconciliation and dialogue. Many constituencies are finding alternative ways to express their dissatisfaction with the dominant configurations governing understandings of the Israel-Palestine conflict.

In his *Out of the Ashes*, Ellis notes that a civil war has developed in the Jewish community between Jews of conscience—who refuse to forget how Israel's politics of occupation produces Palestinian suffering—and Jews who continue to turn a blind eye to what years of Israeli conquest have wrought upon the Palestinian community. Similarly, Avraham Burg in his *The Holocaust is Over, We Must Rise from its Ashes* states that "We, the Jewish Israelis, are the core of the world's Jewish superpower, and must act toward our enemies as a moral superpower: forcefully, uncompromisingly, and fearlessly" (158). In his *The Myths of Liberal Zionism*, Yitzhak Loar argues that Israel's use of Jewish suffering in the Holocaust to justify its territorial expansion and colonization of Palestinian land is reaching a crisis point, with many Jews walking away from what they see as the abuse of the past for political ends.

Many younger, progressive, American Jews, for example, are refusing the facile formulation that Israel's ongoing dispossession of the Palestinian population is about defense or securing the Jewish community against anti-Semitism. This abuse of memory and history has produced a level of cynicism within the Jewish diasporic community, as many younger Jews are refusing to become wholesale defenders of Israel's actions in the West Bank and its increased militarization.[35] This abuse of memory and history has produced a level of uncertainty within the diaspora, as many younger American Jews are resisting to reflexively defend Israel whenever its actions are publically criticized. For these reasons, organizations such as *J Street* are emerging as a political alternative to the American-Israel Public Affairs Committee (AIPAC), otherwise known as one of the major arms of the "Israel Lobby." *J Street* and other progressive organizations have realized that the perversion of the past in the service of a distinct politics—purposefully geared to conflate issues within the Israel-Palestine conflict such as anti-Semitism and Palestinian resistance—prevents meaningful dialogue. These progressive organizations understand that the Holocaust has been effectively employed as a weapon to advance a politics that relies upon a particular activation of the past to serve a distinct politics in the present, as my final example will demonstrate.

The Holocaust and the Israel-Palestine conflict

In January 1998, Yasser Arafat visited the United States as part of a US negotiated peace effort between Israel and the PLO at Camp David. Arafat expressed interest in visiting the Holocaust Museum in Washington D.C. as part of this visit. A great deal of controversy ensued as plans for the proposed visit went forward. Wilhelm Reich, director of the Museum, refused to extend Arafat the standard courtesies given to other world leaders and VIPs, arguing that Arafat's presence at the hallowed sight would be an affront to the memory of the dead. When the Clinton White House learned of Reich's resistance to Arafat's visit, it expressed its displeasure.

The Museum's Board of Directors became involved with deliberations over the visit, reversing Reich's initial decision, insisting that Arafat be allowed to view the Museum and afforded the same privileges during his visit as other world leaders might be. From the Board of Director's perspective, Arafat's visit could be used for public relations purposes: Arafat, as a Palestinian leader, through his very presence at the Museum would represent an open acknowledgment of Jewish suffering in the Holocaust, and by extension, an acknowledgment of the legitimacy of Israel's right to exist as a Jewish state.

The controversy around Arafat's visit was not simply a matter of logistics, it was a battle over political signification, as various factions debated what it would mean for the PLO leader to visit one of the most significant sites devoted to documenting Jewish suffering. The Board of Directors decided that having Arafat visit the museum would signal to the world that Arafat acknowledged the Holocaust as a legitimate event and expressed an interest in learning something about it. What would it mean for a Palestinian leader, in the context of Israeli-Palestinian peace talks, to visit the Holocaust Museum? It was undoubtedly an opportunity ripe for political manipulation as Zionist organization sought to characterize the visit as a Palestinian capitulation to Jewish history, but in actuality to Zionist history. Through his visit to the Holocaust Museum, Arafat would be acknowledging the centrality of the Holocaust for Jews, those Jews living in Israel as well as those in the diaspora. This acknowledgment would help to solidify Zionism's claim that the Holocaust is the event through which Israel gains its legitimacy as a protectorate against any threat to the existence of the Jewish people.

In arguing with Lerher that Arafat should have been allowed to visit the museum, Hyman Bookbinder claimed that "Whatever arguments can be made about not opening wide the welcome gates to an Arafat, they are overwhelmed by the central argument that the museum exists because of its potential—demonstrated over and over again—to move even the most skeptical" (Dorf and Kurtman). As Joseph Massad states in his *The Persistence of the Palestinian Question*, "The fact that neither Arafat nor the PLO had ever denied the Jewish holocaust and had always expressed solidarity with its victims was immaterial to such propaganda" (138). By visiting the museum, Arafat would seemingly be giving tacit endorsement to Zionism's wedding of Jewish and Zionist history and the manipulation of Jewish history to serve Israeli political aims. Once again, the past returned like a boomerang to influence the present, encircling the participants in an emotional drama involving events that have been molded for a specific emotional effect, subjecting all those who enter the scene to be sorted as either "good" or "evil."[36] Given the tendency to sort interlocutors within such discursive environments in this way, as a result of the affect-laden pull that is often at work, it is relatively easy to understand why Rachel Corrie's memory—like Arafat's presence at the Holocaust museum represented an anomaly to some constituencies—symbolized such a monumental threat to some list-serv participants. Instead of substantively engaging the significance of Corrie's actions, it was easier to scapegoat and diminish Corrie and what she supposedly represented, for example, anti-Semitism, anti-Israel activism, anti-Americanism, etc.

Similarly, John Mearsheimer and Stephen Walt faced abuse and vilification for exploring the power of the Israel Lobby in shaping discussion and perceptions about the Middle East in the United States. Mearsheimer and Walt's book *The Israel Lobby* goes to great lengths to make clear that the Israel Lobby does not involve a conspiracy and is not a shadow organization controlled by a Jewish cabal. Indeed, Mearsheimer and Walt insist that the Israel Lobby is the loose coalition of individuals and organizations that actively work to shape U.S. foreign policy in a pro-Israel direction that engages in old fashioned politics, highlighting that the most active elements of the Israel Lobby involve Christian Zionists and not only, or just, Jews.[37] Despite Walt and Mearsheimer's insistence that the Israel Lobby is anything but a conspiracy, Abe Foxman in his *The Most Dangerous Lies* and Alan Dershowitz, in his *The Case Against Israel's Enemies* invoke the anti-Semitic forgery, *The Protocols of the Elders of Zion*, suggesting that Walt and Mearsheimer traffic in anti-Semitic stereotypes in their descriptions of the Lobby's power.[38] Similar tendencies were seemingly at work in the language choices of some WPA list-serv participants, especially among those who insisted that the Corrie award was inherently anti-Semitic and anti-Israel.

In retrospect, what was so fascinating about the WPA discussion was the participants' complete avoidance of international law and the international consensus on a just resolution of the Question of Palestine. Only two participants briefly mentioned UN 242, UN 194, the Fourth Geneva Convention, etc. According to international law, Israel's occupation, by which I mean settlement expansion beyond the established 1967 Green Line, constitutes the major obstacle to a comprehensive peace agreement in the Middle East. President Jimmy Carter asserted as much in his book *Palestine: Peace Not Apartheid*, when he wrote that the major stumbling block to achieving peace in the Israel-Palestine conflict is Israel's unwillingness to comply with international law. It is almost as if the majority of the WPA participants were not aware of the international consensus or the relevant international law, indicating that "what justice would look like in the Middle East" is actually pretty straightforward from the standpoint of the international community, United Nations resolutions, and thousands of pages of human rights reports. Invocations of the region's "tortured history," "complex politics," and "terribly fraught and nuanced situations" are studious ways of avoiding how Israel's militarism and territorial expansionism play a key role in creating the conditions of possibility for "cycles of violence," resistance, and repression. Assertions that the Rachel Corrie Courage in the Teaching of Writing Award represents "a denial of nationalism," "an instance of ignoring history," "a specific case of propaganda," and an instance of "the rhetoric of martyrdom" are clearly diversionary techniques employed to prevent a substantive discussion of the historical and diplomatic record enveloping the conflict. Those participants to the WPA discussion who responded to the call for nominations for the Rachel Corrie award in May 2006 with, "I'm uncomfortable with the anti-Israel rhetoric that seems to be beneath it," were seeking to protect their own knowledge claims about the conflict: I am uncomfortable; therefore, what is making me uncomfortable must be inappropriate. If to state that "Israel is in violation of international law" is beyond the pale, reflecting that one harbors anti-Semites animus, then it is completely understandable why public figures such as Jimmy Carter and Desmond Tutu are so often accused of engaging in anti-Israel rhetoric. This tendency to condemn criticism and critics of Israeli policy as anti-Semites enforces a type of political correctness at the cost of refusing to promote greater understanding about the conditions producing conflict in the Israel-Palestine conflict.

As critical intellectuals, we must make public interventions into debates about the Israel-Palestine conflict. Events such as the ones I have described in this article are relatively representative of the kinds of opportunities that are available to those seeking to identify and clarify the psychological forces and energies infusing the rhetorical situations surrounding these debates. The abuse of history and historical memory in the service of a politics does not enable productive dialogue, but instead creates affective environments that disable the potential for experimentation, risk-taking, and exchange. In such an environment, participants are particularly susceptible to the kinds of inappropriate transfers of the past into the present that I have examined. If we refuse to engage the relevant issues with respect to the Israel-Palestine conflict, particularly when these issues are directly part of our professional conversation (as the discussion of the Rachel Corrie Courage in the Teaching of Writing Award clearly was), then we cede the discursive field to the past, without considering the demands for political and rhetorical action in the present. Indeed, as one participant aptly noted toward the end of the controversy, in an attempt to explain the surprising level of passion and vitriol that had been expressed in a seeming moment of communal division,

> We're revealed as less unified than we might imagine and that we would find comfortable. It's the revelation that what seems "obvious" to us isn't so to others—most significantly, those others we imagined to be so like us. It may be the kind of shock (even betrayal) that I felt when students were no longer like me, that what I thought we shared had sobering limits. I knew I'd have to work harder, but I think I got smarter then, too.

Dealing with such divisions in our professional communities, when we are hit with the realization that we are not as unified as we previously believed ourselves to be, forces a reevaluation of our most sacred and entrenched belief systems. Such moments should be viewed as opportunities for persuasion, rhetorical action, and material interventions.

Postscript

In a report dated 24 March 2008, a Task Force headed by Paul Puccio, and charged by then CCC's chair Cheryl Glenn, offered guidelines to distance the CCCCs from the SIGs (special-interest groups). According to the report, "CCCC respects the right of self-organizing groups to act as their members deem appropriate, as long as those actions are clearly represented as the group's and not, for example, as an aspect of CCCC." Furthermore, the Task Force offered the following policy recommendations:

1   Any award conferred by a SIG or Caucus must include the following disclaimer: "This Award is not sanctioned by CCCC. It represents the sole judgement of the independent group conferring it and does not reflect the opinions or honors of CCCC." SIGs and Caucuses should communicate to award recipients that they must represent the award in any document or venue as SIG/Caucus-based and not as a "CCCC Award." This should be seen by SIGs and Caucuses as an opportunity for proudly claiming their own field of inquiry and practice—as well as authoring their own endorsements and appreciation for accomplishments in those fields.

2   Should such an award be so misrepresented as a "CCCC Award," we propose that the SIG, Caucus, or award recipient responsible for the misrepresentation be approached by the Executive Committee in a

collegial manner and asked to amend the misinformation to the best of his or her ability.

We discussed at some length the thorny issue of consequences for a SIG, Caucus, or individual that does not comply with this policy. Some members of our group favor particular sanctions to be levied against such groups or individuals, while others believe that enforcing this policy would be logistically difficult for the officers or members of the Executive Committee in any case. It was proposed that perhaps CCCC assign a compliance officer to be responsible for the enforcement of this policy; Ira Shor volunteered to serve in that capacity, should the organization pursue this option.

Everyone on the Task Force agreed that it is important for the organization to communicate these policies to all SIG/Caucus representatives annually.

3   Perhaps the Task Force's most arduous discussion revolved around the issue of announcements, calls, and notices regarding SIG and Caucus Awards in CCC. The Task Force could not arrive at a consensus. Some members strongly affirm that SIGs and Caucuses in good standing have a right to access in CCC. Others do not believe that a journal editor should be mandated regarding announcements—especially when announcements, more generally, are at the discretion of the editor because of space constraints. It was also observed that an announcement in CCC can be (mis)read as an indication that an Award is sanctioned by the organization when, in fact, it is a SIG or Caucus Award.

All of these recommendations and issues require further deliberation. Several members of the Task Force wished for a clearer statement of context for the charge of the Task Force; they strongly felt that the exigency for this charge was not explicit enough. Most particularly, they resist opening the door to punitive policy changes in the absence of particular exigencies.

It is difficult not to view the controversy around the Rachel Corrie Courage in the Teaching of Writing on the WPA list in May 2006 as having provided the exigence for the creation of this Task Force and the resulting recommendations. However, no one on the Task Force—in an official capacity—would acknowledge such an exigence.

CHAPTER EIGHT

The perils of separation: Fouzi El-Asmar's *To Be an Arab in Israel* as an allegory of settler-colonial anxiety

I sit in preventive detention.
The reason, see, is that I am an Arab.
An Arab who has refused to sell his soul
who has always striven, sir, for freedom.
An Arab who has protested at the suffering
of his people
Who has carried with him the hope
of a just peace,
Who has spoken out against death
at every corner
Who has called for and has lived
a life of brotherhood.
That is why I sit in preventive detention
Because I carried on the struggle
And because I am an Arab

(FOUZI EL-ASMAR, "Because I Am an Arab")

This chapter seeks to examine the struggles of a Palestinian intellectual, who while living in Israel, resisted attempts to silence his political speech about the Israel-Palestine conflict. The suppression of Fouzi El-Asmar's critical speech about the plight of Israel's Palestinian population indicates that El-Asmar's moderation and keen analytical skills—in dissecting the tacit racist contempt held against Arabs in Israel—in fact constituted threats to Israel's state authorities. El-Asmar's story is worth telling in a book devoted to academic and intellectual freedom precisely because of the key role played by some American intellectuals, who are committed to controlling and blocking critical discussion about the conflict, to marginalize El-Asmar's story and to label El-Asmar as a "terrorist."

Fouzi El-Asmar lived as a Palestinian Arab in Israel for the first 35 years of his life. His poetry, including the lines that form the epigraph of this essay, captures the existential predicament of this condition: Can one "be" an Arab in Israel if one refuses to sell or accede one's soul to the state authorities or protests the suffering of one's people, who live under the oppression of a state that claims to speak for the protection of the Jewish people everywhere and for all time? To be an Arab Israeli, then, is to face a choice imposed by the founding conditions of the state within which one lives as a resident alien—a choice between resistance and submission, between capitulation to the logic of Zionism, which brings with it an automatic admission of one's inferiority as an Arab, or an embrace of Palestinian nationalism that pits one against the national aspirations of the Jewish people. Indeed, the logic of Zionism requires either that the Palestinian citizen of Israel submit—as a third-class citizen—to the Jewish state or face the possibility of being deemed an enemy of the state, with the prospect of transfer to the occupied territories.[1]

There can be no "refusal to choose" in the case of the Palestinian citizen of Israel between these two conditions because such a refusal would constitute a veritable renunciation of any and all identity—an impossibility for such a marked Other within Israel.[2] In other words, the Israeli Arab must become either a Palestinian quisling living in Israel—with the possibility of enjoying some of the benefits of citizenship—or lead a more difficult existence as a subversive and potentially insurgent force living within the Jewish state; there is no "middle way." The activation of the subversive insurgent, the potential terrorist who will strike a blow for his brethren against Israeli occupation, is what the Israeli state guards vigilantly against and inevitably prepares for. With each Israeli Defense Force incursion into Gaza, attempts to crush Hamas's and Al Fatah's displays of resistance, the probability of this activation increases. Securing and checking the loyalties of Israel's Palestinian Arab citizens is the state's paramount concern.[3]

To Be an Arab in Israel tells the story of an El-Asmar's efforts within the Israeli peace movement as he worked with progressive anti-Zionist Jews to address the predicament of Israeli Arabs in their struggle to attain civil protections against discrimination in housing and employment and the specific conditions El-Asmar faced within the Israeli prison, Damon, near

Haifa. Considered a political moderate, El-Asmar was placed in administrative detention because of his political activism against Israeli apartheid. Ironically, Palestinian activism in support of political moderation is considered a threat to the portrait of the fanatical and violent Arab, a portrait that is important for Israel's US supporters to uphold.[4] If politically moderate Palestinians within Israel were to be given a wide hearing in the international press, particularly as they struggle with the assistance of progressive Israeli Jews against Zionism's erasure of their existence, it would disturb the notion that the Palestinian population of Israel is committed to undermining Israel's existence, or its "right to exist" with a legally mandated Jewish majority. To be a Palestinian Arab in Israel at this historical moment is to represent an intractable problem for the demography and long-term "security" of the Jewish state, and a painful reminder of how the founding conditions of Israeli society were built upon the Palestinian Arab's exclusion, transfer, or vulnerable location within an apartheid state. The Palestinian Arab in Israel lives in the shadow of the destruction of Palestinian civil society, which Israel's settler-colonial violence unleashed, and in the aftermath of the Holocaust and the rise of militant Zionism.

In Israel, Jewish suffering provides the framework through which one can understand the history of the state. Fouzi El-Asmar, as a Palestinian Arab who lived in Israel, found that he could not "be" in Israel because his very being posed a threat to the security of the state. As Alan Dershowitz wrote in his 1970 *Commentary* piece, entitled "Terrorism and Preventive Detention: The Case of Israel," "I am personally convinced that . . . Fawzi al-Asmar is the leader of a terrorist group."[5] Dershowitz traveled to Israel's Damon prison to interview El-Asmar for his article in *Commentary*, concluding that Israel's decision to place El-Asmar in preventive decision was the correct one because of El-Asmar's connections to terrorist groups determined to commit acts of violence against Israeli citizens. Much of the evidence Dershowitz cited in his article was rebutted by the great human rights advocate, Israel Shahak, who wrote:

> In spite of what Mr. Dershowitz claims, the main purpose of preventive detention is political and has no conceivable connection with any acts of terrorism. To cite just one example: before the last Israeli elections, about 1,200 Arabs were put into preventive detention for periods of four to six weeks and were freed immediately after the election.[6]

That Israeli Arabs would have to be jailed for the duration of an election underlines the specific problems these politically active Arabs pose to Israeli democracy.

How can a Palestinian Arab "be" in Israel when the state's founding is presupposed on the Palestinian Arab's negation, submission, and suppression, in accordance with Zionist doctrine? To be an Arab in Israel is to live with the prospect of expulsion, or redefinition, depending upon the political conditions obtaining at any one moment, where a crisis could lead one to being labeled an "enemy of the state," although one is an Israeli citizen and has perhaps lived in Israel long before there even was an Israel. To be an Arab in Israel is to be viewed as a cancer on the larger Israeli body politic, a remnant of Israel's settler-colonial beginnings and its apartheid presence, the last vestige of a decimated people on the verge of politicide.[7] El-Asmar recounts the murder of forty-nine Palestinians from Kafr Qasim at the hands of Jewish forces in 1967:

> For me it was a turning point in my political development. I spent much time talking about the incident to my friends, who were also greatly affected in varying degrees. We asked ourselves, "What will happen next? When will our turn come? What had these poor workers done?" We dwelt on these and a thousand other questions. From these unanswerable questions, I arrived at the conclusion that in all truth the massacre had been perpetrated simply because these people were Arabs, despite the fact that Arabs in Israel had kept the peace since the creation of the State.[8]

To be an Arab in Israel, then, is to live in a state of suspended animation—a perpetual reminder of how Israeli statesmen such as Yitzhak Rabin, Moshe Dayan, and Ariel Sharon participated in the wholesale expulsion and ethnic cleansing of thousands of Palestinians from villages such as Deir Yassin, Rammla, and Lydda in 1948. Indeed, to be an Arab in Israel is to be a problem. What does it mean to be this problem, at this moment, in Israel? What does it mean that one—as an Arab living in Israel—represents an existential threat to Israel's existence by virtue of one's capacity to reproduce, and that this capacity poses a demographic danger to Israel's future as a Jewish exclusivist state? To be this problem, as an Arab in Israel, warrants extended analysis and reflection. Although W. E. B. Dubois defined the problem of the twentieth century as the problem of the color line, we can proffer that the problem of the twenty-first will be problem of the Arab in his relation to Israel. What does it mean to be this problem, to live in this precarious condition, and to pose such daunting prospects for Israel's future as a Jewish state?

Ironically, the Palestinian Arab may very well be the antidote that will cure Israel's pathological drive toward becoming a Jewish apartheid state—a drive which may sow the seeds for the entire region's destruction.[9] By insisting upon its right to exist as a racist state dedicated to maintaining a Jewish majority at all costs, rather than the state of its citizens, Israel will continue to face innumerable internal and external threats, threats that seek to deter Israel from continuing to serve as a Western imperial bridgehead in the region, rather than a democracy among all the nations of the Middle East. As part of this pathological drive to destruction, consider Zionism's redemption of the land (Eretz Yisreal) through theft, confiscation, and state terror. As Jonathan Cook notes, "Today, the battle for the land is largely finished: 93 percent of the territory inside Israel is effectively nationalized, held on behalf of Israeli Jews and in trust for the Jewish people around the world rather than for all the country's citizens."[10]

The perils of separation

As El-Asmar's *To Be an Arab in Israel* suggests, separating Jews from Arabs in Israel and throughout historical Palestine has been a deliberate ethno-religious separation, but more importantly it is a civilizational separation between East and West. The Arab represents the spectral other of the West, a reminder of the colonial domination of the Middle East. In this context, the Palestinian Arab living within Israel represents a particular problem for a specific form of Israeli domination. Labor and Likudnik Party calls to transfer the Palestinians living within Israel to the West Bank represent a long-recognized strain of Zionist thinking—containing the Palestinian struggle for liberation requires separating these Arabs from the Israeli territory; they are a reminder that Israeli domination of the Palestinian Other is not complete.[11] Citing a Jaffee Institute Study from 2002, Laurence Louer writes in her *To Be an Arab in Israel*, "In March 2003 31 percent of Israeli Jews said they favoured enforced transfer, while 60 percent endorsed the idea of a less explicit transfer policy, in the shape of incentives to leave the country."[12]

Many Jewish Israelis question the loyalty of Israeli Arabs, believing they will always favor the nationalist aspirations of their people living under occupation in the West Bank and in "the largest open-air prison" on the Gaza Strip. To be an Arab in Israel, then, means living as a perceived traitor of the nation, a latent threat to national security, and a vehicle for the promotion of Arab nationalism. Whether the Arab in Israel will become an active threat will not be determined by his actions but by extrajudicial considerations and by states of exception, to which no rule—not even the rule of international law—appears to apply.

Israel's occupation of the West Bank is illegal according to the Fourth Geneva Convention (which prevents an occupying power from transferring its population into occupied territory) and UN Security Council Resolution 242 (which requires Israel to pull back to the 1967 Green Line, relinquishing its control over the Palestinian West Bank); Gaza, after "disengagement," is perhaps an even greater human catastrophe than it was before Israel's occupation "ended" with 1.5 million inhabitants experiencing near complete social and economic suffocation; the nearly four hundred thousand settlers in the West Bank and around East Jerusalem stand in direct violation of international law; Israeli settlement blocks on the West Bank (Ariel, Maale Adumim, Beitar Illit, and Modin Illit) have been expanding during and after "disengagement" and are cutting off East Jerusalem from the rest of the West Bank. Sara Roy claims "Whatever else it claims to be, the Gaza Disengagement Plan is, at heart, an instrument for Israel's continued annexation of West Bank land and the physical integration of that land into Israel."[13]

According to Zionist thinking, as Yosef Gorny powerfully demonstrates in his *Zionism and the Arabs, 1882-1948: A Study of Ideology*, the Palestinian-Arab population has long posed the main obstacle to the creation and maintenance of an exclusively Jewish state. As Yehoshua Porath points out in his two-volume work on Palestinian nationalism and as Benny Morris has confirmed in his inexhaustible *The Birth of the Palestinian Refugee Problem Revisited*, Palestinian resistance to Zionist conquest arose out of a fear of territorial displacement and not, as is frequently assumed and rhetorically insisted, because of Arab anti-Semitism.[14]

Historical and philosophical foundations

In his *The Jewish State* and *Old, New Land* (*Alteneuland*), Theodore Herzl recognized that the Zionist movement could only transform Jews into European Christians outside of Europe, in Asia—"a rampart against the Arab hordes," whereby industry and hard work European Jews could create a new Europe in Asia. To effect this *transformation*, it would be necessary to take the "Jew" out of these European Jews, who were marked by weakness in Europe, and to make them stronger, that is, New Europeans. Just as importantly, the Palestinians through the European Jews' transformation who would be *judaized*, becoming the new Jews.[15]

It is often believed that the Holocaust provided the moral justification for the creation of Israel as a refuge for Jewish survivors of Hitler's Extermination Plan and that most of the world supported Israel's creation out of guilt for not having done more during the war. In fact, the Holocaust was "abducted" by Zionism to ensure that Jewish history, Zionist history, and Israeli history would become one. By this I mean that Zionism, which was a form of European nationalism, became "Jewish nationalism" through Zionism's mediation of the Holocaust for the Jewish displaced persons, who would be denied immigration to anywhere but Palestine, and the Palestinian Arabs, who would eventually be dispossessed. The Zionization of the Holocaust, then, links Zionist and Israeli history.

As Israel destroys the future of the Palestinian people through various forms of judicial and extrajudicial terror, it also destroys the future of Jews within Israel and without, since it only increases the likelihood that the continued perpetuation of cycles of violence that will inevitably be directed against its own citizens. As the existence of the Palestinians living under Israeli occupation hangs in the balance, the fate of Israel's Jews does as well.[16] The complete biopolitical destruction of Palestine will bring with it the destruction of the basis for Jewish ethics, since—according to Zionism's deal—Israel and Judaism have become one.[17] Through this rhetorical maneuver, Zionism seeks immunity for Israel's immoral and illegal behavior by trading on the historical crimes that have been committed against European Jews. This maneuver has been accepted by the Western world and is rarely questioned. As a projection of the Jewish Other, the Israeli Palestinian—as well as the Palestinian living under occupation—represents a trace of the Jewish past that Israel has sought to suppress. Even supposedly liberal elements of Israeli society are unable to assist the Palestinian in his struggle against erasure, such as relegating the murder of forty-nine Palestinian villages at Kafr Qasim to Orwell's memory hole. As El-Asmar writes:

> I also saw that many Jewish circles in Israel did not protest against what had happened [at Kafr Qasim], and even the writers' union and liberal intellectuals were afraid to do so. All of the political parties, except the Communist Party, reacted to the shock of the murders with silence. It was impossible that such an occurrence should not have been important to them. The greatest effect on me was that it demonstrated yet again that the Arabs did not have equal rights with the rest of the citizens of Israel, and that for a long time to come the Arabs would remain second-class citizens.[18]

The tolerance within Israel of this subordinate status for its Arabs is reminiscent of the dhimmi status accorded many Jews, throughout history, in Muslim countries under Sharia law.

It is often said that Palestinians have been forced to endure the burden of a European crime against the Jewish people. In fact, the Palestinians were viewed as most non-whites throughout the world at the time of the UN partition, that is, insignificant and not worthy of consultation or respect. In other words, no real consideration of the Palestinian sentiment toward Zionist colonization, through Jewish immigration, was registered since the Palestinians were non-Europeans. By wedding Jewish history and Zionist history through the Holocaust, which provides the moral justification for the creation of Israel as a settler-colonial Jewish supremacist state, Zionism conflates Judaism, Zionism, and Israel.

The making of a settler colony

It is one of the tragic ironies of history that Israel's settler-colonial project has done to another people, the Palestinians, what Hitler's *Lebensraum* project sought to do to the Jews: to use separation, expulsion, ethnic cleansing, legal barriers, illegal land appropriation, imprisonment, settlements, and state terror to erase the existence of a people, whose very being represents a metastasis on the Israeli body politic. Those Palestinians in the West Bank, numbering more than 1.5 million, are viral bodies that have to be held at bay, outside the colony if you will. The activation of these viral bodies poses a real threat to Israel's existence as a Jewish racist state—a state with a legally mandated Jewish majority. This majority ensures that Israel will never be a state of its citizens but always the state of, and only for, the Jewish people. Regardless of where these Jews may live, and even if these diaspora Jews have no connection to Israel and object to Israel speaking in their name, Israel will claim to represent them.

Israel's capacity to speak for those Jews—living and dead—who may want nothing to do with Israel's politics of expulsion, terror, and ethnocide, as well as for those Palestinians inside it and just beyond its borders, represents a raw form of discursive power—the power to name, categorize, seize, expel, and memorialize depending upon the state's specific propaganda needs. Resuscitating the memory of dead European Jews, who faced extermination as Hitler sought to make Germany *judenrein*, to justify a politics of expulsion and denial against living Palestinians constitutes a perverse chapter of Zionist history. Containing these living and growing viral Palestinian bodies, before they extend and grow beyond the state's capacity to control them, is the most proximate reason for Israel's commitment to the politicide of the Palestinians within and outside of Israel.

It is these viral bodies, Palestinians living under occupation—whose activation Israel must continually prepare for, particularly in the event that these Palestinians make common cause with those Palestinians who live in Israel—who must be held at bay by any and all means possible. Various antibodies, antidotes to this viral threat if you will, take shape in various pieces of legislation that define the Arab Palestinian as less than human or prohibit a Palestinian Arab (who is an Israeli citizen) from bringing her or his spouse to Israel, if that spouse is a inhabitant of the West Bank; separation walls that divide Jews from Arabs; border checkpoints that remind Palestinians of their "status"; and targeted assassinations that remove those Palestinian leaders who have the temerity to challenge Zionism's supremacist logic.[19]

From the massacre of Palestinian civilians at the Sabra and Shatila refugee camp in 1982—done with the proxy aid of Lebanese Maronite Christians—to Israel's July 2006 bombing of Lebanon's infrastructure, the prospect of the Palestinians activating the Israeli immune system often brings with it extremes of violence.[20] The activation of this immune systems triggers a whole host of reactions, reactions framed as "Palestinian terror" and "Israeli counter-terror," where Arab lives are infinitely expendable and Israeli Jewish lives are wholly sacrosanct. What intense surveillance, 100-kilometer walls, frequent checkpoints, incessant border checks, and illegal expulsions do not accomplish, the science of demographics seeks to. Indeed, there is a growing unease in Israel that the Palestinians Arabs—who comprises just over 20 percent of the Israeli population—will reproduce too quickly, overwhelm the Jewish majority, and threaten the Jewish fabric of the nation.[21] If that happens, the fear is that the rhetoric of democracy will have to be taken seriously, and the Palestinian Arabs will subvert the structure of Zionist supremacy upon which the state is built, exposing the hypocrisy of the Ashkenazi elite that has fattened itself on cheap Arab labor.

This Ashkenazi elite of Israel is threatened politically not only by the Palestinian Arabs, but also by the Oriental Jews, who—although they sometimes make their way into the inner corridors of power—are frequently viewed as "suspect" by ruling elites, as Menachem Begin was when he was elected (as a man of the people) in 1977. The Zionist commitment to upholding a form of Jewish apartheid, with its longing for the recreation of a little Europe in Asia, situates the Ashkenazi ruling elites to lord it over much of the working class in Israel, comprised mainly of Sephardic Jews, who often view themselves as being unseen and disrespected by the Ashkenazi. As Chomsky points in his *The Fateful Triangle: The United States, Israel, and the Palestinians*, "These segments of the population had long regarded the Labor Party and its institutions as an oppressive bureaucracy, representing management and the hated kibbutzim, often islands of wealth and luxury alongside of development towns—notorious for their lack of development— for the Oriental Jews, many of whom serve as the labor force for kibbutz industry."[22] Ashkenazi superiority, which has been present since the state's founding, has its basis in European settler colonialism, which infused the outlooks of Theodore Herzl, Chaim Weizmann, and Golda Meir, all of whom simply denied the existence of the Palestinians, while considering Oriental Jews to be inferiors within an Israeli racial state. By this logic, Ashkenazi Jews, as European-derived Jews and as racially superior beings, should be Israel's statesmen, decision makers, and comprise the ruling class.[23]

The ideology informing the perspective that the Ashkenazi Jew is the original and superior Jew requires the building and maintenance of discursive barriers to separate "lower" Jews from "higher" Jews—just as real barriers must be constructed to separate the Palestinian from all of Israel's Jews. This "supremacist" logic and the perils of separation attending it, however, threaten Israel's survival as it struggles to deal with what Avner Yaniv calls its "dilemmas of security"[24]—by creating a labor system based on ethnic separation and hierarchy that creates intense dissension within its own body politic while also dealing with multiple security threats arising out of its illegal military occupation in the West Bank and its ongoing war with Hamas in Gaza and Hezbollah in South Lebanon, Israel essentially exists as a garrison state controlled by the whims of its top military leaders.[25] It has long been clear that Israel is not a state with an army, but an army with a state, as military correspondent Ben Kaspit once put it.[26] Israel is isolated in the court of world opinion, with its patron, the United States giving it military support at bargain rates, often providing the US government with the necessary battlefield conditions for testing experimental high-tech weaponry on helpless Palestinian and Lebanese civilians.[27]

Consequences of Israel's quest for regional supremacy

A million and a half Gaza Palestinians are said to be no longer living under occupation, due to Israel's attempts to work toward reconciliation and peace through the removal of five thousand Israeli settlers in the spring and summer of 2005. While the evacuation of Gaza's Israeli settlers in actuality translated into the expansion of West Bank settlements, the US media interpreted the evacuation as yet another sign of Israel's commitment to brokering a good-faith peace agreement with the intransigent Palestinians, yet another testament to the subservience of Western intellectuals to Zionism's narrative.[28]

Israel's apologists often argue that—since Israel is surrounded by twenty-two Arab nations—the Palestinians should simply relocate to an adjacent "Arab country," suggesting that all Arabs are essentially the same in terms of cultural orientation and political commitments, an indication of the deeply racist premises guiding much US media discourse about the Israel-Palestine conflict. As Noam Chomsky wrote, in response to the Baker-Peres plan of 1989, which argued that the Palestinians do not need their own state because a Palestinian state already exists in Jordan: "We might ask how [the world] would react to an Arab claim that the Jews do not merit a 'second homeland' because they already have New York, with a huge Jewish population, Jewish-run media, a Jewish mayor, and domination of cultural and economic life."[29] US and Israeli peace efforts, which if accurately described would be labeled "attempts to subvert peace," have treated the Palestinians as itinerant Arabs who can and should be transplanted to any part of the Arab world for the sake of peace.[30] From Oslo to Camp David, the Palestinians have been forced to renounce their claims of territorial dispossession while acknowledging Israel's "right to exist" as a Jewish apartheid state, a tacit admission of the legitimacy of Palestinian dispossession at Israel's hands in 1948 and 1967.[31]

Refusing Zionism's logic

Those who refuse to recognize Israel in this way are forced to deny the Holocaust, or at least its relation to Israel, since not all Arabs are able to refuse Zionism's logic. The only option for them is to deny the Holocaust, that is, since Zionism's logic demands that it is through the Holocaust that Zionist history and Jewish history become one in the form of Israeli history, the natural tendency for these Arab "deniers" is to not recognize the Holocaust as a legitimate event; these Arab deniers of the Holocaust, in Joseph Massad's thinking, are Zionists because the only way for them to reject Zionism's claim that Jewish suffering in the Holocaust grants Israel license to oppress and dispossess the Palestinians is to deny that the Holocaust ever happened.[32] This Arab "Holocaust denial," however, buys wholesale into the implicit Zionist claim that the Holocaust—if one accepts it as an actual event—provides adequate justification for Israel's statehood, Israel's occupation of Palestinian land, and Israel's 60-year long violation of Palestinian human rights. Clearly, the Holocaust's occurrence does not—as a moral matter—allow Israel to humiliate and oppress another people. It is this tenet of Zionist logic, rather than the Holocaust, that these Arab deniers should question.

Only by delinking Zionism from Judaism, by separating Zionist and Jewish history, can—as many Palestinian intellectuals and the PLO have done for several years—not only admit the Holocaust but revere the Holocaust survivors, such as those who fought heroically in the Warsaw Uprising, as heroes. This is precisely the reason why the PLO and Palestinian intellectuals do not refer to Israel as the Jewish state but instead as "the Zionist entity." [33]

Orientalism and the real "New Anti-Semitism"

Is Israel's goal to make the occupied territories "Palästinenser-rein" or Palestinian-free? It seems that once one asks this question, other more perplexing questions—that are equally confusing—develop. Recognizing that anti-Semitism and Orientalism are, historically speaking, "secret sharers" is the key to understanding the dynamics of the Israel-Palestine conflict. In other words, if anti-Semitism—in the form of Orientalism— has transformed the Arab Palestinian into the New Jews, we can perhaps reframe the Israel-Palestine conflict by exposing the mechanisms of these Other-creating discourses.[34] For example, one cannot help but notice the profound and tragic similarities between the discourses of the War on Terror, which represents the Palestinian Arab as a two-legged beast, lecherous, untrustworthy, sneaky, and vile, has a historical analog in one-time European representations of Jews. During the British mandate, men who would one day become Israeli prime ministers—Menachem Begin and Shimon Peres, for example—were wanted as "Jewish terrorists" for engaging in acts of terror against British forces.[35] These historical precedents are important for understanding how representations of a despised group can seize a national imagination.[36]

What is lost in all the purported fierce vigilance to protect Jews from anti-Semitism is the fact that Palestinian Arabs have moved into the subject position once occupied by European Jewish refugees. It is the Palestinians who flee state-sanctioned violence, face constant threats of expulsion, dispossession, and ethnic cleansing. They are the new vulnerables, a testament to the fact that anti-Semitism and Orientalism are closely intertwined.

The very descriptors that were so viciously applied to European Jews throughout Europe in the 1930s and 1940s are quite regularly applied to Arabs, who are framed as terrorists in possession of weapons of mass destruction seeking to destroy Judeo-Christian civilization.[37] That Western media discourses have so readily imbibed these tropes, most recently as part of the War on Terror, to describe Arab peoples throughout the Middle East, should alert one to the fact that it is the Arab, as the new Jew, who is the target of the New Anti-Semitism, and not—as the ADL would have us believe—Jews living in the United States and Europe. In his *Never Again?*, Abe Foxman maintains that "[t]he Jewish people face a threat equal to, if not greater than, the threat they faced in 1933."[38] In fact, Arab peoples face a threat equal to, if not greater than, what European Jews faced in 1933. To counteract this realization, a whole series of discursive sign posts have developed to deter people from comprehending the reality and gravity of the situation. Those who do comprehend it and warn of the dangers ahead face extremes of abuse and vilification.

Calling Israeli apartheid "apartheid"

Former President Carter's use of the word "apartheid" in the title of his book *Palestine: Peace Not Apartheid* racialized the Israel-Palestine conflict in a way most US citizens were wholly unfamiliar. Carter's comparison of the Palestinians living under occupation with the South African blacks in their struggle against the white colonial regime created a new paradigm for American understandings of the conflict. While Carter has claimed the Israel-Palestine conflict does not revolve around racial difference, but rather around religion and land, it is important to demonstrate how Carter's book has helped to highlight an unrecognized racial component of the conflict through his apartheid analogy. In listing and considering the unsavory ways the Israeli government might cope with the Palestinian Question, Carter highlights the problematic apartheid option in the following:

> A system of apartheid, with two peoples occupying the same land but completely separated from each other, with Israelis totally dominant and suppressing violence by depriving Palestinians of their basic human rights. This is the policy now being followed, although many Israeli citizens of Israel deride the racist connotation of prescribing permanent second-class status for the Palestinians.[39]

It should be noted that Carter, with this description of the second-class citizens of Palestinians, is referring to the Palestinians living under occupation, not to Israel's Palestinian Arabs. In fact, Carter would not admit that a system of apartheid exists *within* Israel, acknowledging that Israel's Palestinian citizens are—in theory—allowed to vote and hold public office.

The public outcry against Carter, in response to his drawing a comparison between Palestinian Arabs living under Israeli occupation and South African blacks living under the Verwoerd, Vorster, and Botha regimes, which extended throughout the inner corridors of power in Washington, is quite telling on a number of different levels: (1) This is the first time any president, either in office or out, has taken such a visible and strong public stand on the conflict; (2) Organizations such as the Zionist Organization of America, the American Jewish Committee, and the Anti-Defamation League have furiously attacked Carter (the one US President who has done the most to assure Israel's security) since the book's publication, highlighting the fact that no US citizen—even the Nobel Prize-winning Jimmy Carter—can speak out against the Israeli government's criminal policies without facing a deafening chorus of allegations that one is an "anti-Semite," a racist, or some sort of bigot; this issue is, as Edward Said argued toward the end of his battle with leukemia, the last remaining taboo in American life[40]; (3) The reaction of the Democratic Party, which has distanced itself from Carter, tells one a lot about how US political elites will avoid being even remotely connected to anyone who shows even the slightest critical interest in addressing the issue of Israel's oppression of the Palestinians.

In numerous interviews and commentary pieces about his book, Carter has claimed that he used the word "apartheid" in the title to be provocative, initiate a debate, and facilitate a much-needed discussion about what is openly discussed in Israel and the rest of the world: Israel's continued seizure of Palestinian land in the West Bank with tacit US support, which—rightly or wrongly—the Arab world uses a continued political grievance against the United States.[41] As he writes, "The bottom line is this: Peace will come to Israel and the Middle East only when the Israeli government is willing to comply with international law, with the Roadmap for Peace, with official American policy, with the wishes of the majority of its citizens—and honor its own previous commitments—by accepting its own legal borders."[42] Why, Carter seems to ask, is there a veritable taboo on discussion of such issues in the United States? To compare the Palestinians struggle against Israeli occupation to the black South African struggle against white colonials creates an "epistemological vertigo" for American understandings of the conflict. Given that American understandings of Israel's founding do not normally extend beyond Leon Uris's *Exodus*—filled with heroic resisters—it is unsurprising that so many different political forces have coalesced to denounce and silence Jimmy Carter.

While there is plenty of evidence in such personal testimonies as Fouzi El-Asmar's *To Be an Arab in Israel* and Rafik Halbi's *The Westbank Story*, as well as in scholarly treatments such as David Kretzmer's *The Legal Status of Arabs in Israel*, Elia Zureik's *The Palestinians in Israel*, and Sabri Jiryis *The Arabs in Israel*, that Israel practices apartheid—with Palestinian Arabs treated as distinct third-class citizens—Carter maintains that Israel is a democracy.[43]

In reality, Carter's *Palestine: Peace Not Apartheid* is not critical enough of the United States and Israel's 30-year commitment to preventing a comprehensive diplomatic settlement in the Middle East. For those enclosed within the US media bubble, this statement sounds as if it's from Pluto, where we are reminded that Palestinian rejectionism of Israel's right to exist, and the absence of a Palestinian peace partner, are what stands in the way of Middle East peace. As usual, image and reality have been reversed. The Israeli government has never sought peace with its Arab neighbors; in fact, with key US diplomatic and military cover, it has done everything to subvert a cessation of hostilities—that this insight has been effectively concealed from elite audiences in the United States is a testament to the strength of the American propaganda system.

As I mentioned at the beginning of the book, John Mearsheimer, a University of Chicago professor of political science and Stephen Walt, Professor of International Relations at Harvard, were scandalized within the academic world with the *London Review of Books'* publication of their article on the "Israel Lobby." The article largely recited what has been well known within policy circles about the US-Israel special relationship for quite some time: US support for Israel's oppression of the Palestinians does not further the United States' regional aims or its strategic interests. Mearsheimer and Walt argue that US Middle East policy is largely shaped by the power and influence of a set of powerful special-interest groups, directed mainly by the American Israel Public Affairs Committee, whose influence extends not only into governmental, media, and economic spheres but to academic and intellectual ones as well.[44] By preventing an open discussion of US Middle East policy, and Israel's specific place in it, and punishing politicians who wish to subject the special relationship to interrogation, organizations such as AIPAC are depriving US citizens of vital information that is necessary for understanding how crucial resolving the Israel-Palestine conflict is to securing long-term peace in the Middle East.

What the future may hold

Despite claims that Israel remains a safe haven for World Jewry in the event of the threat of another Holocaust, in reality Israel is the most dangerous place on the planet for a Jew to reside because of the intense militarism at the center of Israeli society and the number of external threats this militarism engenders.[45] If there is a threat of another Holocaust, it exists within Israel and the occupied territories, where Israel's Palestinian Arabs face the prospect of outright expulsion and increased ethnic cleansing.[46] This Holocaust does not pose a threat to Israel's Ashkenazi and Sephardic Jewish inhabitants but to its Palestinian Arab citizens and the nearly three million Palestinian refugees in the West Bank and Gaza. As Massad deftly argues,

"Anti-Semitism is alive and well today worldwide and its major victims are Arabs and Muslims and no longer Jews. The fight should indeed be against all anti-Semitism no matter who the object of its oppression is, Arab or Jew."[47] To this end, Fouzi El-Asmar continues his struggle as a Palestinian Arab and in his refusal to sell his soul. That he continues this struggle, and maintains this refusal in the United States, is a sign that there is still hope that a Palestinian Arab will be able to live as a full citizen of Israel, rather than a third-class citizen in an apartheid—settler-colonial—state.

CHAPTER NINE

Conclusion: What is next for academic freedom and the Question of Palestine?

Universities in context

In this time of increasing corporatization of the American university system, academics struggle to maintain their autonomy in shaping the research agendas within their respective disciplines. The disciplinary structure of the university is coming to reflect the demands of late capitalism, necessitating ideological conformity among its members—something that they would be hesitant to admit. The number of books that have been published in the last 10 years expressing concern about the university intellectual's loss of autonomy and purpose is extensive. From Ellen Schrecker's *The Lost Soul of the University*, to Cary Nelson's *No University is an Island*, to Bruce Wilshire's *The Moral Collapse of the University*, to Bruce Robbins' *Secular Vocations: Intellectuals and the University*, to Bill Readings' *University in Ruins*, to John Michael's *Anxious Intellects: Academic Professionals, Public Intellectuals, and Enlightenment Values*, a common theme emerges: intellectual life in America is in crisis because American universities are becoming increasingly corporatized; indeed, they have become transnational corporations in their basic form.[1]

The academic intellectual's specific location within the transnational global economy is remarkably undertheorized.[2] As Timothy Brennan points out in his *At Home in the World: Cosmopolitanism Now*, "When work of that sort has appeared, the functionalism of the role has often been denied in a recuperation of images of the traditional intellectual, who may be cast, as he or she once was, as a disinterested seeker of truth, but who retains in some accounts an unlikely aura of disinterestedness . . ."[3] Part of the reason for this undertheorization of this location, I believe, results from an unwillingness of academic workers to recognize and admit their complicity in the promotion of state power. For example, it is difficult to find American academics conducting a soul-searching exploration of how their relative silence and complicity in supporting the US government's insistence that Iraq possessed weapons of mass destruction, prior to the US invasion of Iraq in March of 2003, played a large part in generating popular support for the invasion itself. Scholars Richard Falk and Howard Friel, in their *Record of the Paper*, present a compelling case that *The New York Times* deliberately misled the US public in the months prior to the invasion about just how persuasive the evidence the US government had in its possession was, as it insisted that Saddam Hussein possessed weapons of mass destruction. A group of neoconservative intellectuals was also complicit in obscuring that the US invasion was in violation of international law and that weapon inspectors were satisfied that Hussein was not hiding a stash of weapons of mass destruction. Something beyond US fears about Iraq's weapons of mass destruction were driving the United States to war. There has been a good bit of *post hoc* speculation about what this "something" was: unfettered access to Iraqi oil reserves, a desire to solidify US geostrategic dominance in the region, and a desire to free the Iraqi people from the grips of a tyrannical regime are some of the reasons that are often provided. As will become abundantly clear, none of these reasons, in themselves, would have provided the necessary push for war.

Equally resistant to recognition and analysis are the ways in which knowledge production is financed by state and business entities interested in a foregone conclusion and not disinterested investigation: support for and justifications of the military-industrial complex and the continual promotion of war for "reasons of state."[4] Jacques Derrida writes that:

> [I]n order for that which is not yet established elsewhere to take shape through a theoretical institutional analysis that would do justice to it, a new institution must take advantage of a certain capacity to access what is forbidden (repressed, made minor, marginalized, even "unthought") elsewhere. It must therefore access a certain knowledge still deprived of all institutional manifestation. What can claim such a thing, that such a knowledge or foreknowledge exists?[5]

Derrida's focus upon a repressed form of knowledge is important here because he brings attention to how institutions can forbid certain forms of knowing and legitimate the forgetting of certain narratives. Authorizing figures within a disciplinary discourse and, simultaneously, preventing others from speaking allow for an enclosing of a body of knowledge within a protective shell. The promotion of a discipline's status through its incorporation in mainstream institutions and governmental agencies secures a certain prestige for the discipline's understandings of the world. For example, the active promotion of Orientalism at this historical moment within think tanks such as the RAND Corporation, the Washington Institute for Near East Policy, and the Jewish Institute for National Security Affairs coincides with the United States and Israel's push for a transformation of the Middle East. In other words, the demonization of Palestinian Arabs—whose active resistance poses an obstacle to this call for the transformation of the Middle East are portrayed as incapable of governing themselves and in need of a guiding hand—advances a motivated ideology seeking to penetrate the policy making process. When such an ideology attains hegemonic status, it can shape popular perceptions to such a degree that common sense can be defeated, as the media's passivity prior to the US invasion of Iraq demonstrates.

When repressed, minor, or marginalized perspectives attain authority within the academy, a discipline can be pushed in an unexpected and counterintuitive direction, upsetting the discursive foundations upon which it previously rested. Foucault called such turns or unexpected moves epistemic shifts or ruptures.[6] Changes or shifts of this kind are rare because individuals usually do not want to risk the loss of symbolic capital that frequently accompanies the generation of controversy.

Often within the educational institution for example individuals refuse to challenge authority when they feel it might be impolitic or damaging to their status within a department or school. This faith in the maintenance of professional decorum combines with a concern for material and social advancement, ensuring the promotion of bourgeois ethics, virtues, and values. "Guild consciousness" replaces "critical consciousness" or "class consciousness" with the celebration of the professional hierarchy being the first and foremost concern.

Within the university's hierarchy, norms of behavior, codes of silence, and schedules of advancement ensure a solidarity and perhaps necessary uniformity between academic workers. Accreditation, certification by other accredited professionals, examinations, and temporal distance make for a differential field within which gradations of talent can supposedly be measured. Being controversial or engaging in resistance politics impedes the progress through the hierarchy. Of course, disciplines have their authoritative figures and texts which must be invoked and properly read as a sign of appropriate training ("bowing before the disciplinary gods"). Disciplinarity, then, because it is intimately connected to various types of certification and, I would argue, socialization is actively promoted within the university as an exertion of state power and bourgeois culture.

One of the mechanisms for containing thought and promoting conformism is the guild structure of the universities. As Noam Chomsky points out, this structure "has often served as marvelous device for protecting them from insight and understanding, for filtering out people who raise objectionable questions, for limiting research—not by force, but by all sorts of subtle means—to questions that are not threatening." Just as importantly, "[t]here's no academic profession that's concerned with the central problems of modern society. . . . This is a subtle form of design to prevent inquiry into power."[7] The disciplines are constructed so that certain questions cannot be posed.

Although separation may exist between the university and mass culture, public discourse permeates this boundary, shaping the contours of disciplinarity itself in subtle and hidden ways. Postcolonial theory, for example, exposes the institutionalization of orthodoxy and cultural superiority while challenging current conceptions of history, objectivity, and political economy.[8] Central to this challenge resides in the power of cultural and institutional critique. It is these critiques, I assert, that are met with the most psychological resistance by dominant groups. Bourdieu describes the ways in which dominant groups react to threats to their doxa:

> In contrast [to the dominated individuals], dominant individuals, in the absence of being able to restore the silence of the doxa, strive to produce, through a purely reactionary discourse, a substitute for everything that is threatened by the very existence of heretical discourse. Finding nothing for which to reproach the social world as it stands, they endeavor to impose universally, through a discourse permeated by the simplicity and transparency of common sense, the feeling of obviousness and necessity which this world imposes on them; having an interest in leaving things as they are, they attempt to undermine politics in a depoliticized political discourse, produced through a process of neutralization or, even better, of negation, which seeks to restore the doxa to its original state of innocence and which, being oriented towards the naturalization of the social order, always borrows the language of nature.[9]

Oppositional intellectuals find themselves placed within a double bind: they have to ingratiate themselves within a disciplinary discourse before being able to question the methods and conclusions of their masters. Academic hierarchies maintain structures of authority. Any attempt to sidestep this temporal distance or to question the authority of the hierarchy often leads to unfortunate professional repercussions: a crucial letter of recommendation is not written or is written with just the wrong inflection, your promotion does not go through, you are professionally "black-listed" as a troublemaker, or you are overlooked for a pivotal bureaucratic or state post because you failed to utter the requisite *idée reçues*.

I wrote this book in the hopes of identifying and interrogating the political forces within the United States that suppress debate around the Israel-Palestine conflict. These forces seek to keep that debate within narrow bounds, leaving key assumptions unexplored and unidentified. The notion that Israel, supported by the United States, is the key obstacle to peace in the Middle East is something that many will angrily deny. As the title "Out of Bounds" is meant to indicate, it is becoming increasingly difficult for those seeking to bring a proper dose of perspective to the conflict—through reference to the historical and diplomatic record—to remain within the bounds of debate as these have been constructed, ensuring that anyone who strays beyond the "respectable" issues of debate will face the ugly charge of anti-Semitism. Regrettably, these unfortunate tactics may lead some to conclude that anti-Semitism has become trivial because it is used so recklessly to derail serious discussion.[10]

The preservation of a Jewish majority within Israel, as times goes on, will become increasingly difficult to justify as Israel's Arab population grows, and as Israel increases its grip upon the occupied territories, in the hope of fully integrating these territories into a greater Israel. The Israeli government, and its apologists, will have to develop increasingly rigid surveillance mechanisms to police how the relevant issues—Israel's "right to exist" as a Jewish state, the Palestinian refugees' right of return, continued building of settlements, the status of Jerusalem, and reparations for those who endured the Nakba—will be discussed in the US public sphere. Israel's territorial ambitions, usually offered under the mantle of defense, will become increasingly hard to defend. If Israel goes forward with a strike on Iran's nuclear facilities in Natanz, the US public may finally wake up to the fact that much of the conflict in the Middle East is driven by Israel's military aggression. When and if that happens there will presumably be widespread questioning about why the mainstream media and the academy did not play a more active role in apprising the public of the relevant issues. At that time, I believe there will be a renewed interest in many of the figures discussed in this book. Crisis leads to the resuscitation of truth-tellers, particularly when people come to realize that there has been active suppression involved in keeping the public far away from the important issues. This marginalization of the public will have to be accounted for and explained at some point.

As scholars continue to seek out opportunities to engage the public about the facts about the Israel-Palestine conflict, we must support each other and remember the extreme vilification faced by dissidents during far worse periods of intellectual repression. Those of us who are privileged enough to speak from a tenured position in the academy must come to understand the gravity of the situation in Palestine and recognize our own complicity in the knowledge-producing function of the university, particularly as this relates to providing research for the military-industrial complex and rationales for Israel's colonization project. Persuading our colleagues to become more knowledgeable about the issues will not always be easy, but until there is a wider base of support within the university for scholars pursuing supposedly controversial lines of inquiry with respect to Israel-Palestine, we will be stuck with the current configuration—too few people willing to speak out against the suppression of vigorous debate in the academy.

As I discussed in an earlier chapter, in September of 2004 I guest moderated an online exchange between several academic colleagues like Noam Chomsky, and Norman Finkelstein. When discussion turned to the Israel-Palestine conflict, Chomsky and Finkelstein—quite predictably—faced accusations of anti-Semitism for their withering criticism of Israeli military repression in the Middle East. As the guest moderator, I faced questions about why I brought these "virulent critics of Israel" onto the list. Never mind that it became clear, early on, that very few people had actually read anything either Finkelstein or Chomsky have written on the Israel-Palestine conflict.

University scholars are expected to write and speak competently within their areas of expertise, avoiding the injection of extraneous issues—social, political, etc.—into their teaching. Academic freedom protects them in this endeavor.[11] According to the AAUP's "A Statement of the Association's Council: Freedom and Responsibility,"

> It is the mastery teachers have of their subjects and their own scholarship that entitles them to their classrooms and to freedom in the presentation of their subjects. Thus, it is improper for an instructor persistently to intrude material that has no relation to the subject, or fail to present the subject matter of the course as announced to the students and as approved by the faculty in their collective responsibility for the curriculum.[12]

In the humanities and social sciences, what is or is not an extraneous issue may not be clear. As a teacher of rhetoric and writing, I have been able to draw upon a number of examples from the Israel-Palestine conflict that illuminate rhetorical concepts such as the rhetorical situation, adherence, and identification. Just because these examples may be controversial is not a reason for me to avoid them. University scholars are also free to speak on issues of public concern as private citizens, as long as they make it clear that they are not speaking for the institution or on issues relating to their area of expertise. Where does this place the scholar of Middle East history?

The denial of an appointment to Juan Cole at Yale University in 2007 because of pressure from pro-Israel groups raises troubling questions about how someone who is considered an expert on the Middle East can effectively weigh in on issues of public concern without facing possible retaliation in an employment situation. That Cole's appointment was essentially derailed, despite two university-committee recommendations, reveals the significance of the predicament for scholars doing critical scholarship on the Israel-Palestine conflict.[13] Academic appointments should not be subject to a veto orchestrated by wealthy donors to the university, whose only understanding of the scholar's work may be superficial at best and whose partisanship can be primed on a moment's notice by right-wing cultural forces.[14] As the cases at Columbia indicate, Zionist alumni have been emboldened by their ability to influence administrative decision-making, even if they may not win every battle. In both of these cases, alumni sought to subvert the university's personnel decision-making by threatening to withdraw donations to Columbia University if Abu-Haj and Massad, both of whom are Palestinian, were granted tenure.[15] The Committee for the Open Discussion of Zionism has played a key role in publicizing the cases of embattled academics who

have faced attacks to their character and scholarship. See http://www.codz.
org/(accessed on 1 March 2011).

The modern research university operates coextensively with the demands
of transnational capitalism. Israel's role in the circuitry of capitalism has
been ably analyzed in Nitzan and Bichler's *The Global Political Economy
of Israel*. The question then becomes how this transnational role has led
to the reconfiguration of academic freedom with respect to the Israel-
Palestine conflict. Cathy Chaput's *Inside the Teaching Machine* provides an
extensive analysis of how a materialist conception of rhetoric can enable a
fuller understanding of how priorities are established within the research
university, allowing us to avoid the sentimental view of academic freedom,
which is often conceptualized as being under threat because right-wing forces
simply disagree with the views being advanced by progressive scholars.
A historical materialist conception of rhetoric enables us to understand that
the reorganization of the university, including the reconceptualization of
academic freedom, has come in response to the increased expansion of global
capitalism. How we react to this increased expansion of global capitalism,
and the reconceptualizations of academic freedom that will inevitably
follow, will determine how American citizens will come to understand this
vital conflict. In brief, certain knowledge claims about the Israel-Palestine
conflict can no longer be considered out of bounds, outside of the realm of
questioning and exploration.

NOTES

Chapter 1

1　See Byrne's "Academic Freedom as a Special Concern of the First Amendment."

2　"Academic Governance and Academic Freedom," p. 5.

3　P. 295 of *1915 Declaration of Principles on Academic Freedom and Tenure*. See: http://www.aaup.org/report/1915-declaration-principles-academic-freedom-and-academic-tenure.

4　See Stanley Fish's lecture on "Versions of Academic Freedom: From Professionalism to Revolution" (27 September 2012) at http://www.youtube.com/watch?v=fe550vwmzBA (accessed on 19 February 2013).

5　See Stacey, Lynch, Yudoff, Byrne, Post, Van Alystne, and others.

6　See Alan Bloom's *The Closing of the American Mind*, Dinesh D'Souza's *Illiberal Education*, and Roger Kimball's *Tenured Radicals* for representative attacks against the US academic system. Bloom, D'Souza, and Kimball argue that the US academy has been hijacked by political correctness, with concerns about race and gender permeating the curricular offerings of the humanities departments in even the most elite American universities, undermining the basis of classical education. According to Bloom, D'Souza, and Kimball, the basis for the canonization of certain great works over others has been framed as illegitimate by a left-oriented contingent of academic faculty, who argue that minority viewpoints have been systematically excluded from academic curricula through conceptions of merit that are Eurocentric.

7　This model is the dominant one at research universities.

8　Many of these issues are discussed in Ellen Schrecker's *The Lost Soul of Higher Education: Corporatization, The Assault on Academic Freedom, and the End of the American University*, Cary Nelson's *No University Is an Island*, and Neil Hamilton's *Academic Ethics: Problems and Materials on Professional Conduct and Shared Governance*.

9　*AAUP Policy Documents & Reports*, Tenth Edition (Baltimore: Johns Hopkins University Press, 2003), p. 3.

10　This topic is taken up in the following excellent collections: Beshara Doumani, ed. *Academic Freedom after September 11th, 2001* (New York: Zone Books, 2006); Evan Gerstman and Matthew Streb, ed. *Academic Freedom at the Dawn of the New Century: How Terrorism, Governments, and Culture Wars Impact Free Speech* (Stanford: Stanford University Press, 2006); and Louis Menand, ed. *The Future of Academic Freedom* (Chicago and London: University of Chicago Press, 1996).

11 See Walter Metzger and Richard Hofstadter's *The Development of Academic Freedom in the United States* (New York and London: Columbia University Press, 1955).

12 See Said's "America's Taboo" at http://www.newleftreview.org/?view=2285 (accessed on 29 June 2009).

13 See Michael Adams and Christopher Mayhew's *Publish It Not: The Middle East Cover Up* (London: Signal Books, 2006) and Norman Finkelstein's *Beyond Chutzpah: The Misuse of Anti-Semitism and the Abuse of History* (Berkeley: University of California Press, 2008).

14 See Noam Chomsky's *The Fateful Triangle: The United States, Israel, and the Palestinians* (Cambridge: South End Press, 1983).

15 See Naseer Aruri's *The Dishonest Broker: The Role of the United States in Palestine and Israel* (Cambridge: South End Press, 2003).

16 See Jonathan Cook's *Israel and the War for Civilization* (London: Pluto Books, 2008).

17 See Clayton Swisher's *The Truth about Camp David: The Untold Story of the Collapse of the Middle East Peace Process* (New York: Nation Books, 2004) and John Mearsheimer and Steven Walt's *The Israel Lobby and U.S. Foreign Policy* (London: Farrar, Straus, and Giroux, 2007).

18 See Norman Finkelstein's *Image and Reality of the Israel-Palestine Conflict*, 2nd edn (London: Verso, 2003).

19 I would also like to mention Lawrence Davidson's Facebook Page, "To the Point Analyses: Deconstructing the News."

20 See Howard Friel and Richard Falk's *The Record of the Paper: How the New York Times Misreports US Foreign Policy* (London and New York: Verso, 2004) and *Israel-Palestine on the Record: How the New York Times Misreports Conflict in the Middle East* (London and New York: Verso, 2007).

21 See Edward Abboud's *Invisible Enemy: Israel, Politics, Media, and American Culture* (Reston, VA: Vox Publishing Company, 2003).

22 See Baruch Kimmerling's *Politicide* (London: Verso, 2003). As Kimmerling observes: "Two deeply rooted existential anxieties exist within the Jewish military culture: one concerns the physical annihilation of the state, an issue that is frequently used, abused and emotionally manipulated by many Israeli politicians and intellectuals, and the other the loss of the fragile Jewish demographic majority on which the supremacy and identity of the state rest" (18).

23 Grant Smith's *Israel's Defense Line* is also another excellent historical analysis of AIPAC's rise to prominence in American power politics.

24 *Deliberate Deceptions: Facing the Facts about the U.S.-Israeli Relationship* (Washington, DC: American Educational Trust, 1995), p. xxviii.

25 See Janice Terry's *U.S. Foreign Policy and the Middle East: The Role of Lobbies and Special Interest Groups* (London: Pluto Books, 2005).

26 See *The AIPAC College Guide: Exposing the Anti-Israel Campaign on Campus*.

27 See Said's *The World, the Text, and the* (Cambridge: Harvard University Press, 1983), particularly the chapter entitled "Writing Between Culture and System."

28 Karl Marx and Frederick Engels. *The German Ideology* (New York: International Publishers, 1947), p. 64.

29 See Eric Solaro's "Retired Generals Rising Up Against Iraq War" at http://www.seattlepi.com/opinion/266638_solarosub16.html (accessed on 27 February 2011).

30 Ibid.

31 See pp. 229–62 ("Iraq and Dreams of Transforming the Middle East") in Walt and Mearsheimer's *The Israel Lobby and U.S. Foreign Policy* (New York: Farrar, Strauss, and Giroux, 2009).

32 See Adam Shatz's "The Native Informant" at http://www.thenation.com/article/native-informant (accessed on 28 February 2011).

33 *The Israeli Connection: Who Arms Israel and Why* (London: I.B. Taurus & Co., 1989); *Israeli Foreign Policy: South Africa and Central America* (Cambridge: South End Press, 1999).

34 *Israel in the American National Interest* (Urbana: University of Illinois Press, 1999), pp. 332–3.

35 See http://www.richardsilverstein.com/tikun_olam/wp-content/uploads/2008/04/the-petition.pdf (3 August 2008).

36 See exchange between Robert Lieberman and John Mearsheimer and Stephen Walt in *Perspectives on Politics*, Vol. 7, No. 2 (June 2009), pp. 259–73.

37 P. 14.

38 P. 6.

39 P. 9.

40 See Walt and Mearsheimer's *The Israel Lobby and U.S. Middle East Policy*.

41 See Paul *They Dared to Speak Out: Individuals and Institutions Confront the Lobby* and *Deliberate Deceptions: Facing the Facts about the U.S.-Israeli Relationship*.

42 Jimmy Carter spoke of the power of Jewish organizations to prevent open discussion of the Palestinian Question in the United States. As he explained in 15 December 2006 letter to "Jewish Citizens of America":

> I made it clear that I have never claimed that American Jews control the news media, but reiterated that the overwhelming bias for Israel comes from among Christians like me who have been taught since childhood to honor and protect God's chosen people from among whom came our own savior, Jesus Christ. An additional factor, especially in the political arena, is the powerful influence of the American Israel Public Affairs Committee, which is exercising its legitimate goal of explaining the current policies of Israel's government and arousing maximum support in our country. There are no significant countervailing voices. See http://www.cartercenter.org/news/pr/carter_letter_121506.html (accessed on 25 February 2011).

43 I borrow this phrase from the late Palestinian critic, Edward Said, who developed the concept of "structures of attitude and reference" in his classic text, *Culture and Imperialism*, to describe how characters within a novel come to conceptualize their relationship to empire.

44 See Marcy Newman's *The Politics of Teaching Palestine to Americans* (New York: Palgrave Macmillan, 2011).

45 See Abboud's *Invisible Enemy* (Reston: Vox Publishing, 2003) and M. Shahid Alam's *Israeli Exceptionalism: The Destabilizing Logic of Zionism* (New York: Palgrave Macmillan, 2010).

46 See John Rose's *The Myths of Zionism* (London and Ann Arbor: Pluto, 2004).

47 See Abboud and Alam.

48 See U.S. Commission on Civil Rights Campaign to End Anti-Semitism at http://www.usccr.gov/campusanti-semitism.html (accessed on 2 March 2011).

49 See Alan Dershowitz's *The Case Against Israel's Enemies: Exposing Jimmy Carter and Others Who Stand in the Way of Peace* (Hoboken: John Wiley & Sons, 2008).

50 See Norman Finkelstein's "The Ludicrous Attacks on Jimmy Carter: Carter's Real Sin is Cutting to the Heart of the Problem" at http://counterpunch.org/finkelstein12282006.html (accessed on 18 February 2011).

51 See Jonathan Nitzer and Shimshon Bichler *The Global Political Economy of Israel* and Shir Hever *The Political Economy of Israel's Occupation: Repression Beyond Exploitation.*

52 In fact, six internationally recognized experts on the Israel-Palestine conflict peer reviewed *Beyond Chutzpah.*

53 See http://www.alandershowitz.com/publications/docs/response_to_beyond_chutzpah.pdf (accessed on 1 February 2011).

54 See Dershowitz's "Finkelstein's Bigotry" at http://www.campus-watch.org/article/id/3293 (accessed on 1 February 2011).

55 See http://www.alandershowitz.com/publications/docs/depaulletter.htm (accessed on 1 February 2011).

56 See http://www.democracynow.org/2003/9/24/scholar_norman_finkelstein_calls_professor_alan (accessed on 1 February 2011).

57 Atapattu interview with Finkelstein, "How to Lose Friends and Alienate People."

58 See my essay, "William L. McBride and the Enduring Commitment to Intellectual Freedom," in *Revolutionary Hope: Essays in Honor of William McBride.* Eds. Nathan Jun and Shane Wahl (Lanham: Lexington Books, 2013), pp. 7–20.

59 See http://www.logosjournal.com/issue_5.1/dershowitz.htm (accessed on 1 February 2011).

60 See Dershowitz's letter, "Why Finkelstein Was Rejected" in the *Guardian* at: http://www.guardian.co.uk/world/2008/may/29/israelandthepalestinians.lebanon (accessed on 1 March 2011).

61 See *The Politics of Anti-Semitism.* Eds. Alexander Cockburn and Jeffrey St Clair (Oakland: Counterpunch and AK Press, 2003).

62 See Robin Shepherd's *Beyond the Pale: Europe's Problem with Israel* (London: Wiedenfeld and Nicolson, 2009) and Bernard Harrison's *The Resurgence of Anti-Semitism: Jews, Israel, and Liberal Opinion* (Lanham, MD: Rowman and Littlefield Publishers, 2006).

63 London: Wiedenfeld and Nicolson, 2009.

Chapter 2

1   See Lawrence Davidson's *Foreign Policy Inc.: Privatizing American's National Interest* (Lexington: University Press of Kentucky, 2009) and Melanie McAlester's *Epic Encounters: Culture, Media, and U.S. Interests in the Middle East, 1945-2000*, and Zachary Lockman's *Contending Visions of the Middle East* (Cambridge: Cambridge University Press, 2004).

2   There is ample literature on the topic of intellectuals in society and the efforts of oppositional intellectuals to speak truth to power. In this context, I would mention Julian Benda's *The Treason of the Intellectuals*, Trans. Richard Aldington (New York: W.W. Norton & Company, 1928), Max Black's *The Morality of Scholarship* (Ithaca: Cornell University Press, 1969), Paul Bove's influential study, *Intellectuals in Power: A Genealogy of Critical Humanism* (New York: Columbia University Press, 1986), Edward Shils' *Intellectuals and the Powers, and Other Essays* (Chicago: University of Chicago Press, 1983), Alvin Gouldner's *The Future of Intellectuals and the Rise of the New Class* (Oxford: Oxford University Press, 1982), and Edward Said's *Representations of the Intellectual* (New York: Vintage, 1994).

3   See Alvin Rosenfeld's "Progressive Jewish Thought and the New Anti-Semitism" at http://www.ajc.org/atf/cf/%7B42D75369-D582-4380-8395 D25925B85EAF%7D/PROGRESSIVE_JEWISH_THOUGHT.PDF (accessed on 12 April 2010), http://www.ajc.org/atf/cf/%7B42D75369-D582-4380-8395-D25925B85EAF%7D/AntiZionism.pdf (accessed on 12 April 2010), and http://www.ajc.org/site/apps/nl/content3.asp?c=ijITI2PHKoG&b=846637&ct=875059 (accessed on 12 April 2010). Also, see U.S. Commission on Civil Rights Campaign to End Anti-Semitism at http://www.usccr.gov/campusanti-semitism.html (accessed on 12 April 2010).

4   See Yosef Gorny's *Zionism and the Arabs Ideology, 1882-1948: A Study of Ideology* (Oxford: Oxford University Press, 1987) and Simha Flapan's *Israel and the Palestinians* (New York: Barnes and Nobles Books, 1979).

5   See Alan Dershowitz's *The Case for Peace* (New York: Wiley and Sons, 2004) and *The Case Against Jimmy Carter and Other Enemies of Israel* (New York: Wiley and Sons, 2008).

6   Numerous publications on the New Anti-Semitism strike a consistent theme: Israel is criticized because it is a Jewish state and not because of any illegitimate actions it may engage in. See Phyllis Chessler's *The New Anti-Semitism: The Current Crisis and What We Must Do About It* (New York: Jossey-Bass, 2005); Abraham Foxman's *Never Again? The Threat of the New Anti-Semitism* (New York: Harper One, 2004); Gabriel Schoenfeld's *The Return of Anti-Semitism* (New York and London: Encounter Books, 2005); and Ron Rosenbaum's *Those Who Forget the Past: The Question of Anti-Semitism* (New York: Random House, 2004); and Bernard Harrison's *The Resurgence of Anti-Semitism: Jews, Israel, and Liberal Opinion* (Lanham, MD: Rowman and Littlefield Publishers, 2006) for the various arguments with respect to this theme.

7   Rosevale, CA: Institute for Jewish & Community Research, p. 95.

8   See Manfred Gerstenfeld's edited collection, *Academics Against Israel and the Jews* (Jerusalem: Jerusalem Center for Public Affairs, 2007) and Edward Alexander and Paul Bogdanor's edited collection *The Jewish Divide Over Israel: Accusers and Defenders* (New Brunswick and London: Transaction Publishers, 2006).

9   I go into depth about the "subversion of academic freedom" in Chapter 4.

10 See Jonathan Kessler and Jeff Schwaber's *The AIPAC College Guide: Exposing the Anti-Israel Campaign on Campus* (Washington, DC: American Israel Public Affairs Committee, 1984); Abraham Foxman's *The Deadliest Lies: The Israel Lobby and the Myth of Jewish Control* (New York: Palgrave MacMillan, 2007); Manfred Gerstenfeld's *Academics Against Israel and the Jews* (Jerusalem: The Jerusalem Center for Public Affairs, 2007); Gary A. Tobin, Aryeh K. Weinberg, and Jenna Ferer's *The Uncivil University: Politics and Propaganda in American Education* (Roseville, CA: Institute for Jewish and Community Research, 2007).

11 In a chapter entitled "The Case Against Mearsheimer and Walt" in his *The Case Against Israel's Enemies: Exposing Jimmy Carter and Others Who Stand in the Way of Peace* (Hoboken, NJ: Wiley & Sons, 2008), Alan Dershowitz claims that

> Anti-Israel professors continue to dominate Middle East studies programs across the country. The "free speech" argument has become the last recourse of anti-Israel academics who cannot win a debate based on facts. They do not want free speech for all views, but only special protection for their own. Much of what they describe as "censorship" is just ordinary counterspeech from people who disagree with them. (71)

12 See U.S. Commission on Civil Rights Report entitled "Campus Anti-Semitism" at http://www.usccr.gov/pubs/081506campusantibrief07.pdf (accessed on 13 August 2009). Zachary Lockman, President of the Civil Rights Commission at http://www.monthlyreview.org/mrzine/mesa170607.html (accessed on 13 August 2009).

13 P. 103.

14 See Norman Finkelstein's *Beyond Chutzpah: The Misuse of Anti-Semitism and the Abuse of History*, revised edition (Berkeley: University of California Press, 2008).

15 New York: Farrar, Strauss, and Giroux, p. 196.

16 P. 352.

17 New York: Vintage Books, 1992, p. xxi.

18 *Orientalism* (New York: Vintage Books, 1979), p. 12.

19 See Kramer's Ivory *Towers on Sand: The Failure of Middle East Studies in America* (Washington, DC: Washington Institute for Near East Policy, 2001); Pipes' *Militant Islam Reaches America* (New York: W.W. Norton & Co., 2003); Ajami's *Dream Palace of the Arabs: A Generation's Odyssey* (New York: Vintage, 1999); and Lewis's *What Went Wrong? The Clash Between Islam and Modernity in the Middle East* (New York: Harper Perennial, 2003).

20 Consider the work of New Historians such as Benny Morris *The Birth of the Palestinian Refugee Problem, 1947-49* (Cambridge: Cambridge University Press, 1988), Illan Pappe *The Making of the Arab-Israeli Conflict, 1947-1951* (London: I.B. Taurus, 1992), Avi Shlaim *The Iron Wall: Israel and the Arab World* (New York: W.W. Norton Company, 2001), and Nur Masalha *Imperial Israel and the Palestinians: The Politics of Expansion* (London: Pluto Press, 2000).

21 See Stephen Zunes' *Tinderbox: U.S. Middle East Policy and the Roots of Terrorism* (Monroe: Common Courage Press, 2002).

22 In *The Israel Lobby and U.S. Foreign Policy*, Walt and Mearsheimer write:

> Given the harm that this conflict is inflicting on Israel, the United States and especially the Palestinians, it is in everyone's interest to end this tragedy once and for all. Put differently, resolving this long and bitter conflict should not be seen as a desirable option at some point down the road, or as a good way for U.S. presidents to polish their legacies and garner Nobel Peace Prizes. Rather, ending the conflict should be seen as a national security priority for the United States. But this will not happen as long as the lobby makes it impossible for American leaders to use the leverage at their disposal to pressure Israel into ending the occupation and creating a viable Palestinian state. (346)

23 See Victor Kattan's *From Coexistence to Conquest: International Law and the Origins of the Arab-Israeli Conflict, 1891-1949* (London: Pluto Books, 2009), John Quigley's *The Case for Palestine: An International Law Perspective* (Durham and London: Duke University Press, 2005), and John Lucas's *The Israeli-Palestinian Conflict: A Documentary Record 1967-1990* (Cambridge: Cambridge University Press, 1992).

24 Crazy state is not a reference to a psychological state, but instead to a country's tendency to promise to deliver cataclysmic violence to a region if its military demands are not met.

25 See Chomsky's "The New War on Terror" talk (18 October 2001) at http://www.chomsky.info/talks/20011018.htm (4 August 2008).

26 Consider the cases of Margo Ramlal-Nankoe at Ithaca College and Terri Ginsberg at North Carolina State University. See "College Faces Threat of Tenure Lawsuit" at http://theithacan.org/am/publish/news/200809_College_faces_possibility_of_lawsuit.shtml (accessed on 1 March 2011) and "Uphill Battle for Academic Freedom at U.S. universities" at http://electronicintifada.net/v2/article10998.shtml (accessed on 1 March 2011).

27 As the authors write in the conclusion to the book:

> The United States does not support Israel's existence because it makes Americans more secure, but rather because Americans recognize the long history of Jewish suffering and believe it that is desirable for the Jewish people to have their own state. As we have noted repeatedly, there is a strong moral case for supporting Israel's existence, and we believe the United States should remain committed to coming to Israel's aid if its survival were in jeopardy. But Americans should do this because they think it is morally appropriate, not because it is vital to their own security. (338)

28 See Dershowitz's "Debunking the Oldest—and Newest—Jewish Conspiracy: A Reply to the Mearsheimer and Walt Working Paper" at http://www.hks. harvard.edu/research/working_papers/dershowitzreply.pdf (20 June 2008).

29 *The Israel Lobby and U.S. Foreign Policy*, p. 336.

30 Ibid., p. 344.

31 See Oded Yinon's "The Zionist Plan for the Middle East," at http://www. informationclearinghouse.info/pdf/The%20Zionist%20Plan%20for%20 the%20Middle%20East.pdf (accessed on 9 June 2013); Shahak's *Open Secrets: Israeli Foreign and Nuclear Policies* (London: Pluto Press, 1997); and Chomsky's *The Fateful Triangle: The United States, Israel, and the Palestinians* (Cambridge: South End Press, 1983).

32 See http://www.boston.com/news/globe/editorial_opinion/oped/ articles/2006/12/21/why_wont_carter_debate_his_book/, http://www.nytimes. com/2007/01/09/opinion/09ross.html?_r=1, and http://www.meforum. org/1633/my-problem-with-jimmy-carters-book (all accessed on 11 July 2009).

33 See "Target Ford" (18 May 2006) at http://www.thenation.com/doc/20060605/ sherman (28 July 2008).

34 *They Dared to Speak Out*, p. 247.

Chapter 3

1 See the Appendix A at the end of the book for my online writings about the case as it developed.

2 See Steven Plaut's "The Next Piece of Housekeeping at DePaul?" at: http:// www.frontpagemag.com/readArticle.aspx?ARTID=28030 (accessed on 13 July 2009).

3 To distinguish between the event and the propaganda phenomenon, Finkelstein uses a lower-case "h" when he speaks of the event, the holocaust, and a capital "h" when he is referring to the propagandistic effects that have been created around the historical event—the Holocaust. See p. 3 of *The Holocaust* Industry: *The Exploitation of Jewish Suffering*, 2nd edn (London and New York: Verso Books, 2003). Finkelstein writes in the footnote on that page, "In this text, *Nazi holocaust* signals the actual historical event, *The Holocaust* its ideological representation."

4 See http://www.normanfinkelstein.com/article.php?pg=11&ar=1 (accessed on 30 June 2009).

5 This debate on *Democracy Now* is the focus of another chapter.

6 See http://www.democracynow.org/2003/9/24/scholar_norman_finkelstein_ calls_professor_alan (accessed 6 July 2009).

7 See http://www.democracynow.org/2003/9/24/scholar_norman_finkelstein_ calls_professor_alan.

8 *Israel's Sacred Terrorism*. Shrewsbury, MA: Association of Arab-American University Graduates, Inc., 1980.

9   See Pappe's *The Ethnic Cleansing of Palestine.*

10 See http://www.frontpagemag.com/readArticle.aspx?ARTID=8063 (accessed on 3 July 2009).

11 http://www.normanfinkelstein.com/in-praise-of-smoking-guns-the-dershowitz-file/(accessed on 6 July 2009).

12 See Jon Wiener's "Giving Chutzpah New Meaning" at http://www.thenation.com/doc/20050711/wiener and a subsequent exchange ("Tsuris Over Chutzpah") between Wiener and Dershowitz at http://www.thenation.com/doc/20050829/exchange (accessed on 13 July 2009).

13 According to Jon Wiener, the UC Press explained in a statement accompanying review copies that "Professor Finkelstein's only claim on the issue was speculative. He wondered why Alan Dershowitz, in recorded appearances after his book was published, seemed to know so little about the contents of his own book. We felt this weakened the argument and distracted from the central issues of the book. Finkelstein agreed." See Jon Wiener's "Giving Chutzpah New Meaning" at http://www.thenation.com/doc/20050711/wiener/2 (accessed on 13 July 2009).

14 In a letter to the editors of the Nation, in response to Jon Wiener's "Giving Chutzpah New Meaning," Dershowitz wrote:

> I wrote to the directors of the University of California Press (with a copy and cover note to the Governor) emphasizing that "I have no interest in censoring or suppressing [Norman] Finkelstein's freedom of expression." In a further letter, I made it clear that "I am not trying to get the Governor to prevent the publication of Finkelstein's book." The purpose of my letters was to encourage the UCP to give "serious consideration" to its decision to publish a defamatory lie (that I did not write *The Case for Israel*). (See http://www.thenation.com/doc/20050829/exchange (accessed on 13 July 2009))

15 As Jon Wiener notes in his *Nation* article "Giving Chutzpah New Meaning":

> The Finkelstein book was originally under contract to the New Press, and Dershowitz claims he succeeded in persuading the New Press to drop it. He told me in an e-mail that after he wrote the New Press pointing out "numerous factual inaccuracies in Finkelstein's manuscript, New Press cancelled it's [*sic*] contract with him." New Press publisher Colin Robinson says that's not true: "We did not cancel the agreement to publish Norman's book and never wanted to do so." Finkelstein said the same thing in an e-mail: "I was the one who pulled out of the contract when publication was delayed due to Dershowitz's letters. In fact, Colin urged me to reconsider the decision and stay with New Press." (See http://www.thenation.com/doc/20050711/wiener (accessed on 13 July 2009))

16 See Steven Weiss's "Dershowitz Fires Back at His Critics" in the *Jewish Forward* at: http://www.forward.com/articles/3515/(accessed on 13 July 2009).

17 See Jon Wiener's "Giving Chutzpah New Meaning" at http://www.thenation.com/doc/20050711/wiener (accessed on 6 July 2009).

18 See http://www.law.harvard.edu/faculty/dershowitz/statement.html (accessed 6 July 2009).

19 See Jon Wiener's "Giving Chutzpah New Meaning" at http://www.thenation.com/doc/20050711/wiener (accessed on 13 July 2009).

20 Dershowitz writes: "American Jews need more chutzpah. Notwithstanding the stereotype we are not pushy or assertive enough for our own good and for the good of our more vulnerable brothers and sisters in other parts of the world" (*Chutzpah*, 1).

21 See Rokach's *Israel's Sacred Terrorism*.

22 See Ze'ev Schiff *Israel's Lebanon War* (New York: Simon and Schuster, 1984) and *A History of the Israeli Army: 1874 to the Present* (New York: Macmillan, 1985); Benny Morris's *The Birth of the Palestinian Refugee Problem* (Cambridge: Cambridge University Press, 1987) and *The Birth of the Palestinian Refugee Problem Revisited* (Cambridge: Cambridge University Press, 2003).

23 See Cockburn's "Alan Dershowitz, Plagiarist" at http://www.thenation.com/doc/20031013/cockburn (accessed on 13 July 2009). An additional exchange took place between Dershowitz and Cockburn at http://www.thenation.com/doc/20031215/letter (accessed on 13 July 2009). Also, see Frank Menetrez's "Plagiarism, Cover Up, and Misrepresentations: The Case Against Alan Dershowitz" at http://www.counterpunch.org/menetrez02122008.html (accessed on 13 July 2009) and Menetrez's "Dershowitz v. Finkelstein, Who's Right and Who's Wrong?" at http://www.counterpunch.org/menetrez04302007.html (accessed on 13 July 2009) and Kim Petersen's "Harvard Besmirched" at http://dissidentvoice.org/2008/03/harvard-besmirched/(accessed on 13 July 2009).

24 One of the most intriguing of Dershowitz's gaffes, the Felix Frankfurter Professor's reference to George Orwell's "turnspeak" in two separate instances in *The Case for Israel*, has yet to be properly explained. Orwell coined the phrase "Newspeak"; "turnspeak"—"the cynical inverting of facts"—was coined by Peters in *From Time Immemorial*. In a letter to New Press editor, Colin Robinson, Dershowitz admitted that he attributed the phrase "turnspeak" to Huxley. How did Huxley get introduced into this melee?

25 My postmodernist friends will have to excuse me for using this phrase, "the historical record," in this context. As it turns out, it is a useful phrase, one repeatedly employed by historians and serious political analysts.

26 See Kolsky's *Jews Against Zionism: The American Council of Judaism, 1942-48*. Philadelphia: Temple University Press, 1998.

27 See Raul Hilberg's and Avi Shlaim's comments about Finkelstein's scholarship in May 2007 at http://www.democracynow.org/2007/5/9/it_takes_an_enormous_amount_of (accessed on 13 July 2009). Noteworthy here is Hilberg's comment: "It takes an enormous amount of courage to speak the truth when no one else is out there to support him."

28 Consider Noam Chomsky's powerful reflection in *Towards a New Cold War*:

> To put it in the simplest terms, a talented young journalist or a student aiming for a scholarly career can choose to play the game by the rules,

with the prospect of advancement to a position of prestige and privilege and sometimes even a degree of power; or to pursue an independent path, with the likelihood of a minor post as a police reporter or in a community college, exclusion from major journals, vilification and abuse, or driving a taxi cab. Given such choices, the end result is not very surprising. Few options are open to isolated individuals in a basically depoliticized society lacking popular organizations that question the legitimacy of existing structures of domination and control, state or private. (14–15)

29 *Beyond Chutzpah*, p. 17; emphasis in original.

30 See http://www.normanfinkelstein.com/the-book-burners-boast/(accessed 6 June 2009) and http://www.ajc.org/atf/cf/%7B42D75369-D582-4380-8395-D25925B85EAF%7D/PROGRESSIVE_JEWISH_THOUGHT.PDF (accessed 6 June 2009).

31 *Beyond Chutzpah*, p. 83.

32 P. 82.

33 See Joseph Massad's "Palestinians and the Limits of Racialized Discourse" in *Social Text*, no. 34 (1994): 94–114.

34 "Palestinians and the Limits of Racialized Discourse," p. 98.

35 *Beyond Chutzpah*, p. 94.

36 See Paul Breines' *Tough Jews: Political Fantasies and the Moral Dilemma of American Jewry* (New York: Basic Books, 1992).

37 See http://www.logosjournal.com/issue_5.1/dershowitz.htm, http://www.logosjournal.com/issue_4.4/abraham.htm, and http://www.logosjournal.com/issue_5.1/abraham.htm (all accessed on 6 July 2009).

38 See http://www.btselem.org/English/Press_Releases/20050329.asp (accessed on 11 July 2009).

39 See http://www.logosjournal.com/issue_5.1/dershowitz.htm (accessed on 14 July 2009).

40 See Wiener's "Giving Chutzpah New Meaning" at http://www.thenation.com/doc/20050711/wiener/2 (accessed on 13 July 2009).

41 See Sara Roy's "A Dubai on the Mediterranean" at http://www.lrb.co.uk/v27/n21/roy_01_.html (accessed on 6 July 2009).

42 See Halper's *An Israeli in Palestine* (London: Pluto Books, 2008).

43 See Meron Benevisti's "Bantustan Plan for Apartheid Israel: Sharon's Separation Scheme is Doomed to Fail Once It Becomes Clear What It Means." *Guardian*, 25 April 2004. http://www.guardian.co.uk/world/2004/apr/26/comment (accessed on 6 June 2013).

44 See http://www.iop.harvard.edu/events_forum_archive.html (accessed on 6 July 2009).

45 See http://www.thenation.com/doc/20001113/gordon (accessed on 6 July 2009).

46 See http://www.csun.edu/~vcmth00m/finkelstein.html (accessed on 5 July 2009).

Chapter 4

1   As Chomsky noted in the *Democracy Now* interview:

> Chomsky: The whole thing is outrageous. I mean, he's an outstanding scholar. He has produced book after book. He's got recommendations from some of the leading scholars in the many areas in which he has worked. The faculty—the departmental committee unanimously recommended him for tenure. It's amazing that he hasn't had full professorship a long time ago.

> Goodman: And, as you were saying, there was a huge campaign led by a Harvard law professor, Alan Dershowitz, to try in a desperate effort to defame him and vilify him, so as to prevent him from getting tenure.

> Chomsky: The details of it are utterly shocking, and, as you said, it got to the point where the DePaul administration called on Harvard to put an end to this.

2   The distinction between an individual's right to academic freedom and the institution's right to academic freedom is amply discussed in a great deal of law review literature. In particular, see Robert Post, "The Structure of Academic Freedom," and Judith Butler, "Academic Norms, Contemporary Challenges: A Reply to Robert Post on Academic Freedom," in *Academic Freedom after September 11*, ed. Beshara Doumani (New York: Zone Books, 2006), pp. 61–142. It's clear that the institution's right to decide who may teach, what may be taught, how it should be taught, and who may be admitted for study, has far more basis in law than the individual's right to pursue innovative or controversial lines of inquiry that may upset or work around established scholarly norms. Indeed, one of the reasons DePaul may have chosen to deny Finkelstein tenure by claiming that his scholarship was contrary to DePaul's Vincentian mission was because such a rationale would have probably been viewed as a justifiable reason for denying tenure, at least from a legal perspective. Ultimately, DePaul argued that Finkelstein posed a threat to the academic freedom of others.

3   Recent cases involving scholars critical of Zionism include Joseph Massad, Nadia Abu El-Haj, Joel Kovel, Margo Ramlal-Nankoe, Terri Ginsberg, Nicholas De Genova, Thaddeus Russell, William Robinson, and Kristofer Petersen-Overton.

4   In his *Patriotic Correctness: Academic Freedom and Its Enemies*, John K. Wilson (2008: 115) notes, "In reality, left-wing activists are rare in academia. There is an overwhelming emphasis on obscure research in academia and a strong tendency to avoid political activism."

5   The three members of DePaul's Political Science Department who opposed Finkelstein's tenure bid were not scholars on the Middle East or the Israel-Palestine conflict.

6   J. D. Bindenagel, DePaul's Vice President for Community, Government, and International Affairs and a Holocaust compensation official in the Clinton administration, called University of Chicago Professor John Mearsheimer (one of the external reviewers of Finkelstein's tenure case) in September of 2007, shortly after Finkelstein's resignation from the University, requesting

a meeting with Mearsheimer so Bindenagel could explain "DePaul's position on the Finkelstein case." What exactly needed explaining? That the Israel Lobby's financial and political clout, which was brought to bear on DePaul, necessitated Finkelstein's firing?

7　The relevant section of Chapter 4 ("Reappointment and Separation," 2) reads as follows:

> When deciding whether or not to renew the contract of a nontenured faculty member, the University follows two general principles. DePaul is obligated to select, given available resources, faculty members who will best contribute to its distinctive goals and academic mission. *Consequently, the University has the utmost latitude, within the limits of academic freedom, in determining which nontenured faculty members will be retained. The University should be left without a reasonable doubt as to the faculty member's qualifications for tenure before it reaches a favorable decision on a reappointment to which tenure is attached.* (emphasis added)

8　On DePaul's Office of the General Counsel: In a memorandum dated 8 June 2007, Chief General Counsel, Jose Padilla, argued to Anne Bartlett, DePaul Faculty Council President, that no appeals process existed through which a tenure decision could be contested.

9　As Bill Williams (2007) noted in his "Commissar Two-Step at DePaul: Defamation Zionist Style":

> In May 2004, a mere one month before fifty Jenner and Block attorneys attended a Jewish United Fund/Jewish Federation of Metropolitan Chicago Lawyer's Division dinner in Chicago, where Alan Dershowitz delivered the keynote address on "The Case for Israel," John Simon, *a Jenner and Block partner*, was elected Chair of DePaul's Board of Trustees. In October 2004, he assumed the position of *chair of the Board of Trustees* after having served as a Trustee since 1990.

10　DePaul's Faculty Governance Council sent a letter to Harvard's leadership (Harvard Law School Dean, Elena Kagan, and its President, Derek Bok) in November 2006, requesting that Dershowitz's outside interference be stopped, while also noting the harm that was being done to the "sanctity" of DePaul's tenure and promotion process. The irony, of course, is that the reasons Dershowitz cited as to why Finkelstein should have been denied tenure, very closely mirrored the actual reasons DePaul adopted to deny Finkelstein tenure.

11　Here are the details of my exchange with Dershowitz during the Q&A session at Northwestern:

> Abraham: "Professor Dershowitz, thank you for being here tonight. Tomorrow, DePaul's University Tenure and Promotion Committee will meet to vote on Norman Finkelstein's tenure case. You are obviously opposed to seeing Finkelstein receive the academic privilege of a tenured position. You have called his scholarship "One-side agit prop."" (Dershowitz breaks in: "It is. . . .")
>
> Abraham: "There's only one problem with your position: The leading scholars on the Holocaust and the Israel-Palestine conflict not only say that Finkelstein's scholarship is accurate—devastatingly so—but have praised his

work as a vital correction to current dogma and illusion. For example, Raul Hilberg, the leading scholar on the Nazi Holocaust, has clearly indicated that Finkelstein's work is moving in the right direction."

Dershowitz: "Hilberg is a scholar on the Holocaust, not on the use of the Holocaust, which Finkelstein began writing about in 1995."

Abraham: "Avi Shlaim, professor of international relations at Oxford, has stated that Finkelstein's work is a devastating indictment of much propaganda that passes as scholarship on the conflict."

Dershowitz: "He's a hard leftist, hardly a serious scholar."

Abraham: "What about your own colleague at Harvard, Middle East scholar, Sara Roy?"

Dershowitz: "She's a radical leftist! I am putting DePaul University on notice! If it grants Finkelstein tenure, it will ruin its reputation as a serious university devoted to serious academic study. I guarantee you this: Finkelstein will be fired within ten years, if he receives tenure. Is it merely a coincidence that the same people who supported Ward Churchill are now supporting Finkelstein? What does it mean that a scholar on the Middle East would commission a Brazilian neo-nazi to portray me masturbating in rapturous joy to the sight of dead Lebanese civilians? What kind of person would include that as part of his tenure file?"

Dershowitz stated that "Finkelstein was invited to the Iranian Holocaust Denial Conference, along with another American Professor—Professor David Duke." According to Dershowitz, "Finkelstein declined the invitation, because he got into an argument with the conference organizers. Apparently, they wouldn't give him as much time as he wanted to speak."

12 According to Jon Wiener (2009):

> In what *The Chronicle* called "language similar to that used by Mr. Dershowitz," the dean wrote, "I find the personal attacks in many of Dr. Finkelstein's published books to border on character assassination and, in my opinion, they embody a strategy clearly aimed at destroying the reputation of many who oppose his views."

13 Drawing on the following analogy from Henry Louis Gates' essay, "Critical Race Theory and Freedom of Speech," in Louis Menand's edited collection, *The Future of Academic Freedom* (Chicago: University of Chicago Press, 1996), where Gates tries to show how, what would normally be considered straightforward hate speech "addressed to a black freshman at Stanford," can be embedded in perfectly acceptable academese; Finkelstein shows us how insidious the discourse of civility can be in delivering a personally wounding insult:

> Person A: Lavon, if you find yourself struggling in your classes here, you should realize it isn't your fault. It's simply that you are the beneficiary of a disruptive policy of affirmative action that places under-qualified, underprepared, and often undertalented black students in demanding educational environments like this one. The policy's egalitarian aims may be well intentioned, but given the fact that aptitude tests place African-Americans almost a full standard deviation below the mean, even controlling for socioeconomic disparities, they are probably misguided. The

truth is, you probably don't belong here, and your college experience will probably be a long downhill slide.

Person B: Out of my face jungle bunny.

As Gates notes, "Surely, there is no doubt which is likely to be more wounding and alienating to its intended audience" (146).

14 From a 7 December 2007 meeting about the status of my own formal review.

15 Professor John Mearsheimer (R. Wendell Harrison Distinguished Service Professor, University of Chicago), in his "Defense of Academic Freedom" conference talk, stated:

> Almost everyone admits that significant pressure was brought to bear on DePaul to deny Finkelstein tenure. Alan Dershowitz's intervention in this regard is the most visible example of outside interference, but he was surely not the only outside to weigh in against Finkelstein. DePaul's leaders all but acknowledge the outside pressure but deny it had any effect on the final decision. Of course, what else are they going to say? They are certainly not going to admit that they caved into pressure from the Israel lobby. But there is little doubt that they did, as there is no other plausible explanation for the top administrators' decision to override the recommendation of the political science department and the college-wide tenure committee.

16 Here is the essence of DePaul's position, as elaborated in the settlement statement: "Professor Finkelstein has expressed the view that he should have been granted tenure and that third parties external to the University h outside interest about the tenure decision. This attention was unwelcome and inappropriate. In the end, however, it had absolutely no impact on either the process or the final outcome. Professor Finkelstein is a prolific scholar and an outstanding teacher. The University thanks him for his contributions and service." Settlement statement available at newsroom.depaul.edu/NewsReleases/showNews.aspx?NID=1655 (accessed on 3 February 2011). Also, see Finkelstein and Bernabai interview about settlement agreement with Amy Goodman on *Democracy, Now!*, www.democracynow.org/2007/9/10/professor_norman_finkelstein_and_depaul_end (accessed on 2 February 2011). As I have demonstrated, there was plenty of inside interference, which was coordinated with outside interference, to create an insurmountable obstacle for Finkelstein to receive a fair tenure hearing.

17 For a personal example, see condor.depaul.edu/~mabraha5/utkmaterials.htm (accessed on 26 March 2011).

18 "The Fate of an Honest Intellectual," in P. Mitchell and J. Schoeffel (eds), *Understanding Power: The Indispensable Chomsky*. New York: New Press, 2002, p. 245. Finkelstein left the Middle East Studies Program for the Politics Department, from which he received his Ph.D.

19 Dershowitz's response to this review can be viewed at www.logosjournal.com/issue_5.1/dershowitz.htm (accessed on 6 February 2011). My reply to Dershowitz's reply can be viewed at www.logosjournal.com/issue_5.1/abraham.htm (accessed on 6 February 2011).

20 Throughout the 2007–08 academic year, Finkelstein was considered for a visiting professorship at California State Northridge Despite the support of

the CSU-Northridge Provost, Harry Hellenbrand, Finkelstein's appointment was never ultimately approved. It is an open question as to the role of outside interference in President Joleen Koester's seemingly last-minute "policy decision not to hire visiting faculty at CSUN, even if a request to do so originates at the department level" (Klein 2008–09).

Chapter 5

1 Stanley Fish. "Don't Blame Relativism" as part of a colloquium entitled "Can Postmodernists Condemn Terrorism?" in *Responsive Community* (www.gwu. edu/~ccps), Summer 2002. As William McBride remarked, "We don't need him [Fish] to remind us!"

2 13 July 2002, *NY Times* Op-Ed. For equally problematic discussions of Said and postcolonial theory after 9/11, consider Stanley Kurtz's "Edward Said, Imperialist: The Hegemonic Impulse of Post-Colonialism" in *The Weekly Standard* (http://www.weeklystandard.com) and Dinesh D'Souza's "Two Cheers for Colonialism" in *The Chronicle Review* (http://chronicle.com/free/ v48/i35/35b00701.htm).

3 As will become clear in this section, the rhetoric of the American and Israeli (pro-Zionist) Right is similar in the enforcement of "objectivity" and "truth." Consider Edward Said's reflection in *The Question of Palestine*:

> The Arabs and Islam *represent* viciousness, veniality, degenerate vice, lechery, and stupidity in popular and scholarly discourse. On this collective representation of the Arabs and Islam, Zionism, like its Western ideological parents, drew. (26)

4 For a discussion of the problematic usages of the term "post-colonialism" see Anne McClintock and Ella Shohat in *Social Text* 31/32, pp. 85–98 and pp. 99–113 (1980).

5 22 September 2001, *NY Times* Op-Ed.

6 See Said's "The Clash of Ignorance" in *The Nation* (22 October 2001), Samuel P. Huntington's "The Clash of Civilizations?" in *Foreign Affairs* (Summer 1993) and Huntington's book *The Clash of Civilizations: Remaking of World Order* (New York: Touchstone Books, 1996).

7 22 September 2001, *NY Times* Op-Ed.

8 22 September 2001, *NY Times* Op-Ed. Hitchens took issue with both Noam Chomsky and Norman G. Finkelstein who seemed to view 9/11 as a direct outcome of US foreign policy in the Middle East.

9 In the July 2002 issue of *Harper's*, Said writes that

> American public discourse has been grappling most energetically with our enemies, Islamic fundamentalism, terrorism, the axis of evil, and so on, but not with any particularly useful results that I know of. Reflective, disinterested research on delicate matters of faith or history appears to be out of the question—and isn't what the market requires, at any rate. (Said in *Harper's* "Impossible Histories: Why Many Islams Cannot be Simplified," 70)

10 In his July 2002 *Harper's* articles, Said stated that

> Above all, "we" cannot go on pretending that "we" live in a world of our own; certainly, as Americans, our government is deployed literally all over the globe—militarily, politically, economically. So why do we suppose that what we say and do is neutral, when in fact it is full of consequences for the rest of the human race? In our encounters with other cultures and religions, therefore, it would seem that the best way to proceed is not to think like governments or armies or corporations but rather to remember and act on the individual experiences that really shape our lives and those of others.? (74)

11 See Dominick LaCapra in *Writing History, Writing Trauma* (Baltimore: Johns Hopkins University Press, 2000), pp. 142–3 and Peter Lowenberg in *Decoding the Past: A Psychohistorical Approach* (New York: Knopf, 1983). LaCapra, in an interview with Yad Vashem, states:

> The basic sense of transference in Freud is a process of repetition: specifically, the repetition of the oedipal scene in later life, the relationship between parent and child in situations such as that of teacher/student, or analyst/patient in ways that may be inappropriate. Although oedipal relations have an obvious importance in a society in which the nuclear family becomes the typically overcharged locus of emotion and often a more or less mystified "haven in a heartless world," I think that transference extends beyond the Oedipal relationship and that it's confinement within that scenario amounts to a domestication that may well divert attention from one's implication in institutions and social relations that extend beyond but of course include and help to shape the family.

12 *Writing History, Writing Trauma*, p. 148.

13 *The Responsive Community*, p. 28.

14 In his July 2002 *Harper's* article Fish writes that

> [t]he point of the public sphere is obvious: it is supposed to be the location of those standards and measures that belong to no one but apply to everyone. It is to be the location of the universal. The problem is not that there is no universal—the universal, the absolutely true, exists, and I know what it is. The problem is that you know, too, and that we know different things, which puts us right back where we were [a few sentences ago], armed with universal judgments that are irreconcilable, all dressed up and nowhere to go for an authoritative adjudication. (37)

15 For a perhaps more convincing analysis see Michael Walzer's "Can There be a Decent Left?" in *Dissent* (Spring 2002). For a less critical appraisal see Peter Berkowitz in *The New Republic Express* (28 June 2002) http://www.thenewrepublic.com.

16 I will not divulge the identity of this individual but only say that, in a communication widely-circulated within the department, he or she attempted to initiate a boycott of the roundtable through what might be called "a minor propaganda campaign." Another individual—believing that the roundtable was deliberately stacked against Israel—sent a communication to one of my roundtable co-hosts entitled "20 Facts on the Middle East" that was written by

Jack Kemp and Jeane Kirkpatrick. The implication was clear: anyone speaking up for Palestinian human rights was badly misinformed.

17 See Said in *The Question of Palestine* (New York: Vintage Books, 1980), pp. 56–114, Ella Shohat in "Sephardim in Israel: Zionism from the Standpoint of its Jewish Victims" in *Social Text* (Fall 1988), and Ronald Aronson in "Never Again? Zionism and the Holocaust," in *Social Text* 3 (Fall 1980).

18 See *Nation and Narration*, ed. Homi Bhaba (New York: Routledge, 1990).

19 Many were disturbed to see the jubilant celebration of the 9/11 attacks in the West Bank.

20 See Peter Novick in *The Holocaust in American Life* (New York: Mariner Books, 2000), pp. 161–9.

21 On these matters, see Laurence J. Silberstein's *The Postzionism Debates: Knowledge and Power in Israeli Culture* (New York: Routledge, 1998). Peter Novick's *The Holocaust in American Life* (New York: Mariner Books, 2000), Norman G. Finkelstein's *The Holocaust Industry: The Exploitation of Jewish Suffering* (London: Verso, 2002), Tim Cole's *Selling the Holocaust: From Auschwitz to Schindler's List (How History is Bought, Packaged and Sold)* (New York: Routledge, 2000) and Dominick LaCapra's *Representing the Holocaust* (Ithaca: Cornell University Press, 1996), *History and Memory After Auschwitz* (Ithaca: Cornell University Press, 1998) and, *Writing History, Writing Trauma* (Baltimore: Johns Hopkins University Press, 2000). Also see Pierre Vidal-Naquet's *Assassins of Memory: Essays on the Denial of the Holocaust*, trans. with a forward by Jeffrey Mehlman (New York: Columbia University Press, 1992).

22 Compare Bennett's statement to Said's anguished reflection after 9/11:

> Israel is now cynically exploiting the American catastrophe by intensifying its military occupation and oppression of the Palestinians. Since 11 September, Israeli military forces have invaded Jenin and Jericho and have repeatedly bombed Gaza, Ramallah, Beit Sahour and Beit Jala, exacting great civilian casualties and enormous material damage. All of this, of course, is done brazenly with US weaponry and the usual lying cant about fighting terrorism. Israel's supporters in the US have resorted to hysterical cries like "we are all Israelis now," making the connection between the World Trade Center and Pentagon bombings and Palestinian attacks on Israel an absolute conjunction of "world terrorism," in which and Arafat are interchangeable entities. What might have been a moment for Americans to reflect on the probable causes of what took place, which many Palestinians, Muslims and Arabs have condemned, has been turned into a huge propaganda triumph for Sharon; **Palestinians are simply not equipped to defend themselves against both Israeli occupation in its ugliest and most violent forms and the vicious defamation of their national struggle for liberation.** (*Al-Aharam Weekly*, September 2001, emphasis added)

23 Ibid., p. 213.

24 "Academic History Caught in the Cross-Fire: The Case of Israeli-Jewish Historiography" *in History and Memory*, Vol. 7, No. 1 (1995), p. 47.

25 Silberstein, p. 167.

26 According to Brunner,

> Aharon Megged accused the New Historians of disseminating anti-Zionist propaganda and declared that anyone who called the Zionist movement and policies colonialist identifies with the Palestinians—i.e., Israel's threatening and destructive other. Megged leaves no doubt that as a fighting participant in the founding state he has a strong personal identification with Israel's collective self-image. Those who interpret this conflict from an angle that differs from that of the Zionist actors are accused of completely negating the existence of the latter. (282)

27 Brunner in *History and Memory*, p. 283.

28 "Politics and Collective Memory" in *History and Memory*, Vol. 7, No. 1, p. 26.

Shapira goes on to write

> Thus, one cannot speak of objective facts, and even less so of historical truth. As a result, facts are but a vain illusion invented by historians, whose approaches were conditioned by their a-priori positions. There are no "objective" or "non-objective" historians: there are only historians who recognize the relativity of their data and those who refute it. This view is meant to serve as the basis for the return of ideology to historiography: every historian has a political agenda, whether overt or covert. Thus, the ideological approach is legitimate when analyzing historical material. History, according to this version, is a "narrative," that is, a story invented by historians out of their own ideological needs. The conclusion to be drawn is that no story is more authentic than any other; each is meant to further the political or social ends of its author or the interest group he or she represents. (26)

29 Shapira writes that

> [i]f the deconstructionist trend followed by some of the "new historians" gains strength, then it will become clear we are facing a total crisis in all that concerns the human sciences and the domain of history in particular. For if no historical reality exists to be uncovered, if there are no agreed-upon research principles of what is permitted and forbidden, accepted, and unaccepted, if there is no methodological rules, then there can be no common language between historians. (34)

30 Shapira, p. 27.

31 See Erik Cohen's "Israel as a Post-Zionist Society," in *Israel Affairs*, Vol. 1, No. 3 (Spring 1995), p. 210.

32 Noa Gedi's and Yigal Elam's "Collective Memory—What Is It?" in *History and Memory*, Vol. 7, No. 2 (1995), pp. 31–50 and José Brunner's "Pride and Memory: Nationalism, Narcissism and the Historians' Debates in Germany and Israel" in *History and Memory*, Vol. 9, Nos. 1 and 2 (1997), pp. 256–300.

33 Cohen, p. 211.

34 Said, "The Public Role of Writers and Intellectuals," *The Nation*, 17 September 2001.

35 Discussions of "contrapuntal reading" and "structures of attitude and reference" appear most prominently in *Culture and Imperialism*.

36 Shapira, p. 33.

37 See Rashid Khalidi's *Palestinian Identity: The Construction of Modern National Consciousness* (New York: Columbia University Press, 1997). Harvard law professor, Alan Dershowitz, in his *Why Terrorism Works: Understanding the Threat, Responding to the Challenge* (New York: New York University Press, 2002), writes that "[i]t is impossible to understand the terrible events of September 11, 2001, without understanding the dynamics—and the success—of PALESTINIAN terrorism" (36, emphasis mine).

38 See Barbara Herrnstein Smith's *Contingencies of Value: Alternative Perspectives for Critical Theory* (Cambridge, MA: Harvard University Press, 1987), pp. 54–5 and pp. 96–9 and Smith's *Belief and Resistance: The Dynamics of Contemporary Intellectual Controversy* (Cambridge, MA: Harvard University Press, 1999), pp. 21–2.

39 See Peter Novick's. *That Noble Dream: The Objectivity Question and the American Historical Profession* (Cambridge: Cambridge University Press, 1988), p. 3. Novick describes the "objectivity question in the historical profession" as being similar to "Nailing jelly to the wall." He writes that

> [t]he objective historian's role is that of a neutral, or disinterested, judge; it must never degenerate into that of advocate or, even worse, propagandist. The historian's conclusions are expected to display the standard judicial qualities of balance and evenhandedness. As with the judiciary, these qualities are guarded by the insulation of the historical profession from social pressure or political influence, and by the individual historian avoiding partisanship or bias—not having any investment in arriving at one conclusion rather than another. (2)

Also see Thomas L. Haskell's "Objectivity is Not Neutrality: Rhetoric versus Practice in Peter Novick's *That Noble Dream*" in *Objectivity is Not Neutrality* (Baltimore: Johns Hopkins, 1998), pp. 145–73.

40 In "Academic History Caught in the Cross-Fire," Kimmerling claims that, "[h]istoriography, any historiography, is part of a sociopolitical hegemony and is committed to serving it" and that "[t]o challenge a hegemonic body of knowledge is far more complicated than the struggle against a politically directed elite" (58).

41 In the United States Code and in military manuals "terrorism" is defined as "the calculated use of violence or the threat of violence to attain political, religious, or ideological goals through intimidation, coercion, or the instilling of fear." Noam Chomsky argues that this definition cannot be accepted by the United States and Israel because all of the wrong consequences follow with respect to the Palestinian intifada in the occupied territories: the United Nations has established that this definition does not apply to people resisting racist occupations or suffering under human rights violations. Noam Chomsky has argued that—contrary to popular opinion—terrorism and violence usually do work to effect political changes. According to Chomsky, "terrorism is not the weapon of the weak but, overwhelmingly, the weapon of the strong. Terrorism is often ascribed to the weak because the strong control the doctrinal systems that fashion the definitions." (October 2001 lecture at MIT)

42 Shortly after the 9/11 attacks, Said wrote:

Political rhetoric in the US has overridden [reasoned deliberation] by flinging about words like "terrorism" and "freedom" whereas, of course, such large abstractions have mostly hidden sordid material interests, **the efficacy of the oil, defense and Zionist lobbies now consolidating their hold on the entire Middle East** and an age-old religious hostility to (and ignorance of) "Islam" that takes new forms every day. The commonest thing is to get TV commentary, run stories, hold forums, or announce studies on Islam and violence or on Arab terrorism, or any such thing, using the predictable experts (the likes of Judith Miller, Fouad Ajami, and Steve Emerson) to pontificate and throw around generalities without context or real history. **Why no one thinks of holding seminars on Christianity (or Judaism for that matter) and violence is too obvious to ask.**

(Al-Haram 12).

43 Said writes that

[t]he sad truth is that where discussion of Israel is concerned, the United States is well below Israel itself in norms of truth and methods of debate. Here there is a perfect illustration of Richard Hofstader's "paranoid style" in American political life. This is not, alas, a matter of the left being better than the right. The young progressives who publish *Radical History* conscientiously avoid discussion of the Palestinians. Those who know better are cowed by the Israeli lobby. (Edward Said's "Conspiracy of Praise" in *Blaming the Victims: Spurious Scholarship and the Palestinian Question*. London: Verso, 1986, p. 30)

44 *The Question of Palestine*, pp. 40–1.

45 See Toine van Teeffelen's "Tragic Heroes and Victims in Zionist Ideology" in *Khamsin*, Vol. 9, p. 127.

46 The case of Norman G. Finkelstein will be considered in the next chapter. Also see Paul Findley's *They Dare to Speak Out: People and Institutions Confront Israel's Lobby* (Westport: Lawrence Hill & Company, 1985) and Said's *The Question of Palestine*, p. 43.

47 One might object to this claim by pointing out that President George W. Bush has called for the creation of a Palestinian state. However, there is a huge difference between Palestine and a Palestinian state. The use of the name "Palestine" acknowledges that a cohesive people, the Palestinians, existed in what is now present-day Israel and confirms the forceful removal of the Palestinians from that area in 1947–48.

48 See Said's "American Zionism—The Real Problem" at http://www.mediamonitors.net/edward12.html.

49 See Van Teeffelen, p. 130.

50 See Benny Morris's "The New Historiography: Israel Confronts Its Past" in *Tikkun*, Vol. 3, No. 6 (November/December 1988), pp. 19–22, pp. 99–102 and *The Birth of the Palestine Refugee Problem: 1947-49* (Cambridge: Cambridge University Press, 1996).

51 Morris in "The New Historiography: Israel Confronts Its Past" in *Tikkun*, Vol. 3, No. 6 (November/December 1988), p. 102. Interestingly enough, Morris undertook a dramatic reversal in some of his advocacy for Israeli negotiations

with the PLO and Arafat in February 2002, claiming that today the Palestinian leadership really denies Israel's legitimacy. See his "Peace? No Chance," in the *Guardian* (21 February 2002). For a response to Morris's *Guardian* article, see Avi Shlaim's "A Betrayal of History," in the *Guardian* (22 February 2002). For a refutation of "Benny Morris's 'Born by War not by Design' Thesis" see Norman G. Finkelstein's *Image and Reality in the Israel-Palestine Conflict* (London: Verso, 1996) (Chapter 3). See Morris's "Response to Finkelstein and Masalha" in *Journal of Palestine Studies*, Vol. 21, No. 1, pp. 88–114 and Norman Finkelstein's "Rejoinder to Benny Morris" Ibid., No. 2 (Winter 1992), pp. 161–71.

52 Edward Said and Jean Mohr. *After the Last Sky* (New York: Pantheon, 1982), p. 133.

53 See Edward Alexander's "Professor of Terror" in *Commentary* (August 1989), pp. 49–50, Hillel Halkin's "Whose Palestine? An Open Letter to Edward Said," in *Commentary* (May 1980), pp. 21–30 and Justin Reid Weiner's "'My Beautiful Old House' and Other Fabrications by Edward Said" in *Commentary* (September 1999).

54 *Nightline*, 29 April 2002.

55 *The Nation*, "Beat the Devil" Column, 16 May 2002.

56 See Said's heated debate with Robert J. Griffin and Daniel and Jonathan Boyarin in "An Exchange on Edward Said and Difference," *Critical Inquiry*, Vol. 15 (Spring 1989), pp. 611–33. As a follow-up to that exchange, see the letters from Geoffrey Hartman, Said, and Masao Miyoshi, and the editors in *Critical Inquiry* 16 (Autumn 1989), pp. 199–204; Edward Alexander's "The Professor of Terror," *Commentary*, Vol. 88, No. 2 (August 1989), pp. 48–50; Mark Krupnick's "Edward Said and the Discourse of Palestinian Rage," *Tikkun*, Vol. 4, No. 6 (November/December 1989), pp. 21–4; Hilel Halkin's "Whose Palestine? An Open Letter to Edward Said," *Commentary*, Vol. 69, No. 5 (May 1980), pp. 21–30; Justus Reid Weiner's "'My Beautiful Old House' and Other Fabrications by Edward Said" Commentary, Vol. 108, No. 2 (September 1999), pp. 23–31; and the Bruce Robbins-Catherine Gallagher exchange in *Diacritics*, prompted by the publication of Robbins' review of Said's *The Question of Palestine* and *The World, the Text, and the Critic*. See Robbins' "Homelessnes and Worldliness," *Diacritics* (Fall 1983), 69–77, Gallagher's "Politics, the Profession, and the Critic," *Diacritics*, Vol. 15, No. 2 (Summer 1985), pp. 37–43; and Robbins' "Deformed Professions, Empty Politics," *Diacritics*, Vol. 16, No. 3 (Fall 1986), pp. 67–72.

57 See Said's "The Role of Writers and Intellectuals <http://www.thenation. com/doc/20010917/essay> (accessed on 20 February 2010). The essay is reproduced in Said's *Humanism and Democratic Criticism* (New York: Pantheon Books, 2004).

58 See Said's *Journal of Palestine Studies* essay on "U.S. Policy and the Conflict of the Powers in the Middle East" (1973), Vol. 20.

59 See Said's "Opponents, Audiences, Constituencies, and Community," *Critical Inquiry* (September 1982), pp. 1–26.

60 Said discusses Northup Frye's *The Great Code: The Bible and Literature*, Harold Bloom's *Kabbalah and Criticism*, and others in the final chapter of *The World, the*

Text, and the Critic. Also, see the special issue of *Boundary 2* on "The Problems of Reading in Contemporary American Criticism," Vol. 8, No. 1 (Autumn 1979). Of note here are the contributions by Donato, Logan, Warner, and Crites.

61 See Said's "The Problem of Textuality: Two Exemplary Positions" in *Critical Inquiry*, Vol. 4, No. 4 (1978).

62 See Sokmen's and Ertur's *Waiting for the Barbarians: A Tribute to Edward Said* (London: Verso, 2008), Radha Radhakrishnan's *History, the Human, and the World Between* (Durham: Duke University Press, 2008), and William Spanos's *The Legacy of Edward W. Said* (Urbana: University of Illinois Press, 2009).

63 See Shaheen's *Reel Bad Arabs: How Hollywood Vilifies a People*, 2nd edn (Brooklyn: Olive Branch Press, 2009).

64 See Said's "Dignity, Solidarity, and the Penal Colony," *Counterpunch* 29 January 2010, http://www.counterpunch.org/said09252003.html.

65 "Said, Palestine, and the Humanism of Liberation," *Critical Inquiry*, Winter 2005, p. 451.

66 Roseville, CA: Institute for Jewish Community and Research, p. 56.

67 See John Mearsheimer and Stephen Walt's *The Israel Lobby and U.S. Foreign Policy* (London: Farrar, Giroux, and Strauss, 2007).

68 See Jacqueline Rose's *The Last Resistance* (London: Verso, 2007) and James Le Sueur's *Uncivil War: Intellectuals and Identity Politics during the Decolonization of Algeria* (Lincoln: University of Nebraska Press, 2005).

69 *Humanism and Democratic Criticism* (New York: Columbia University Press, 2004), p. 123.

70 See Said's "Dignity, Solidarity, and the Penal Colony" in *Counterpunch* 29 January 2010, http://www.counterpunch.org/said09252003.html.

Chapter 6

1 *For Reasons of State* (New York and London: The New Press, 2003).

2 See Chomsky's *Toward a New Cold War*, Edward Said's *The World, the Text, and the Critic* (Cambridge, MA: Harvard University Press, 1983) and James Merod's *The Political Responsibility of the Critic* (Ithaca: Cornell University Press, 1983).

3 *Toward a New Cold War* (New York: New Press, 2003), pp. 14–15.

4 See my *Guardian* article, "Finkelstein Case: Academic Freedom Loses to Israel Lobby," at http://electronicintifada.net/v2/article7055.shtml (5 May 2008).

5 See Noam Chomsky, et al. *The Cold War & The University* (New York: New Press, 1997) and Christopher Simpson's edited collection, *Universities and Empire: Money and Politics in the Social Sciences During the Cold War* (New York: New Press, 1998).

6 See Noam Chomsky and Edward Herman's *Manufacturing of Consent: The Political Economy of the Mass Media* (New York: Pantheon, 2002).

7 Jesse Lemisch. *On Active Service in War and Peace: Politics and Ideology in the American Historical Profession* (Toronto: New Hogtown Press, 1975).

8 According to Irwin Unger, New Left scholarship was "scholarship as an opportunity for a political harangue" (Lemisch's *On Active Service*, p. 44).

9 See Chomsky and Herman's *The Political Economy of Human Rights*, Vols. I and II (Cambridge: South End Press, 1979).

10 See Geoffrey Stone's *Perilous Times: Free Speech in Wartime from the Sedition Act of 1798 to the War on Terrorism* (New York: W.W. Norton, 2005) and Ellen Shrecker's *No Ivory Tower* (Oxford: Oxford University Press, 1988), *Many are the Crimes: McCarthyism in America* (Princeton: Princeton University Press, 1999), and *Cold War Triumphalism: The Misuse of History after the Fall of Communism* (New York: New Press, 2006).

11 See Chomsky's "The Fate of an Honest Intellectual" in *Understanding Power: The Indispensable Chomsky*, eds. Noam Chomsky, John Schoeffel, and Peter Mitchell (New York and London: New Press, 2002), pp. 246–9. Norman Finkelstein, who was recently denied tenure at DePaul University, exposed Joan Peters' *From Time Immemorial: The Origins of the Arab-Israel Conflict Over Palestine* (New York: JKAP Publications, 1984) as a "threadbare hoax" in 1986 while a graduate student of Politics at Princeton University. Peters' book, heralded as a breakthrough in historical scholarship by the leading lights of American Arts and Letters, claimed that the Palestinians never really existed as a society, but in fact were random Arabs who emigrated into historical Palestine a few years prior to Israel's creation. Since that exposure of Peters' book, Finkelstein's persona and scholarship have been under fierce attack, despite his publication of five internationally acclaimed books on the Israel-Palestine conflict and the Nazi Holocaust.

12 See Timothy Brennan's "Meanwhile, in the hallways" in *Class Issues: Pedagogy and the Public Sphere*, ed. Amitava Kumar (New York: New York University Press, 1997), pp. 221–36.

13 See my "Academic Freedom as a Rhetorical Construction: A Response to Powers and Chaput," a response essay to Karen Powers and Catherine Chaput's "Anti-American Studies in the Deep South: Dissenting Rhetorics, the Practice of Democracy, and Academic Freedom in Wartime Universities." *College Composition and Communication*, Vol. 59, No. 3 (February 2008), pp. 512–17.

14 See Ward Churchill's "The Myth of Academic Freedom: Personal Experience of a Liberal Principle in the Neoconservative Era (Fragments of a Work in Progress)" in *Social Text 90*, Vol. 25, No. 1 (Spring 2007), pp. 17–39.

15 See the *Anti-Chomsky Reader*, ed. Peter Collier and David Horowitz (San Francisco: Encounter Books, 2006).

16 As Brennan writes: "The United States continues to invade other countries, but the invasion is not now supposed to be an invasion: rather, the nation extends its shadow, becomes the elsewhere, decenters itself. To what extent current theory helps the United States perform this function with relative impunity is a vital question, it seems to me," (*At Home in the World: Cosmopolitanism Now*, p. 6). Chomsky writes that: "In an age of science and technology, it is inevitable

that their prestige will be employed as an ideological instrument—specifically that the social and behavioral sciences will in various ways be made to serve in defense of national policy or as a mask for special interest. It is not merely that intellectuals are strongly tempted, in a society that offers them prestige and affluence, to take what is now called a 'pragmatic attitude' (in a perverse sense of 'pragmatism' which is, sad to say, not without some historical justification, as shown in the Dewey-Bourne interchange during World War I—see Introduction, pp. 5–7), that is, an attitude that one must 'accept', not critically analyze or struggle to change, the existing distribution of power, domestic or international, and the political realities that flow from it, and must only for 'slow measures of improvement' in a technological, piecemeal manner." (*American Power and the New Mandarins*, 317). Also, see Gopal Balakrishnan's edited collection *Debating Empire* (London: Verso, 2003).

17   In their *Multitude: War and Democracy in the Age of Empire*, Hardt and Negri write: "Our point of departure [in *Empire*] was the recognition that contemporary global order can no longer be understood adequately in terms of imperialism as it was practiced by the modern powers, based primarily on the sovereignty of the nation-state extended over foreign territory. Instead, a 'network power', a new form of sovereignty, is now emerging, and it includes as its primary elements, or nodes, the dominant nation-states along with supranational institutions, major capitalist corporations, and other powers" (xii).

18   See Paul Berman's *Terror and Liberalism* (New York: W.W. Norton Co.), pp. 144–53.

19   This argumentative rigor can be observed in Chomsky's *The Fateful Triangle: The United States, Israel, and the Palestinians* (Cambridge: South End, 1983), *World Orders: Old and New* (New York: Columbia University Press, 1998), *The Political Economy of Human Rights*, Vols. I and II (Cambridge: South End Press, 1979).

20   See Appendix B at the end of the book.

21   See Julien Benda's *The Treason of the Intellectuals (La Trahison Des Clercs)*, trans. Richard Altington (New York: W.W. and Norton Company, 1928) and Masao Miyoshi's "A Borderless World? From Colonialism to Transnationalism and the Decline of the Nation-State," *Critical Inquiry*, Vol. 19, No. 4 (Summer 1993), pp. 726–51.

22   See Joseph Massad's "Policing the Academy" at http://weekly.ahram.org. eg/2003/633/op2.htm (4 June 2008).

23   In his review of *Chomsky's The Fateful Triangle: The United States, Israel, and the Palestinians*, entitled "The Permission to Narrate," Edward Said writes: "[Chomsky's] isolation from the actual arena of contest, his distance from power as a fiercely uncompromising intellectual, his ability to tell the dispassionate truth (while no longer able to write in previously hospitable places like the *New York Review of Books*) have made it possible for him to avoid the ideological traps and the dishonesty he perceives in Israeli and US apologists. There is, of course, no state worship in Chomsky, nor is there any glossing over uncomfortable truths or indecent practices that exist within one's own camp. But are isolation, the concern for justice, the passion to record injustice, sufficient to ensure one's own freedom from ideology?

When Chomsky claims to be dealing with facts, he does deal with more facts than his opponents. *But where are facts if not embedded in history, and then reconstituted and recovered by human agents stirred by some perceived or desired or hoped for historical narrative whose future aim is to restore justice to the dispossessed?* In other words, the reporters of fact, like Chomsky, as well as the concealers of fact, like the 'supporters of Israel', are acting within history, according to codifiable norms of representation, in a context of competing ideological and intellectual values. When he states the facts as widely, as clearly, as completely as any person alive, Chomsky, is not merely performing a mechanical reporting chore, from some Archimedean point outside propaganda and cliché: he is doing something extremely sophisticated, underpinned by standards of argument, coherence, and proof that are not derived from the merely 'factual.' But the irony is that Chomsky does not reflect theoretically on what he does; he just does it. So, on the one hand, he leaves us to suppose that telling the truth is a simple matter while, on the other hand, he compiles masses of evidence showing that no one can really deal with the facts. How can we then suppose that one man can tell the truth? Does he believe that in writing this book he will lead others to tell the truth also? What makes it possible for us as human beings to state the facts, to manufacture new ones, or to ignore some and focus on others? Answers to these questions must reside in *a theory of perception, a theory of intellectual activity, and in an epistemological account of ideological structures as they pertain to specific problems as well as to concrete historical and geographical circumstances.* None of these things is within the capacity of a solitary individual to produce, and none is possible without some sense of communal or collective commitment to assign them a more than personal validity. It is this commitment that national narratives authorize and represent, although Chomsky's understandable reluctance to hew to any national or state line prevents him from admitting it" (*The Politics of Dispossession: The Struggle for Palestinian Self-Determination, 1969-1994* (New York: Vintage, 1995), pp. 267–8, emphasis mine).

24   See http://www.americanempireproject.com/bookpage.asp?ISBN=0805076883 (23 March 2008).

25   Consider the prominence of conceptions such as "empire," "biopolitics," "command centers," and "multitudes," which in fact serve to glorify and mystify operations of power rather than to elucidate them. These large structures, which represent projections of power, becoming relatively meaningless in helping one to predict and discuss how power actually works in the world. I would wager that these structures in fact serve to confuse those seeking to learn about how power actually works.

26   In his *Wars of Positions: The Cultural Politics of Left and Right* (New York: Columbia University Press, 2006), Timothy Brennan writes of "the post-turn," when "political belonging was ejected from the idea of identity" and when many left intellectuals ran away from "any politics seeking to enter or make claims on the state" (X). On a related note, in his *Acts of Resistance: Against the Tyranny of the Market*, Bourdieu writes: "[Globalization] is a myth in the strong sense of the word, a powerful discourse, an *idée force*, an idea which has social force, which obtains belief. It is the main weapon in the battles against the gains of the welfare state" (34).

27 See Avner Yaniv's *Dilemmas of Security: Politics, Strategy, and the Israeli Experience in Lebanon* (Oxford: Oxford University Press, 1987).

28 *Welcome to the Desert of the Real* (New York and London: Verso, 2006), pp. 126–34.

29 As Chomsky wrote in that context: "Here the question of 'lack of knowledge' does arise. To review the familiar and well-documented facts, in mid-1981 a US-brokered truce was established on the Israel-Lebanon border (we can go into what happened before, but to the limited extent that it is relevant to the 1982 invasion, it simply reinforces what we learned by looking at the period after the truce). For the next year, Israel carried out a series of murderous and destructive attacks against Lebanon, apparently trying to elicit some PLO response that could be used as a pretext for the planned invasion. There was none, apart from some very minor and symbolic retaliations to Israeli attack. Failing to construct the desired pretext of Palestinian incursions and attacks, Israel invaded anyway, pretending that this was a response to an assassination attempt against the Israeli Ambassador to London—though Israel knew at once that the attempt was carried out not by the PLO, but by Abu Nidal, who was at war with the PLO and had been condemned to death by them. The Israeli invasion began with the bombing of Sabra-Shatila Palestinians refugee camp, including its hospital, killing 200 people, according to the eyewitness testimony of the US Mideast scholar Cheryl Rubenberg. Then came the invasion, killing perhaps another 20,000 (victims are rarely counted accurately by the powerful) and leaving vast destruction. The actual reasons were not concealed: the goal was to put an end to the PLO efforts at a negotiated settlement, which were becoming an embarrassment and to impose an Israeli client regime in Lebanon. *So yes, knowledge is useful, and lack of knowledge can indeed be a problem.*" The full *Pretext* interview with Chomsky can be found in Appendix B at the end of the book. (http://www.pre-text.com/ptlist/reinvw.html, emphasis mine, 23 March 2007).

30 See Chomsky's *The Fateful Triangle: The United States, Israel, and the Palestinians* (Boston: South End Press, 1983), pp. 289–97.

31 Such tales continue to be produced in contemporary rhetorical scholarship, as Carol Winkler illustrates in her *In the Name of Terrorism: Presidents on Political Violence in the Post-World War II Era* (Albany: SUNY Press, 2006): "In the Middle East, the frequency and deadlines of terrorist attacks spiked after Israel responded to terrorist raids across its border by invading Lebanon in June 1982. The resulting violence prompted the United States to send the Marines into Lebanon as part of a multinational peacekeeping force" (66).

32 See *Image and Reality in the Israel-Palestine Conflict,* 2nd edn (London and New York: Verso, 2004).

33 See Zeev Maoz's *Defending the Holy Land: A Critical Analysis of Israel's Security of Foreign Policy* (Ann Arbor: University of Michigan Press, 2006).

34 *Open Secrets: Israeli Foreign and Nuclear Policy* (London and Ann Arbor: Pluto Books, 1997).

35 P. 128.

36 Chomsky, Noam. *Manufacturing Consent: Noam Chomsky and the Media, The companion book to the award-winning film by Peter Wintonick and Mark Achbar* (Boston: Black Rose Books, 1994), p. 21.

37 *Critical Inquiry*, Vol. 28, No. 2 (Winter 2002), pp. 573–79.

38 See http://human-nature.com/nibbs/01/chomky.html (30 March 2008).

39 See http://www.venezuelanalysis.com/news/1954 (30 April 2008).

40 Chomsky in 9 June 2004 *Pretext* post.

41 As Chomsky noted:

> Suppose the press had not just reported the sale, but done it as honest
> journalism would: that is, report that after several days of Israeli bombing
> of civilian targets with US helicopters, with dozens killed and wounded,
> and facing no credible threat., Clinton made the biggest deal in years to
> send new military helicopters to Israel, with no conditions on their use, the
> Pentagon revealed. Would people have been willing to accept that? I doubt
> it. And one can only assume that editors and American intellectuals doubt
> it too. That's why they suppressed it. It's undoubtedly very important news,
> and even apart from my personal experience with what I suppose is the
> most liberal group of editors in the country, and other reactions among elite
> intellectuals when informed, how else can one account for the unanimous
> refusal to report it? Furthermore, pretty normal practice. (Chomsky email
> message to author, 8 April 2004)

42 See Roy's Introduction to Chomsky's *Reasons of State*, p. xviii.

43 See Berube's "Peace Puzzle" in the 15 September 2002 issue of the *Boston
Globe* at: http://www.boston.com/news/packages/iraq/globe_stories/091502_
bush.htm (12 March 2008), Chomsky's 9/22/02 "Letter to the Editor" in the
Boston Globe, and Berube's 9/22/02 rejoinder. Also, see Berube's article for
The Center for Book Culture at http://www.centerforbookculture.org/context/
no10/berube.html (10 April 2008). Also, see Christopher Hitchens in *The
Nation* at http://www.thenation.com/doc.mhtml?i=special&s=hitchens20010
924 (15 March 2008).
  Chomsky's reply is available at: http://www.thenation.com/doc/20011015/
chomsky20011001 (19 April 2008); Hitchens' rejoinder: http://www.
thenation.com/doc/20011015/hitchens20011004 (20 April 2008); Chomsky's
reply to Hitchens' rejoinder is available at: http://www.thenation.com/
doc/20011015/chomsky20011004 (30 April 2008).

44 "Language, Politics, and Composition: A Conversation with Noam Chomsky."
Journal of Advanced Composition, Vol. 11 (1991), p. 6.

45 See Finkelstein's interview with Y. M. D. Fremes at: http://www.
normanfinkelstein.com/article.php?pg=4&ar=17 (26 May 2008).

46 In his *What's Liberal About the Liberal Arts? Classroom Politics and "Bias"
in Higher Education* (New York: W.W. Norton, 2007), Michael Berube
writes:

> "Another bunch, further off to the left, finds figures like Noam Chomsky so
> persuasive when it comes to American wickedness at home and abroad—
> not capriciously, either, for that wickedness is often real enough—that
> they become utterly indiscriminate about 'dissent,' valuing even its most
> counterproductive forms" (120); "The wholly uncritical Chomsky fans seem
> to me to have abdicated some of the tasks of critical thinking in precisely
> the same way that the wholly uncritical Bush worshippers have done, and

I wish the campus left, especially, would be a domain of ideas, where every citizen is obligated to scrutinize every idea on its merits." (121)

47 See Christopher Hitchens' "A Rejoinder to Noam Chomsky," *Nation*, 4 October 2001, http://www.thenation.com/doc/20011015/hitchens20011004 (30 April 2008).

48 In Sudan and Afghanistan, of course, civilian targets were, in fact, hit. In Sudan, a pharmaceutical factory; in Afghanistan, a wedding party. The termination of food-aid shipments in Afghanistan in 2001 could have resulted in "a silent genocide" (not Chomsky's words but that of Amnesty International).

49 Timothy Brennan and Keya Ganguly, "Crude Wars," *South Atlantic Quarterly*, Vol. 105, No. 1 (Winter 2006), pp. 29–30.

50 In their *Multitude: War and Democracy in the Age of Empire*, Hardt and Negri write: "In the contradictory new global economic order that is emerging through international agreements, there are woven together both globalizing tendencies and resurgent nationalist elements, both liberal proposals and self-interested perversions of liberal ideals, both regional political solidarities and neocolonial operation of commercial and financial domination" (171).

51 See Richard Faulk and Howard Friel's *The Record of the Paper: How the New York Times Misreports U.S. Foreign Policy* (New York and London: Verso, 2004).

52 *World Orders, Old and New*, p. 240.

53 *After the Cataclysm: Postwar Indochina and the Reconstruction of Imperial Ideology* (Cambridge: South End, 1979), p. 295.

54 See Cohn's "Holocaust Denial" in the *Anti-Chomsky Reader*; Windschuttle's "Unmasking Noam Chomsky" at http://www.cis.org.au/Policy/winter03/polwin03-6.pdf (4 June 2008); and Eliot Abram's letter to the editor of the *Index on Censorship* at http://normanfinkelstein.files.wordpress.com/2007/04/abrams.pdf (4 June 2008).

55 See http://www.normanfinkelstein.com/article.php?pg=4&ar=6 (19 March 2008).

56 Ibid.

57 27 October 2004 email to the author.

58 *For Reasons of State*, p. xli.

Chapter 7

1 See http://condor.depaul.edu/~mabraha5/pretext1.pdf; http://condor.depaul.edu/~mabraha5/pretext2.pdf; http://condor.depaul.edu/~mabraha5/pretext3.pdf; http://condor.depaul.edu/~mabraha5/pretext4.pdf; http://condor.depaul.edu/~mabraha5/pretext5.pdf. http://condor.depaul.edu/~mabraha5/pretext6.pdf (accessed on 1 September 2010).

2 In his *Multidirectional Memory: Remembering the Holocaust in the Age of Decolonization*, Michael Rothberg, drawing upon Hannah Arendt's *Origins of Totalitarianism* and Aime Cesaire's *Discourse of Colonialism*, develops the notion of *choc en retour*, literally "boomerang effect," "backlash," or "reverse shock" (23).

3   See Cheryl Glenn's *Unspoken: The Rhetoric of Silence*. Glenn writes, "Silence
    exists in overlapping states: environmental, locational, communal, personal. It
    can be self- or other-initiated, self- or other-derived. Silence can be something
    one does, something that is done to someone, or something one experiences"
    (9). Last year, a former editor of *College Composition and Communication*
    in an "Afterword" questioned whether an edited collection devoted to the
    examination of a "critical rhetoric on the Israel-Palestine Conflict" should be
    "burned," arguing that the collection was being published under false pretenses
    with a major commercial publisher in Rhetoric and Composition. This former
    CCC's editor claimed that she had been led to believe that the collection would
    explore positions on the conflict through rhetorical analysis, instead the essays
    she was handed supposedly engaged in "entrenched position-taking." Within
    the Afterword, this former CCC's editor characterized Norman G. Finkelstein,
    the son of Holocaust survivors, as "a denier of historical fact," suggesting that
    Finkelstein "denies" the Holocaust. Actually, Finkelstein has argued that the
    Holocaust is often used as an ideological weapon to silence critics of Israel's
    human rights record and its continual violation of international law. It's ironic
    that this former CCC's editor called for full scholarly accountability, when she
    herself did not meet the minimum benchmark for accountability.

4   See Jimmy Carter's *Palestine: Peace Not Apartheid* and Barack Obama's
    19 May 2011 State Department Speech. Carter notes, "The bottom line is this:
    Peace will come to Israel and the Middle East when the Israeli government is
    willing to comply with international law, with the Roadmap for Peace, with
    official American policy, with the wishes of a majority of its own citizens—and
    honor its own previous commitments—by accepting its legal borders. All Arab
    neighbors must pledge to honor Israel's right to exist in peace *under these
    conditions*. The United States is squandering international prestige and good
    will and intensifying global anti-American terrorism by unofficially condoning
    or abetting the Israeli confiscation and colonization of Palestinian territory"
    (216, emphasis added). As Obama noted in this speech, "The borders of Israel
    and Palestine should be based on the 1967 lines with mutually agreed swaps,
    so that secure and recognized borders are established for both states. The
    Palestinian people must have the right to govern themselves, and reach their
    potential, in a sovereign and contiguous state." Also, see Zalman Amit and
    Daphna Levit's *Israeli Rejectionism: A Hidden Agenda in the Middle East
    Peace Process*.

5   See http://condor.depaul.edu/~mabraha5/utk materials.htm (accessed on
    2 January 2013) for an example of how university administrators may not
    always support scholarship promoting peace, human dignity, and justice.

6   For a list of all the emails posted on the topic of the Rachel Corrie Courage in
    the Teaching of Writing Award, see http://condor.depaul.edu/~mabraha5/Chart
    (final).pdf (accessed on 6 January 2013).

7   See Bruce Ticker's "The Case Against Rachel Corrie" and Joshua Hammer's
    "The Death of Rachel Corrie." For a critique of Hammer's article, see Pham
    Nguyen's "Mother Jones Smears Rachel Corrie Specious Journalism in Defense
    of Killers."

8   See Hussein.

9   See Barbara Herrnstein-Smith's *Belief and Resistance: The Dynamics of Intellectual Controversy* (Cambridge: Harvard University Press, 1999), p. vii.

10 The call for nominations read as follows:

Fourth Annual Rachel Corrie Award for Courage in the Teaching of Writing 2007
RACHEL CORRIE

Rachel Corrie was a 23-year-old peace activist and senior at The Evergreen State College in Olympia, Washington. She was killed on March 16, 2003 in Rafah in the Gaza Strip. She was on leave from school to work in Palestine with the International Solidarity Movement, a group using and promoting "nonviolent, direct-action methods of resistance to confront and challenge illegal Israeli occupation forces and policies." Rachel was attempting to block an Israeli military bulldozer from demolishing the house of a pharmacist and his family when the driver of the bulldozer ran over her, then backed up and ran over her again. Wearing a bright orange jacket and using a bullhorn, Rachel was, by all eyewitness accounts and in horrifying photographs published on the Internet, exceptionally visible. Her parents, some members of Congress, and grassroots organizations including several Jewish peace groups have called for an independent US investigation into her death. Such an investigation has yet to happen, and the US media virtually buried the story—though it was featured prominently in the United Kingdom and in many other countries.

Corrie took courses like "Labor and the Environment" and "Public Art and the Middle East Conflict"; she also wrote detailed emails from Palestine. The late Edward Said, who met with her parents in May, 2003, wrote, "Her letters back to her family are truly remarkable documents of her ordinary humanity that made for very difficult and moving reading. . . ."

THE AWARD

The Progressive SIGs and Caucuses Coalition (PSCC) of the CCCC wishes to honor the memory of this extremely courageous student by recognizing a teacher in the CCCC who has taken professional risks in order to promote social justice through the teaching of writing. It is well known that the politics of hiring, tenure, and promotion often motivate graduate students and junior faculty to write, teach, and serve in "safe" subject and project areas; many are encouraged by mentors to shy away from genuinely "controversial" or "risky" subjects until they are tenured. In making this award, the PSCC hopes, conversely, to encourage writing teachers early in their careers to take on research, pedagogy, and service projects that promote commitment to peace, justice, and human dignity—even when hazarding the ire of deans, chairs, editors, and hiring and review committees.

Also, see http://www.discoverthenetworks.org/groupProfile.asp?grpId=7046.

11 See my "The Rhetoric of Academic Controversy after 9/11: Edward Said in the American Imagination," for a discussion about how transference can develop around an individual or school of thought.

12 See Shlomo Sand's *The Invention of the Jewish People*.

13 See Rory McCarthy's "British activist saw Rachel Corrie die under bulldozer, court hears."

14 For eyewitness accounts of Corrie's death, see Dale et al.'s "Four Eyewitnesses Describe the Murder of Rachel Corrie."

15 See Sandersock's *Peace Under Fire: Israel/Palestine and the International Solidarity Movement* for the eyewitness testimony of those who were near Rachel Corrie when she was attempting to block the bulldozer's path.

16 See *Multidirectional Memory: Remembering the Holocaust in the Age of Decolonization*.

17 See Patricia Roberts-Miller's *Deliberate Conflict: Argument, Political Theory, and Composition Classes*.

18 See Dominick LaCapra's *History in Transit* and *History and Memory after the Holocaust*.

19 Thomas Rickert makes this observation, through LaPlanche, in his *Acts of Enjoyment: Rhetoric, Žižek, and the Return of the Subject*.

20 According to Thomas Rickert in his *Acts of Enjoyment: Rhetoric, Žižek, and the Return of the Subject*, "Žižek understands trauma to be our response to an impossible limit or radical antagonism; it is an experience of constitutive anxiety or unease at the terrifying prospect of the impossibility of achieving harmonious resolutions to personal and social relations. Furthermore, trauma is more intensified by the fact that is also 'resists' symbolization, totalization, symbolic integration (*Sublime* 6)" (219).

21 See Freud's "From the History of an Infantile Neurosis."

22 See Ian Lustick's "Abandoning the Iron Wall: Israel and the Middle Eastern Muck," "To Build and to Be Built By: Israel and the Hidden Logic of the Iron Wall," and "Negotiating Truth: The Holocaust, Lehavdil, and Al-Nakba."

23 See the Introduction to *Judaic Perspectives in Rhetoric and Composition*, p. 3. Greenbaum and Holdstein allege that anti-Semitism has crept into composition studies, citing comments made during the WPA list-serv debate about the Rachel Corrie Courage in the Teaching of Writing Award.

24 See Norman Finkelstein's *Beyond Chutzpah: The Misuse of Anti-Semitism and the Abuse of History*. For additional perspectives on the "New Anti-Semitism" and Alexander Cockburn and Jeffrey St Clair's *The Politics of Anti-Semitism*. For a contrasting view, see Bernard Harrison's *The Resurgence of Anti-Semitism: Jews, Israel, and Liberal Opinion*.

25 See Judith Butler's "It's Not Anti-Semitic" and Sara Roy's "Short Cuts."

26 See pp. 210–11 of Dershowit'z *The Case for Israel* for a list of features constituting the New Anti-Semitism.

27 See LaCapra's *Writing History, Writing Trauma*.

28 In speaking to the disconnect between popular and scholarly knowledge on the Israel-Palestine conflict and the attacks that have been enabled against serious scholarship on the conflict, Joseph Massad notes, "What makes these anti-scholarship attacks possible and popular is the existence of a major discrepancy, even a radical disconnect, between popular knowledge and media coverage about the Palestine/Israel conundrum and established scholarly knowledge about the topic. It is this disconnect that the witch hunters mobilize against scholarship as proof that it is not media and popular knowledge,

which defends Israeli policy and Zionism's axioms, that is ideological, but rather academic scholarship which has largely uncovered unsavory facts about both." See Massad's "Targeting the University: Witch hunt at Columbia."

29 This phrase appears in Theodore Herzl's *The Jewish State*. According to Joseph Massad,

> Herzl affirms that it is not a question of taking Jews away from "civilized regions into the desert," but rather the transformation "will be carried out in the midst of civilization. We shall not revert to a lower stage we shall rise to a higher one." (119)

30 See Norman Finkelstein's *Image and Reality in the Israel-Palestine Conflict*.

31 See Jonathan Cooke's *Israel and the Clash of Civilizations: Iran, Iraq, and the Plan to Remake the Middle East*.

32 In his *Writing the Arab-Israeli Conflict: Pragmatism and Historical Inquiry*, Jonathan Isacoff uses the phrase "teleological exceptionalism" to describe how "some of Israel's most cosmopolitan elites, such as [Abba] Eban," described the unique circumstances surrounding Israel's birth in terms that did not conform to traditional liberation movements, emphasizing the reuniting of the Jewish people with the land after a nineteen-hundred-year separation (55).

33 For very thoughtful discussions of "conflation of memory," see Michael Bernard-Donals "Conflations of Memory; or, What They Saw at the Holocaust Museum after 9/11" in *Forgetful Memory: Representation and Remembrance in the Wake of the Holocaust*. Albany: SUNY Press, 2009, pp. 125–43.

34 See Yuri Slezkine's *The Jewish Century* and Karen Brodkin's *How Jews Became White Folks and What That Says About Race in America*.

35 See Norman G. Finkelstein's 16 September 2009 interview with Amy Goodman on *Democracy Now* about the Goldstone report at http://www.normanfinkelstein.com/democracy-now-analysis-of-goldstone-report/(accessed on 31 August 2010).

36 Ultimately, Arafat chose not to visit the Museum at all, bringing the controversy to a premature end. For news coverage of the controversy, see Baer's "Holocaust Museum Reverses Self, Offers VIP Tour to Arafat"; Kurtzman's "Controversy Bedevils U.S. Holocaust Museum Again"; *Washington Post*, "U.S. Holocaust Museum Scuttles Visit by Arafat"; and Miller's "Arafat at Holocaust Museum? Issue Stirs Emotions in Israel."

37 According to Walt and Mearsheimer,

> We use "Israel Lobby" as a convenient shorthand term for the loose coalition of individuals and organizations that actively work to shape U.S. foreign policy in a pro-Israel direction. The lobby is not a single, unified movement with a central leadership, however, and the individuals and groups that make up this broad coalition sometimes disagree on specific policy issues. Nor is it some sort of cabal or conspiracy. On the contrary, the organizations and individuals who make up the lobby operate out in the open and in the same way that other interest groups do. (112)

38 Dershowitz writes, in his *The Case Against Israel's Enemies: Exposing Jimmy Carter and Others Who Stand in the Way of Peace*,

> To summarize: Mearsheimer and Walt accuse American Jews of creating a mechanism of social and political control in order to further their loyalty to Israel—which, Mearsheimer and Walt imply, trumped American Jews' loyalty to the United States—by steering U.S. foreign policy in directions that suited Israel's and not America's interests. American Jews and their friends are not only disloyal, Mearsheimer and Walt suggest, but dangerous to the United States. (52)

Furthermore, as Dershowitz claims, "The accusations leveled by Mearsheimer and Walt share the same themes as the notorious *Protocols of the Elders of Zion,* the czarist forgery whose motifs became a staple of anti-Semitic propaganda" (52).

In his *The Deadlies Lies: The Israel Lobby and the Myth of Jewish Control,* Foxman contends,

> Naturally, scholars like Mearsheimer and Walt don't directly tap into this vein of fantasy ("the whole bizarre rigmarole of paranoid fantasies that finds its classic expression in the notorious czarist forgery *The Protocols of the Elders of Zion*"). In fact, they explicitly disavow it. But the tenor of their argument, intentionally or not, activates that fantasy and draws upon the emotions it evokes. (109)

Chapter 8

1 See Yosef Gorny's *Zionism and the Arabs, 1882-1948: A Study of Ideology.* Oxford: Clarendon Press, 1987.

2 See "Richness of Muslim Identities" in Chapter 4 (Religious Affiliations and Muslim History) in Amartya Sen's *Identity and Violence* (New York and London: W.W. Norton & Company, 2006), pp. 59–83.

3 In his *Blood and Religion: The Unmasking of the Jewish and Democratic State* (London and Ann Arbor: Pluto Books, 2006), Jonathan Cook notes how Israel's Arab citizens faced a predicament in September of 2000, when the Second Intifada began, expressing sentiments in sharp contrast to what they demonstrated in their behavior since 1976:

> The veteran Israeli journalist Gideon Levy, who has reported from the occupied territories for many years for *Ha'aretz,* argued that the sudden outpouring of anger by the minority in October 2000 should be seen in the context of decades of quiescence. Ever since 1976, when six Arab demonstrators were killed by the security forces during protests against a wave of land confiscations, Arab citizens had demonstrated unswerving loyalty, he observed. "Twenty five years of exemplary, almost exaggerated loyalty, almost groveling obedience to the state whose wars are not their wars, whose national anthem is not their anthem, whose language is not their language, whose holidays are not their holidays." (48; Levy quote from "Only through Force," *Ha'aretz,* 8 October 2000)

4 See Alan Dershowitz's *Why Terrorism Works: Understanding the Threat, Responding to the Challenge* (New Haven: Yale University Press, 2002).

5   See Dershowitz's "Terrorism & Preventive Detention" in December 1970
    Commentary, p. 70. As El-Asmar responded: "I was astonished to read in Alan
    M. Dershowitz's article, 'Terrorism and Preventive Detention: The Case of
    Israel' [December 1970], facts and views imputed to me which are untrue"
    (June 1971 letter to the editor, *Commentary*, p. 33).

6   June 1971 letter to the editor, *Commentary*, p. 36.

7   According to the late Baruch Kimmerling, "politicide" refers to the Israeli
    government's attempts to completely destroy Palestinian civil society. See
    Kimmerling's *Politicide: Ariel Sharon's War Against the Palestinians* (London
    and New York: Verso, 2003). As Kimmerling observes: "Two deeply rooted
    existential anxieties exist within the Jewish military culture: one concerns the
    physical annihilation of the state, an issue that is frequently used, abused and
    emotionally manipulated by many Israeli politicians and intellectuals, and
    the other the loss of the fragile Jewish demographic majority on which the
    supremacy and identify of the state rests" (18).

8   See *To be an Arab in Israel*, p. 50.

9   See Chapter 7 (The Road to Armageddon) in Noam Chomsky's *The Fateful
    Triangle: The United States, Israel, and the Palestinians* (Boston: South End
    Press, 1983).

10 *Blood and Religion*, p. 8.

11 Reflecting a "Separatist" ideology, Israeli military historian Martin van Creveld
    writes:

    > [The only solution is] building a wall between us and the other side, so tall
    > that even the birds cannot fly over it . . . so as to avoid any kind of friction
    > for a long, long time in the future. . . . Unfortunately, the Israeli army insists
    > against all military logic on being present on both sides of the wall. We
    > could formally finish the problem, at least in Gaza, in forty-eight hours, by
    > getting out and building a proper wall. And then of course, if anybody tries
    > to climb over a wall, we kill him. (qtd. in Kimmerling's *Politicide*, p. 169)

12 *To Be an Arab in Israel* (New York: Columbia University Press, 2003).

13 See Sara Roy's "A Dubai on the Mediterranean" (http://www.lrb.co.uk/v27/
    n21/roy_01_.html) from the 3 November 2005, *London Review of Books*
    (7 March 2008).

14 See Yehoshua Porath's *The Emergence of the Palestinian Arab National
    Movement: 1918-1929* (New York: Routledge, 1995) and *The Palestinian
    Arab National Movement, 1929-1939: From Riots to Rebellion* (New York:
    Routledge, 1977). Benny Morris's *The Birth of the Palestinian Refugee
    Problem Revisited* (Cambridge: Cambridge University Press, 2004).

15 By this logic, according to Michael Selzer in his *The Aryanization of the Jewish
    State* (New York: Blackstar Publishing, 1967), "The sallow, emaciated, cringing
    Jew of the European shtetl, with his long beard and greasy caftan, the Fagin
    and the Shylock, had in Israel given way to a rugged new type—pioneering and
    adventurous, blond, sturdy and fearless, who typically spent his days ploughing
    fields with a modern tractor and his nights around the campfire making love to a
    succession of fair maidens who could have walked straight out of Wagner's own
    Vallhalla" (49). *The Jewish State*, pp. 136–52 and *Old New Land*, pp. 115–81.

16 As Kimmerling writes, "The hard facts are that a Palestinian people exists, no matter how 'old' it is, and that the possibility of their politicide—or their being cleansed from the country—without a fatal outcome for Israel is nil" (*Politicide*, 214).

17 See Massad's "The Persistence of the Palestinian Question," in *The Persistence of the Palestinian Questions: Essays on Zionism and the Palestinians.* New York: Routledge, 2006, pp. 166–78.

18 *To Be an Arab in Israel*, p. 50.

19 In his *On The Border*, trans. Levi Laub (Cambridge: South End Press, 2005), Michael Warschawski writes: "The acknowledgment of the other, of the non-Jew as a possible victim, is an important break with the Zionist narrative; the recognition that he may be our victim is another. It is this realization that enables one to back away from the tribe and to come closer to the border that separates the tribe from the rest of humanity" (54). Consider also Massad's reflections:

> After all, Israeli racism only manifests in its flag, its national anthem, and a bunch of laws that are necessary to safeguard Jewish privilege, including the Law of Return (1950), the Law of Absentee Property (1950), the Law of the State's Property (1951), the Law of Citizenship (1952), the Status Law (1952), the Israel Lands Administration Law (1960), the Construction and Building Law (1965), and the 2002 temporary law banning marriage between Israelis and Palestinians of the occupied territories. (from "Israel's Right to be Racist" at http://electronicintifada.net/v2/article6679.shtml, 9 March 2008)

20 See Bayan Nuwayhed al-Hout's *Sabra and Shatila (September 1982)* (Pluto Books: London and Ann Arbor, 2004) and Franklin Lamb's *The Price We Pay: A Quarter-Century of Israel's Use of AMERICAN WEAPONS Against Civilians in Lebanon (1978-2006)* (Beirut, London, and Washington, DC: Lamont Press LTD, 2007).

21 According to Kimmerling, ". . . politicide is a multilevel process, not necessarily anchored to a coherent socio-military doctrine. It is a general approach, with many of the decisions being made in the field, but who cumulative effects are twofold. The first is the destruction of the Palestinian public sphere, including its social and material infrastructure. The second effect is to make everyday life for the Palestinians increasingly unbearable by destroying the private sphere and any possibility of normalcy" (*Politicide*, 211).

22 P. 118.

23 As Selzer writes in his *The Aryanization of the Jewish State*:

> [All the instances of cultural genocide being perpetuated against the Oriental Jew in Israel] add up [however,] to one thing: *A unique situation has arisen in Israel where, despite the absence of legal discrimination, a minority ethnic group enjoys such power and prestige that it is able to set up its own values and practices as normative and to imbue with a sense of inferiority and alienation the majority ethnic group.* (68–9)

24 Avner Yaniv, *Dilemmas of Security: Politics, Strategy, and the Israeli Experience in Lebanon* (Oxford: Oxford University Press, 1987).

25 See Chapter 3 (Rejection and Accommodation) in Chomsky's *The Fateful Triangle: The United States, Israel, and the Palestinians* and Shlomo Brom's

"An Intelligence Failure," *Strategic Assessment* (Jaffee Center Strategic Studies, Tel Aviv University), Vol. 6, No. 3 (November 2003), pp. 1–10.

26 See Kaspit's "When the Intifada Erupted, it was finally clear to all: Israel is Not a State with an Army but an Army with a State," *Ma'ariv*, 6 September 2002, pp. 8–11.

27 See Franklin Lamb's *The Price We Pay: A Quarter-Century of Israel's Use of AMERICAN WEAPONS Against Civilians in Lebanon (1978-2006)* (Beirut, London, and Washington, DC: Lamont Press LTD., 2007).

28 See Ilan Pappe's "The Gaza Disengagement and the Prospect for Further Human Rights Violations" at http://www.adalah.org/newsletter/eng/aug05/ar1.pdf (10 March 2008).

29 See *Letters from Lexington: Reflections on Propaganda,* new updated edition, Paradigm 2004, p. 19.

30 For example, Israel's 6 June 1982 invasion of Lebanon was launched to subvert a "PLO peace offensive," which was becoming an embarrassment to Israel's attempts to draw the Palestinians into a war. See Ze'ev Schiff and Ehud Yahari's *Israel's Lebanon War* (New York: Touchstone, 1985).

31 See Joseph Massad's "Israel's Right to be Racist" at http://electronicintifada.net/v2/article6679.shtml (accessed on 28 February 2011).

32 See Massad's "Semites and Anti-Semites, That is the Question," at http://weekly.ahram.org.eg/2004/720/op63.htm (*Al-Ahram Weekly*, Issue No. 720, December 2004). As Massad writes:

> Those Arabs who deny the holocaust accept the Zionist logic as correct. Since these deniers reject the right of Zionists to colonise Palestine, the only argument left to them is to deny that the holocaust ever took place, which, to their thinking, robs Zionism of its allegedly "moral" argument. But the fact that Jews were massacred does not give Zionists the right to steal someone else's homeland and to massacre the Palestinian people. The oppression of a people does not endow it with rights to oppress others. If those Arab deniers refuse to accept the criminal Zionist logic that justifies the murder and oppression of the Palestinians by appealing to the holocaust, then these deniers would no longer need to make such spurious arguments. All those in the Arab world who deny the Jewish holocaust are in my opinion Zionists. (11 March 2008)

33 See Joseph Massad's "Palestinians and Jewish History: Recognition or Submission?" *Journal of Palestine Studies*, No. 7 (Fall 2000), pp. 52–67.

34 In his *Orientalism* (New York: Vintage Books, 1979), Edward Said writes: "[B]y an almost inescapable logic, I have found myself writing the history of a strange, secret sharer of Western anti-Semitism. That anti-Semitism and, as I have discussed it in its Islamic branch, Orientalism resemble each other very closely is a historical, cultural, and political truth that needs only to be mentioned to an Arab Palestinian for its irony to be perfectly understood" (*Orientalism* 28). As Massad points out:

> As Edward Said demonstrated a quarter of a century ago in his classic *Orientalism*, "what has not been sufficiently stressed in histories of modern anti-Semitism has been the legitimation of such atavistic designations by Orientalism, and . . . the way this academic and intellectual legitimation has

persisted right through the modern age in discussions of Islam, the Arabs, or the Near Orient." Said added: "The transference of popular anti-Semitic animus from a Jewish to an Arab target was made smoothly, since the figure was essentially the same." In the context of the 1973 War, Said commented that Arabs came to be represented in the West as having clearly "Semitic" features: sharply hooked noses, the evil moustachioed leer on their faces, were obvious reminders (to a largely non-Semitic population) that "Semites" were at the bottom of all "our" troubles. ("Semites and Anti-Semites, That is the Question")

35 See J. Bower Bell's *Terror Out of Zion: Irgun Zvai Leumi, Lehi and the Palestine Underground, 1929-1949* (New York: St. Martin's Press, 1977).

36 See "Rejection and Accomodationism" (Chapter 3) in Chomsky's *The Fateful Triangle: The United States, Israel, and the Palestinians* (Boston: South End Press, 1983).

37 See my "History, Memory, and Exile: Edward Said, the New York Intellectuals, and the Rhetorics of Accommodation and Resistance." *MMLA* special issue on "History, Memory, and Exile" ed. Michael Bernard-Donals, Vol. 39, No. 2 (2006), pp. 133–55.

38 Foxman, Abraham H. "Never Again?" *The Threat of the New Anti-Semitism* (New York: HarperCollins, 2003).

39 *Palestine: Peace Not Apartheid* (New York: Simon & Schuster, 2006), p. 215.

40 See "America's Last Taboo" at http://www.flwi.ugent.be/cie/said.pdf (1 April 2008).

41 See http://www.guardian.co.uk/commentisfree/story/0,,1970058,00.html (15 March 2008).

42 *Palestine: Peace Not Apartheid*, p. 216.

43 *The West Bank Story* (New York and London: Harcourt Brace Jovanovich Publishers, 1981); *The Legal Status of Arabs in Israel* (Boulder, San Francisco, and Oxford: Westview Press, 1990); *The Palestinians in Israel* (London, Boston, and Henley: Routledge & Kegan Paul, 1979); *The Arabs in Israel: 1948-1966* (Beirut: The Institute for Palestine Studies, 1986).

44 "The Israel Lobby," 23 March 2006.

45 See Gil Troy's *Why I am a Zionist: Jewish Identity and the Challenge of Jewish Identity* (Bronfman Educational Center: Montreal, 2002).

46 According to Kimmerling, "A new Palestinian Nakba ('Catastrophe') would be accompanied by a new Jewish Holocaust if the Israeli Jews and the Palestinians fail to conclude that their fates are intertwined, that their interests are mostly mutual and not intertwined" (*Politicide*, 217).

47 See Massad's "Semites and Anti-Semites, That is the Question."

Chapter 9

1 *The Moral Collapse of the University: Professionalism, Purity, and Alienation* (Albany: State University Press of New York, 1990); *Secular Vocations: Intellectuals, Professionalism, Culture* (London: Verso, 1993);

The University in Ruins (Cambridge, MA: Harvard University Press, 1996); *Anxious Intellects: Academic Professionals, Public Intellectuals, and Enlightenment Value* (Durham: Duke University Press, 2002). Also, see Sheila Slaughter and Bruce Rhoades' *Academic Capitalism and the New Economy: Markets, State, and Higher Education* (Baltimore: Johns Hopkins University Press, 2004).

2   See James Merod's *The Political Responsibility of the Critic* (Ithaca: Cornell University Press, 1987), Timothy Brennan's *At Home in the World: Cosmopolitanism Now* (Cambridge, MA: Harvard University Press, 1999), and Stephen Bronner's *Blood in the Sand* (Lexington: University of Kentucky Press, 2006).

3   *At Home in the World*, p. 6.

4   This is an acknowledgment to Noam Chomsky's book, *For Reasons of State* (New York and London: The New Press, 2003).

5   Jacques Derrida. *Who's Afraid of Philosophy?* (Stanford: Stanford University Press, 2002), p. 14.

6   See Chapter 4 ("The Formation of Enunciative Modalities") and Chapter 5 ("The Formation of Concepts") in Foucault's *The Archaeology of Knowledge & the Discourse on Language*. (New York: Pantheon Books, 1972).

7   See Milan Rai's *Chomsky's Politics* (London: Verso, 1999), p. 131.

8   See Gayatri Spivak's *Outside the Teaching Machine* (New York: Routledge, 1993) and *A Critique of Postcolonial Reason: Toward a History of the Vanishing Present* (Cambridge, MA: Harvard University Press, 1999).

9   Pierre Bourdieu. *Language and Symbolic Power* (Stanford: Stanford University Press, 1991).

10   See the essays in Alexander Cockburn and Jeffrey St Clair's *The Politics of Anti-Semitism* (London: AK Press, 2003).

11   According to the American Association of University Professor's "Committee A Statement on Extramural Utterances," "*The 1940 Statement of Principles* asserts the right of faculty members to speak or write as citizens, free from institutional censorship or discipline. At the same time, it calls attention to the special obligations of faculty members arising from their position in the community: to be accurate, to exercise appropriate restraint, to show respect for the opinion of others, and to make every effort to indicate that they are not speaking for the institution" (*AAUP Policy Documents and Reports*, Ninth Edition, 2006). Additionally, according to the AAUP's "A Statement on Professional Ethics,"

> As members of the academic institution, professors seek above all to be effective teachers and scholars. Although professors observe the stated regulations of the institution, provided the regulations do not contravene academic freedom, they maintain their right to criticize and seek revision. Professors give due regard to their paramount responsibilities within their institution in determining the amount and character of work done outside it. When considering the interruption or termination of their service, professors recognize the effect of their decision upon the program of the institution and give due notice of their intentions. (172)

12 *AAUP Policy Documents and Reports*, p. 174.

13 See Weiss's "Burning Cole" at http://www.thenation.com/doc/20060703/weiss (accessed on 23 July 2009); Scott Jaschik's "Blackballed at Yale" at http://www.insidehighered.com/news/2006/06/05/cole (accessed on 23 July 2009); Steve Lipman's "Opening the Ivy Doors" at http://www.campus-watch.org/article/id/3005 (accessed on 23 July 2009); Michael Rubin's "Cole is Poor Choice for Middle East Position" at http://www.yaledailynews.com/articles/view/17496?badlink=1 (accessed on 23 July 2009); and Jessica Marsden's "Cole May Join Univ. Faculty" at http://www.yaledailynews.com/articles/view/17475 (accessed on 23 July 2009).

14 As Cole noted after his appoint to Yale's faculty had been derailed:

> I am a Middle East expert. I lived in the area for nearly 10 years, speak several of its languages, and have given my life to understanding its history and culture. Since September 11, 2001, my country has been profoundly involved with the region, both negatively and positively. Powerful economic and political forces in American society would like to monopolize the discourse on these matters for the sake of their own interests, which may not be the same as the interests of those of us in the general public. Obviously, such forces will attempt to smear and marginalize those with whom they disagree. Before the Internet, they might have had an easier time of it. Being in the middle of all this, trying to help mutual understanding, is what I trained for. Should I have been silent, published only years later in stolid academic prose in journals locked up in a handful of research libraries? And this for the sake of a "career"? The role of the public intellectual is my career. And it is a hell of a career. I recommend it. (See *The Chronicle of Higher Education*. Washington: 28 July 2006. Vol. 52, No. 47; pg. B.9).

15 See Anna Kelner's "Joseph Massad's Tenure and Its Implications for Columbia's Liberal, Jewish Student Body" at http://www.huffingtonpost.com/anna-kelner/joseph-massads-tenure-and_b_223659.html (accessed on 23 July 2009). Like many news commentators, Kelner successfully conflates Judaism, Zionism, and Israel, without even really that is what she is doing. Kelner writes that, "The Jewish community of alumni and current students has previously exercised its will and sheer manpower to prevent anti-Semitic or anti-Israeli opinions from gaining University support." It is important to point out that an ad hoc committee that was tasked by Columbia University President Lee Bollinger with the task of investigating the charges of anti-Semitism leveled at Massad decided that the charges held no merit. Also, see John Gravois's "Alumni Group Seeks to Deny Tenure to Middle Eastern Scholar at Columbia" at: http://chronicle.com/article/Alumni-Group-Seeks-to-Deny/39398 (accessed on 23 July 2009).

WORKS CITED

"AAUP Statement on Controversy in the Classroom." (2004). www.aaup.org/
AAUP/comm/rep/A/controversy.htm (accessed 3 February 2011).

Abboud, Edward. *Invisible Enemy: Israel, Politics, Media, and American Culture.*
Reston, VA: Vox Publishing Company, 2003.

Abraham, Matthew. "The Rhetoric of Academic Controversy after 9/11: Edward
Said in the American Imagination." *JAC* 24, 3 (2004): 113–42.

—. Rev. of *Beyond Chutzpah. Logos* 4(4). www.logosjournal.com/issue_4.4/
abraham.htm (accessed 6 February 2011).

—. "Responding to Complaints about *Beyond Chutzpah*" *Logos* 5(1), 2005. www.
logosjournal.com/issue_5.1/abraham.htm (accessed 6 February 2011).

—. "Showdown at DePaul: Why DePaul Faculty Must Speak Out Now." *Dissident
Voice*, 23 June 2007. dissidentvoice.org/2007/06/showdown-at-depaul-why-
depauls-faculty-must-speak-out-now/ (accessed 30 January 2011).

—. "Academic Freedom as a Rhetorical Construction: A Response to Powers
and Chaput," a response essay to Karen Powers and Catherine Chaput's
"Anti-American Studies in the Deep South: Dissenting Rhetorics, the Practice
of Democracy, and Academic Freedom in Wartime Universities." *College
Composition and Communication* 59, 3 (February 2008): 512–17.

—. "William L. McBride and the Enduring Commitment to Intellectual Freedom,"
in Nathan Jun and Shane Wahl (eds), *Revolutionary Hope: Essays in Honor of
William McBride*. Lanham: Lexington Books, 2013, pp. 7–20.

Adams, Michael and Christopher. Mayhew. *Publish It Not: The Middle East Cover
Up*. London: Signal Books, 2003.

AIPAC. *The AIPAC College Guide: Exposing the Anti-Israel Campaign on
Campus*. Washington, DC: AIPAC, 1984.

Ajami, Fouad. *Dream Palace of the Arabs: A Generation's Odyssey*. New York:
Vintage, 1999.

Alam, M. Shahid. *Israeli Exceptionalism: The Destabilizing Logic of Zionism*.
New York: Palgrave Macmillan, 2009.

Alexander, Edward "The Professor of Terror." *Commentary*, 88, 2 (August 1989),
48–50.

Alexander, Edward and Paul Bogdanor, (eds), *The Jewish Divide Over Israel:
Accusers and Defenders*. New Brunswick and London: Transaction Publishers,
2006.

—. "Professor of Terror." *Commentary* 88 (August 1989): 49–50.

Alvin Rosenfeld's. "Progressive Jewish Thought and the New Anti-
Semitism" at http://www.ajc.org/atf/cf/%7B42D75369-D582-4380-8395
D25925B85EAF%7D/PROGRESSIVE_JEWISH_THOUGHT.PDF (accessed
on 12 April 2010), http://www.ajc.org/atf/cf/%7B42D75369-D582-4380-

8395-D25925B85EAF%7D/AntiZionism.pdf (accessed on 12 April 2010), and
http://www.ajc.org/site/apps/nl/content3.asp?c_ijITI2PHKoG&b_846637&
ct_875059 (accessed on 12 April 2010).

Amit, Zalman and Daphna Levit. *Israeli Rejectionism: A Hidden Agenda in the
Middle East Peace Process*. London and New York: Pluto Press, 2011. Print.

Apatu, D. (2001). "A Conversation with Norman Finkelstein: How to Lose Friends
and Alienate People." *CounterPunch*, 13 December. www.counterpunch.org/
finkelstein1.html (accessed 3 February 2011).

Arendt, Hannah. *Origins of Totalitarianism*. New York: Houghton Mifflin
Harcourt, 1973.

Aronson, Ronald. "Never Again? Zionism and the Holocaust." *Social Text* 3
(1980): 60–72.

Aruri, Naseer. *The Dishonest Broker: The Role of the United States in Palestine
and Israel*. Cambridge: South End Press, 2003.

Baer, Susan. "Holocaust Museum Reverses Self, Offers VIP Tour to Arafat,"
Baltimore Sun, 21 January 1998. http://articles.baltimoresun.com/1998-01-21/
news/1998021138_1_holocaust-museum-visit-the-museum-arafat-visit (accessed
1 September 2010).

Balakrishnan, Gopal, ed. *Debating Empire*. London: Verso, 2003.

Beit-Hallahmi, Benjamin. *The Israeli Connection: Who Arms Israel and Why*.
London: I. B. Taurus & Co., 1989.

Bell, J. Bower. *Terror Out of Zion: Irgun Zvai Leumi, Lehi and the Palestine
Underground, 1929-1949*. New York: St. Martin's Press, 1977.

Benda, Julian. *The Treason of the Intellectuals*, trans. Richard Aldington.
W.W. Norton & Company, 1928.

Bennett, William. *Why We Fight: Moral Clarity and the War on Terror*.
Washington, DC: Regnery Pub., 2003.

Berg, Avraham. *The Holocaust is Over: We Must Rise From Its Ashes*. New York:
Palgrave, 2008.

Berkowitz, Peter. *The New Republic Express*, 28 June 2002. www.thenewrepublic.
com/docprint.mhtml?i = express&s = berkowitz062802 (30 December 2003).

Bernard-Donals, Michael. *Forgetful Memory*. Albany: SUNY Press, 2009.

Berube, Michael. *What's Liberal about the Liberal Arts? Classroom Politics and
"Bias" in Higher Education*. New York: W.W. Norton, 2007.

—. "Peace Puzzle" in the 15 September 2002 issue of the *Boston Globe* at: http://
www.boston.com/news/packages/iraq/globe_stories/091502_bush.htm (12
March 2008).

—. Berube's 9/22/02 rejoinder to Chomsky in the *Boston Globe*.

—. Berube's article for The Center for Book Culture at http://www.
centerforbookculture.org/context/no10/berube.html (10 April 2008).

Bickerton, Ian. *The Arab-Israeli Conflict: A Guide for the Perplexed*. New York:
Continuum, 2011.

Birmingham, P. (2007). "Academic Freedom on Trial: Norman Finkelstein and
the Minority Report." *Dissident Voice*, 13 August. dissidentvoice.org/2007/08/
academic-freedom-on-trial-norman-finkelstein-and-the-minority-report/
(accessed 30 January 2011).

Black, Max. *The Morality of Scholarship*. Ithaca: Cornell University Press, 1969.

Bloom, Harold. *Kaballah and Criticism*. London and New York: Bloombury
Academic, 2005.

Bourdieu, Pierre. *Language and Symbolic Power*. Stanford: Stanford University Press, 1991.

Bove, Paul. *Intellectuals in Power: A Genealogy of Critical Humanism*. New York: Columbia University Press, 1986.

Boyle, Francis A. *Palestine, Palestinians, and International Law*. Atlanta: Clarity Press, 2003.

Breines, Paul. *Tough Jews: Political Fantasies and the Moral Dilemma of American Jewry*. New York: Basic Books, 1992.

Brennan, Timothy. "Meanwhile, in the hallways," in Amitava Kumar (ed.), *Class Issues: Pedagogy and the Public Sphere*. New York: New York University Press, 1997.

—. *At Home in the World: Cosmopolitanism Now*. Cambridge, MA: Harvard University Press, 1999.

—. *Wars of Position: The Cultural Politics of Left and Right*. New York: Columbia University Press, 2006. Print.

Brennan, Timothy and Keya Ganguly. "Crude Wars." *South Atlantic Quarterly* 105, 1 (Winter 2006): 29–30.

Brodkin, Karen. *How Jews Became White Folks and What That Says About Race in America*. New Brunswick: Rutgers University Press, 1998.

Bronner, Stephen. *Blood in the Sand*. Lexington: University of Kentucky Press, 2006.

Brunner, Jerome. "Pride and Memory: Nationalism, Narcissism and the Historians' Debates in Germany and Israel." *History and Memory* 9, 1–2 (1997): 256–300.

Butler, Judith. "It's Not Anti-Semitic." *London Review of Books* 26, 16 (21 August 2003).

—. "Academic Norms, Contemporary Challenges: A Reply to Robert Post on Academic Freedom," in Beshara Doumani (ed.), *Academic Freedom after September 11*. New York: Zone Books, 2006, pp. 61–106.

Byrne, Peter. Academic Freedom: A "Special Concern of the First Amendment." *Yale Law Journal* 99, 2 (November 1989): 251–340.

Byrne, Robert. "Academic Freedom: A Special Concern of the First Amendment." *Yale Law Journal* 99, 2 (1987): 251–340.

Carter, Jimmy. *Palestine: Peace Not Apartheid*. New York: Simon & Schuster, 2006.

Cesaire, Amie. *Discourse of Colonialism*. New York: Monthly Review Press, 2001.

Chaput, Catherine. *Inside the Teaching Machine*. Tuscaloosa: University of Alabama Press, 2008.

Chessler, Phyllis. *The New Anti-Semitism: The Current Crisis and What We Must Do About It*. New York: Jossey-Bass, 2005.

Chicago Manual of Style. Chicago: University of Chicago Press, 2003.

Chomsky, Noam. *After the Cataclysm: Postwar Indochina and the Reconstruction of Imperial Ideology*. Cambridge: South End Press, 1979.

—. *The Political Economy of Human Rights*, Vols. I and II. Cambridge: South End Press, 1979.

—. *The Fateful Triangle: The United States, Israel, and the Palestinians*. Cambridge: South End Press, 1983.

—. *World Orders: Old and New*. New York: Columbia University Press, 1998.

—. "The Fate of an Honest Intellectual," in P. Mitchell and J. Schoeffel (eds), *Understanding Power: The Indispensable Chomsky*. New York: New Press, 2002, pp. 244–8.

—. *Manufacturing of Consent: The Political Economy of the Mass Media.* New York: Pantheon, 2002.

—. *Hegemony or Survival? America's Quest for Global Dominance.* New York: Henry Holt and Company, 2003.

Chomsky, Noam and Edward Herman. *Manufacturing of Consent: The Political Economy of the Mass Media.* New York: Pantheon, 2002.

Chomsky's 9/22/02 "Letter to the Editor," in the *Boston Globe*, Also, see Christopher Hitchens in *The Nation* at http://www.thenation.com/doc.mhtml?i _ special&s _ hitchens20010924 (15 March 2008).

Chomsky's reply is available at: http://www.thenation.com/doc/20011015/chomsky 20011001 (19 April 2008); Hitchens' rejoinder: http://www.thenation.com/ doc/20011015/hitchens20011004 (20 April 2008); Chomsky's reply to Hitchens' rejoinder is available at: http://www.thenation.com/doc/20011015/chomsky 20011004 (30 April 2008). "Language, Politics, and Composition: A Conversation with Noam Chomsky." *Journal of Advanced Composition*, 11 (1991), 6.

Christison, Kathleen. *Perceptions of Palestine: Their Influence on U.S. Middle East Policy.* Berkeley: University of California Press, 2001.

Churchill, Ward. "The Myth of Academic Freedom: Personal Experience of a Liberal Principle in the Neoconservative Era (Fragments of a Work in Progress)." *Social Text 90* 25, 1 (Spring 2007): 17–39.

Cockburn, Alexander and Jeffrey St. Clair (eds), *The Politics of Anti-Semitism.* Petrolia and Oakland: Counterpunch and AK Press, 2003.

Cohen, Erik. "Israel as a Post-Zionist Society." *Israel Affairs* 1, 3 (1995): 210–11.

Cole, D. "The New McCarthyism: Repeating History in the War on Terrorism." *Harvard Civil Rights-Civil Liberties Law Review*, 38, 1 (2003): 1–30. www.law. harvard.edu/students/orgs/crcl/vol38_1/cole.pdf (accessed 3 February 2011).

Cole, J. "The New McCarthyism." *The Chronicle Review* 52, 3 (2005): B7–8.

Cole, Tim. *Selling the Holocaust: From Auschwitz to Schindler's List: How History is Bought, Packaged and Sold.* New York: Routledge, 2000.

College Personnel Committee (2007). Memo, 22 March. english.sxu.edu/sites/ kirstein/archives/680 (accessed 13 March 2011).

Collier, Peter and David Horowitz, ed. *Anti Chomsky Reader.* San Francisco: Encounter Books, 2006.

Cooke, Jonathan. *Blood and Religion: The Unmasking of the Jewish and Democratic State.* London and Ann Arbor: Pluto Books, 2006.

—. *Israel and the Clash of Civilizations: Iran, Iraq, and the Plan to Remake the Middle East.* London: Pluto Books, 2008.

Crowley, Sharon. *Toward a Civil Discourse: Rhetoric and Fundamentalism.* Pittsburgh: University of Pittsburgh Press, 2006. Print.

Dale, Tom, et al. "Four Eyewitness Describe the Murder of Rachel Corrie." *Electronic Intifada*, 19 March 2003, 6 January 2012. http://electronicintifada. net/content/four-eyewitnesses-describe-murder-rachel-corrie/4460. Web.

Davidson, Lawrence. *America's Palestine: Popular and Official Perceptions from Balfour to Israeli Statehood.* Gainesville: University Press of Florida, 2001.

DePaul-Finkelstein Settlement Statement, newsroom.depaul.edu/NewsReleases/ showNews.aspx?NID=1655.

Derrida. *Who's Afraid of Philosophy?* Stanford: Stanford University Press, 2002.

Dershowitz, A. (n.d.). "The Hazards of Making the Case for Israel." *JBooks.* www. jbooks.com/interviews/index/IP_Dershowitz.htm (4 February 2011).

—. *Why Terrorism Works: Understanding the Threat, Responding to the Challenge.* New York: New York University Press, 2002.

—. *The Case for Israel.* New York: John Wiley & Sons, Inc., 2003.

—. (2005a). Chapter 16 in *The Case for Peace: How the Arab-Israeli Conflict Can Be Resolved.* Boston: Wiley, pp. 167–88. www.law.harvard.edu/faculty/ dershowitz/Chapter_16.pdf (accessed 10 February 2011).

—. (2005b). "Letter to Matthew Abraham." www.logosjournal.com/issue_5.1/ dershowitz.htm (accessed 6 February 2011).

—. (2006). DePaul Letter. www.alandershowitz.com/publications/docs/depaulletter. htm (accessed 10 February 2011).

—. (2007). "Norman Finkelstein: The Case Against." *Guardian*, 14 June. www. guardian.co.uk/commentisfree/2007/jun/14/finkelsteinthecaseagainst (accessed 3 February 2011).

—. *The Case Against Israel's Enemies.* New York: Wiley & Sons, 2008.

Discover the Network. "Rachel Corrie Award." 18 August 2010. http://www. discoverthenetworks.org/groupProfile.asp?grpId=7046. Web.

Doumani, Beshara, ed. *Academic Freedom after September 11.* New York: Zone Books, 2006.

Dror, Yeshekel. *Crazy States: A Counterventional Strategy.* Lexington: Heath Lexington Books, 1971.

D'Souza, Dinesh. *Illiberal Education: The Politics of Race and Sex on Campus.* New York: Free Press, 1991.

—. "Two Cheers for Colonialism." 10 May 2002. *The Chronicle Review.* http:// chronicle.com/free/v48/i35/35b00701.htm (1 January 2004).

Edward Shils'. *Intellectuals and the Powers, and Other Essays.* Chicago: University of Chicago Press, 1983.

Elam, Gedis and Yigal. "Collective Memory—What Is It?" *History and Memory* 7, 2 (1995): 256–300.

El-Asmar, Fouzi. *To Be an Arab in Israel.* New York: Columbia University Press, 2003.

Ellis, Marc. *Out of the Ashes: The Search for Jewish Identity in the Twenty-First Century.* London: Pluto Press, 2002.

—. *Judaism ≠ Israel.* New York and London: New Press, 2009.

Eric Solaro's. "Retired Generals Rising Up Against Iraq War" at http://www.seattlepi. com/opinion/266638_solarosub16.html (accessed on 27 February 2011).

Felshman, J. (2005). "Whose Holocaust Is It Anyway?: Why Alan Dershowitz Wants Norman Finkelstein Fired." *Chicago Reader*, 26 August. www. chicagoreader.com/pdf/050826/050826_cover.pdf (accessed 3 February 2011).

Findley, Paul. *They Dare to Speak Out: People and Institutions Confront Israel's Lobby.* Chicago: Lawrence Hill Books, 1989.

—. *Deliberate Deceptions: Facing the Facts about the U.S.-Israeli Relationship.* Washington, DC: American Education Trust, 1993.

Finkelstein, Norman G. "Rejoinder to Benny Morris." *Journal of Palestine Studies,* 21, 2 (Winter 1992): 161–71.

—. *The Holocaust Industry: Reflections on the Exploitation of Jewish Suffering,* 2nd edn. London: Verso, 2003.

—. *Image and Reality in the Israel-Palestine Conflict,* 2nd edn. London: Verso, 2003.

—. "How to Lose Friends and Alienate People." Interview with Don Atapattu, *Counterpunch*, 13 December 2001. http://www.counterpunch.org/finkelstein1. html (3 January 2004).

—. (2007a). "Moment of Truth: Will Dershowitz Release the Letters?" www. normanfinkelstein.com/moment-of-truth/(accessed 4 February 2011).

—. (2007b). "In Praise of Smoking Guns: The Dershowitz File." www. normanfinkelstein.com/in-praise-of-smoking-guns-the-dershowitz-file/ (accessed 6 February 2011).

—. *Beyond Chutzpah: The Misuse of Anti-Semitism and the Abuse of History*, 2nd edn. Berkeley: University of California Press, 2008.

—. Finkelstein interview with Y. M. D. Fremes at: http://www.normanfinkelstein. com/article.php?pg_4&ar_17 (26 May 2008).

—. "Civility in Academic Life." *Works & Days, Special Issue: Academic Freedom in the Post-9/11 University* 26 and 27 (2009): 307–22, ISSN 0886-2060.

Finkelstein and Bernabai interview about settlement agreement with Amy Goodman on *Democracy, Now!*, www.democracynow.org/2007/9/10/professor_norman_finkelstein_and_depaul_end (accessed 2 February 2011).

Finkin, Matthew and Robert Post. *The Common Good: Principles of American Academic Freedom*. New Haven: Yale University Press, 2009.

Fish, Stanley. *There's No Such Thing as Free Speech and It's a* Good Thing *Too*. Oxford: Oxford University Press, 1994.

—. *The Trouble With Principle*. Cambridge, MA: Harvard University Press, 2001.

—. "Postmodern Warfare: The Ignorance of Our Warrior Intellectuals." *Harper's Magazine* (July 2002): 33–40. http://www.thinkingwithshakespeare.org/files/Fish-In-Harpers.pdf

Flapan, Simha. *Israel and the Palestinians*. New York: Barnes and Nobles Books, 1979.

—. *The Birth of Israel: Myths and Realities*. New York: Pantheon, 1998.

Foucault, Michel. *The Archaeology of Knowledge & the Discourse on Language*. New York: Pantheon Books, 1972.

Foxman, Abraham. *Never Again? The Threat of the New Anti-Semitism*. New York: Harper One, 2004.

—. *The Most Dangerous Lies: The Israel Lobby and the Myth of Jewish Control*. New York: Palgrave Macmillan, 2007.

Freud, Sigmund. "From the History of an Infantile Neurosis." *The Standard Edition of the Complete Psychological Works of Sigmund Freud*, trans. James Strachey. London: Hogarth, 1964.

Friel, Howard and Richard Falk. *The Record of the Paper: How the New York Times Misreports US Foreign Policy*. London and New York: Verso, 2004.

—. *Israel-Palestine on the Record: How the New York Times Misreports Conflict in the Middle East*. London and New York: Verso, 2007.

Frye, Northup. *The Great Code: The Bible and Literature*. New York: Mariner Books, 2002.

Gallagher, Catherine. "Politics, the Profession, and the Critic." *Diacritics*, 15, 2 (Summer 1985): 37–43.

Gerstenfeld, Manfred, ed. *Academics Against Israel and the Jews*. Jerusalem: Jerusalem Center for Public Affairs, 2007.

Gerstman, Evan and Matthew Streb. *Academic Freedom at the Dawn of a New Century: How Terrorism, Governments, and Culture Wars Impact Free Speech*. Stanford: Stanford UP, 2006.

Glenn, Cheryl. *Unspoken: Rhetoric of Silence*. Carbondale: Southern Illinois University Press, 2004.

Goldberg, Michelle. "Osama University?" November 2003. http://www.salon.com/news/feature/2003/11/06/middle_east/print.html (28 December 2003).

Goodman, A. (2003). "Scholar Norman Finkelstein Calls Alan Dershowitz's New Book a Hoax." *Democracy, Now!*, 24 September. www.democracynow. org/2003/9/24/scholar_norman_finkelstein_calls_professor_alan (accessed 10 February 2011).

—. (2007). "Noam Chomsky Accuses Alan Dershowitz of Launching a 'Jihad' to Block Norman Finkelstein From Getting Tenure at Depaul University." www. democracynow.org/2007/4/17/noam_chomsky_accuses_alan_dershowitz_of (accessed 26 March 2011).

Gorny, Yosef. *Zionism and the Arabs Ideology, 1882-1948: A Study of Ideology.* Oxford: Oxford University Press, 1987.

Gouldner, Alvin. *The Future of Intellectuals and the Rise of the New Class.* Oxford: Oxford University Press, 1982.

Gravois, John. "Alumni Group Seeks to Deny Tenure to Middle Eastern Scholar at Columbia" at: http://chronicle.com/article/Alumni-Group-Seeks-to-Deny/39398 (accessed on 23 July 2009).

Green, Stephen. *Taking Sides: America's Secret Relations with Militant Israel.* New York: William, Morrow & Co., 1983.

Grose, Peter. *Israel in the Mind of America.* New York: Knopf, 1983.

Grossman, R. (2007). "Controversial professor denied tenure at DePaul." *Chicago Sun Times*, 10 June. www.normanfinkelstein.com/article.php?pg=11&ar=1074 (accessed 11 February 2011).

Halkin, Hillel. "Whose Palestine? An Open Letter to Edward Said." *Commentary* 79 (May 1980): 21–30.

Halper, Jeff. *An Israeli in Palestine.* London: Pluto Books, 2008.

Hammer, Joshua. "The Death of Rachel Corrie." *Mother Jones*, September/October 2003, 31 August 2010. http://motherjones.com/politics/2003/09/death-rachel-corrie. Web.

Harkabi, Yehoshafat. *Israel's Fateful Hour.* New York: Harper and Row Publishers, 1986.

Harrison, Bernard. *The Resurgence of Anti-Semitism: Jews, Israel, and Liberal Opinion.* Lanham: Rowman and Littlefield, 2006.

Harrison, George. *The Resurgence of Anti-Semitism: Jews, Israel, and Liberal Opinion.* Lanham, MD: Rowman and Littlefield Publishers, 2006.

Haskell, T. (1996). "Justifying the Rights of Academic Freedom: Academic Freedom in the Era of Power/Knowledge," in L. Menand (ed.), *The Future of Academic Freedom*. Chicago: University of Chicago Press, p. 54.

Haskell, Thomas L. "Objectivity is Not Neutrality: Rhetoric versus Practice. *That Noble Dream*," in Peter Novick (ed.), *Objectivity is Not Neutrality*. Baltimore: Johns Hopkins, 1998, pp. 145–73.

Herzl, Theodore. *Old-New Land*, trans. Lotta Levensohn. New York: Block Publishing Company and Herzl Press, 1960.

—. *The Jewish State.* New York: Dover Publications, 1988.

Hever, Shir. *The Political Economy of Israel's Occupation.* London: Pluto Books, 2010.

Holdstein, Deborah and Andrea Greenbaum. *Judaic Perspectives in Rhetoric and Composition.* Creskill: Hampton Press, 2008.

Hollinger, D. (2005). "What Does It Mean to Be Balanced in Academe?" hnn.us/articles/10194.html (accessed 3 February 2011).

Holtschneider, D. (2007). Letter to Norman D. Finkelstein. www. normanfinkelstein.com/pdf/tenuredenial/Finkelstein,Norman06.08.2007.pdf (accessed 4 February 2011).

al-Hout, Bayan Nuwayhed. *Sabra and Shatila* (September 1982). Pluto Books: London and Ann Arbor, 2004.

Hunter, Jane. *Israeli Foreign Policy: South Africa and Central America*. Cambridge: South End Press, 1999.

Huntington, Samuel. "The Clash of Civilizations." *Foreign Affairs* (Summer 1993): 22–49.

—. *The Clash of Civilizations: Remaking of World Order*. New York: Touchstone Books, 1996.

Hussein, Abu Hussein. "Rachel Corrie: Blaming the Victim." *Common Dreams*, 2 September 2012, 6 January 2013. https://www.commondreams.org/view/2012/09/02-6. Web.

Isacoff, Jonathan B. *Writing the Arab-Israeli Conflict: Pragmatism and Historical Inquiry*. Lanham: Rowman and Littlefield, 2006. Print.

Jaschik, Scott. "Blackballed at Yale" at http://www.insidehighered.com/news/2006/06/05/cole (accessed 23 July 2009).

Jenner and Block (n.d.). John B. Simon Bio. www.jenner.com/people/bio.asp?id=361 (accessed 10 February 2011).

—. "Attorneys Hear Dershowitz Make Compelling 'Case for Israel' at JUF Annual Lawyers Division Dinner." www.jenner.com/news/news_item.asp?id=12626724 (accessed 10 February 2011).

John, Mearsheimer and Stephen Walt. "The Blind Man and the Elephant in the Room: Robert Lieberman and the Israel Lobby." *Perspectives on Politics* 7, 2 (June 2009): 259–73.

Karsh, Ephraim. *Fabricating Israeli History: The 'New Historians'*. London: Frank Cass & Co., 1997.

Kattan, Victor. *From Coexistence to Conquest: International Law and the Origins of the Arab-Israeli Conflict, 1891–1949*. London: Pluto Books, 2009.

Kelner, Anna. "Joseph Massad's Tenure and Its Implications for Columbia's Liberal, Jewish Student Body" *Huffington Post* at http://www.huffingtonpost.com/anna-kelner/joseph-massads-tenure-and_b_223659.html (accessed 23 July 2009).

Kessler, Jonathan and Jeff Schwaber's. *The AIPAC College Guide: Exposing the Anti-Israel Campaign on Campus*. Washington, DC: American Israel Public Affairs Committee, 1984.

Khalidi, Rashid. *Palestinian Identity: The Construction of Modern National Consciousness*. New York: Columbia University Press, 1997.

Kimmerling, Baruch. "Academic History Caught in the Cross-Fire: The Case of Israeli-Jewish Historiography." *History and Memory* 7, 1 (1995): 41–65.

—. *Politicide*. London: Verso, 2003.

Klein, D. (2008–09). "Why Is Norman Finkelstein Not Allowed to Teach?" *Works & Days*, special double issue on Academic Freedom in the Post-9/11 University, 26/27(51–4), pp. 307–22.

—. "Why is Norman Finkelstein Not Allowed to Teach?" *Works & Days, Special Issue: Academic Freedom in the Post-9/11 University* 26 and 27 (2009): 307–22, ISSN 0886-2060.

Kolsky, Thomas A. *Jews Against Zionism: The American Council of Judaism, 1942-48*. Philadelphia: Temple University Press, 1998.

Kramer, Martin. *Ivory Towers on Sand: The Failure of Middle East Studies in America*. Washington, DC: The Washington Institute for Near East Policy, 2001.

Krupnick, Mark. "Edward Said and the Discourse of Palestinian Rage." *Tikuun* 4, 6 (November/December 1989): 21–4.

Kurtz, Stanley. 19 June 2003 testimony on Title-VI funding before the House of Representatives, 5 November 2003. http://edworkforce.house.gove/hearings/108th/sed/title/titlevi61903/kurtz.htm (28 December 2003).

—. "Edward Said, Imperialist: The Hegemonic Impulse of Post-Colonialism." *The Weekly Standard*, 21 November 2001. http://www.weeklystandard.com/Utilities/....er_preview.asp?idArticle=284&R=2B0D38B71 (29 December 2003).

Kurtzman, Daniel. "Controversy Bedevils U.S. Holocaust Museum Again," J-Weekly.com, 26 June 1998. http://www.jweekly.com/article/full/8610/controversy-bedevils-u-s-holocaust-museum-again/ (accessed 1 September 2010).

LaCapra, Dominick. *Representing the Holocaust*. Ithaca: Cornell University Press, 1996.

—. *History and Memory after Auschwitz*. Ithaca: Cornell University Press, 1998.

—. *Writing History, Writing Trauma*. Baltimore: Johns Hopkins University Press, 2001.

—. *History in Transit*. Ithaca: Cornell University Press, 2004.

Lamb, Franklin. *The Price We Pay: A Quarter-Century of Israel's Use of AMERICAN WEAPONS Against Civilians in Lebanon (1978-2006)*. Beirut, London, and Washington, DC: Lamont Press LTD, 2007.

Laor, Yitzhak. *The Myths of Liberal Zionism*. London and New York: Verso, 2009.

Lawrence Davidson's *Foreign Policy Inc.: Privatizing American's National Interest*. Lexington: University Press of Kentucky, 2009.

Le Sueur, James. *Uncivil War: Intellectuals and Identity Politics during the Decolonization of Algeria*. Lincoln: University of Nebraska Press, 2005.

Lemisch, Jesse. *On Active Service in War and Peace: Politics and Ideology in the American Historical Profession*. Toronto: New Hogtown Press, 1975.

Lewis, Bernard. *What Went Wrong? The Clash Between Islam and Modernity in the Middle East*. New York: Harper Perennial, 2003.

Lieberman, Robert C. "'The Israel Lobby' and American Politics." *Perspectives on Politics* 7, 2 (June 2009): 235–57.

—. "Rejoinder to Mearsheimer and Walt." *Perspectives on Politics* 7, 2 (June 2009): 275–81.

Lilienthal, Alfred. *The Zionist Connection: What Price Peace?* New York: Dodd, Mead, 1977.

Lipman, Steve. "Opening the Ivy Doors" at http://www.campus-watch.org/article/id/3005 (accessed 23 July 2009).

Lowenberg, Peter. *Decoding the Past: A Psychohistorical Approach*. New York: Knopf, 1983.

Lucas, John. *The Israeli-Palestinian Conflict: A Documentary Record 1967-1990*. Cambridge: Cambridge University Press, 1992.

Lustick, Ian. "To Build and to Be Built By: Israel and the Hidden Logic of the Iron Wall." *Israeli Studies* 1, 1 (Spring 1996): 196–223.

—. "Negotiating Truth: The Holocaust, Lehavdil, and Al-Nakba." *Journal of International Affairs* 60, 1 (Fall/Winter 2006): 51–77.

—. "Abandoning the Iron Wall: Israel and the Middle Eastern Muck." *Middle East Policy* XV, 3 (Fall 2008): 30–56.

Lynch, Rebecca Gose. "Pawns of the State or Priests of Democracy? Analyzing Professors' Academic Freedom Rights Within the State's Managerial Realm." *California Law Review* 91 (2003): 1063–1108.

Maoz, Zeev. *Defending the Holy Land: A Critical Analysis of Israel's Security of Foreign Policy*. Ann Arbor: University of Michigan Press, 2006.

Marsden, Jessica. "Cole May Join Univ Faculty" at http://www.yaledailynews.com/articles/view/17475 (accessed 23 July 2009).

Martin, B. (2007). "Urgent Need to Right Wrongs at DePaul University." *Revolution*, Fall, revcom.us/a/099/martin-en.html (accessed 30 January 2011).

Marx, Karl and Frederick Engels. *The German Ideology*. New York: International Publishers, 1947.

Masalha, Nur. *Imperial Israel and the Palestinians: The Politics of Expansion*. London: Pluto Press, 2000.

Massad, Joseph. "Palestinians and the Limits of Racialized Discourse." *Social Text* 34 (1994): 94–114.

—. "Israel's Right to be Racist" at http://electronicintifada.net/v2/article6679.shtml (accessed 28 February 2011).

—. "Palestinians and Jewish History: Recognition or Submission?" *Journal of Palestine Studies* 7 (Fall 2000): 52–67.

—. "Targeting the University." *CounterPunch*, 3 June. www.counterpunch.org/massad06032005.html, 2005 (accessed 3 February 2011).

—. *The Persistence of the Palestinian Question: Essays on Zionism and the Palestinians*. London and New York: Routledge, 2006.

—. "Semites and Anti-Semites, That is the Question." *Al-Ahram Weekly*, 9–15 December 2006. http://weekly.ahram.org.eg/2004/720/op63.htm (accessed 27 February 2011).

McAlister, Melanie. *Epic Encounters: Culture, Media, and U.S. Interests in the Middle East, 1945-2000*. Berkeley: University of California Press, 2005.

McCarthy, Rory. "British activist saw Rachel Corrie die under bulldozer, court hears." *Guardian*. http://www.guardian.co.uk/world/2010/mar/10/rachel-corrie-civil-case-israel (accessed 25 August 2010).

McClintock, Anne. "The Angel of Progress: Pitfalls of the Term 'Post-Colonialism.'" *Social Text* 31/32, 1 (1994): 85–98.

McClintock, Anne and Ella Shohat in *Social Text* 31/32, pp. 85–98 and 99–113 (1980).

Mearsheimer, John and Stephen Walt. *The Israel Lobby and U.S. Middle East Policy*. London: Giroux & Strauss, 2007.

Menetrez, F. (2007). "Dershowitz v. Finkelstein: Who's Right, Who's Wrong." *CounterPunch*, 30 April. www.counterpunch.org/menetrez04302007.html (accessed 4 February 2011).

—. (2008). "The Case Against Alan Dershowitz." *CounterPunch*, 12 February. counterpunch.org/menetrez02122008.html (accessed 4 February 2011).

Merod, James. *The Political Responsibility of the Critic*. Ithaca: Cornell University Press, 1987.

Metzger, Walter and Richard Hofstadter's. *The Development of Academic Freedom in the United States*. New York and London: Columbia University Press, 1955.

Miller, Marjorie. "Arafat at Holocaust Museum? Issue Stirs Emotions in Israel," Sunsentinel.com, 25 January 1998 (accessed 1 September 2010).

Miyoshi, Masao. "A Borderless World? From Colonialism to Transnationalism and the Decline of the Nation-State." *Critical Inquiry* 19, 4 (Summer 1993): 726–51.

Morris, Benny. *The Birth of the Palestinian Refugee Problem, 1947-1949*. Cambridge: Cambridge University Press, 1988.

—. "The New Historiography: Israel Confronts Its Past." *Tikkun* (November/December 1988): 19–22 and 99–102.

—. "Response to Finkelstein and Masalha." *Journal of Palestine Studies* 21, 1 (1988): 88–114.

—. "The Eel and History: A Reply to Shabtai Teveth." *Tikkun* 89 (January/ February 1990): 19–22 and 79–86.

—. "Response to Finkelstein and Masalha." *Journal of Palestine Studies* 21, 1 (1991): 98–114.

—. "Peace? No Chance," in the *Guardian* (21 February 2002).

—. *The Birth of the Palestinian Refugee Problem Revisited*. Cambridge: Cambridge University Press, 2004.

—. "Peace? No Chance," in the *Guardian* (21 February 2002). For a response to Morris's *Guardian* article, see Avi Shlaim's "A Betrayal of History," in the *Guardian* (22 February 2002).

Newman, Marcy *The Politics of Teaching Palestine to Americans: Pedagogical Perspectives*. New York: Palgrave Macmillan, 2011.

Nguyen, Phen. "Mother Jones Smears Rachel Corrie Specious Journalism in Defense of Killers." *If Americans Knew*. http://www.ifamericansknew.org/cur_sit/mj.html (accessed 31 August 2010).

Nitzan, Jonathan and Shimson Bichler. *The Global Political Economy of Israel*. London and Ann Arbor: Pluto Press, 2002.

Novick, Peter. *That Noble Dream: The Objectivity Question and the American Historical Profession*. Cambridge: Cambridge University Press, 1988.

—. *The Holocaust in American Life*. New York: Mariner Books, 2000, pp. 161–9.

Obama, Barack. "State Department Speech." 19 May 2011, 29 May 2012. *YouTube*. http://www.youtube.com/watch?v=FwmxLT8F2io. Web.

Pappe, Illan. *The Making of the Arab-Israeli Conflict, 1947-1951*. London: I.B. Taurus, 1992.

—. *The Ethnic Cleansing of Palestine*. London: Oneworld Publications, 2007.

—. *Out of Frame: Academic Freedom in Israel*. London and Ann Arbor: Pluto Books, 2010.

Peters, Joan. *From Time Immemorial: The Origins of the Arab-Jewish Conflict Over Palestine*. New York: J.KAP Pub., 1984.

Pipes, Daniel. *Militant Islam Reaches America*. New York: W.W. Norton & Co., 2003.

Plaut, S. (2007a). "The Finkelstein Affair." *Front Page*, 23 April. archive. frontpagemag.com/readArticle.aspx?ARTID=26229 (accessed 4 February 2011).

—. (2007b). "The Passion of Norman Finkelstein." *Front Page*, 17 September. archive.frontpagemag.com/readArticle.aspx?ARTID=28143 (accessed 4 February 2011).

—. (2007c). "Will America's Largest Catholic University Give Tenure to a Fan of Hezbollah?" *Front Page*, 5 April. archive.frontpagemag.com/readArticle. aspx?ARTID=26012 (accessed 4 February 2011).

Porath, Yehoshua. *The Emergence of the Palestinian Arab National Movement: 1918-1929*. New York: Routledge, 1995.

—. *The Palestinian Arab National Movement, 1929–1939: From Riots to Rebellion*. New York: Routledge, 1977.

Post, Robert. "The Structure of Academic Freedom," in Beshara Doumani (ed.), *Academic Freedom after September 11*. New York: Zone Books, 2006, pp. 61–106.

Powers, Karen and Catherine Chaput. "Anti-American Studies in the Deep South: Dissenting Rhetorics, the Practice of Democracy, and Academic Freedom in Wartime Universities." *College Composition and Communication* 58, 4 (June 2007): 648–81.

Puccio, Paul. *Report of the Task Force on CCCC Awards and Guidelines*, 24 May 2008. Print.

Quigley, John. *The Case for Palestine: An International Law Perspective*. Durham and London: Duke University Press, 2005.

Radhakrishnan, Radha. *History, the Human, and the World Between*. Durham: Duke University Press, 2008.

Rai, Milan. *Chomsky's Politics*. London: Verso, 1999.

Rickert, Thomas. *Acts of Enjoyment: Rhetoric, Zizek, and the Return of the Subject*. Pittsburgh: University of Pittsburgh Press, 2007.

Ridgen, D. and Rossier, N. (dirs.). *American Radical: The Trials of Norman Finkelstein*. U.S.: Baraka Productions, 2009.

Robbins'. "Homelessnes and Worldliness." *Diacritics* 13 (Fall 1983): 69–77, 37–43.

—. "Deformed Professions, Empty Politics." *Diacritics* 16, 3 (Fall 1986): 67–72.

Roberts-Miller, Patricia. *Deliberate Conflict: Argument, Political Theory, and Composition Classes*. Carbondale: SIU Press, 2007.

Rokach, Livia. *Israel's Sacred Terrorism*. Shrewsbury, MA: Association of Arab-American University Graduates, Inc., 1980.

Rose, Jacqueline. *The Last Resistance*. London: Verso, 2008.

Rosenbaum, Ron. *Those Who Forget the Past: The Question of Anti-Semitism*. New York: Random House, 2004.

Rothberg, Michael. *Multidirectional Memory: Remembering the Holocaust in the Age of Decolonization*. Stanford: Stanford University Press, 2009.

Rothstein, Edward. *New York Times* Op-Ed. "Attacks on U.S. Challenge Postmodern True Believers." 22 September 2001. http://www.uoregon.edu/~dgalvan/intl240-f03/pomo&9-11-rothstein1.htm (2 January 2004).

—. *New York Times* Op-Ed. "Moral Relativity Is a Hot Topic? True. Absolutely." 13 July 2002. http://0 November 2002.

Roy, Arundithi. Introduction to Chomsky's *For Reasons of State*. New York: New Press, 2003, p. xviii.

Roy, Sara. "Short Cuts." *London Review of Books* 26, 7 (1 April 2004).

Rubin, Michael. "Cole is Poor Choice for Middle East Position" at http://www.yaledailynews.com/articles/view/17496?badlink=1 (accessed 23 July 2009).

Said, Edward. *The Question of Palestine*. New York: Pantheon Books, 1979.

—. *Orientalism*. New York: Vintage Books, 1979.

—. "Opponents, Audiences, Constituencies, and Community." *Critical Inquiry* (September 1982): 1–26.

—. *The World, the Text, and the Critic*. Cambridge: Harvard University Press, 1983.

—. "Introduction," in Said and Christopher Hitchens (eds), *Blaming the Victims: Spurious Scholarship and the Palestinian Question*. London: Verso, 1986, p. 1.

—. "An Exchange on Edward Said and Difference III: Response." *Critical Inquiry* 15 (Spring 1989): 636.

—. *Culture and Imperialism*. New York: Vintage Books, 1993.

—. *Representations of the Intellectual*. New York: Vintage, 1994.

—. *The Politics of Dispossession: The Struggle for Palestinian Self-Determination, 1969-1994*. New York: Vintage, 1995.

—. "Islam and the West Are Inadequate Banners," *London Observer*, 16 September 2001.

—. "American Zionism—The Real Problem." http://www.mediamonitors.net/edward12.html (11 April 2002). Published as "America's Last Taboo" in Roane Carey's *The New Intifada: Resisting Israel's Apartheid.*

—. "Impossible Histories: Why the many Islams cannot be simplified." *Harper's Magazine*, July 2002, 69–74.

—. "The Public Role of Writers and Intellectuals," *The Nation*, 17 September 2001. http://www.journalism.uts.edu.au/subjects/ppc1_2000/said.html (30 December 2003).

—. *Humanism and Democratic Criticism.* New York: Columbia University Press, 2004.

—. "Collective Passion: can the voice of rationality be heard over the war drums?" *Al-Ahram*, 20 September 2001. http://weekly.ahram.org.eg/2003/658/_edsaid.htm (3 January 2004).

—. "Dignity, Solidarity, and the Penal Colony." *Counterpunch*, 29 January 2010. http://www.counterpunch.org/said09252003.html.

Said, Edward and Mohr. Jean. *After the Last Sky: Palestinian Lives.* New York: Columbia University Press, 1982.

Said's heated debate with Robert J. Griffin and Daniel and Jonathan Boyarin in "An Exchange on Edward Said and Difference." *Critical Inquiry* 15 (Spring 1989): 611–33. As a follow-up to that exchange, see the letters from Geoffrey Hartman, Said, and Masao Miyoshi, and the editors in *Critical Inquiry* 16 (Autumn 1989): 199–204.

Salaita, Steven. *Anti-Arab Racism in the USA: Where It Comes from and What It Means for Politics Today.* London and Ann Arbor: Pluto Press, 2006.

Sand, Shlomo. *The Invention of the Jewish People.* London and New York: Verso, 2010. Print.

Sandersock, Joyce, et al. *Peace Under Fire: Israel/Palestine and the International Solidarity Movement.* London and New York: Verso, 2004. Print.

Schiff, Ze'ev. *Israel's Lebanon War.* New York: Simon and Schuster, 1984.

—. *A History of the Israeli Army: 1874 to the Present.* New York: Macmillan, 1985.

Schoenfeld, Gabriel. *The Return of Anti-Semitism.* New York and London: Encounter Books, 2005.

Schrecker, Ellen. *No Ivory Tower: McCarthyism and the Universities.* Oxford: Oxford University Press, 1986.

—. *Many are the Crimes: McCarthyism in America.* Princeton: Princeton University Press, 1999.

—. *Cold War Triumphalism: The Misuse of History after the Fall of Communism.* New York: New Press, 2006.

—. *The Lost Soul of Higher Education: Corporatization, the Assault on Academic Freedom, and the End of the American University.* New York and London: The New Press, 2010.

Selzer, Michael. *The Aryanization of the Jewish State.* New York: Blackstar Publishing, 1967.

Sen, Amartya. *Identity and Violence.* New York and London: W. W. Norton & Company, 2006, pp. 59–83.

Shahak, Israel. *Open Secrets: Israeli Foreign and Nuclear Policies.* London: Pluto Press, 1997.

Shapira, Anita. "Politics and Collective Memory: The Debate over the 'New Historians' in Israel." *History and Memory* 7, 1 (1995): 9–40.

Shatz, Adam. Ajami. "The Native Informant," *The Nation*, 28 April 2008. http://www.thenation.com/article/native-informant# (accessed 5 September 2013).

Sheehan, Jack. Shaheen's *Reel Bad Arabs: How Hollywood Vilifies a People*, 2nd edn. Brooklyn: Olive Branch Press, 2009.

Sheila Slaughter and Bruce Rhoades *Academic Capitalism and the New Economy: Markets, State, and Higher Education*. Baltimore: Johns Hopkins University Press, 2004.

Shepherd, Robin. *Beyond the Pale: Europe's Problem with Israel*. London: Wiedenfeld and Nicolson, 2009.

Sherman, Scott. "Target Ford" (18 May 2006), *Nation* at http://www.thenation.com/doc/20060605/sherman (28 July 2008).

Shlaim, Avi. "A Betrayal of History," in the *Guardian*, 22 February 2002.

—. *The Iron Wall: Israel and the Arab World*. New York: W.W. Norton Company, 2001.

Shohat, Ella. "Notes on the 'Post-Colonial'." *Social Text* 31/32, 1 (1994): 99–113.

Silberstein, Laurence J. *The Postzionism Debates: Knowledge and Power in Israeli Culture*. New York: Routledge, 1999.

Slezkine, Yuri. *The Jewish Century*. Princeton: Princeton University Press, 2004.

Smith, Barbara Herrnstein. *Contingencies of Value: Alternative Perspectives for Critical Theory*. Cambridge, MA: Harvard University Press, 1987.

—. *Belief and Resistance: The Dynamics of Contemporary Intellectual Controversy*. Cambridge, MA: Harvard University Press, 1999.

Smith, Grant. *Israel's Defense Line: The Justice Department's Battle to Register the Israel Lobby as Agents of a Foreign Government*. Washington, DC: Institute for Research, 2003.

Sokmen, Muge and Basak Ertur, ed. *Waiting for the Barbarians: A Tribute to Edward Said*. London: Verso, 2008. Print.

Spivak, Gayatri. *Outside the Teaching Machine*. New York: Routledge, 1993.

—. *A Critique of Postcolonial Reason: Toward a History of the Vanishing Present*. Cambridge, MA: Harvard University Press, 1999.

Stacey, Stacey E. "Who Owns Academic Freedom? The Standard for Academic Free Speech at Public Universities." *Washington and Lee Law Review* 59 (2002): 299–360.

Sternhell, Zeev. *The Founding Myths of Israel*, trans. David Maisel. Princeton: Princeton University Press, 1999.

Stone, Geoffrey. *Perilous Times: Free Speech in Wartime from the Sedition Act of 1798 to the War on Terrorism*. New York: W.W. Norton, 2005.

Spanos, William. *The Legacy of Edward W. Said*. Urbana: University of Illinois Press, 2009.

Suchar, Charles. (2007). "Letter to the University Board on Tenure and Promotion." *CAMERA*, 12 April. blog.camera.org/archives/2007/04/depaul_dean_slams_finkelstein.html (accessed 26 March 2011).

Swisher, Clayton. *The Truth about Camp David: The Untold Story of the Collapse of the Middle East Peace Process*. New York: Nation Books, 2004.

Terry, Janice. *U.S. Foreign Policy and the Middle East: The Role of Lobbies and Special Interest Groups*. London: Pluto Books, 2007.

Ticker, Bruce. "The Case Against Rachel Corrie." *Israel National News*. http://www.israelnationalnews.com/Articles/Article.aspx/3735 (accessed 31 August 2010).

Tobin, Gary A., Aryeh K. Weinberg, and Jenna Ferer. *American Higher Education*. Roseville, CA: Institute for Jewish Community and Research, 2009. Print.

Troy, Gil. *Why I am a Zionist: Jewish Identity and the Challenge of Jewish Identity.* Bronfman Educational Center: Montreal, 2002.

U.S. Commission on Civil Rights Campaign to End Anti-Semitism at http://www.usccr.gov/campusantisemitism. html (accessed on 12 April 2010).

Van Teeffele, Toine. "Tragic Heroes and Victims in Zionist Ideology." *Khamsin* 9 (1988): 127.

Van Alystne. Academic Freedom and the First Amendment in the Supreme Court of the United States: An Unhurried Historical Review. *Law and Contemporary Problems* 53, 3 (1990): 79–154.

Vidal-Naquet, Pierre. *Assassins of Memory: Essays on the Denial of the Holocaust*, trans. Jeffrey Mehlman. New York: Columbia University Press, 1992.

Walt, S. and J. Mearsheimer. *The Israel Lobby and U.S. Foreign Policy.* London: Farrar, Straus and Giroux, 2008.

—. "The Art of Smear." http://walt.foreignpolicy.com/posts/2012/12/17/the_art_of_the_smear (accessed 19 December 2012).

Walzer, Michael. "Can There be a Decent Left?." *Dissent*, April 2002. http://www.dissentmagazine.org/wwwboard/wwwboard.shtml (30 December 2003).

Washington Post (in *LA Times* collection of articles), "U.S. Holocaust Museum Scuttles Visit by Arafat." http://articles.latimes.com/1998/jan/17/news/mn-9140, 17 January 1998 (accessed 1 September 2010).

Weiner, Justin Reid. "'My Beautiful Old House' and Other Fabrications by Edward Said." *Commentary* 98 (September 1999): 23–31.

Weiss, Phillip. "Burning Cole" at http://www.thenation.com/doc/20060703/weiss (accessed 23 July 2009).

Wiener, J. (2009). "The Chutzpah Industry." *The Nation*, 21 May. www.thenation.com/doc/20070521/wiener (accessed 13 July 2009).

Williams, B. (2007a). "The Poisoning of Academic Freedom: Strange Calculus at DePaul." *CounterPunch*, 28 June. www.counterpunch.com/williams06282007.html (accessed 30 January 2011).

—. (2007b). "The Commissar Two-Step at DePaul." *CounterPunch*, 2 July. www.counterpunch.org/williams07022007.html, Web (accessed 30 January 2011).

Wilson, John K. *Patriotic Correctness: Academic Freedom and Its Enemies.* Boulder and London: Paradigm Publishers, 2008.

Winkler, Carol. *In the Name of Terrorism: Presidents on Political Violence in the Post-World War II Era.* Albany: SUNY Press, 2006.

Worsham, Lynn. "Going Postal: Pedagogic Violence and the Schooling of Emotion." *JAC* 18, 2 (1998): 213–45. Print.

Writing Program Administration (WPA) archive, 14 May–19 May 2006, 6 January 2013. https://lists.asu.edu/cgi-bin/wa?A0=WPA-L. Web.

Yaniv, Avner. *Dilemmas of Security: Politics, Strategy, and the Israeli Experience in Lebanon.* Oxford: Oxford University Press, 1987.

Yinon, Oded. "Zionist Plan for the Middle East." http://www.informationclearinghouse.info/pdf/The%20Zionist%20Plan%20for%20the%20Middle%20East.pdf Web (accessed 9 June 2013).

Yudof, Mark G. "Three Faces of Academic Freedom." *Loyola Law Review* 32, 4 (Winter 1987): 831–58.

Zunes, Stephen. *Tinderbox: U.S. Middle East Policy and the Roots of Terrorism.* Monroe: Common Courage Press, 2003.

APPENDIX A

Debating the Finkelstein case

Letter to Matthew Abraham on *Beyond Chutzpah* Review

by
Alan Dershowitz

To the Editor:

It is difficult to write a rebuttal against a writer whose own article so readily discredits itself. Matthew Abraham, an English professor, uses such outlandish and intemperate language, makes such wild historical fabrications, and parrots so many verifiably false accusations, that I cannot help but suspect that he has written his review of Norman Finkelstein's *Beyond Chutzpah* as an example for his students on how not to write well. His article reads like a cheap agitprop parody. Before I begin, then, I will let Abraham, the Rachel Corrie Courage in Teaching Award winner, speak for himself.

Abraham concurs with Finkelstein that "American Jewish Zionists" are involved in "a lucrative extortion racket" designed to enrich and shield ourselves "from much-deserved scrutiny in [our] toadying for special dispensations as oppressed 'chosen people.'" Abraham says that the Anti-Defamation League is a "U.S. Front operations for the Israeli government" engaged in "a form of ruthless grave robbery for the glorification of that massive land-based U.S. aircraft carrier, Israel." Abraham places full blame on "America and Israel" for "block[ing] resolution" of the Middle East conflict. He calls Israel a "crazy state," concludes that it is not a democracy, and places the full blame on "America and Israel" for "block[ing] resolution" of the Middle East conflict." The "historical record," writes Abraham, "confirms that the PLO and the Arab states have overwhelmingly been in favor of peace." He repeats Arafat's Bantustan accusation – that Palestine was offered cantons of land, rather than the contiguous state on over 95% of the occupied territories that the Camp David maps show – and twice insists that Israel has ethnically cleansed Palestinians from Israel, as if simply repeating the accusation were enough to make it true. My favorite Abraham claim is his wild assertion that "American Jewish Zionists" (there's that phrase again) "blocked" Holocaust survivors from coming to America! I've heard of many "Jewish conspiracies," but this is the first time I've heard of a Jewish conspiracy to keep Jews out of America.

Then there is Abraham's breathless praise of Finkelstein "a well-respected, Princeton trained political scientist with several internationally recognized books to his credit." Hardly. While Finkelstein's books have found a welcoming audience in the neo-Nazi demographic, mainstream media sources have uniformly dismissed Finkelstein as a Jew-hating crank, and he has been fired from several universities for shoddy scholarship and abusive treatment of students. In 2000, Finkelstein published a scandalous screed, called *The Holocaust Industry*, in which he railed against American Jewish leaders who were seeking justice for Holocaust survivors. In his book and in public lectures, Finkelstein accused Jewish leaders of being part of a worldwide Jewish conspiracy, whose members included Elie Wiesel, Leon Uris, Steven Spielberg, Stuart Eizenstat, Abba Eban, Abraham Foxman, Edgar Bronfman, and Burt Neuborne. The problem was that Finkelstein simply made up his alleged facts, his quotations, and his citations. Moreover, since he cannot read German, and since many of the most important sources relating to the Holocaust are in German, he faked his research. This is what University of Chicago Professor Peter Novick, whose work *The Holocaust in American Life* Finkelstein characterized as "the initial stimulus for [his] book," said about Finkelstein:

> As concerns particular assertions made by Finkelstein . . . the appropriate response is not (exhilarating) "debate" but (tedious) examination of his footnotes. Such an examination reveals that many of those assertions are pure invention. . . . No facts alleged by Finkelstein should be assumed to be really facts, no quotation in his book should be assumed to be accurate, without taking the time to carefully compare his claims with the sources he cites.

Novick called *The Holocaust Industry* "trash" and a "twenty-first century updating of the '*Protocols of the Elders of Zion*.'" Omer Bartov, who reviewed *The Holocaust Industry* for *The New York Times*, called it an "irrational and insidious" "conspiracy theory," "verg[ing] on paranoia," full of "dubious rhetoric and faulty logic," "indifference to historical facts," and "sensational 'revelations' and outrageous accusations." In sum, Bartov called the book "a novel variation on the anti-Semitic forgery, *The Protocols of the Elders of Zion*." Marc Fisher, a columnist for the *Washington Post*, observed that "Norman Finkelstein [is] a writer celebrated by neo-Nazi groups for his Holocaust revisionism and comparisons of Israel to Nazi Germany."

In his many pages of vague invective against "American Zionist Jews," Abraham manages to level two substantive charges against me, both of which are easily disproved. First, Abraham's claims that I "wag[ed] an astounding campaign to kill off Finkelstein's retort [*Beyond Chutzpah*]." But as I wrote to the University of California Press: I have no interest in censoring any publication. But I do insist that a book, 'a large part of which is devoted to Alan Dershowitz' has been checked for accuracy and that all appropriate measures have been taken to assure that its biased and defamatory author does not include within it maliciously false information. Among Finkelstein's defamations are his allegations that I "almost certainly didn't write" *The Case for Israel*, "and perhaps [he] didn't even read it prior to publication." Finkelstein even suggests that all of my books are written for me by the Israeli Mossad: "[I]t's sort of like a Hallmark line for Nazis. . . . [T]hey churn them out so fast that he has now reached a point where he doesn't even read them."

Finkelstein has attempted to frame *Beyond Chutzpah*'s publication as a triumph for academic freedom. This dispute, though, has never been about academic freedom. Nobody ever tried to prevent Finkelstein from publishing his bigoted falsehoods. The dispute has always been about academic standards. In order to deflect attention away from their lack of academic standards and hard-left anti-Israel bias, Finkelstein and his publisher have lied about the issue of academic freedom. Nobody has ever tried to censor Finkelstein's drivel. He can always publish it with presses that acknowledge their anti-Israel bias. The issue is, and has always been, one of academic standards: how could the University of California Press publish a work so lacking in standards, so filled with misquotations, falsifications, and faked data by a failed academic with a well deserved reputation for the "pure invention" of his sources? No objective university press would have published this sequel to a book the *New York Times* called a "variation on the anti-Semitic forgery, the *Protocols of the Elders of Zion*."

Second, Abraham writes, "Rarely has anyone committed to upholding a party line exceeded Dershowitz' loyalty to one revered state, and that state is Israel." Relatedly, he claims that "pro-Zionist Jews" lie about anti-Semitism because we are afraid of being "no longer perceived as the world's greatest victims." These charges come straight from Finkelstein, who alleges that Jews will cry "anti-Semite" at anyone who criticizes Israel. Finkelstein subtitles his book "On the Misuse of Anti-Semitism and the Abuse of History," explaining his thesis as follows: "Like the Holocaust, 'anti-Semitism' is an ideological weapon to deflect justified criticism of Israel and, concomitantly, powerful Jewish interests. In its current usage, 'anti-Semitism,' alongside the "war against terrorism," serves as a cloak for a massive assault on international law and human rights.

This allegation, though, is belied by a simple scan of the themes and theses of my own books. Only eight years ago, I wrote an entire book discussing challenges facing American Jews now that institutional anti-Semitism is all but nonexistent and personal anti-Semitism has been relegated to the marginalized extremes of the political spectrum. As I put it in *The Vanishing American Jew*, "The thesis of this book is that the long epoch of Jewish persecution is finally coming to an end. . . ." And in both *The Case for Israel* and *The Case for Peace*, I was clear that criticism of Israel and anti-Semitism are not the same thing. Considering my extensive and well-documented history of criticizing particular Israeli policies and politicians, Finkelstein's obsessive focus on me and my book ensures that *Beyond Chutzpah* amounts to nothing more than an attempt to blow over a straw man of Finkelstein's – and Abraham's – own construction.

Abraham praises as "intrepid" Finkelstein's underlying question, "Do American Zionist Jews, *qua* Jews, use their ethnic privilege to advance Israel's morally-bankrupt agenda toward increasing militarization in its ethnic cleansing and annexation of the West Bank?" He answers with a resounding yes. It's a shame that a professor of rhetoric, who repeatedly accuses others of "toeing the party line," would rely on so many tired and false clichés in the service of his extremist anti-Jewish (or as Abraham would have it, his anti-"American Zionist Jew") agenda.

The case for Norman Finkelstein

Norman Finkelstein, the famed critic of Israel, has been denied tenure by DePaul University. What does it mean for academic freedom?

- Matthew Abraham
- guardian.co.uk, Thursday 14 June 2007 08.00 BST

On Friday, June 8, DePaul University President Dennis Holtschneider announced that he had decided to uphold the university's tenure and promotion board's ruling denying outspoken political science professor Norman Finkelstein tenure. In a press release, the president is quoted as saying that academic freedom "is alive and well at DePaul University". Not surprisingly, the announcement of Finkelstein's tenure denial has spawned a national discussion. Academics everywhere have been forced to ponder the implications for the future of academic freedom in the United States, especially those who dare to criticize US and Israeli policy in the Middle East.

Finkelstein, the son of Holocaust survivors, has been relentless in exposing what he calls "The Holocaust Industry": the institutions and organizations that have used the holocaust (the actual historical event) to justify Israel's criminal assault upon the Palestinian population and international law. Among these organisations, he includes the World Jewish Congress, the Anti-Defamation League, the American Jewish Committee, and a host of other fellow travellers. There is no doubt that Finkelstein's work has stoked controversy. But that shouldn't detract from what makes his tenure treatment so worrying: Finkelstein is undoubtedly a path-breaking and serious scholar.

Raul Hilberg, the leading scholar on the Nazi holocaust, has called Finkelstein's The Holocaust Industry "a breakthrough" and states that Finkelstein "was on the right track" in his documentation of how the World Jewish Congress, with the aid of the Clinton administration, extorted billions of dollars from Swiss banks in the name of Holocaust survivors, only to pocket the money for Jewish organisations. And, although *The Holocaust Industry* is Finkelstein's most frequently cited book in defamatory attempts to cast him as a "Holocaust denier" and a "denier of justice to Holocaust survivors", *Image and Reality in the Israel-Palestine Conflict* – a thorough criticism of the central political and philosophical tenets informing Zionism – is his most scholarly and substantial work. But Finkelstein's detractors avoid discussion of *Image and Reality* for exactly that reason: it is considered a first-rate piece of scholarship.

Finkelstein argues that most US commentators obscure or avoid the clear historical and diplomatic record in examining the Israel-Palestine conflict by ignoring or downplaying international law, fooling the US public into believing that Israel's occupation is just, necessary, and lawful. One such example is the failure of the 2000 Camp David talks – a failure that has been attributed, at least in elite circles within the United States, to Yasir Arafat's intransigence. In actuality, what Bill Clinton and Ehud Barak offered Arafat was something no Palestinian leader could accept: a Bantustan state reminiscent of the African national territories.

Finkelstein's latest exposure of US and Israeli apologetics for state violence was of famed Harvard Law Professor Alan Dershowitz, who was at the centre of Finkelstein's analysis in *Beyond Chutzpah: The Misuse of Anti-Semitism and the Abuse of History*. In August 2003, Dershowitz published *The Case for Israel*, which Finkelstein uses as a foil in *Beyond Chutzpah*, demonstrating that Dershowitz misrepresents key diplomatic, legal and historical aspects of the conflict. Dershowitz attempted to block publication of *Beyond Chutzpah* by inundating the University of California Press with threatening letters from the major New York law firm of Cravath, Swaine, and Moore throughout the spring and summer of 2005, stating he would sue the press if it did not ensure that every claim Finkelstein made about Dershowitz was factually correct. *Beyond Chutzpah* was vetted by six experts of the Israel-Palestine conflict and several libel attorneys. When he could not prevail upon the press or the University of California's Board of Regents, Dershowitz asked Governor Arnold Schwarzenegger to intervene. Schwarzenegger refused to do so on grounds of academic freedom. Finkelstein wasn't so lucky at DePaul.

But, by all accounts, Finkelstein far exceeds DePaul's teaching and publication requirements; indeed, he has the teaching and publication record for full professorship. His tenured colleagues in the political science department voted 9-3 in favour of his tenure and promotion to associate professor. (And the three professors who voted against Finkelstein's tenure are not experts on the Israel-Palestine conflict or the holocaust.) The college's personnel committee unanimously upheld the department's recommendation in a 5-0 vote.

In a memo dated March 22, Dean of Liberal Arts and Sciences Charles Suchar withheld support of Finkelstein's tenure application and agreed with the authors of the minority report, arguing that Finkelstein's tendency to engage in demeaning and reputation-damaging attacks compromised the quality of his scholarship. The dean invoked "Vincentian Personalism" as a tenure criterion, and reported to the university's board that Finkelstein has an "apparent penchant of reducing an argument and oppositional views to the inevitable personal and reputation damaging attack, demeaning those with whom he disagrees." Surprisingly, these concerns had never been raised about Finkelstein's work previously by DePaul's administration.

To thank for these new concerns we have Alan Dershowitz, who distributed an "information packet" to the faculty and waged a one-man war against Finkelstein. Throughout the months of April and May, Dershowitz availed himself of the pages of the *New Republic*, *FrontPage* magazine and even the *Wall Street Journal* to attack a world-renowned scholar and one of DePaul University's most accomplished teachers. Dershowitz has maintained that the Finkelstein case is not about academic freedom but about academic standards. DePaul administrators ended up rationalizing the tenure denial along similar lines. That Finkelstein's opponents have succeeded should give pause to anyone concerned about academic freedom in the United States.

Norman Finkelstein: the case against

The denial of tenure to Norman Finkelstein is not about academic freedom. It's about unscholarly propaganda.

- Alan Dershowitz
- guardian.co.uk, Thursday 14 June 2007 21.00 BST

Matthew Abraham's account of the denial of tenure to Norman Finkelstein is filled with errors. Finkelstein's tactic was to try to create a feud with me so that he could blame his tenure denial on me rather than on his lack of scholarship.

In her 1951 bestseller, *The Groves of Academe*, Mary McCarthy described a failed academic who, realized he wouldn't get tenure, became a communist so that he could claim that he was being denied tenure because he was a Red rather than a lousy scholar.

A version of that ploy was used by Finkelstein who brags that "never has one of [his] articles been published in a scientific magazine". By his own account he has been fired by "every school in New York", including Brooklyn College, Hunter and NYU. His chairman at one of these colleges said that Mr Finkelstein was fired for "incompetence", "mental instability" and "abuse" of students with politics different from his own. His prospects seemed bleak, so when radical Islamist Aminah McCloud – a follower of Louis Farrakhan – helped him land a job at DePaul, a school that Mr. Finkelstein describes as "a third-rate Catholic university", he accepted "exile."

His prospects did not improve when he wrote a screed against Holocaust survivors called *The Holocaust Industry*. The scholar whose work on the Holocaust was the "stimulus" for this volume, University of Chicago professor Peter Novick, warned: "No facts alleged by Finkelstein should be assumed to be really facts, no quotation in his book should be assumed to be accurate, without taking the time to carefully compare his claims with the sources he cites . . . Such an examination reveals that many of those assertions are pure invention."

Nor was he helped when *New York Times* reviewer Prof Omer Bartov, an authority on genocide, characterized his book as "a novel variation on the anti-Semitic forgery, The *Protocols of the Elders of Zion* . . . brimming with indifference to historical facts, inner contradictions, strident politics . . . indecent . . . juvenile, self-righteous, arrogant and stupid."

On the other hand, Mr. Finkelstein is supported by hard-leftists like Noam Chomsky and Alexander Cockburn. They regard him as a scholar in a class with Ward Churchill (the Colorado professor who called the 9/11 victims "little Eichmanns") – a characterisation with which I would not quarrel.

Facing tenure denial, Mr. Finkelstein opted for a tactic that fitted the times. He expressed views so *ad hominem*, unscholarly and extreme that he could claim the decision was being made not on the basis of his scholarship, but rather on his politics.

Mr. Finkelstein does not do "scholarship" in any meaningful sense. Although his writings center on Israel (which he compares to Nazi Germany) and the Holocaust, he has never visited Israel and cannot read or speak German – precluding the possibility of original scholarship.

Prof. Bartov described his work as an irrational Jewish "conspiracy theory". The conspirators include Steven Spielberg, NBC and Leon Uris. The film *Schindler's List*, Mr. Finkelstein argues, was designed to divert attention from our Mideast policy. "Give me a better reason! . . . Who profits? Basically, there are two beneficiaries from the dogmas [of *Schindler's List*]: American Jews and American administration."

NBC, he says, broadcast Holocaust to strengthen Israel's position: "In 1978, NBC produced the series Holocaust. Do you believe, it was a coincidence, 1978? Just at this time, when peace negotiations between Israel and Egypt took place in Camp David?"

He argues that Leon Uris, the author of Exodus, named his character "Ari" in order to promote Israel's "Nazi" ideology: "Because Ari is the diminutive for Aryan. It is the whole admiration for this blond haired, blue eyed type." (Ari is a traditional name dating back to the Bible.)

He has blamed September 11 on the US, claiming that we "deserve the problem on our hands because some things Bin Laden says are true.") He says that most alleged Holocaust survivors – including Elie Wiesel – have fabricated their past.

Like other anti-Semites, Mr. Finkelstein generalizes about "the Jews"; for example: "Just as Israelis . . . courageously put unruly Palestinians in their place, so American Jews courageously put unruly blacks in their place." He says "the main fomenters of anti-Semitism "are 'American Jewish elites' who need to be stopped." Normally, no one would take such claims seriously, but he boasts that he "can get away with things which nobody else can" because his parents were Holocaust survivors.

And then, of course, there is me. In a recent article, Should Alan Dershowitz Target Himself for Assassination? Mr. Finkelstein commissioned a cartoon by a man who was placed second in the Iranian Holocaust-denial cartoon contest. The Hustler-type cartoon portrayed me as masturbating in joy while viewing images of dead Lebanese on a TV set labeled "Israel peep show", with a Star of David prominently featured.

Mr. Finkelstein has accused me of not having written "The Case For Israel" but when I sent his publisher my handwritten draft, they made him remove that claim. He has accused virtually every pro-Israel writer, including me, of "plagiarism". I asked Harvard to conduct an investigation of this absurd charge. Harvard rejected it, yet he persists.

The final part of Mr. Finkelstein's quest for tenure is to blame his tenure problems on "outsiders". His surrogate, Mathew Abraham, claims that I intruded myself into the DePaul review process, neglecting to mention that I was specifically asked by the former chairman of DePaul's political science department to "point [him] to the clearest and most egregious instances of dishonesty on Finkelstein's part". I responded by providing hard evidence of made-up quotes and facts – a pattern that should alone disqualify him from tenure.

Nevertheless, Mr. Finkelstein's radical colleagues voted for tenure, having cooked the books by seeking outside evaluations from two of his ideological soulmates. The dean, however, recommended against tenure, as did the university-wide tenure committee and the President.

Like the character in *The Groves of Academe*, Mr. Finkelstein generated protests by students and outsiders. He has encouraged radical goons to email threatening messages; "Look forward to a visit from me," reads one. "Nazis like [you] need to be confronted directly." He has threatened to sue if he loses – while complaining about outside interference. No university should be afraid of truth – regardless of its source – especially when truth consists of Mr. Finkelstein's own words.

Even without tenure, Mr. Finkelstein will persist in his unscholarly, *ad hominems* against supporters of Israel, Holocaust survivors and the US. But his bigotry will no longer receive the imprimatur of the largest Catholic university in the America.

This is not a denial of academic freedom. It is a denial of tenure for unscholarly, *ad hominem* propaganda.

June 27, 2007

The Dershowitz Style

The Smearing of Robert Trivers

By MATTHEW ABRAHAM

Robert Trivers is a professor of anthropology at Rutgers University in New Brunswick, N.J. He has written on topics ranging from natural selection, selfish genetic elements, to self deception. Both of Trivers' sisters married Lebanese men, according to a recent article by Scott Jaschik in *InsideHigherEd*, which led Trivers to learn much about Lebanon because he has family there. His most recent work has focused on how sustaining myths of the nation depend upon the operation of various types of self deception, leading people who undoubtedly conceptualize themselves as good people and upstanding citizens to suppress critical instincts-that would normally be operative in condemning bad actions by others-when it comes to justifying one's own evil deeds. It would seem, given his academic training and family connection to Lebanon, that Trivers would be well-equipped to understand how techniques of self deception would be operative in the context of intellectual rationalizations for illegitimate war, particularly when it comes to analyzing how this phenomenon works in the case of someone who works overtime to justify the military actions of Israel, actions which often pose a threat to the stability of the Middle East. In a letter dated April 15, 2007, he wrote this to Harvard Law Professor Alan Dershowitz:

"Dear Alan,

You have long been known as a rancid defender of Israeli fascism toward its Arab neighbors but this summer you wrote an article rationalizing Israeli attacks on civilians while Israel was visiting a mini-holocaust on Lebanon. When Human Rights Watch published evidence of war crimes, you stitched together a set of lies suggesting otherwise, which lies you did not retract (of course) when they were shown to be falsehoods.

Now you try to block from tenure someone who has the courage and integrity to expose your history of lies and your resemblance this summer to classic nazi-apologists. This after earlier attempting to block publication of his work and even sliming the memory of his mother. Norman Finkelstein has integrity and intellectual quality you will never experience first-hand.

Regarding your rationalization of Israeli attacks on Lebanese civilians, let me just say that if there is a repeat of Israeli butchery toward Lebanon and if you decide once again to rationalize it publicly, look forward to a visit from me. Nazis-and nazi-like apologists such as yourself-need to be confronted directly.

Robert Trivers"

As part of his never-ending campaign of vilification against Norman Finkelstein's tenure bid at DePaul University, Dershowitz wrote in his May 4th op-ed *in The Wall Street Journal*, entitled "Finkelstein's Bigotry":

"Like the character in the 'Groves of Academe,' Mr. Finkelstein generated protests by students and outsiders. He has encouraged radical goons to email threatening messages; "Look forward to a visit from me," reads one. "Nazis like [you] need to be confronted directly." He has threatened to sue if he loses – while complaining about outside interference. No university should be afraid of truth – regardless of its source – especially when truth consists of Mr. Finkelstein's own words." (emphasis mine)

In his May 14th *Cambridge Diarist* article in *The New Republic*, entitled "Taking the Bait", where he asserted that he was invited into DePaul's tenure and promotion process by the former chair of DePaul's political science department and that Finkelstein was crying "outside interference" to justify his lack of scholarship, Dershowitz wrote:

"In the past months, I have received threatening calls and letters. The Rutgers biologist Robert Trivers, for one, has warned, "Nazi-like apologists as [you] need to be confronted directly." Suddenly I'm the Nazi? And a masturbating one to boot! I'm not shy about entering arguments, but I can't help feeling like I walked into a trap. How could I not argue against Finkelstein? But, when I raise my voice, I know that I'm supplying essential ammunition. I guess when you've got no scholarship to make your tenure case, you need all the outside interference you can get. "(emphasis mine)

As Trivers pointed out in his May 21st letter to the *Wall Street Journal* editors, entitled "What I Said to Dershowitz" in the May 23 rd issue:

"What I Said to Dershowitz

Wall Street Journal, May 23, 2007; Page A15

In regard to Alan Dershowitz's commentary "Finkelstein's Bigotry" (editorial page, May 4): In it he asserts that "He [Norman Finkelstein] has encouraged radical goons to email threatening messages; 'Look forward to a visit from me,' reads one. 'Nazis like [you] need to be confronted directly.'"

But all of this is untrue. I wrote the letter in question (April 15, 2007), but without Prof. Finkelstein's knowledge, interest or approval. The key sentences had nothing to do with Prof. Finkelstein: "Regarding your rationalization of Israeli attacks on Lebanese civilians, let me just say that if there is a repeat of Israeli butchery toward Lebanon and if you decide once again to rationalize it publicly, look forward to a visit from me. Nazis and Nazi-like apologists such as yourself need to be confronted directly."

As for being an academic goon: I am late responding because I was in Europe lecturing after receiving the Crafoord Prize from the Royal Swedish Academy of Sciences.

Robert Trivers

Professor of Anthropology and Biological Sciences

Rutgers University"

Norman Finkelstein is quoted in Christine Flow's June 16th, 2007 *Harvard Crimson* article, "Dershowitz Foes Face Scrutiny", confirming Trivers' account: "I wish I could claim people of that stature as my friends," Finkelstein said. "But how could we be friends? I have no idea what he's talking about [in his work]. We might as well be talking from Earth to Mars." So much for Dershowitz's assertion that Finkelstein "encouraged radical goons to email threatening messages" to him. Also, notice how Dershowitz recasts what Trivers actually wrote: he removes the crucial qualifying portion of the sentence, ". . . if there is a repeat of Israeli butchery toward Lebanon and if you decide once again to rationalize it publicly," leaving the reader to believe that Trivers wrote "Look forward to a visit from me. Nazis like [you] need to be confronted directly," which he clearly did not.

Trivers was scheduled to speak at Harvard's Program for Evolutionary Dynamics on Friday, May 25th. About an hour before his talk, Trivers was informed by Michael Nowak, PED's director and a professor of mathematics and biology at Harvard, who had pleaded with Trivers for several months to commit to the engagement at Harvard, that the talk, as well as the reception to be held in Trivers' honor, had been cancelled because Trivers had supposedly called a Harvard professor a Nazi, as reported in the *Boston Globe*. In an email to *InsideHigherEd*, Dershowitz confirmed that his "office routinely sends letters that can be construed as threatening to the Harvard police" "The Trivers letter fit into that category. I am and always have been opposed to the cancellation of speeches of any kind, whether it be of David Duke, Norman Finkelstein, or Robert Trivers. I do favor counter speech such as leafleting," Dershowitz wrote. Indeed, as reported in Flow's *Harvard Crimson* article, Dershowitz, upon learning that PED would be holding a celebration for Trivers after his talk, decided he would not attend, but would instead stand outside the hall where the celebration was scheduled, handing out copies of Trivers' April 15th letter to Dershowitz to those entering. As it turns out, Dershowitz sits as a faculty affiliate on PED and was retained as a defense lawyer for Jeffrey Epstein, who was indicted for soliciting prostitution and donated 6.5 million dollars to PED. "I don't think you should have a party at which a Harvard faculty doesn't feel comfortable,"

Dershowitz wrote to *InsideHigherEd*. "I have a right to go anywhere at Harvard without feeling a risk to my bodily integrity." Trivers has insisted that he, at no point, intended for the letter to be read as promising to deliver on a physical threat.

As one can see for themselves, by reading Trivers' April 15th letter in its entirety, that Trivers did not label Dershowitz a Nazi, but instead noted the resemblance between Dershowitz's apologetics for Israel's bombing of South Lebanon last summer and the performances of classic Nazi-apologists. Similarly, in the last line of his letter, Trivers notes that "Nazis-and nazi-like apologists such as yourself-need to be confronted directly," which clearly suggests that he was calling Dershowitz a "nazi-like" apologist not a Nazi or Nazi-apologist. The difference between a "nazi-like apologist" and a "classic Nazi-apologist" should be wholly clear to those who are familiar with the operations of the English language. The appellation "nazi-like apologist" would apply to someone who provided rationalizations for indiscriminate bombings of civilian areas that resembled the apologetics provided by those in pay to the Nazi regime.

There can be little doubt that the Israeli air force engaged in indiscriminate bombing last summer throughout South Lebanon. Similarly, there can be little doubt that Alan Dershowitz sought to justify these bombings under various arguments, including that Hezbollah was using the civilian population as a human shield to protect its soldiers and armaments from Israeli attack. Dershowitz's most egregious claim, and the one that probably inspired Trivers's letter, is that all Lebanese were legitimate targets because an overwhelming majority supported resistance to the Israeli invasion. Trivers, without naming Dershowitz or drawing a comparison between Dershowitz and Nazis, states that Nazis should be confronted directly. Who could disagree? Trivers then clearly designates that Dershowitz is a nazi-like apologist, i.e. someone who intellectualizes about and provides rationalizations for state violence against civilians. That's precisely what Alan Dershowitz did do last summer during Israel's thirty-three days of bombing in South Lebanon.

Finally, we must consider whether or not Trivers' letter constituted a legitimate physical threat against Dershowitz's bodily integrity in its promise to make good on "a visit" if Dershowitz decided to publicly rationalize a future Israeli butchery in Lebanon. Trivers did not write "expect me to come up to Cambridge and punch your lights out" in the event of another Israeli air strike in Lebanon and another Dershowitzian rationalization of that action, nor did he write to Dershowitz that "I will kill you if you rationalize future Israeli air strikes in South Lebanon." All Trivers promised to do was to pay Dershowitz a visit ". . . if there is a repeat of Israeli butchery toward Lebanon and if you decide once again to rationalize it publicly."

Given that Dershowitz cannot, or at least pretends not to be able to, distinguish between a "Nazi apologist" and a "Nazi-like apologist," why should he be given the benefit of the doubt in his attempts to make Trivers' promise of a "visit", in the event of another Israeli butchery in south Lebanon, tantamount to a physical threat? The answer is simple for those familiar with Dershowitz's favorite tactic: when he has no defense for his attempts to justify U.S. and Israeli war crimes, he attempts to shift the focus of the debate, poses as the victim, and vilifies those who have exposed him. It's a familiar tactic, especially for one practiced in the Stalin-like school of vilification. Below, one can see my many attempts to get some clarification from Dershowitz on the exact contents of Trivers' letter, before Trivers himself sent it to me, and how-yet once again-Dershowitz misrepresents what Trivers actually wrote.

Matthew Abraham is an assistant professor of English at DePaul University in Chicago. He can be reached at: matthew.mabraha2@gmail.com

_____ Forwarded message _____

From: Alan Dershowitz <<mailto:dersh@law.harvard.edu> dersh@law. harvard.edu>

Date: May 26, 2007 6:05 PM

Subject: Re: letter

To: MATTHEW ABRAHAM <<mailto:matthew.mabraha2@gmail.com> matthew.mabraha2@gmail.com>

The correspondence is over. Any further emails from you will be harassment.

Sent via BlackBerry from Cingular Wireless

_____ Original Message _____

From: "MATTHEW ABRAHAM" <<mailto:matthew.mabraha2@gmail. com> matthew.mabraha2@gmail.com>

Date: Sat, 26 May 2007 17:48:15

<mailto:To:dersh@law.harvard.edu> To:dersh@law.harvard.edu

Subject: Re: letter

What should one conclude if the _WSJ_ doesn't publish the Trivers' letter, which you have now apparently sent to the _WSJ_ editors? Is there a way to independently verify that you sent them the letter?

I'm afraid I don't understand why you are now telling me not to email you any further. What fantasy world am I living in exactly? Please be specific.

Thanks, MA

On 5/26/07, Alan Dershowitz <<mailto:dersh@law.harvard.edu> wrote: Our correspondence is over. I sent the Trivers letter the [to] *WSJ*. If they publish it you will learn the truth. Otherwise you can continue to live in your fantasy world but leave me out of it. Do not email me any further.

Sent via BlackBerry from Cingular Wireless

_____ Original Message _____

From: "MATTHEW ABRAHAM" <<mailto:matthew.mabraha2@gmail.com> matthew.mabraha2@gmail.com

Date: Sat, 26 May 2007 13:45:11

To:dersh@law.harvard.edu

Subject: Re: letter

Dear Professor Dershowitz:

The fact of the matter is that yesterday you said "Ask him [Trivers]. Or send me your fax #," under the pretense that you were going to send me Trivers' letter if I sent you my fax # (as you know, I sent it to you immediately (yesterday) and I did again just a few minutes ago). When I didn't receive the letter yesterday, I began to get a little skeptical if what you claimed the letter said in the "middle paragraph" about Trivers' reference to you as a "Nazi apologist" in the context of the Finkelstein case was true. As you know, Trivers maintains that Finkelstein was never mentioned in the letter.

In one of your messages to me today, you mentioned that intended to fax me Trivers' letter after you get back to Cambridge, but now will not because I doubted your word without having actually seen the letter Trivers sent to you. Given your record of truth-telling on various matters pertaining to the Holy State and its dealings with the Palestinians, and your own record of deceit and apologetics on the matter, which have been repeatedly exposed by Professors Chomsky and Finkelstein over the last several years, you might imagine why I was taken aback by your moral outrage at my proclivity to believe that you *might" be (yet, once again) misrepresenting someone's correspondence to you, i.e. Trivers' letter. I replied that you could have Mitch Webber, your research assistant, send Trivers' letter to me right away by writing to or calling him (with your Blackberry) and telling him to fax Trivers' letter to me. Presumably that's what research assistants are around for, right? To be at the beck and call of famous Harvard Law Professors such as yourself. I also wrote that it was a perfect opportunity through which to prove me wrong in expressing skepticism about what you *claim* the letters states, and to show that Trivers lied in the letters pages of the *WSJ*. In addition, I also think it would provide you with a perfect opportunity to blast the *WSJ* editors for publishing a letter containing a gross mischaracterization about the context within which the "Nazi and Nazi-apologist" allegation was made (Trivers' April 15th letter to you). As Trivers wrote in his *WSJ* letter, his letter to you doesn't even mention Finkelstein and that he sent it to you without requesting the permission of or consulting with Finkelstein. Since the letter was written to you, one can reasonably presume that you received it, read it, and are still in possession of it. Therefore, I would kindly request that you fax me the letter since I provided you with my fax # (personal information) when you asked for it.. Now, you have made a new demand because I've expressed skepticism about whether or not you're telling the truth about the Trivers' letter: "Will you agree to publicly apologize and admit you made up a defamatory accusation if I quoted the letter correctly?" The evidentiary burden, as you know, for proving that a public figure like yourself has been subjected to a "defamatory accusation" is quite high. I would also imagine in your case—given your history of misrepresenting matters that are of public record such as your claim from 1973 that Shahak was legitimately ousted as the chair of the Israeli League of Human Rights, which Chomsky has decisively documented was a lie (available on the internet, as I understand it)—the evidentiary burden would be considerably higher than for most human beings. Since you're a lawyer, I'm sure you'll correct me if I'm wrong. You also know that truth is a defense to the allegation that one has been defamed or slandered. So, before I answer your most recent question, may I ask who will evaluate whether I "made up a defamatory accusation if [you] quoted [Trivers'] letter correctly." A reasonable person? You? Webber? Derek Bok? Elena Kagan? Larry Summers? Your wife? A third-party agreed upon beforehand by the two of us? I'm interested in pursuing the exercise, I just need some more information before going forward. If I don't receive a response from you, or you evade the question, I'll be sure to place this most recent correspondence with you in my "Dershowitz-didn't-answer-the-question file," which has grown quite large in light of some of your recent public statements.

Thanks, MA

On 5/26/07, Alan Dershowitz <<mailto:dersh@law.harvard.edu> dersh@law.harvard.edu wrote: Will you agree to publicly apologize and admit you made up a defamatory accusation if I quoted the letter correctly? If not don't bother to reply

Sent via BlackBerry from Cingular Wireless

_____ Original Message _____

From: "MATTHEW ABRAHAM" <<mailto:matthew.mabraha2@gmail.com> matthew.mabraha2@gmail.com:

Date: Sat, 26 May 2007 12:27:37

To:dersh@law.harvard.edu

Subject: Re: Fwd: letter to D.

Why not prove me wrong, and convince me that I'm wrong, in questioning your word by faxing me Trivers' letter? It would seem, if given what you say about the language in Trivers 'letter, which apparently*now*describes you as a "classic nazi apologist" "in [Trivers'] paragraph explicitly [sic] referencing finkelstein," that you would be eager to demonstrate that Trivers' is a liar and that I was wrong to doubt you. Just write to Webber and have him fax me the letter at 773-325-7328. Seems to me like a moment of truth for you, your entourage, and the agitprop you produce.

Thanks, MA

On 5/26/07, Alan Dershowitz <<mailto:dersh@law.harvard.edu> dersh@law.harvard.edu: <wrote: . I was going to fax the letter when I got back to Cambridge. It would show that he used the precise words "classic nazi apologists" in his paragraph explicitly referencing Finkelstein. But since u question my word without even checking I will have no further correspondence with you

Sent via BlackBerry from Cingular Wireless

_____ Original message _____

From: MATTHEW ABRAHAM<

<mailto:matthew.mabraha2@gmail.com>matthew.mabraha2@gmail.com:

To: dersh@law.harvard.edu>

Dear Professor Dershowitz:

There's a huge difference between a "Nazi apologist" and a "Nazi-like apologist." The phrase "Nazi apologist" does not appear in Trivers' letter, which is why I presume you have not faxed me the letter. In addition, I'm left to wonder if Finkelstein is mentioned at all in Trivers' letter of April 15th, 2007, as you claim he is in "the middle paragraph." Here is what Trivers wrote: "Regarding your rationalization of Israeli attacks on Lebanese civilians, let me just say that if there is a repeat of Israeli butchery toward Lebanon and if you decide once again to rationalize it publicly, look forward to a visit from me. Nazis — and Nazi-like apologists such as yourself — need to be confronted directly."

Thanks, MA

On 5/25/07, Alan Dershowitz <mailto:dersh@law.harvard.edu> dersh@ law.harvard.edu: wrote:

Ask him. Or send me your fax #

Sent via BlackBerry from Cingular Wireless

_____ Original Message _____

From: "MATTHEW ABRAHAM"<:

<mailto:<mailto:dersh@law.harvard.edu>dersh@law.harvard.edu>: >

Subject: Re: Trivers

Could you kindly reproduce the middle paragraph of Trivers' letter?

On 5/25/07, Alan Dershowitz <mailto:dersh@law.harvard.edu> dersh@ law.harvard.edu

: wrote: Middle paragraph

Sent via BlackBerry from Cingular Wireless

_____ Original Message _____

From: "MATTHEW ABRAHAM"<

<mailto: <mailto:dersh@law.harvard.edu> dersh@law.harvard.edu>

Subject: Re: Trivers

Dear Professor Dershowitz:

Could you kindly point me to the potions of Trivers' letter, where he "refer explictely to f and in that very calls [you] a nazi apologist"? I trust, from what you claim below, that you have actually seen the entire letter.

Thanks, MA

On 5/23/07, Alan Dershowitz <<mailto:dersh@law.harvard.edu> dersh@ law.harvard.edu: wrote: Ask him for his entire letter and you will see he is lying. He refers explicitly to f and in that very sentence calls me a nazi apologist. By the way do you agree with that characterization? No evasion. A direct answer please.

Sent via BlackBerry from Cingular Wireless

_____ Original Message _____

From: " MATTHEW ABRAHAM"<

Subject: Trivers

Dear Professor Dershowitz:

In today's *WSJ*, Rutgers professor Robert Trivers responded to your recent "Finkelstein's Bigotry," and by extension your recent "Taking the Bait," which appeared in *TNR*. Do you have a response to his charge that you misrepresented the context of his remarks, i.e., that they had nothing to do with the Finkelstein case, as you suggested? I trust that you would never deliberately misrepresent someone's remarks on such a highly charged topic as the Israel-Palestine conflict.

Thanks, MA

This article, "The Dershowitz Style: The Smearing of Robert Trivers," originally appeared in Counterpunch magazine. See: http://www.counterpunch.org/2007/06/27/the-smearing-of-robert-trivers/

Showdown at DePaul: Why DePaul's Faculty Must Speak Out Now

by Matthew Abraham / June 23rd, 2007

DePaul University's Promotion and Tenure Board's decision to deny tenure to Professors Norman G. Finkelstein and Mehrene Laurdee on June 8th, 2007 has placed DePaul University on the brink of a legitimacy crisis, a legitimacy crisis that threatens to irrevocably harm the very fabric of a university that has placed social justice and activism at the very heart of its Vincentian mission since 1898. What does it mean that this Vincentian University has denied tenure to two passionate advocates of social justice who not only met the tenure requirements of their departments and the College of Liberal Arts and Sciences but clearly surpassed them? What would St. Vincent de Paul have made of this year's tenure and promotion decisions? Would he have agreed with them? From what I know of St. Vincent de Paul's life and work, I'm almost certain he would be distressed by what has transpired under the name of "Vincentian tenure standards," which are transparent code words for "proving one's ideological serviceability to the interests of the powerful," in this case DePaul's would-be patrons. Finkelstein and Larudee apparently failed that test.

Norman Finkelstein has written passionately about the plight of the Palestinians living under Israeli occupation, indicting powerful elites who capitalize upon the moral capital of the Holocaust for financial gain while demonstrating indifference toward the suffering of those on the receiving end of US high-tech weaponry in the Palestinian occupied territories and South Lebanon. Larudee, the sister of International Solidarity Movement leader Paul Larudee who was jailed in Israel for a brief time, is a specialist on international organizations and developing countries. During their time at DePaul, Finkelstein and Larudee have inspired numerous students to create a better world, sparked vigorous debate on the issues of our age, and dared to speak truth to power, which is an era of clichés and political correctness is the minimum intellectual responsibility requires.

As an untenured assistant professor on this campus, who thought serious scholarship would find a site of articulation within the university named after St. Vincent de Paul, I have questioned not only my DePaul colleagues' commitment to academic freedom, but the motivations and rationalizations of many of my colleagues who remain silent in the wake of the grave injustice that took place on June 8 th, 2007, when Finkelstein and Larudee received their denial letters from President Dennis Holtschneider.

Outside the student center at the Lincoln Park campus stands a giant statue of the famous 20th century priest, Monsieur John Egan, who asks "What are you doing for justice?" At DePaul these days, it seems the students are doing more by way of affirmatively answering Egan's question than the faculty. Students have staged protests of some sort every day since the tenure denials were made official. At this moment, a handful of these students are staging a hunger protest outside the Lincoln Park student center. DePaul's students are standing on principle, and as one protester's rally sign declared, "You can silence our professors, but you can't silence their ideas."

Professional decorum dictates that administrative decisions, whatever they may be and regardless of whether or not they make sense, should be accepted with grace and without undue skepticism, and certainly without resistance, by the faculty. This situation, however, demands fierce resistance. I am calling on all of my DePaul colleagues to launch an intellectual revolt against the suppression of academic freedom on our campus. Although President Holtschneider maintains that academic freedom is alive and well at DePaul, and Provost Epp's insists that the denial of tenure to Larudee and Finelstein were "faculty decisions," it is high time to call out these PR strategies for what they are: convenient smokescreens designed to appease, obfuscate, and confuse.

Over the last three months, I have provoked, teased, begged, and cajoled tenured faculty at DePaul to be vigilant about the Finkelstein case, stating quite clearly that it was a test case that would have wide ranging implications for the future of academic freedom and academic freedom protections in the United States. Regrettably, only about four faculty members at DePaul took this warning seriously, with most believing the tenure processes at DePaul have essentially been fair and would, over time, weed out any early expressions of bias and unfairness. Indeed, some faculty members stated unequivocally that they would lead the charge if the University Board denied Finkelstein tenure. As one senior faculty member proudly proclaimed, "The faculty will revolt if Finkelstein is denied."

Now, that the results are final and Finkelstein and Larudee have been the victims of egregious violations of academic freedom and due process per the faculty handbook, faculty members at DePaul must stand up, speak out, and not settle for a summer of fun, relaxation, and a convenient amnesia. It is high time for the faculty to identify and mobilize against the forces within DePaul University that conspired to deny Finkelstein and Larudee what they rightfully earned; organize in support of academic freedom by creating a solid lobbying effort against illegitimate external influences in DePaul's tenure and promotion processes; and perhaps most importantly, insist upon a thorough investigation of what happened at the University Promotion and Tenure Board hearings in May that led to majority votes against Finkelstein and Larudee's tenure and promotion to associate professor.

If a Task Force were formed to interrogate the faculty members who served on this year's committee, there is the possibility that someone would emerge to tell the truth about what influence, if any, was placed on the faculty members who served to vote in a particular way. This needs to happen not just to answer the questions that have emerged over the last two weeks about how the UPTB arrived at its decisions, but to prove that DePaul's administration has absolutely nothing to hide. If there is nothing to hide, there is no reason why those who served on the UPTB would object to being interviewed by the Task Force. The administration's insistence that there is no appeals process only contributes to an already tense situation filled with suspicion about the UPTB's deliberations from last April and May.

That Finkelstein and Larudee received overwhelming support from their respective departments and unanimous support from the LA&S College personnel committee that heard their cases, only to have the UPTB reach entirely different conclusions about their scholarship than the lower levels in what essentially amounts to a retrying each case, suggests that the seven voting members of the UPTB either learned a great deal about the US-Israel-Palestine conflict and international studies in a month's time, were denied crucial pieces of information, or were coerced to vote a certain way to produce a desired outcome. In any event, all three scenarios are extremely troubling.

One thing is clear: US supporters of Israel, who have not hesitated in the past to use psych-op smear tactics against individuals committed to upholding international law and the international consensus on the Israel-Palestine conflict, may very well have successfully corrupted DePaul University's tenure and promotion processes through DePaul's Board of Trustees in a blatant attempt to remove political opponents from the largest Catholic university in the United States.

Matthew Abraham is the 2005 Rachel Corrie Courage in the Teaching of Writing Award Winner.

This article, orginally appeared here in *Dissident Voice*: http://dissidentvoice.org/2007/06/showdown-at-depaul-why-depauls-faculty-must-speak-out-now/

September 5, 2007

A Defining Moment

Standing Firm with Norman Finkelstein and DePaul's Heroic Students

By MATTHEW ABRAHAM

I am an untenured, assistant professor at DePaul University in Chicago, where
Norman G. Finkelstein, the most heroic critic of U.S. and Israeli policy in
Palestine ever to set foot in the U.S. academy, was denied tenure over nearly
three months ago. I was, and am, deeply saddened that DePaul University,
the institution where I have chosen to make a career, has so effectively
undermined its social justice mission in a series of actions that have put us,
as a faculty body, in grave peril.

By capitulating to the threats, antics, and pressures of Alan Dershowitz, the
Israel Lobby, and its numerous affiliates, DePaul has compromised something
so integral to an educational institution's mission, that once so compromised,
it is impossible to regain. That something is *institutional autonomy*. An
institution's ability to withstand outside pressure, and economic coercion-
which can often be tantamount to blackmail-is a must in an age of corporate
scandal, sleazy deal making, and political cover-ups. The general public used to
look to the academy for leadership, vision, and most importantly, uncorrupted
knowledge. Not anymore. DePaul is now even more vulnerable than it was
before President Dennis Holtschneider signed Norman G. Finkelstein's tenure
denial letter on June 8 th. Despite the legalistic obfuscations about the how
the Finkelstein denial is not about academic freedom, but about professional
conduct, the denunciation of so-called "conspiracy theories" which have
cropped up over the summer, and the holier-than-thou pronouncements
about how this past year's tenure and promotion decisions were the result of
a "clean process," DePaul University is more vulnerable than ever to the next
assault upon its integrity and autonomy-no matter how many millions of
dollars have poured into its coffers because of the Finkelstein tenure denial,
we are vulnerable.

Today, Wednesday (September 5th, 2007), is the biggest day in DePaul
University's history as Norman G. Finkelstein returns to campus to begin his
terminal year after being denied tenure on June 8th. Finkelstein has been placed
on "administrative leave" because of his supposed behavior on June 13 th and
June 14th, when he confronted faculty in the Political Science Department,
individuals who voted against his tenure, and Dean Charles Suchar, who
recommended against tenure in a memo dated March 22 nd to the University
Board on Tenure and Promotion. Because of these confrontations and because
of recommendation made by a special committee within the Political Science
Department, according to a memo written by Provost Helmut Epp, Finkelstein

has been removed from the classroom and will not be allowed to teach the courses that were assigned to him as late as ten days ago.

Over the last few months I have been forced to ask some hard questions about DePaul's institutional mission, its commitment to preserving tenure as a special accolade for the best and the brightest in the academy, and its defense of academic freedom in the context of the Israel-Palestine conflict, which so often is subject to institutional surveillance, censorship, and silencing. Most importantly, I have come to question DePaul's administration and faculty's commitment to upholding academic freedom, as a serious institutional value, which enables critical thinking and meaningful dissent around important, albeit, taboo subjects such as Israel's human rights record in the occupied territories and the special role that U.S. taxpayers fill in contributing to that record. Indeed, the silence of many tenured faculty here at DePaul, in the face of egregious violations of academic freedom and due process in the Finkelstein case, is in many ways the same silence that plagues the American public when it comes to speaking out about the forty-year Israeli occupation of Palestine. This faculty silence is perhaps the hardest thing for me, as a new faculty member, to understand and reconcile with DePaul's Vincentian heritage and mission. If there was ever a time for Vincentian personalism to manifest itself, it is now, in this moment, when Norman Finkelstein steps onto campus this morning. If faculty find themselves unable to rally around him, too busy with the usual duties that attend preparing for the beginning of the academic year, perhaps DePaul faculty should ask themselves why they are in this business of opening young minds to new ideas, when they are incapable of seeing that our campus is on the brink of devolving into something reminiscent the Red Scare of the McCarthy Era. Will those faculty associated with, and standing in support of Finkelstein, be the next targets of DePaul's administration? If so, I would certainly be a likely target. I am ready to accept that challenge.

Faculty and administrators that I respect, people to whom I have turned to for advice and guidance in the short time I have been at DePaul, have repeatedly cowered in the face of various pressures within and external to the university around the political persecution of Norman G. Finkelstein. Most DePaul faculty have preferred to simply stay out of the way, justifying their inaction with statements such as "Perhaps the administration has information that we don't" or "We don't know what happened in that room when Finkelstein met with the University Board." "Finkelstein is difficult" I've heard people say or "He's not collegial and is a polemicist" someone else dismissively points out. "He's saying things, which might be true, but people aren't ready to hear such things as yet" another announces. These are excuses, I know, that well-meaning people generate to justify their decision to remain silent, realizing perhaps the fight for this dissident is not going to yield anything for them personally or professionally.

DePaul's decision to deny Norman G. Finkelstein tenure in such a clumsy and blatantly foolish way, really beggars the imagination. The administration maintains that Finkelstein does not show adequate respect for the views of his political opponents in his scholarship, which is a transparent admission that, since it could not find serious flaws in his teaching or scholarship, the administration had to concoct a reason to deny Finkelstein tenure. That which Suchar called "Vincentian personalism" and what Holtschneider referenced as "a tendency to simplify and polarize debates which require subtle and layered consideration," are admissions that DePaul, under no circumstances, was to make a positive recommendation on the Finkelstein tenure case. Indeed, that is more likely than not what key members on DePaul's Board of Trustees told the administration over a year ago-"Find a way to do this. We don't care how." Perhaps realizing that most DePaul faculty would prefer to hold on to their academic privilege, instead of rocking the boat and making noise about the persecution of a dissenting colleague, the administration made a cynical calculation: "No one will care if Finkelstein is denied tenure. We can pull this off with minimum cost." Therein lay a miscalculation: There are a group of people who care about the political persecution of Norman G. Finkelstein–DePaul's heroic students, who are at this moment standing by their favorite professor as he prepares for the fight of his life. Regardless of whether or not the faculty joins these students in this day's heroic struggle is of little consequence. A mighty victory has been won for the idealism of the young. With them and Finkelstein I will stand firm.

Matthew Abraham is an assistant professor of Writing, Rhetoric, and Discourse at DePaul University. He was the 2005 Rachel Corrie Courage in the Teaching of Writing award winner. He can be reached at matthew.mabraha2@gmail.com.

This article, "Standing Firm with Norman Finkelstein and DePaul's Heroic Students," originally appeared here in *Counterpunch*: http://www.counterpunch.org/2007/09/05/standing-firm-with-norman-finkelstein-and-depaul-s-heroic-students/

Weekend Edition
September 8 / 9, 2007

Finkelstein's Legacy at DePaul

Climbing Jacob's Ladder, One Rung at a Time

By MATTHEW ABRAHAM

"It is time for me to move on and hopefully find new ways to fulfill my own mission in life of making the world a slightly better place on leaving it than when I entered it."

Norman G. Finkelstein on 9/5/07

When Norman Finkelstein announced last Wednesday that he and DePaul University had reached a negotiated settlement, ending his nearly year-long battle to gain tenure in the face of the highly unusual set of circumstances created by the extramural campaign of hate and intimidation launched by Alan Dershowitz, the Israel Lobby, and its numerous affiliates, one could have almost have felt as if the whole controversy had come to an anti-climactic end. It was a sad moment for many who had defended Finkelstein throughout the year, in the hope the administration could be brought to its senses about the deadly blow that had been delivered against academic freedom and this world-class intellectual, who brought a determination to his work few will be able to match.

In exchange for his immediate resignation from DePaul's faculty, DePaul would essentially admit that Finkelstein had met the University's tenure and promotion requirements ("Professor Finkelstein is a prolific scholar and an outstanding teacher"), while also providing Finkelstein with an undisclosed amount of money, along with a backhanded acknowledgment of the public outrage that had been generated in response to the tenure denial ("We understand that Professor Finkelstein and his supporters disagree with the University Board on Promotion and Tenure's conclusion that he did not meet the requirements for tenure.") Well, the obvious reason Finkelstein and many of his supporters disagreed with the University Board on Promotion and Tenure's conclusions is because Finkelstein consistently earned among the highest, if not the highest, teaching evaluations in the political science department for six years in a row. Coupled that with the five books which he has published to international acclaim, the most recent being his *Beyond Chutzpah: On the Misuse of Anti-Semitism and the Abuse of History* with the University of California Press, which Dershowitz's campaign of abuse and vilification could not censor, one might naturally understand why Finkelstein and his supporters have drawn the logical inference that something else-other than the usual DePaul standards-might have been in play.

Given that the University has now settled with Finkelstein under confidential terms, the logical inference, that outside political interference was the real reason Finkelstein was denied tenure, is most certainly correct. The administration's repeated rejoinder that Finkelstein just did not measure up to the institution's standards is clearly absurd. To recap: The tenure members of Finkelstein's own department voted 9-3 supporting his tenure bid; The five members of the Liberal Arts and Science's College Personnel Committee voted 5-0 to support Finkelstein's tenure and promotion to full professor; two outside reviewers, of international acclaim, enthusiastically endorsed Finkelstein's application. In late March, an administrative intervention, in the form of Dean Chuck Suchar, took place because the faculty, if left to its own devices, was going to give Finkelstein tenure. Suchar alleged that he could not support Finkelstein's tenure bid because his scholarship was at odds with DePaul's institutional mission, which apparently requires DePaul professors to respect the God-given dignity of political opponents such as Alan Dershowitz. In brief, according to Suchar, tenuring Finkelstein would be problematic since the latter engages in *ad hominem* and reputation-demeaning attacks.

In my opinion, all of this discussion about whether or not Finkelstein engages in *ad hominem* attacks, and whether or not his doing so should be legitimate grounds for denying him tenure, seems to completely miss the larger point: Finkelstein's colleagues within his department and College overwhelmingly supported his tenure bid. The tenured members of his department, the people who worked with him on a daily basis, voted to support his tenure and promotion to associate professor. The three members of the department who voted against him filed a minority report, arguing that Finkelstein was uncollegial to them personally. The College Personnel Committee voted unanimously to support the Department's majority recommendation. Surely, no one is going to claim that the nine people who voted for Finkelstein in his own department, and the five people who supported him on the College Personnel Committee, did so because they are anti-Semites or self-hating Jews, right?

Realizing that faculty support for Finkelstein would pose a huge problem for the administration's long-ago hatched plan to deny him tenure, the Dean intervened and claimed that Finkelstein's scholarship–which has been published to international acclaim and praised by the likes of the leading experts on the Israel Palestine conflict (Avi Shlaim (Oxford), Sara Roy (Harvard), the late Baruch Kimmerling (Hebrew Univ. of Jerusalem), William Quandt, and Beshara Doumani (Berkeley) and the Nazi Holocaust (the late Raul Hilberg, the founder of Holocaust Studies who was actually doing serious work on the Holocaust long before it became politically convenient and ideologically serviceable to do so, Joachim Fest, Arno Mayer, Christopher Browning, and Ian Kershaw)–just did not comport with what it means to embody Vincentian personalism.. Finkelstein's five books have undergone forty-six different translations-more than the entire faculty within DePaul's College of Liberal Arts and Sciences combined. That doesn't sound very controversial to me.

In his report, the Dean bases his argument that Finkelstein's scholarship doesn't meet DePaul's standards on a single chapter from *The Holocaust Industry*. As it turns out, the Dean, in the course of advancing his argument, reveals he hasn't read any of Finkelstein's books, much less the one he is referencing. Suchar got so confused in his borrowings from another text, which was perhaps provided to him by Dershowitz or some other third party, that he misspelled the word "huckster" as "huxter"-just as Dershowitz misspelled it in his propaganda package, [see p. 5 of 21], which he sent Finkelstein's former department chair. In addition, note that Suchar places the Israeli historian Benny Morris in the same company as Dershowitz, Elie Wiesel, and Daniel Goldhagen. As anyone who has read Finkelstein's work surely knows, Morris is someone Finkelstein holds in high regard and is not someone he would mention in the same breath as Dershowitz, Wiesel, and Goldhagen-all of whom he has referred to as "hoaxers" and "hucksters"; not, as Suchar (and Dershowitz) would have it, "hoaxters and huxters." After Suchar's memo withholding support for Finkelstein's tenure came out in late March, fourteen members of the political science department, including all the junior faculty members, refuted what was alleged about Finkelstein's supposed incivility, stating they found him to be a great colleague who made a tremendous contribution to the department.

The University Board, which voted 4-3 against tenure, embraced the minority report written by the three people in Finkelstein's department who voted against him, none of whom are experts on the Middle East or the Nazi Holocaust, while ignoring the majority vote from Finkelstein's department, the unanimous vote of the College Personnel Committee, and the enthusiastic endorsements of two distinguished outside reviewers, whose views and opinions about Finkelstein's record were solicited by DePaul's political science department. This year's university committee consisted of faculty members from Psychology, Law, Theatre Arts, Management, Mathematics, Communications, and Education. Is one to understand that these faculty members were in a better position to judge Finkelstein's record than his own department, his College, and the distinguished reviewers? Note that President Holtscheider, in summarizing the University Board's reasoning, doesn't even offer one example of the *ad hominem* attacks in Finkelstein's work, which apparently necessitated the tenure denial.

In examining the evidence at hand, it's fairly clear that Finkelstein was not denied tenure because of his supposed *ad hominem* attacks or his lack of collegiality. He was denied tenure at DePaul because tremendous outside pressure was placed on the university to remove an effective critic of U.S. and Israeli policy in the Middle East from its precincts. I wish the administration would stop repeating the bald-face lie that Finkelstein's scholarship did not meet DePaul's tenure and promotion standards. It's embarrassing and an insult to the intelligence. Apparently, Rubinstein and Associates, the PR firm DePaul hired to help it with its public relations image, thought the repeated invocation of this lie would pass muster; it clearly did not.

Private giving to DePaul doubled between 2006 and 2007. I have no doubt that DePaul receiving that money was dependent upon the administration ensuring that Finkelstein be denied tenure. It's to DePaul's credit that it hired and retained Finkelstein for six years. There was plenty of pressure placed on the university during that time period to get rid of him because he was writing and speaking, with great effectiveness, about Israel's terrible human rights record against the Palestinians in the occupied territories, which is sustained by the United States' crucial material, military, and diplomatic support. Indeed, it's often difficult for U.S. intellectuals to hear that they might be contributing to a cultural milieu that condones and turns its eyes away from U.S.-supported war crimes. When Finkelstein exposed Dershowitz's *The Case for Israel*, in his *Beyond Chutzpah*, to be a "hoax concocted from another hoax," Finkelstein in fact exposed how our own elite intellectual culture works. How else does one explain that Henry Louis Gates praised *The Case for Israel* as a great book? Maybe he didn't read it before he wrote a positive blurb for it?

In October of 2004, I had the distinct honor of interviewing Professor Finkelstein for an online discussion of his books. Although he became impatient with the participant's seemingly, complete lack of comprehension of his work, which were supposed to be the basis of participant questions, he tried to provide some comic relief. His dismissal of Derrida and his work, the day after Derrida's passing, was in meant to force discussion participants to think about why Derrida's thinking had come to dominate so much contemporary discussion within the humanities; that's what iconoclasts are supposed to do. They force us to question why we embrace certain figures, theories, and approaches, attacking them when they become all too sacred.

Below, I've pasted in Finkelstein's final post to the discussion list, which struck me as ironic and insightful. I'd prefer tenure to be an honor we bestow upon people who are saying provocative and timely things about the important issues of the day, rather than an accolade with which we buy people's silence and good behavior. All too often that's unfortunately how tenure operates. Robert Jensen wrote a powerful essay about this problem a few months ago, considering what it would mean for the U.S. academy if Finkelstein were denied tenure. I'm afraid Jensen's words were prescient.

If there are those in the public sphere who have actually read Finkelstein's books and grappled with his arguments who wish to offer up some examples of Finkelstein's supposed *ad hominem* attacks, I'm sure they could be analyzed and discussed. For example, are Finkelstein's charts documenting Dershowitz's reliance upon Joan Peters' *From Time Immemorial* in his *The Case for Israel ad hominem*?

For someone to state that they've heard that Finkelstein is a nasty piece of work, a self-hating Jew, and an anti-Semite based on third parties, who have a vested interest in silencing him, seems inconsistent with what responsible public intellectualism is all about. Let's not forget that Finkelstein is Jewish, the son of Holocaust survivors, and had much of his family exterminated during the holocaust. The dedication of his *Image and Reality in the Israel-Palestine Conflict* reads as follows:

To my beloved parents,
Maryla Husyt Finkelstein,
survivor of the Warsaw Ghetto,
Maidanek concentration camp

and

Zacharias Finkelstein,
survivor of the Warsaw Ghetto,
Auschwitz concentration camp.

May I never forget or forgive what was done to them

Thanks, Norm, for all you have done for your colleagues and students at DePaul. In the end, you proved to have had far more integrity, intelligence, determination than those who were in a position to judge you. As you helped humanity climb Jacob's ladder, one rung at a time, you have inspired all of us to make this world a better and more humane place.

Wed, 27 Oct 2004 08:11:02 -0500

Reply-To: Scholarly Book Review List <PRETEXT@LISTSERV.UTA.EDU>

Sender: Scholarly Book Review List <PRETEXT@LISTSERV.UTA.EDU>

From: "Vitanza, Victor" <sophist@uta.edu>

Subject: nf (PRE/TEXT)

Content-Type: multipart/alternative;

Date Sent: Wednesday, October 27, 2004 01:21 AM

From: Norman Finkelstein <normangf@hotmail.com>

To: mabraha2 <mabraha2@utk.edu>

Cc: NormanGF <NormanGF@hotmail.com>

One reason for the right-wing's ascendancy in the United States is that, at any rate, in some departments, and especially those where I can lay reasonable claim to personal and professional knowledge, what reactionaries have to say, however painful it might be to confess, contains a grain, and then some, of truth. It is frequently alleged in these right-wing quarters that universities have been effectively hijacked by semi-literate, politically correct blowhards spouting an incomprehensible and vacuous jargon, not to mention one with the tonal aesthetic of a tin can, which, rather than be a badge or shame, is for these post-whatevers a point of preening and, what's yet more a matter commanding consternation among those still preserving a jot of rationality, for them a signifier of superiority to the common herd who, God forbid, make themselves generally understood. I am old enough to have passed through multiple of these epochs in non-thought. When I was coming of age politically, Althusser and his acolytes like Poulantzas were all the rage. Who can forget that prose that induced the same aesthetic effect as it was chewed over in the mind as tin foil does when chewed over in a mouth filled with cavities? This fashion passed expeditiously enough when Poulantzas jumped off a towering edifice (showing enough consideration for humanity by, reportedly, carrying his books with him as he plunged to eternity), quickly to be followed by Althusser strangling his wife to death, all in the fateful academic year 1979. (On a personal note, having been a student in Paris at the time, I still vividly recall these untimely deaths, attended by the almost simultaneous passings of Sartre and Roland Barthes, the latter run down by a car.) This lunatic craze however was almost immediately superseded by the Foucault cult, when every half-baked, ill-educated dimwit imagined him or herself a philosopher after having dabbed in (excerpts from, if even that much) Nietzsche, Heidegger and the Paris master-thinker himself. Shortly thereafter began the Derrida fad with a fresh wagon-load of cliché and jargon unloaded at navel-contemplating conferences, pawned off as radical and cutting edge whereas it possessed all the intellectual and political content of marsh mellow topped with Redi-Whip; and – will the Lord ever forgive them for this sin- unloaded on unsuspecting students. I have on occasion, mostly for light amusement after a hard day's work, picked up some of these texts, and wonder how poor, unsuspecting, innocent, young people have borne such utter rubbish. To inflict it on them is – and here I write as a committed, if atheistic, educator – truly a sin beyond redemption. Fortunately adults such as myself, and not bound by the constraints, whether of political correctness or academic fashion, still preserve the liberty – which I, at any rate, do not intend to abdicate – of calling this what it is. For all I know he might have been the most decent fellow going, but as an influence on academic life Derrida was an abomination – or, more exactly, a too-long running joke. I do not in the least lament his passing, except in the sense of the truism that for those who knew him personally, his loss, like the loss of human life generally, must be a source of sorrow. Beyond that, good riddens. The reactions to my posting on this listserv have fallen into three main categories: 1) studied disgust at my lack of academic couth – which is a useful pretext (if I might appropriate that word) for avoiding discussion of substantive issues; 2) incomprehensible gibberish about my "rhetoric," "representations," intermixed with words I've never heard of like "aporia" and "irenic" – or, to be precise, words I have heard of, but don't think it's worth the trouble of learning their definition, although I love dictionaries – my last great hope is that if reincarnation is yet a transcendental and temporal truth, I come back as a Webster's unabridged; and although reveling in the exquisite delights of learning new words: yet as a point of principle I refuse to invest the energy requisite for such lexicological investigation simply to satisfy the pitifully deformed ego of a pedant; and 3) factual points of difference. Almost none of the postings fit under the last head. I will limit my remarks here to two interrelated point.

I asserted that one evidence that Holocaust studies is a non-field is the sorts of questions it ponders: e.g. the fanatical insistence on proving the "uniqueness" of the Nazi holocaust. It was then asserted in response by one listserv member that this concern is hardly peculiar to Holocaust studies. Let's then, put forth a simple challenge. Consider this illustrative rendering from a leading light of this purported field. Professor Steven T. Katz has published the first of a projected three volume study (Oxford University Press) harnessing over 5,000 titles the purpose of which is to prove that "the Holocaust is phenomenologically unique by virtue of the fact that never before has a state set out, as a matter of intentional principle and actualized policy, to annihilate physically every man, woman and child belonging to a specific people." Clarifying his thesis, Katz explains: ""? is uniquely C. "? may share A, B, D, . . . X with?£ but not C. And again "may share A,B,D, . . . X with all £ but not C . . ."| lacking C is not ". . . . By definition, no exceptions to this rule are allowed.?£ sharing A,B,D, . . . X with "? may be like "? in these and other respects . . . but as regards our definition of uniqueness any or all?£ sharing A,B,D, . . . X with "? may be like "? in these and other respect . . . but as regards our definition of uniqueness any or all?£ lacking C are not "?. . . . Of course, in its totality "? is more than C, but it is never "? without C." To avoid any confusion, Katz further elucidates that he uses the term phenomenological "in a non-Husserlian, non-Shutzean, non-Schelerian, non-Heideggerian, non-Merleau-Pontyian sense." Translation: the Katz enterprise, like Holocaust studies generally, is phenomenal non-sense. Now here's my question: Please cite even a single article in the vast output of scholarship on American slavery that even remotely echoes such insane preoccupations. Or, point to me a single article in the scholarly literature on American slavery making the claim that it "leads into darkness," "negates all answers," "lies outside, if not beyond, history," "defies both knowledge and description," "cannot be explained nor visualized," is "never to be comprehended or transmitted," marks a "destruction of history" and a "mutation on a cosmic scale," is "non-communicable"– "we cannot even talk about it." I am, or course, quoting here the high-priest of Holocaust studies, Elie Wiesel. Does this sound to anyone on the listserv like rational inquiry or is it, as I've suggested, a highly lucrative and politically useful mystery religion?

Matthew Abraham is an assistant professor of Writing, Rhetoric, and Discourse at DePaul University. He was the 2005 Rachel Corrie Courage in the Teaching of Writing award winner. He can be reached at matthew.mabraha2@gmail.com.

Why Finkelstein was rejected

Alan M Dershowitz

May 28, 2008

The Guardian

Your article about Norman Finkelstein's exclusion from Israel (US academic deported and banned for criticising Israel, May 26) claims that Finkelstein was refused tenure at De Paul University for attacking pro-Israel supporters, such as me. This is entirely false. Finkelstein's denial of tenure was based on his lack of scholarship and professionalism. The minority report written by three members of the political science department lays out the basis for his tenure denial.

Finkelstein and his followers have access to this minority report, but they have deliberately suppressed it, releasing instead a rebuttal to the report, while withholding the report itself. I have challenged Finkelstein to release the report, which he is entitled to do, but he has refused.

The result is that newspapers such as yours mischaracterise the reason for his tenure denial, in a way they would not be able to do if they had the minority report available to them.

On the merits of his exclusion from Israel, I categorically disagree with Israel's decision. Finkelstein should be allowed to speak in Israel. His views should be exposed to the marketplace of ideas, where they will be rejected as they have in most other parts of the world.

Alan M Dershowitz

Harvard law school, Cambridge, Massachusetts

This article, "Climbing Jacob's Ladder One Rung at a Time," originally appeared in *Counterpunch* at: http://www.counterpunch.org/2007/09/08/climbing-jacob-s-ladder-one-rung-at-a-time/

APPENDIX B

Pretext Re/Interview

PreText Discussion with Noam Chomsky and Norman Finkelstein

In September and October 2004, MIT Institute Professor Noam Chomsky and DePaul Professor Norman Finkelstein fielded questions through email about Chomsky's *Hegemony or Survival? America's Quest for Global Dominance* and Finkelstein's *Holocaust Industry* and *Beyond Chutzpah: The Misuse of Anti-Semitism and the Abuse of History*, as part of a Pretext Re/Interview. The guest moderator was Matthew Abraham, who was then a faculty member at the University of Tennessee at Knoxville. In the text below, the questions are followed by Professor Chomsky's and Finkelstein's responses.

Question:

You have searched, endlessly without success, for over thirty years for a reference in American academic scholarship to "the U.S. invasion of South Vietnam." The death toll from the Indochina wars was somewhere around 4 million; 5 million might, in fact, be more accurate. The publication of the Pentagon Papers revealed just how badly the government misled the public on Vietnam. Similar internal documents may reveal an equal amount of deception at work in the case of Cuba, Nicaragua, and Iraq. The strength of, what you refer to as, "the doctrinal system" makes the production of the sentence, "The U.S. invaded South Vietnam," highly unlikely, perhaps impossible. Similarly, how many people are familiar with "the Case of Nicaragua," i.e. that the United States was found guilty of "international terrorism" by a World Court and in violation of several security council resolutions, only to dismiss and ridicule the Court's judgment while escalation international terrorism? You heap a great deal of blame, some might even say abuse, upon North American intellectuals for not resisting the temptations (security, pleasures, accolades, etc.) of adhering to state doctrine. "North American intellectuals" covers a lot of people. This group, in conjunction with the Western press, has—in your opinion—vetoed the facts on Vietnam and Nicaragua out of history—dispatching them to Orwell's memory hole. You claim that, after the Cold War, a new menace had to be constructed to dupe the paymasters, American taxpayers, about the real aims of state planners. As the blame could no longer be laid at the Kremlin's door, U.S. planners turned their attention to the threat of the technological sophistication of Third World nationals. Arab nationalism, not the spread of communism, became the real threat. Clearly, 9/11, and seemingly everything that has happened since with the New War on Terror, confirms what you have been writing for some time. Do you really believe North American intellectuals, U.S. ones in particular, could have make a fundamental difference in challenging the aims of state as these are laid out in internal planning documents?

Noam Chomsky:

I do not see how there can be much doubt about this. True, it is not easy. There have been times when crucial sectors of the intellectual community refused to take part in distorting or effacing crucial policy issues. In such cases we find that they are generally disregarded or marginalized, and new "experts" are created to serve the role of advocates of power, or of critics who content themselves with lamentations about the failure of good intentions and similar forms faint damns, effectively cutting off serious critical analysis. Nevertheless, there can be little doubt that the influence could be, and sometimes has been, highly significant.

Question:

The events of 9/11 brought with them the expected expression of sympathy for American suffering from the around the world. However, as you've repeatedly acknowledged, there were starkly different reactions to the events "on both sides of the Irish Sea." While world opinion expressed sympathy for the loss of innocent life, it also registered a recognition of the U.S. government's complicity in supporting low-intensity conflict throughout the world. Central American countries, such as Nicaragua, have end endured their own Armageddon, albeit in slow motion. 9/11 was historic because it represented a radical historical shift: the "guns" were pointed in the opposite direction, i.e., at an imperial power. As you note, that is new, radically new. You write:

> The atrocities of 9/11 serve as a dramatic reminder of what has long been understood: the rich and the powerful no longer are assured the near monopoly of violence that has largely prevailed throughout history; and with modern technology, the prospects are horrendous indeed. Though terrorism is rightly feared everywhere and is indeed an intolerable "return to barbarism," it is not surprising that perceptions about its nature differ rather sharply at opposite ends of the guns, a fact that is ignored at their peril by those whom history has accustomed to immunity while they perpetrate terrible crimes, quite apart from the moral cowardice so starkly revealed (209).

In the wake of 9/11 and with the re-declaration of the War on Terror, this stance has made you remarkable unpopular among left liberals. Why do you believe you have received such a negative response from this group of intellectuals when the stance you take seems relatively commonsensical, trivial perhaps?

Noam Chomsky:

I agree that the stance is relatively trivial, and commonsensical. But to consider it would be uncomfortable for people who have a not inconsiderable share of responsibility for crimes of state. It is always easier to condemn the other fellow's misdeeds than to look into the mirror: to be a hypocrite, as defined in the Gospels. It's a common human failing, and power and privilege provide defenses against what honesty would require. Examples are all too easy to find. The record of international tribunals, to select only one important and revealing case.

Question:

I would like to know how you suggest academics be motivated to at least investigate their culpability in supporting abusive US practices, if not come to ethical terms with that culpability. Academics are, generally, as jingoistic and parochial as their less educated countrymen in their willingness to discuss the ethics/morality of war, issues of sovereignty, and human rights, not that level of education determines much of anything in ethical and moral practices. It seems to me that throughout the book and underpinning your answers is the assumption that, somehow, academics as well as most contemporary Americans, have abdicated their ethical responsibilities as citizens. Would you care to elaborate on this?

Noam Chomsky:

The only way I can think of to "elaborate on . . . the assumption that, somehow, academics as well as most contemporary Americans, have abdicated their ethical responsibilities as citizens" is to provide illustrations. That is what I have tried to do in writing about these topics for the past 40 years. How successfully is for you to decide. Without such evidence, the assumption should simply be disregarded. I also know of no way to motivate people to investigate the question of their possible culpability other than by bringing forth illustrations, whether we have in mind academics, children, or anyone else.

Question:

Several years ago, you sat down with Gary Olson and Lester Faigley for an interview for the *Journal of Advanced Composition*. Upon being asked if you had a theory of rhetoric, you answered with the following:

I don't have any theory of rhetoric, but what I do have in the back of my mind is that one should not try to persuade; rather, you should try to lay out the territory as best you can so that other people can use their own intellectual powers to work out for themselves what they think is right or wrong. For example, I try particularly in political writing, to make it extremely clear in advance exactly where I stand. In my view, the idea of neutral objectivity is largely fraudulent. It's not that I take the realistic view with regard to fact, but the fact is that everyone approaches complex and controversial questions—especially those of human significance—with an ax to grind, and I like that axe to be apparent right up front so that people can compensate for it. But to the extent that I can monitor my own rhetorical activities, which I probably not a lot, I try to refrain my efforts to bring people to reach my conclusions (6-7).

In *Hegemony or Survival? America's Quest for Global Dominance*, the word "rhetoric" is used at least eight times to describe the language of concealment of today's imperial planners:

p. 24: "exalted rhetoric"
p. 45: "rhetoric"
p. 46: "rhetoric:
p. 47: "rhetoric in internal documents"
p. 63: "rhetoric of contemporary planners"
p. 109: "rhetoric"
p. 129: "lofty rhetoric:
p. 136: "democratization rhetoric"

Throughout the book your tone is urgent, but also hopeful as you clearly see the "great beast" of public opinion emerging as challenges to power by modern state planners. The word "cynical" has been used repeatedly to describe the tone of your later political writings. Some say the gentle, caring tone of the 60s is gone and you are much more strident in your delivery. How has your "rhetoric" changed over the last forty years?

Through a number of books—*American Power and the New Mandarins, For Reasons of State, Turning the Tide, Toward a New Cold War, The Culture of Terrorism, The Fateful Triangle: The United States Israel, and the Palestinians, The Washington Connection and Third World Fascism, After the Cataclysm: Postwar Indochina and the Reconstruction of Imperial Ideology*, and *Manufacturing Consent: The Political Economy of the Mass Media*—you have documented, quite carefully, the level of complicity and deceit Western intellectuals have attained in disguising the historical record, while making grave atrocities more palatable. This critique of the Western intelligentsia continues in *Hegemony and Survival: America's Quest for Global Dominance*. In the context of discussing the level of devastation leveled against Iraq by the U.S. and the fact that the "war" didn't lead "uprooted Iraqis to see war as a path to lost homes," you write:

> There has been no inquiry into whether Kurds and Colombians, uprooted with extreme violence, apparently in even greater numbers, might also see war as a path to lost homes. The proposal would, in fact, be outlandish. Washington could alleviate the misery and perhaps clear the way to a more substantial solution to deeply rooted problems by simply withdrawing its support for atrocities. But that would require at the very least a willingness on the part of the educated classes to look into the mirror instead of restricting themselves to lamentations on the crimes of official enemies, about which there is often little that can be done (53).

Part of the problem, of course, is that the mirror is never really held up to the faces of those who constitute the intellectual class. Although you tried to bring some attention to it through a meeting with newspaper editors in October 2000, the unprecedented $500 million Blackhawk helicopter and Apache spare-parts sale to Israel in late 2000 and, then again, in early 2001 didn't merit mention in a single, major U.S. periodical. Is this the sort of thing you're talking about? Why the media blackout? Discussed on p. 181 of *Hegemony or Survival*? More extensive coverage in your introduction to Roane Carey's *The New Intifada: Resisting Israel's Apartheid*.

Noam Chomsky: It is true that the term "rhetoric" ("rhetorical") has a rather negative connotation for me, as illustrated by the uses that you cite in *H&S*, also in comments to Olson-Faigley about persuasion.

On "speaking truth to power," I assume that the powerful either already know what we are trying to tell them, or else, as you say, are too indoctrinated to care. But I have, and have expressed (e.g., in a talk to writers conference reprinted in Powers and Prospects), what seem to me more serious reservations. I don't think we should claim to be able to be able to speak the truth. We do our best, but even in physics one can't make that claim.

As long as there is a category of "decision-makers," it makes very good sense for people to try to make their voices heard—to "persuade" them, if one wants to use the term, but not necessarily (and in fact rarely) by argument: rather, by changing their calculus of costs. That involves many means. I don't have anything particular to say about "intellectuals," as distinct from others. People do vary a lot in privilege (including access to resources, options for running their own lives, etc.). Their responsibilities vary with their opportunities. Thus those with greater privilege have correspondingly greater responsibilities, including the responsibility to participate in efforts to influence decision-makers (or to eliminate them in favor or more democratic structures). That can take the form of talks, discussions, writing, solidarity and support activity, demonstrations, resistance . . . it is quite a range. Some of these activities are called "intellectual" and those who take part in them are sometimes called "intellectuals"—though we should bear in mind that throughout history, with the rarest of exceptions, those regarded as "intellectuals" are servants of power, often in the most sordid ways.

These considerations hold for just about every case that should concern us, such as the one you describe, which was quite remarkable. To repeat the basic facts, when the Intifada began (rarely going beyond stone-throwing), Israel responded with extreme violence. The Israeli military command was shocked later when the full reports came in. One high military officer commented with disgust that the army had fired "a bullet for each child." The casualty figures showed it: 20–1 in the first month, all within the occupied territories. And as you say, Israel at once used US military helicopters (Israel doesn't produce helicopters) to attack civilian targets, killing and wounding dozens of people. That was reported. Not reported, however, was that right in the midst of these reports of US-Israeli atrocities in the first days of the Intifada, Clinton made the biggest deal in a decade to send new military helicopters to Israel, also spare parts for recently sent helicopters, with no constraints on their use, as the Pentagon informed journalists. The press was silent, despite efforts to induce editors to publish the facts. Even a protest by Amnesty International was not reported. The reaction, unfortunately, is not unusual. Nor is the unanimity in suppressing obviously crucial facts, without central authority or presumably interaction. Evidently it is just understood that it is improper to allow the public to know of our ongoing crimes, in which they are participating, without their knowledge. What does this case tell us about "speaking truth to power"? "Power" in this case is decision-makers in the media; no one bothered to inform the White House of what they knew perfectly well.

What we learn from the case, along with innumerable others like it, many at the same time, is the usual lesson. Those who are privileged enough to be able to find out the facts for themselves should make every effort they can to bring them to the general public. In this case the efforts have mostly failed. Almost no one knows, except those who attend talks, read the independent ("alternative") press, take part in activist movements, etc. That's normal. There are examples of vastly greater scale and horror, right now. The lesson is to try harder.

Question: "As long as there is a category of "decision-makers," it makes very good sense for people to try to make their voices heard—to "persuade" them, if one wants to use the term, but not necessarily (and in fact rarely) by argument: rather, by changing the calculus of costs." I don't see in what follows an elaboration of what such a rhetorical move (from "argument" to "calculus of costs") might look like, unless you are saying, in what follows, that somehow when people (e.g., "tax-payers") become aware of what their money is being used for, they will rise up against those in power who are presumably using their tax-dollars in an inappropriate ("unethical"?) way. Perhaps you could address specifically what "changing the calculus of costs" means, for I think it may be a much more important culture-specific rhetorical tool for a Western, liberal, capitalist audience, than say, "argument".

Noam Chomsky:

My comment about changing the calculus of costs, to which you refer, was followed by this passage:

"That involves many means. I don't have anything particular to say about "intellectuals," as distinct from others. People do vary a lot in privilege (including access to resources, options for running their own lives, etc.). Their responsibilities vary with their opportunities. Thus those with greater privilege have correspondingly greater responsibilities, including the responsibility to participate in efforts to influence decision-makers (or to eliminate them in favor of more democratic structures). That can take the form of talks, discussions, writing, solidarity and support activity, demonstrations, resistance, ...—it is quite a range."

Those means are available to us, over a wide range, and fortunately for the country and the world, the means are available to us, over a wide range, and fortunately for the country and the world, the means have often been used. That's how rights have been won and protected over the centuries, until the present.

Maybe I'm missing the point, but that seems to me the answer to the question you raise.

There are innumerable examples, not just in winning rights (of minorities, women, freedom of speech, . . .) but also in recognizing the rights of others. Take, say, the Indochina wars. For years, the US hammered South Vietnam brutally without protest. Finally, after many years, protest and resistance developed, and they did change the calculus of costs of decision-makers. That's why something still survives the wreckage of Indochina. When the Reaganites tried to duplicate the Kennedy-Johnson-Nixon policies in Central America, they had to back down and resort to "clandestine" terror—"clandestine" in that everyone knew all about it except American citizens. That was bad enough but nothing like saturation bombing, chemical warfare, and the other massive crimes of Indochina. By 1989, the Bush I administration recognized (in leaked documents) that wars against "much weaker enemies" would have to be won "decisively and rapidly," or political support would erode, because it was by then think, unlike the happy days of the 1960s. The US attack in Fallujah killed hundreds or maybe thousands of people, but the military had to back off. Had this taken place in South

Vietnam, the problem would have been quickly resolved with B-52s and mass murder operations. This country had become more civilized, thanks to the use of the many means to change the calculus of costs. There are innumerable examples of the use of these means, to which we owe just about everything that is decent.

Question: At a couple of points within *Hegemony or Survival?* (specifically in the Afterword, p. 11), you mention the propaganda problem Emmanuel Constant from Haiti, now living safely in Queens, NY, presents to the Washington commissars. Who is Constant and why will he never be extradited back to Haiti where he should be standing trial for major crimes? What does this case tell us about the rule of force in international affairs?

Noam Chomsky:

It is an interesting case. Constant was the leader of the Haitian paramilitary force FRAPH that was responsible for murdering thousands of poor Haitians under the military dictatorship that overthrew the democratically elected government in 1990. He was also on the CIA payroll.

The vicious military junta and its wealthy supporters were supported by George Bush I, and even more so by Bill Clinton. Both of them not only openly violated the embargo imposed by the Organization of American states, but even secretly authorized shipments of oil—the core element of an embargo—to the junta in violation of presidential directives. The facts were leaked and were the lead story on the AP wires, repeated over and over, the day before the Marines were scheduled to land in Haiti, when every news desk in the country had eyes glued to the wire service (just as I did). It was impossible to miss. I wrote an article about all of this the next day, but it was for *Z Magazine*, and wouldn't be out for six weeks, so I wrote about it in past tense, taking for granted it would be reported. My naiveté. Actually it was reported in oil industry journals and there was a brief report in the *Wall St. Journal*, and in a very small newspaper around the country, but discipline held: few know about this, because it would have been inconsistent with the image of the noble humanitarian intervention to protect human rights and restore democracy, the official story until today—acceptable if one excludes all relevant facts, including these.

Constant fled to the US. He was tried in absentia in Haiti and convicted. Haiti has repeatedly requested that the US extradite him to face trial there, but with one or another bureaucratic excuse, it hasn't happened, and he is living in Queens. He is one of many world class international terrorists who are welcomed on US soil, if their crimes were carried out with the open or tacit approval and cooperation of the US. The most famous, perhaps, is Orlando Bosch, one of the leading international terrorists, accused by the FBI of dozens of serious terrorists atrocities, some committed on US soil.

The Justice Department sought to deport him as a threat to US national security, but Bush I intervened and granted him a presidential pardon. He's living happily in Florida, presumably taking part in further terrorist crimes (against Cuba). His main associate, Luis Carilles Posada, was tried and jailed in Venezuela, but somehow "escaped" and made his way to El Salvador, where he was able to take part in Reagan's terrorist war against Nicaragua. He was just recently sentenced for a serious terrorist crime, but immediately granted a presidential pardon, and is thought now to be in Honduras. The energetic researcher can learn these matters. They are not entirely suppressed. That would be front-page news, repeatedly, with full commentary and explanation, in a country that valued its freedom.

There are other cases. We may recall that a leading principle of the Bush II doctrine is, in the president's words, that "those who harbor terrorists are as guilty as the terrorists themselves" must be treated accordingly. The prominent strategic analyst Graham Allison of Harvard describes this as the most important element of the Bush Doctrine, which has "already become a *de facto* rule of international relations." Commentators are kind enough to point out that Bush was calling for bombing the US.

None of this poses a propaganda problem, however, because it is all kept under cover, with very rare and limited exceptions, and the significance is virtually never discussed. As for what it tells us about the educated classes, and about the rule of force in international affairs, I think it should hardly be necessary to comment.

Interlocutor: Due to family and personal history, I feel a strong emotional attachment to the State of Israel and also strong feelings about the past, present, and future state of Israel, and its terrible situation, the atrocities that have been committed against its citizens, and also the atrocities its military has committed. How could one adequately express the grief at watching one's family walk the sad trail from victim to victimizer and back again?

Noam Chomsky: I share the emotional attachment, since childhood. But having lived intimately with all of this all my life, and followed the events closely, I wouldn't describe what has happened as you do. I think that does not accurately convey the balance of terror and crimes. But that's a separate matter. In answer to your question, it is very hard to watch "one's family walk the sad trail from victim to victimizer," particularly when there is no "back again," but rather going on to carry out still worse crimes.

And let us be clear about the use of the word "victims." Jews have certainly been victims, in fact victims of some of the worst crimes in human history. But in their interaction with Palestinians for the past century, it is overwhelmingly the Palestinians who have been the victims.

Interlocutor: Having said that, it will not surprise you that I take exception with the idea that anything regarding Israel would be an uncontroversial matter of fact.

Noam Chomsky: Is this just with regard to Israel, or is it true generally? For example, is it an uncontroversial matter of fact that suicide bombers have carried out murderous attacks in Israel? If you think it is uncontroversial, then it is your responsibility to explain the distinction. If you think it is controversial (I don't), then you might want to explain why. Either way, I think you have the burden of explanation to meet.

Of course, there is a sense in which no empirical matter is strictly uncontroversial. But plainly that is not relevant here.

Interlocutor:

For me, this is misleading in terms of understanding the Middle East conflict and also misleading in terms of epistemology and rhetoric.

Noam Chomsky:

Same question. Does this also hold for suicide bombings targeting Israelis? If not, it is your responsibility to justify the distinction you are making.

Interlocutor:

The next reinterview will focus more on the Middle East. I hope you will be sticking around for that. For now, because of your disciplinary background, I am interested in learn more about why "rhetoric" is negative for you.

Noam Chomsky:

I think that was explained in the reference that were given. What was left out?

Interlocutor:

You have not been one to passively accept the most common view or the political and economic reality, so it puzzles me that you would take the most common view of "rhetoric."

Noam Chomsky:

I don't know if the most common view of "rhetoric" has the negative connotations I feel. But if it does, I don't see the relevance. Are you puzzled that I take the common view of terrorist atrocities against Jews? Or about the sun rising in the morning? Why shouldn't one take the common view when it is correct?

Interlocutor:

I will continue with the Israeli example. Few "knowledgeable people," in my view, deny that the Israeli's military has used unproportional and counterproductive violence;

Noam Chomsky: The phrase "unproportional and counterproductive violence" is, in my opinion, a rhetorical device that should be seriously questioned. Would you say that about Palestinians (who have carried out far less violence than Israelis)? Or Al-Qaeda, or the Russians in Afghanistan? In what sense was the Israeli invasion of Lebanon, for example "unproportional and counterproductive violence"?

however, it does not follow that when isolated facts are controversial, "there is no serious issue about truth."

Noam Chomsky: It certainly does not follow. That would be an error in logic. And you are certainly right that 'when isolated facts are controversial, "there is no serious issue about truth".' But I see no relation between that statement and anything that was discussed.

Logic aside, is there a serious issue about truth in the specific case to which the statement referred? Is there some controversy about the facts? If so, what?

Interlocutor:

Even with a fact as a mutual starting place or "common ground," unless one is a pre-modern representational artist or fancies one's self as some sort of neutral court reporter on the world stage, issues of truth never disappear. What should be taken as the significance of the fact is a question of truth. What should be policy is a question of truth. In what way the historical context should be taken into account when considering the fact is a question of truth.

Noam Chomsky:

I do not see any relation between these comments, whatever their merit, and what was discussed.

Interlocutor:

I do not pretend to be educating you or anyone else on this list. You yourself have just said, "I don't think we should claim to be able to 'speak the truth.'" What I don't understand is: Given this stated epistemological humility, what negative connotation of "rhetoric" do you endorse? We all know the negative connotations of its everyday usage, but what negative meanings of it do you endorse?

Noam Chomsky: I don't "endorse" any connotation of the term "rhetoric." Rather, the term has negative connotations for me. The reasons were indicated in the examples cited in the questions to which I responded. I'm not sure what new question you are asking.

Interlocutor: Thank you for your work and for making yourself available in this forum.

Noam Chomsky: A pleasure.

Question: In an expanded e-book version of *Hegemony or Survival* (p. 1002, footnote 509), you do mention the Samson option, a reference to Israel's nuclear arsenal and its implications for the stability of the Middle East region.

Seymour Hersh has written a pretty extensive book on this topic for which he received considerable criticism. For the benefit of the lists' subscribers, could you please provide some background about the Samson option and why intellectuals, or anyone concerned with issues of hegemony or survival, should be concerned about it? You cite Werner Farr of the U.S. Army in footnote 509. You write: "Like other analysts he assumes that one purpose of Israeli nuclear weapons, not often stated, but obvious, is that their 'use' on the United States," presumably to ensure consistent U.S. support for Israeli policies. The concept "we will go crazy ("nishtagea") if challenged goes back to the Labor government of the 1950s. In your exhaustive *The Fateful Triangle: The United States, Israel, and the Palestinians*, you cover some of this material in Chapter 7 (4.2.2). Some might say that this theory is over the top and inherently anti-Semitic—or at least anti-Israel—and feeds worldwide anti-Semitism. How do you respond to these concerns/criticisms?

Noam Chomsky: The phrase "Samson option" refers to the biblical account of Samson's greatest achievement, pulling down the Temple walls in a suicide operation, and killing more Philistines than in his entire lifetime. Exercising the "Samson option" means risking total destruction by undertaking huge mass slaughter to prevent some undesired outcome. As discussed in *Fateful Triangle*, the source is high Israeli officials in the 1950s. After nuclear weapons were developed, it becomes more extreme, of course. The matter is commonly discussed in Israeli commentary. I don't recall Hersh's account in detail, but I am sure he cites many examples.

Israeli doves often condemn this stance—in fact, so did Prime Minister Sharett, in his diaries, one of the original sources in the 1950s, cited in *FT*, which also cites Aryeh (Lova) Eliav, one of Israel's best-known and intellectual doves, who writes that the attitude of "those who brought the 'Samson complex' here, according to which we shall kill and bury Gentiles around us while we ourselves shall die with them," is a form of "insanity."

As for the criticisms you mention, plainly they are misdirected. They should be directed to high Israeli officials and prominent Israeli commentators. And once that is recognized, the absurdity of the criticisms should be evident.

Question: So, in your estimation, is Warner correct when he states that it's well known in U.S. and Israeli intelligence circles that these nuclear weapons can be used against the U.S. to ensure support (military, diplomatic, economic) for harsh and repressive policies in the occupied territories and beyond? Or is it that these weapons could be unleashed in the Middle East itself, causing such chaos that the U.S. must inevitably comply with extremely dangerous policies or put the petroleum reserves ("the world's greatest material asset") themselves in jeopardy? You might understand why some might find this "theory" and the described scenarios extremely unlikely, bizarre perhaps— part of the lunatic fringe, likely to be banished to the dissident literature. Is this Samson option a likely scenario?

Noam Chomsky:

I have no way to judge whether Warner is correct about US and Israeli intelligence circles. It sounds plausible, and he is not alone from within these circles in similar suggestions. It has also been suggested that Israel's missile programs very visibly targeting southern Russia were intended as a warning to the US: push us too far and we'll bomb Russia, bringing down the Temple wall on you too. Without access to classified documents, it is impossible to verify such suggestions, though one might ask what other purpose there might be.

That Israel might attack the oil fields in reaction to US pressure has been discussed in the Israeli press, for example, at the time of the Saudi peace plan in 1981. The matter is discussed in my *The Fateful Triangle* (chap. 3, chap. 7,), citing the journal of the Israeli Labor Party, *Davar*, which "found Israel's reaction—including military flights over Saudi Arabia—to be so 'irrational' as to cause foreign intelligence services to be concerned over Israel bombing of Saudi oil fields." It was interpreted as a warning to the US not to support this peace initiative; unnecessary, as it turned out. There's some discussion of this in my *Middle East Illusions* (chap. 9) and *Hegemony or Survival* (chap. 7).

How seriously to take high-level Israeli commentators and press, US intelligence analysts, and others, we have to judge for ourselves. It would, however, be a strange judgment to consign them to the "lunatic fringe."

Question:

Does this kind of bargaining ploy work best when it is unclear—if the other participants aren't sure just how far the threatener will go? In discursive situations in which one person is playing the canny but irrational person who must be placated at all costs, it's important that the other people not know if s/he means it or doesn't, whether s/he has any limits at all, or exactly what would constitute "provocation." A set of documents which actually laid out the policy/plan, like a set of rules that someone agreed to, would reduce the uncertainty, and bring it back into the realm of the rational.

I'm not saying that's what Israel is doing (although this strategy was, explicitly, the "rationale" behind mutually assured destruction in US foreign policy, and I'm running across it in regard to proslavery writings all over the place), but I am saying that I don't know how one could know. If this were a very pubic strategy (as it was with proslavery), then you'd have a lot of bellicose posturing, but if its strategy within intelligence circles, how could one know?

Noam Chomksy:

In this case, the strategy was not confined to intelligence circles. As usual, there is a public record too, some of which I have cited in print maybe in this discussion too. But a good deal is, of course, surmise, as in all such cases.

Question:

As I understand it, neither the Israeli government nor the United States has confirmed or denied the existence of nuclear weapons at Dimona or elsewhere in Israel. After Mordechai Vanunu was kidnapped by Israel for "spilling the beans" about the nuclear weapons programs in Israel, he was tired and jailed for nearly twenty years. Vanunu actually worked at the Dimona facility (http://www.globalsecurity.org/wmd/world/israel/dimona.htm). Heavily influenced by existential philosophy, Sartre in particular, Vanunu—in an apparent act of humanitarian intervention and self-purification—told the world press about the existence of nuclear weapons at Dimona. It's a pretty remarkable story. Noam will be able to provide the exact details around the Vanunu case. But I think ____ is getting at something important when she asks, "Doesn't this kind of bargaining ploy work best if it's unclear—if the other participants aren't sure just how far the threatener will go?"

Noam Chomsky:

Vanunu released information on the Dimona nuclear weapons facility to the *London Sunday Times*. I don't think the information was much of a surprise to those who have been following these matters, and I doubt that foreign intelligence services learned anything of significance. He was kidnapped in Europe, brought to Israel and subjected to a show trial that was a complete farce, and then placed in solitary confinement for (I think) 12 years, under conditions that meet any reasonable definition of torture. Most of this is unknown because of US support for Israeli actions.

Vanunu was finally allowed some contact with the outside world, and has just been released—technically; he is still kept under strict controls, under the pretext, which few believe, that he might reveal some secrets.

I don't think his testimony changed the terms of the "bargaining ploy"— if that's what it was—in any substantial way. I doubt that US or foreign intelligence services disagree with the judgment of the former head of the US Strategic Command, General Lee Butler, that Israel's possession of nuclear weapons is "dangerous in the extreme," in part because of the obvious impact on further proliferation in reaction.

However, as I wrote already, I am not trying to second-guess Israeli planners.

Question:

In the early 1970s the Trilateral Commission published a study entitled "The Crisis of Democracy" with essays by Samuel Huntington, Jo Jo Watanuki, and Michael Crozier. The study, written at the height of student protests over the Vietnam War, reached some startling conclusions—Western industrial powers, such as the United States, England, and Japan had a problem on their hands: common people were actually believing that democracy ("rule by the people") was a realizable goal and began to expect the dominant institutions to practice it. "The Crisis of Democracy" could be handled through a sort of self-selection process, whereby educational and other mainstream institutions would remove troublemakers who sought to give the restless masses too much inspiration. The "study" recommended that value-oriented intellectuals, those who are naïve enough to believe in truth, honor, integrity, etc., be removed from the institutions of higher learning, and that those dedicated to preserving the privileges of an articulate elite be cultivated and promoted (the technical specialists, i.e., the intelligentsia). There's little doubt that this intelligentsia has a great deal of control over intellectual and cultural life in the United States. In many ways, it's this type of intellectual you're attempting to "out" in *H&S* through your documentation of the intellectual failures of "the change of course doctrine" and "humanitarian intervention." In many ways, the historical record has been written by this group of specialists in conjunction with the manipulation of the public relations industry. Without the efforts of figures such as Joyce and Gabriel Kolko, William Appleman Williams, Howard Zinn, Gore Vidal, Robert Fisk, Irene Gendzier, Edward Said, and Eqbal Ahmed the history of American empire could conceivably remain unknown. In your *The Culture of Terrorism*, a book that has a number of resonances with *H&S*, you write:

> The general subservience of the media to the state propaganda system does not result from direct government order, threats of coercion, centralized decisions, and other devices central to totalitarian states, but

from a complex interplay of more subtle factors. A similar complex of inducements—access to privilege and prestige, class interest, penalties for straying beyond acceptable limits, and the like—produces a systematic bias in the scholarship that is concerned with foreign policy and its formulation, servicing to protect the basic system of social, economic, and political decision-making from scrutiny. It is by no means necessary to yield to these pressures, certainly in a society that lacks the forms of coercion and punishment found elsewhere. But the temptation to do so is considerable, and those who choose a different path often find their opportunities to do their work or reach more than a marginal audience are limited or excluded (11).

The doctrinal system presents many such challenges, but there are always a few individuals who manage to find their way around them. If a stable framework emerges to bring these isolated individuals together, it's a tremendous threat to concentrated power. Within the contexts I've outlined here, are you able to identify the types of intellectual communities that could come together at this historical moment in the United States to demand and enact desperately needed change in the harsh and repressive U.S.-supported policies currently fueling much of the unrest in the Middle East? Much sound and fury has been made about the various "divest from Israel" campaigns on many college campuses, with anti-divestment petitions garnering as much as the divestment ones. Alan M. Dershowitz, Felix Frankfurter Professor of Law at Harvard, claims that academics who push for such divestment are engaging in a nasty sort of "educational malpractice." Issues such as this one are incredibly complex and require careful thinking by value-oriented intellectuals. However, in light of the cultural and intellectual terrain I've described, what chance does the value-oriented intellectual have in enacting any sort of social change animated by a commitment to justice (a word rhetoricians have to regard with suspicion) in light of Lyotard's différend. It seems as if she has very little chance.

Noam Chomsky:

I read the Trilateral study as soon as it appeared, and began to lecture and write about it right away. It was quite revealing, I thought, particularly because of its origins: the more liberal internationalist end of the ideological spectrum in the industrial democracies; the Carter administration, for example, was drawn almost entirely from the ranks of the Commission. The study expressed concern over the "excess of democracy" in the 1960s as normally passive and apathetic sectors of the population—in fact, most of the population—began to try to enter the political arena to press for their interests and concerns. Implicit, but unstated, is that they are beginning to crowd out the sector that acts in the public arena by right: the concentration of private power. The study called for more "moderation in democracy," in effect, return to greater passivity and obedience. It distinguished the "value-oriented intellectuals" from the "technocratic and policy-oriented intellectuals"; in the case of the Soviet enemy we distinguish the "dissidents" from the "commissars/apparatchiks," praising the former and condemning the latter, but at home values are commonly reversed, in this case too. The study also warned that the institutions responsible for "the indoctrination of the young"—schools, universities, churches, etc.—are being delegitimated by the "value-oriented intellectuals," threatening what the Trilateral commentators regard as "democracy." It was even concerned that the media were getting out of hand, and might have to be subjected to some sort of controls.

The study brought to mind the triumphalist conceptions of "end of ideology" in the 1950s, shattered by the unanticipated activism of the years that followed; and many earlier similar episodes in a familiar cycle.

My personal judgment, for what it's worth, is that the most constructive reaction to such regular efforts to impose obedience and to marginalize critical thought is not to create communities of intellectuals, though there is nothing wrong with that and it can be useful. More significant, I think, is that for those who are privileged enough to be considered "intellectuals" to engage in popular struggles and activism, to which they can make a substantial contribution. I don't think the terrain is any more difficult that it has been in the past; quite the contrary in fact. Though there are cycles of progress and regression over the centuries, the trajectory seems to me generally upward, and I think struggles for more justice and freedom can be carried out from a higher plane that was commonly the case in earlier periods.

Interlocutor:

While I think the charge of anti-Semitism can be used too readily to shut down discussion, I do think there is a factor of "simplification" at work in this discourse. Simplification is a rhetorical strategy for putting an end to reflection and spurring action. The point is to polarize and moralize an immensely complicated situation so that a desired course of action will seem like an obvious necessity. In this case, the goal of action is to drive a wedge between the U.S. and Israel. While throwing around claims of "anti-Semitism" can also be a strategy of simplification, employed with the opposite motive, many who want to end the U.S.-Israel alliance in order to decrease terrorism against the U.S., such as Pat Buchanan, do not mind putting anti-Semitic feeling (and money) to work.

In this discourse of simplification, substantiated and unsubstantiated facts are piled together in such a way that it produces the image of the hysterical Jew. The development of nuclear weapons, wherever it occurs, brings the fear of a general disaster. But the attraction to the discourse about "Samson" for simplification is that it displaces this apocalyptic feature of all nuclear arsenals onto the image of the Jew. This displacement, we are told, has no element of anti-Semitism, because Jews have themselves discussed this disturbing part of Israeli history. So we have one claim: Jews are victimizers. While of course Chomsky will not go along with Islamic extremists who go ahead and claim that ALL Jews are victimizers and deserving of death, Chomsky's response to my earlier post indicated some discomfort with my view that Israelis are simultaneously victims and victimizers in the same sense that U.S. citizens are. To make the "Samson" issue work for simplification, the statements of Israeli doves count as evidence, but this simplification simultaneously puts the Israeli doves into the general category of hysterical victimizers.

Breaking the U.S.-Israeli alliance might end the State of Israel and change the nature of the disaster but would not likely end the disaster. The suppression of the Palestinians would once again fall to the Syrians and the Jordanians who, we must remember, were rather slow in admitting the existence of Palestinians as a discrete population. The Palestinian cause functions for Islamic states as a means to redirect anger caused by the lack of democracy and free speech in those states. While the popular sympathy for Palestinians is real, it would be foolish to think the surrounding governments are truly interested in Palestinian autonomy for its own sake.

Obviously, none of this justifies the actions of the Israeli military. Simplification and polarization, whether employed by the Right or the Left, should be shunned as counter-democratic tendencies. See Žižek's *Welcome to the Desert of the Real*, where he advocates simplification as part of his shift away from democratic commitment. If forced, I would choose Liberal analysis-paralysis over Rightist or Leftist brinkmanship.

Noam Chomsky:

I'm afraid I do not follow. Whose goal is to "polarize," "moralize," "drive a wedge between the U.S. and Israel"? The high-level Israeli officials who discussed these plans in the 1960s? The respected Israeli intellectuals who commented on these policies and condemned the "Samson complex" as "insanity"? What is the implication of the innuendo?

I also do not understand why you think that citing these sources "simultaneously puts the Israeli doves into the general category of hysterical Jewish victimizers." I am also unaware of the "discomfort" you sensed in my response. I recall no discomfort.

You write that "Chomsky will not go along with Islamic extremists who go ahead and claim that ALL Jews are victimizers and deserving death." Should I return the compliment by writing that "_____ will not go along with (Jewish) extremists who go ahead and claim that ALL (Arabs) are victimizers and deserving death"?

I'm afraid I do not see the relevance of the further comments. And, frankly, do not see how to conduct serious discussion in these terms.

Question:

Although the letter below (on the next page) appears in Chapter 4 of your *Pirates and Emperors, Old and New*), I think it has some relevance for discussions about H&S and some of the questions that have arisen in the last week about intellectual intervention and affairs of state. Elliot Abrams, now head of Middle East Affairs for the National Security Council, wrote this letter in 1986 (when he was head of Central American Affairs at the State Department to the editor of *The Index on Censorship*, a journal devoted to exposing censorship throughout the world. Abrams was indicted for lying to Congress in 1986, but was pardoned by Bush I. What's remarkable about the letter is that it was written on State Department letterhead, suggesting that the *Index on Censorship* had not done an effective enough job in censoring your views on the Middle East and that Abrams was, in fact, speaking as a U.S. government official. Abrams wrote his letter in response to your "American Thought Control: The Case of the Middle East," an article that questioned the very vocabulary framing discussions of the Israel-Palestine conflict. In this article, you discussed in detail how the phrase "peace process"—through a form of Newspeak—has been completely evacuated of meaning. Within the Newspeak lexicon, the whole world waits for the Palestinians to climb aboard the peace process. It's not necessary, of course, to ask whether the U.S. or Israel are aboard because the peace will be fashioned on their terms. You suggest that there is a doctrinally enforced unwillingness among the American intelligentsia to critically probe some of the propositions that govern the U.S.-Israel occupation of the Palestinians. This Newspeak: 1) leaves out mention of the rights of the indigenous Palestinian population (can't be mentioned); 2) can't articulate, much less fathom, that the U.S. and Israel have been actually blocking a comprehensive diplomatic settlement in the region for over thirty years (bombing of Lebanon occurred in 1982 because of the prospect of peace); 3) won't recognize the racist assumptions that govern the "rejectionist" stance, (Palestinians are portrayed as rejecting the territorial rights of Israel, but the converse can't be articulated) which if stated openly, would not be tolerated by the American general public, e.g., that Arabs are somehow civilizationally deficient; and 4) assures that the "security threats" will be those that Israel faces; no one ever asks whether or not Israel and the U.S. pose a security threat to the Palestinians. As a thought experiment, notice how when a "six-week cessation in violence" or a "new outbreak of violence" is reported by the U.S. press, it's when Palestinians commit violence. However, when Palestinians are murdered it's not considered murder or violence. All in all, your article highlighted the degree of discipline and level of commitment that can be maintained within a well-functioning propaganda system. Why do you cherish Abram's letter so much and what does it mean that your article caught the attention of a state department official? For a state department official to write to an English journal, devoted to examining censorship, is perhaps comparable to a Soviet commissar writing to *In These Times* here in the U.S. because it published the views of a Soviet dissident. What does the controversy that ensued, when the article was published, tell us about the intellectual communities within which we all travel?

Mr. Dan Jacobson
36 Cranbourne Gardens
London NW OHP
England
Dear Dan:

Forgive me for writing to you again in your capacity as a Director and Member of the Editorial Board of *Index on Censorship*, but I can't resist. In the latest issue which I have, July/August 1986, there appears a truly astonishing article, beginning on p. 2 and continuing at great length. This article is an attack on the United States, the United States government, and the United States press by Noam Chomsky.

You probably know about Chomsky: he is a fanatical defender of the PLO who has set new standards for intellectual dishonesty and personal vindictiveness in his writings about the Middle East. There really isn't anyone left in the U.S.—with regard to politics—who takes Chomsky seriously in view of his astonishing record. I therefore find it inexplicable that he is given fully three pages to go on with his attack on one of the freest presses in the world. Clearly giving him this much space lends a certain respectability to his disreputable efforts. Can it be that your editors simply do not know who Chomsky is and are unfamiliar with his record? Can it be, fully familiar with this, they nevertheless decided to give him this platform?

Sincerely,

Elliot Abrams

Noam Chomksy:

The story is in fact more interesting and complex. Some of it is mentioned in Chapter 4, and considerably more in the article by Alexander Cockburn cited in the footnote, based on material leaked to journalists in England. There's more, in fact, not uninteresting. Perhaps it will be told one day.

On the significance of the letter itself, my own view is expressed in the chapter: "What the letter reveals is the deep totalitarian streak in the mentality of leading figures in the Reagan administration: not even the tiniest opening must be allowed to unacceptable thought." And as I go on to say, they are not alone, though they were an extreme end of the spectrum, and their current inheritors are clustered even more at that extreme. We can add more about the significance today: Abrams was appointed by Bush II to the top position on Middle East policy in the National Security Council.

Turning to your question—"What does the controversy that ensued, when the article was published tells us about the intellectual communities within which we travel"—I think it might be rephrased: "What does the lack of controversy that ensued tell us about the intellectual communities within which we travel." In England, the tremendous and unprecedented attack on the journal and its editor for daring to step out of line did elicit some controversy, mostly denials from those implicated. In the US, I don't recall anything beyond the Cockburn article. I don't recall anything in print about the Abrams letter. Perhaps—probably—I've forgotten some reactions, but I'm pretty sure they were slight at most. That presumably means that the events are considered quite normal and appropriate within the dominant intellectual culture.

Turning to your analogy, the reaction would no doubt have been dramatically different, which tells us something, perhaps.

Noam Chomsky:

Very little of this seems addressed to me. I'll comment below on the few fragments that may be.

I would, however, like to make a suggestion to facilitate discussion. When a questioner raises a point about something I (or others) said earlier, it would be a good idea to repeat it. I just don't have time to do extensive research through huge files.

(I write maybe 100 letters a day) to try to find what the questioner may be referring to. That happens to be particularly relevant here.

Interlocutor:

What I find disappointing about Matthew Abraham's line of questioning here is its persistent rhetoric of "Dean Noam Chomsky, isn't Israel awful?"

I'm saddened to see this list go in this direction. Where is the intellectual discussion which has marked all of the other Re/Interviews I've seen and participated in?

This line here: "This Newspeak: 1) leaves out mention of the rights of the indigenous Palestinian population (can't be mentioned); 2) can't articulate, much less fathom, that the U.S. and Israel have actually been blocking a comprehensive diplomatic settlement in the region for over thirty years (bombing of Lebanon occurred in 1982 because of the prospect of peace);

3) won't recognize the racist assumptions that govern the 'rejectionist' stance, (Palestinians are portrayed as rejecting the territorial rights of Israel, but the converse can't be articulated) which if stated" doesn't speak to Newspeak but lack of knowledge regarding Middle East history, the question of nationalism in the Middle East (and when Palestinian nationalism is born), the rhetoric of the PLO, Hamas, and Jihad regarding a so called "peace" and what that means, and the Palestinian incursions into Northern Israel (and take over Lebanon) which prompted the Lebanese invasion in the first place.

Noam Chomsky:

Perhaps this is addressed to me. If so, the question didn't come up, so the lack of response to the non-question cannot, as a matter of logic, reflect "lack of knowledge regarding Middle East history." However, those who are interested in the topic can find answers easily, e.g. in the standard work of Yehoshua Porath on Palestinian nationalism, and much other scholarship.

"the role of Egypt and Jordan in preventing a Palestinian state (which _____ alluded to and was dismissed by Chomsky). . . ."

I checked earlier letters of _____ and my responses, and could not find anything about this. However, if someone were to raise the issue, it is easily answered. Egypt and Jordan have officially supported a Palestinian state since the matter reached the international agenda in the mid-1970s. Further discussion is plainly impossible until we are informed what the writer has in mind in referencing the role of Egypt and Jordan in preventing a Palestinian state.

"the rhetoric of the PLO, Hamas, and Jihad regarding a so called "peace" and what that means . . ."

The "rhetoric of the PLO" since the mid-1970s is a topic I've discussed elsewhere, in print. Since the topic didn't come up in any relevant form in this discussion, this charge goes the same way as the others. As for Hamas and Jihad, the same.

"and the Palestinian incursions into Northern Israel (and takeover of Lebanon) which prompted the Lebanese invasion in the first place . . ."

Here the question of "lack of knowledge" does arise. To review the familiar and well-documented facts, in mid-1981 a US brokered truce was established on the Israel-Lebanon border (we can go into what happened before, but to the limited extent that it is relevant to the 1982 invasion, it simply reinforces what we learn by looking at the period after the truce). For the next year, Israel carried out a series of murderous and destructive assaults against Lebanon, apparently trying to elicit some PLO response that could be used as a pretext of Palestinian incursions and attacks, Israel invaded anyway, pretending that this was a response to an assassination attempt against the Israeli Ambassador to London—though Israel knew at once that the attempt was carried out not by the PLO, but by Abu Nidal, who was at war with the PLO and had been condemned to death by them. The Israeli invasion began with the bombing of the Sabra-Shatila Palestinian refugee camp, including its hospital, killing over 200 people, according to the eyewitness testimony of the US Mideast scholar Cheryl Rubenberg. Then came the invasion, killing perhaps another 20,000 (victims are rarely counted accurately by the powerful) and leaving vast destruction. The actual reasons were not concealed: the goal was to put an end to the PLO efforts at a negotiated settlement, which were becoming an embarrassment and to impose an Israeli client regime in Lebanon.

So, yes, knowledge is useful, and lack of knowledge can indeed be a problem.

Interlocutor:

Dear Matthew, heard of the attack at Metulla?

Please. Is this a discussion or simple Israel bashing? And is this what is to be expected from the next round of Middle East threads which will follow this one?

Here's a question:

____Will our next prompts be: Tell us, how can we hate Israel more?

Thanks for the clarification. Since there's a lot of interpolation, I'll comment below

Noam Chomsky

[Samson strategy, and the importance of lack of clarity]

That could be. If so, the best strategy for Israeli advocates of the Samson option would be to retain ambiguity. But they don't want or need my advice, and I'm not trying to offer it.

I'm sorry I was unclear—I was thinking about your argument regarding hegemony. One of the many things I like about your work is that the conditions of falsifiability are generally very clearly spelled out. And I think that's useful for public discourse, and a helpful question in class: I often ask students if they can articulate the conditions under which they would change their stance on a topic. If there aren't any, then I say it isn't a political belief but a religious belief, and not a good topic for deliberative rhetoric.

One of the problems with hegemony is that the conditions of falsifiability are (intentionally?) obscured. People hear one side of the story, and may even be told that statement has been verified. In our current American public discourse, in which group loyalty is the highest value, then asking for verification/falsification is a sin (and I chose the word carefully).

I think America is in great danger of making a religion of politics. (Like many, I have high hopes of the Internet, but China's behavior show how that may now work.)

So, I was trying to ask if the hypothesis about the Samson strategy is verifiable/falsifiable, but that was just a way to get to another, more important (to me, anyway) question: how do we argue about topics that can't be verified/falsified, not because we can't articulate the conditions, but because others won't meet the conditions?

Noam Chomsky: There are several hypotheses; am not sure which one you mean. One is that the Samson strategy was articulated by high Israeli officials and harshly condemned by well-known Israeli intellectuals. That one is falsifiable, namely, by checking the sources cited and determining whether they are accurate. That's straightforward. Another hypothesis is the one advanced by the US military analyst cited. The best way to evaluate that would require access to classified documents, which we don't now have, so we have to resort to the usual procedure in discussing policies, and world affairs generally. Nothing special in this case.

On "topics that can't be verified/falsified" because "others won't meet the conditions," the only way that I can think of to proceed is to consider the matter carefully to see if we have proposed the right conditions, and if we are persuaded, to consider their reasons for refusing to meet them and to respond to those reasons. Not very helpful, but I don't see what other response there can be, whether we are talking about quantum physics or human affairs.

Question:

Dr. Chomsky, I'm going to ask one of the less intelligent questions in this discussion, but it's a matter that has been troubling me for some time. A couple of years ago, you spoke at The University of Texas campus, where the room was packed. People were willing to stand in the overflow hallway just for the chance to hear you speak on loudspeakers. Sadly, I didn't get the chance to hear you speak, but I was glad that you visited our campus. One of my friends who heard you speak told me that it was a powerful night of "badly needed information circulation."

Having said that, however, I'm wondering exactly what you think the role of "information" plays on the left. It seems to me that the problems we're talking about here—the crises in the Middle East and U.S. involvement, the war in Iraq, etc.—are often treated as symptomatic problems of "uninformed bodies." The left's treatment seems to be a heavy dosage of information: publicly circulating "information" and "facts" about the connections made between U.S. governmental agencies and state-sponsored terrorism, etc. The left seems to be operating under the belief that we are suffering from poor information-circulation that's cutting off the flow of (potentially) activist blood in our collective bodies.

Noam Chomsky: I don't think this has anything particular to do with "the left."

Suppose we believe that some policy (government or otherwise) should be adopted, or rejected. How do we proceed? One way would be to coerce those who disagree with us so that they follow our orders, maybe by torture, or threats or use of violence. Another way would be to delude them by propaganda, drugs, etc. And we can add others of the same variety.

The alternative would be to try to discuss the matter with them, bring up information that we think they may not have that seems relevant to us, and considerations that they may not have thought of that would be relevant. Whether left, right, center, or indifferent, that seems to me the right way. I presume we agree about this. I don't see, then, what question arises.

I personally doubt that this is the problem.

Noam Chomsky: If it isn't, then those who are opposed to coercion, deception, and other means can proceed no further.

But before I say much more. I'm wondering if you would give us some thoughts on what role you think "information circulation" plays in the struggle of the left.

Noam Chomsky: What I just described. And again, it's nothing special about the left.

What happens, for example, once deliberative bodies become "informed" of the situations you and Matthew are talking about here?

Noam Chomsky: Lots of things happen. Many become activists struggling for peace and justice. That's how constructive social and cultural change takes place, whether it's overcoming slavery, gaining rights for women, preventing nuclear war or environmental disaster, and on, and on.

What is the effect of becoming informed?

Noam Chomsky: That's for the person to decide.

And how exactly do we come to explain "informed bodies who feel passionate opposition to the war with Iraq . . . and still do absolutely nothing about it?

Noam Chomsky: If we are honest with ourselves, we can easily find the answers by looking into the mirror. Take, say, the Rwanda slaughter 10 years ago: about 800 people were killed a day for 100 days. We have recently been lamenting our failure to do anything to stop that horror by some kind of military intervention (not a trivial matter, but it presumably could have been done). Now let's look a step beyond. It takes very little research to discover that every day about 800 children die in southern Africa from easily treatable diseases. That's Rwanda-level killing, not for 100 days but every day, and just children, just southern Africa. And we can easily stop it, not by the difficult and dangerous means of military intervention, but by bribing drug companies to produce medicines for them. Do we do it? If we ask why we don't, we find some of the thousands of answers to the question. We might go on. What does it say about our society that the only way to stop this slaughter is by bribing virtually unaccountable private tyrannies, vastly subsidized by citizens and supported by state power? What do we do about that?

Dr. Chomsky, I would not know whether you felt actual discomfort. Obviously, that is not what I meant but, in any case, I am glad you are feeling well.

Noam Chomsky: My comment about feeling no discomfort was in response to your assertion: "Chomsky's response to my earlier post indicated some discomfort."

I only voice disagreement with you as a normal part of showing you the respect you deserve. We only humor those we fear, feel contempt, or want to use.

Let me take another tack:

___ How do you account for disagreement among intelligent people regarding Israel (or regarding anything else for that matter)?

Noam Chomsky: There is even disagreement among intelligent people about the nature of arithmetic. How could there fail to be disagreement on more contentious issues? There cannot be a general answer about how to account for it. It depends on the case.

Interlocutor:

This is from your post to me:

"There is some disagreement among intelligent people about the nature of arithmetic. How could there fail to be disagreement on more contentious issues? There cannot be a general answer about how to account for it. It depends on the case."

This is from your post to _____:

"The alternative would be to try to discuss the matter with them, bring up information that we think they may not have that seems relevant to us, and considerations that they may not have thought of that would be relevant"

A lot of questions on this list have been asking, in a number of different ways, "Assuming that we accept your picture of things as factual, how do we respond? How can we convince other to pull support away from the right? In other words, how can we convince people of this and get them to actually change their behavior."

Putting together your replies to and myself, your response seem to be—we need to find all of the available means of persuasion for each given situation. I this fair, or am I mischaracterizing your position?

Noam Chomsky: First, I should make clear that I don't think people who receive these communications, or anyone else, should simply accept my "picture of things as factual." As least not if it seems controversial. They have to find out for themselves, and in such matters there is always plenty of room for various interpretations and perspectives.

But if someone does settle, always tentatively, on a "picture of things," whether it conforms to mine or not, and thinks that others should share that picture, then I don't see what honest choice there is apart from the alternative you quote below. That does not, however, entail using "all of the available means of persuasion." Many of these means are entirely improper, and should not be used. Properly undertaken, "persuasion"—like teaching—should be a process of encouraging people to think matters through for themselves, sometimes by suggesting information and considerations that they might not have attended to.

Interlocutor:

Dr. Chomsky, I think most rhetoricians would agree with your common sense statement on persuasion. but many differ regarding the degree to which we/they believe people are capable of thinking for themselves (or willing to) and capable of and willing to putting enlightened thought (for lack of a better phrase) into action. And many differ regarding whether there can be persuasion without coercion.

Sloterdijk and Žižek argue that critical distance tends to devolve into cynical distance. That is to stay: corrected information does not translate into new behavior. Marx, they argue, was wrong that people were merely drugged by ideology. Even when people know their behavior is "ideological" they continue that same behavior. I hope I am being clear here. I do not try to be opaque but my last email seemed to be the first one you understood (or at least admitted to understanding—again, how would I know?). If I am unclear maybe other will step in and articulate this well-known theme better. We can talk about being counter-hegemonic but we have to participate in this economic system or choose hermitage. I would very much like to hear your thoughts on this theme of cynicism. Are you a Sloterdijk fan?

Noam Chomsky:

I don't have any special insight into how well persuasion can succeed without coercion—interpreting the term "coercion" in a broad sense, including deluding, fabrication, exploitation of fear, etc. At this point questions of value arise. If the only way to persuade is to coerce, I'd rather not persuade. Not only is it wrong its itself, in my opinion, but it also reveals, I think that we have not right to even try to persuade. We can never be certain that we are right, or even close to that, which means that the only honest approach leaves open—in fact, very open—the prospect of being persuaded ourselves by the interaction.

I quite agree that we either participate in this economic system or to a mountaintop in Montana with a survival kit. Did that question come up?

I'm not a Sloterdijk fan. Or a Žižek or Marx fan (at least on these topics).

Sorry if I did not understand your earlier communications. However, if you think, as you indicate, that I may just be deceiving you, why bother to even pursue the discussion? I have to say I find these very curious assumptions, and suspect I must be missing something.

Thank you for agreeing to take time to talk w/Re/Inter/View subscribers about your new book. I have some broad questions that, unfortunately, do not stem directly from this recent work, and as such I understand that your response may well be limited.

In a recent interview w/Elisabeth Roudinesco, J. Derrida makes reference to your defense of Robert Faurisson, a literature professor in Lyon who wrote articles to newspapers about the "'rumor of Auschwitz," on the grounds of freedom of speech and the right to expression. (Faurisson, for those unfamiliar, claims that the gas chambers did not exist.) (For *What Tomorrow*)

There was no defense of Faurisson: rather, a defense of his right to freedom of expression. The difference is quite crucial. Those who fail to see this distinction have some serious problems to resolve for themselves.

Though it is irrelevant to the issue of principle, that fact is that at the time there were no articles or newspapers that had been brought to my attention by his harshest critics, so I presume that they did not exist. Rather, Faurisson was accused of having privately published some pamphlets on gas chambers, and as a result had been barred from the university on grounds that he could not be protected from violence, and was facing trial for "Falsification of History." He was later sentenced, in a most astonishing judgment, which accused him of using documents improperly and "allowing others" to use his work for nefarious purposes. Zhdanov and Goebbels would have enjoyed the spectacle greatly.

To be clear, even if he had written such articles at the time, nothing would have changed: he still has the right of freedom of expression. Those who do not understand this, again, have some serious problems to resolve. But I think we all understand it. To take one of many illustrations, a few months ago, Gordon Wood, wrote a review in the *NY Times Book Review* in which he referred in passing to the "elimination" of several hundred thousand native Americans in the course of the conquest of the continent. In fact, it was several million—maybe 10 million or so. There was no comment. I've brought it up occasionally, and no one seems to see anything wrong with it, though I presume the reaction would be different if some leading German historian were to write in *Die Zeit* that several hundred thousand Jews were "eliminated" by the Germans during World War II. Should Wood be censured? Brought to trial? Expelled from the university? Should the *NY Times* be sued? Such suggestions would be utterly outrageous, and we all know exactly why.

The issues arise in the case of Faurisson because he is marginal, defenseless, and an easy target. If he had not been given extraordinary publicity by prominent Paris intellectuals, he would have remained as unknown as many others, in the US as well (including tenured professors at major universities), who make even more extreme and ludicrous claims about the Holocaust. We can speculate about their reasons, but the fact is clear. Also clear—extremely clear—is that the basic issue is whether we adopt the doctrines of the Nazis and Stalin, specifically, that the state has the right to determine Historical Truth and to punish deviation from it. We can either reject their doctrines, in which case there is not issue about "defending Faurisson"—that is, defending his right of freedom of speech. Or we can accept Nazi and Stalinist doctrine. If the latter, we can either do so honestly (that is, announcing clearly that that is what we are doing) or we can do so dishonestly (that is, pretending that is not what we are doing). I'm afraid it's as simple as that.

Derrida says that it is your use of the Constitution to allow "the unacceptable to pass" that he finds "worrisome, as a paradox or a perversity" (132).

I have no idea whether Derrida said that, but let's suppose that someone does. First question: What does it mean? Here are several possibilities: (1) we should call upon the state to silence the "unacceptable," thus adopting the doctrines of the Nazis or Stalin (as in the Faurisson case). (2) We should respond to the "unacceptable," say, writing an article to refute it. (3) We should ignore it as ridiculous. The last of these options is the one we almost always adopt, quite properly, thus consigning all of this to the oblivion where it belongs. The second option is legitimate, if it is somehow felt to be worthwhile. The first option is utterly outrageous. There is nothing "worrisome," and no "paradox" or "perversity," or at least to those who accept minimal standards of freedom and justice—which incidentally have little do with the US Constitution, or Bill or Rights, which, contrary to much illusion, gave only weak protection to freedom of speech; that came much later, in the latter part of the 20th century.

Although Derrida says that "it is imperative that we allow anyone whatever to speak"—even Faurisson, he confesses "with embarrassment"—Derrida seems most concerned with your defense of Faurisson as a right.

Since there was no "defense of Faurisson" there can be no concern about it, as a simple matter of logic. It seems to me remarkable that some cannot distinguish between "defense of X" and "defense of X's right to freedom of expression" when it is under severe attack.

He suggests, further, that this may broadly be a difference between European and American intellectuals, which as far as the latter are concerned, seem to more often place "the weight of the customs . . . and it's Constitution" on any given argument.

It is true that since the 1960s, the US has reached a level of protection of freedom of speech that is, probably, unique in the world, reaching the standards of Enlightenment thinkers. Bentham for one. That's a great achievement, traceable in no small measure to the civil rights movement and other popular movements. It's not "custom" or the "Constitution." And if some European intellectuals are unwilling to rise to the level of the Enlightenment, and prefer the doctrines of fascism and Stalinism, they have a lot to answer for.

Although I am curious about your take on Derrida's thoughts, I want to stretch Derrida's concern over the defense of the "rights of citizens" to the work of Giorgio Agamben, particularly his notion of the "camp." I don't know if you are familiar w/Agamben's work anymore than this recent exchange between Roudinesco-Derrida, but I see Agamben's work turning on this difficult issue of rights.

I have no familiarity with any of this.

Agamben says, in connection to the production of "bare life," which is "the threshold between nature and culture" (–and incidentally, is his working out of Foucault's idea of "biopower" –_ that "Western politics is biopolitics from the very beginning, and that every attempt to found political liberties in the rights of the citizen is, therefore, in vain" (_Homo Sacer_ 181).

To the (limited) extent that I understand this, it seems to me nonsensical.

My primary concern is how you would respond to Derrida's concern over your defense of Faurisson's legal rights, and do you see a connection—as I do—between D's concern and Agamben's thoughts on a condition that always exists prior to "rights" as such? What role does the defense of rights play in our thinking about the Israeli and Palestinian conflict, keeping in mind that Agamben's notion of "camp is much broader than this single example.

I'm afraid I do not understand. First, in France freedom of speech is not protected by law. Therefore Faurisson did NOT have legal rights, as the Courts determined, in a disgraceful judgment. Correcting the facts, I don't understand how Derrida's concerns or Agamben's thoughts bear on what seems to be a very simple and straightforward question about basic and elementary rights. I see no connection to the Israel-Palestine conflict.

Second, as I have found it necessary to work out of other theorists to formulate this question. I am curious of your take on working out of such ideas at all. Do you see any value in arguments that work out of such ontological arguments as, say, Heidegger, who both Agamben and Derrida often reference in the formulation of their thinking? Does the reference to specific, and often tragic dates, combined with death tolls stand somehow in conflict w/such "intellectual work"? (This is a broad question about how intellectuals might go about their "work," which seems to be part of the current discussion thread . . .)

I know very little about this work, primarily, because when I try to read it I am not impressed or interested enough to proceed. I can't respond, for that reason.

Finally, I admit an interest in how you might respond to Roudinesco's response to Derrida's thoughts on your work. She say, "Finally, I wonder what unconscious reason there could be for a Jewish intellectual like Chomsky—a leftist, a civil libertarian hostile to anti-Semitism, a specialist in cognitive rationality, an enemy of what he calls the irrational, and a staunch opponent of Freudian theories—to adopt such a position (toward Faurisson)" (133).

This is a very interesting comment, reflecting a deep commitment of many intellectuals to totalitarian doctrine. Given that quite profound commitment, they cannot understand that someone might defend freedom of speech, and therefore seek "unconscious reasons," etc. If we abandon fascist/ Stalinist doctrine, it is all quite straightforward, and there is no need to see unconscious reasons, or to raise absurd questions about Jewish intellectuals,

cognitive rationality, etc.—all transparent devices to evade the obvious, that is, to evade the fact that their commitments are extremely ugly.

I presume it is unnecessary to expand on the truism that either we defend freedom of speech for views that we detest, or we oppose freedom of speech in principle. Even Stalin and Hitler approved of freedom of speech for view which they approved. It is embarrassing even to write these words, but in dealing with significant strains of intellectual discourse, apparently it is necessary to reiterate truisms.

To clarify: As I read Derrida, he seems to be responding precisely to your defense of Faurission's right to freedom of expression. His concern appears to be over the grounds, the aporia inclination, of such an argument. While he admits it is "imperative" that anyone, even Faurisson, be allowed to speak, he seems to want to have a discussion about aporia aspects of this imperative.

I do not understand what the "aporia aspects of this imperative" are. Nor do I understand why the question arises in this case as distinct from innumerable others, many of them far less straightforward than this one. Thus, I sign innumerable statements protesting the silencing and punishment of people all over the world, often on the basis of very skimpy evidence, and without extensive research; or any. I'm sure you do too, and Derrida as well. Does that raise the same questions? If so, how come I haven't heard about it (except from various infuriated commissars, who we all dismiss with contempt)? If not, why is this case different? Or take the case I mentioned in my first response to you: Wood and the *New York Times*. Suppose that he was suspended from teaching on grounds for Falsification of History and condemned for the crime of denying the Historical Truth established by state power, and the *NYT* was sentenced or perhaps closed. Suppose that you, or I, or Derrida wrote in defense of his right to freedom of expression—as I am sure we would. Would that raise questions about the "aporia aspects of this imperative"? Why is this case different?

More generally, do we really have to spend time discussing why we believe in freedom of speech and oppose the demand that the Holy State will determine Historical Truth and punish deviation from its declarations? And of course there is a background truism: either we defend freedom of speech for views we detest, or we do not believe in freedom of speech at all; Hitler, Stalin, and other tyrants had no problem defending freedom of speech when they agreed with what was said.

Is such questioning an effort to push "totalitarian doctrine"?

How else can it be possibly be understood? Suppose in Stalinist Russia someone had raised similar questions in response to defense of freedom of speech of a dissident. Would we doubt that the person is effectively advocating totalitarian doctrine?

What role do you see philosophy (or rhetoric) playing if one cannot question the grounds of a given issue, even as one admits to the imperative of a given singularity such as Faurisson?

You haven't explained why this is a "singularity." Again, issues of freedom of speech arise precisely when we object to the views expressed. So this is the normal case, in fact, a particularly clear example, since it is not only a matter of defending freedom of speech but also opposing the utterly outrageous doctrine that the state has the right to determine Historical Truth and punish deviation from its commands. I don't see that philosophy or rhetoric have anything to say about these matter, which appear to be truisms.

To my broad question concerning working out of other theorists (such as Heidegger-Derrida-Roudinesco-Agamben) to formulate questions, rather than recourse solely to tragic dates and body counts, and how intellectuals might go about their "work," you say:

> I know very little about this work, primarily, because when I try to read it I am not impressed or interested enough to proceed. I can't respond, for that reason.

A slightly different—but no less broad—question might be to ask what are the conditions necessary for a given reading to impress you?

My conditions are the same as everyone's, as far as I know. Yours I presume. The conditions are, first of all, that we understand what the person is saying, and second, that we think it is informative, illuminating, insightful, suggestive, and other familiar virtues.

Are there living writers-theorists-philosophers-friends today, who, based on their interest in any given any work that you were not initially interested enough in, would incline you towards a re-reading of such a work? Does this often happen?

All the time. That's why I often order books from the library, or buy them, after reading reviews, scholarly articles, etc. Sometimes in the case of books I'd looked at, even read, but learn that I did not really understand. Isn't this true of all of us?

How important are "first impressions"?

Time and energy are finite. We therefore all have to make choices about what we will read. Often these choices are, and must be, made on the basis of first impressions. In some of these cases you mention I've gone beyond casual scanning, but unless the work in question meets the conditions that we all apply, after some effort, I react the same way we all do: by putting it aside.

Finally, I am curious what you are currently reading. I gathered at the beginning of this discussion that you are quite busy answer letters and that effort, coupled w/Re/Inter/View!, is no doubt a full-time job.

I spend many hours a day responding to inquiries from all over the world, but that does not keep me from being in the middle of quite a few books all the time, on a wide range of topics. Don't think it is appropriate to go beyond that, unless you have something specific in mind.

At the height of the Faurisson affair, when members of the French intellectual community found themselves apparently unable to distinguish between "The defense of Faurisson's findings" and "The defense of Faurisson's right to say X in his findings," you expressed some regrets about allowing Serge Thion to publish your essay, "Some Elementary Remarks on Free Expression" as a preface. In fact, you never knew the essay was going to be published as a preface to Faurisson's text. You never knew it would appear as a preface because Thion had asked you to write an essay dealing with free expression, never mentioning how it might be used. As a matter of logic, then, you never wrote a preface to Robert Faurisson's book. If what I've recounted above is incorrect, please say so.

It is correct that I did not publish a preface. Rather, I wrote a statement on freedom of expression, after Paris intellectuals went into a fit of rage over a standard civil rights petition of the kind that we all sign without much attention all the time. Since they were unable to distinguish defense of the right of free expression from defense of the views expressed, I wrote a brief and embarrassingly trivial statement on the matter, at the request of the organizer of the petition, the prominent Southeast Asia scholar Serge Thion. I told him to use it as he liked, and he added it as an "avis" to Faurisson's "memoire" in response to accusations of "Falsification of History" in the matter of gas chambers, for which he was being brought to trial. I knew nothing about any of that.

When you learned the essay would be attached to Faurisson's text, you did try to have the essay retracted at the last minute; at this point, the affair was getting out of hand within Parisian intellectual circles. You've received a lot of criticism for that retraction. In retrospect, you've stated that it probably was a mistake to retract the essay and that you should have said, "Let it run." Again and again, this retraction comes up. What's the significance of the retraction? Why has it been made relevant? This retraction, in the minds of some, impugns your credibility in this case.

I did try to have the essay retracted when I learned about it. But I have never heard a word of criticism about that, though it should have been criticized. Therefore I cannot respond to your question. The criticisms I have heard— and there are mountains of them—have to do with my willingness to defend

his right to freedom of expression (often interpreted by fanatic and mostly ridiculous intellectuals as a defense of his views).

My reasons for requesting retraction had nothing to do with matters of principle: rather, with my failure to appreciate properly the hysterical and quasi-totalitarian atmosphere reigning among Paris intellectuals—as I explained at the time, almost 25 years ago.

Turning to the question of principle, there would be no reason to object to the use of the "avis," just as in any other case of denial of elementary rights. I believe I mentioned earlier in this discussion a recent review by a fine American historian in the NY Times Book Review, in which he casually mentioned that hundreds of thousands of Indians (in fact, many millions) were "eliminated" in the course of expansion over the national territory. If he, and the NY Times, were brought to trial for "falsification of History" I would have had no objection to signing a petition of protest against that, and in the (unimaginable) circumstance that the petition would have been interpreted as defense of this extreme case of denial of mass extermination (in our own history, not someone else's history, which makes it far worse of course), I would have no objection to writing a statement making clear the distinction between defense of freedom of speech and defense of the views expressed, and having it added as an "opinion" to some memoir they wrote in reaction to such outrageous behavior on the part of the state authorities.

All of this is elementary. The only interest in the affair is that it is not understood to be in some sectors, including respected intellectuals—which tells us something about their standards.

In your response to ___, you stated that Faurisson was an easy, defenseless target for those wishing to parade as righteous defenders of the memory of the victims of the Holocaust. Here are your remarks on this score:

The issues [state control of historical truth, removal from an academic position for violating state truth, facing lawsuits for violating academic doctrine, etc.] arise in the case of Faurisson because he is marginal, defenseless, and an easy target. If he had not been given extraordinary publicity by prominent Paris intellectuals, he would have remained as unknown as many others, in the US as well (including tenured professors at major universities), who make even more extreme and ludicrous claims about the Holocaust. We can speculate about their reasons, but the fact is clear. Also clear—extremely clear—is that the basic issue is whether we adopt the doctrines of the Nazis and Stalin, specifically, that the state has the right to determine Historical Truth and to punish deviation from it. We can either reject their doctrines, in which case there is no issue about "defending Faurisson"—that is, defending his right of freedom of speech. Or we can accept Nazi and Stalinist doctrine. If the latter, we can either do so honestly (that is, announcing clearly that that is what we are doing) or we can do so dishonestly (that is, pretending that is not what we are doing). I'm afraid it's as simple as that.

In your estimation, how did your "involvement"—or the conflation of your defense of Faurisson's right to express himself with your defense of Faurisson and his findings—change the very nature of the Faurisson affair?

For Paris intellectuals, it helped enormously in their efforts to provide Faurisson with as much publicity as possible, so that they could then parade as courageous defenders of the reality of the Holocaust, joining 100% of others who any of us would even take seriously. In the US, the reaction is more interesting. Faurisson became very famous among American intellectuals, thought it is unlikely that those who posture dramatically about him have ever read a word he has written or would even know how to find it. And of course they would know nothing about him if it were not for the extraordinary efforts of intellectuals who claim to be offended by him to offer him maximum possible publicity. In contrast, tenured professors in American universities who publish hardcover books denying the Holocaust are ignored—rightly. The reason they are ignored is that it is understood that they do have the right of freedom of speech. In contrast, the Faurisson affair, being remote and obscure, can be converted into an ideological weapon to use against their hated enemies and to puff their own reputations as courageous defenders of Truth. It is all quite comical, actually, and perhaps will be understood that way, some day, if we ever get to the point where honest intellectual history can be written about the current period—not only with regard to this silly and trivial matter.

Question:

Several years ago, you stated in the movie, *Manufacturing Consent*, that the requirement of "concision" (making statements between commercials, in ten-second sound bytes, through the use of clichés, etc.) protects conventional ideas from serious analysis within the mainstream media and is a central part of any propaganda system. Do you have any contemporary examples of where the requirement of concision is blocking discussion/analysis of serious social issues? Any specific examples you'd like to point to from H&S?

The term "concision" is one that I learned from the person who did the planning for "Nightline." I think his name was Jeff Greenfield. I'll assume so. I was being interviewed by a radio station in the mid-West—community radio, so fairly free from doctrinal constraints. The interview began with a clip from an interview with Greenfield, in which he was asked why they never had me on. After some ranting about how I was "from Neptune," he said that I lacked "concision," which meant that I did not give answers in a few short snappy sentences but went on with background, evidence, etc. All of this is in print somewhere; maybe something by David Barsamian, who follows these matters closely.

The statement that I lack "concision" is correct. The demand for "concision" is largely a principle of US mass media, though there are a few exceptions.

It is far less true in radio-TV outside the US, where it is expected that responses will be explained, not simply crammed in slogans between two commercials. Whatever the motive for "concision" may be, it has a very strong doctrinal and disciplinary effect. It entails that either you say something that fits within conventional doctrine, in which case no evidence or argument is considered necessary, or you say something unexpected and sound as though you are "from Neptune," because you are not given the opportunity to explain. Thus if someone says that Qaddafi or Arafat is a "terrorist," they can do so under the requirement of "concision." But if someone were to say—accurately— that Reagan, Bush, Clinton, Peres, Sharon, etc. are terrorists, that would be "from Neptune" under the standards of concision, since there is no time to explain what you mean.

I don't watch TV much, but do so occasionally, for special reasons. One involved Nightline. I was in fact invited to be a commentator right after the fall of the Berlin Wall. Since it was easy to predict what they had in mind, I refused. Shortly after I received a call from my friend Alex Cockburn (I think he won't mind me mentioning this), telling me they'd contacted him. I advised him not to agree, but he decided to proceed. I watched to see what would happen. It was (as I expected) something like this. The program began with scenes of crowds acclaiming the fall of the Wall, and then the anchor shifted to Cockburn in their studio, asking something like "What do you have to say about THAT, Mr. Cockburn," in the interests of concision, designed, in this case, to depict him as a Stalinist apologist, a representative of "the left" who are supposed to be embarrassed by the collapse of Soviet tyranny—called "socialism" in the propaganda system.

This is from memory, so I don't vouch for the details. But it was something roughly like that. Concision is a common and useful device to enforce orthodoxy and undercut independent thought.

Current examples are endless. Take, say, the doctrine-accepted by supporters and critics alike—that Bush has a "messianic vision" of bringing democracy to Iraq, the Middle East, the world, and that that was the "deep reason" for the Iraq invasion (other pretexts having collapsed). When I'm interviewed about this in Canada, UK, Europe, elsewhere, I have an opportunity to explain why the claim lacks the slightest credibility, is overwhelmingly denied by Iraqis, and faces mountain of counter-evidence. If the question comes up in an interview in the mass media here, the person interviewed can either endorse the doctrine, joining about 100% of commentators (including critics, who say that the noble ends are unattainable, etc.), or can express criticism and disbelief, and therefore comes "from Neptune," since the overwhelming evidence against the doctrine cannot be presented under the requirement of "concision."

It's easy to list case after case.

A quick follow-up on where Derrida goes after Chomsky-Faurisson: Rather than argue the constitutionality of Faurisson's freedom of speech, Derrida points to a documentary about Fred A. Leuchter called *Mr. Death* (1999). Leuchter, like Faurisson, doubts the existence of the Nazi gas chambers, and in this film—one that I had the opportunity to see sometime ago—Leuchter steals his way into various concentration camp sites to collect rock samples to prove that there are no measurable traces of Zyklon-B.

There is no question of the constitutionality of F's freedom of speech. French law does not guarantee freedom of speech: in fact, it permits the state to determine Truth and to punish deviation from its commands, as in this case. Many Paris intellectuals, and they are not alone, prefer to evade this crucial matter. As in this case. If it was the US, there is constitutional protection of freedom of speech in the sense that Supreme Court decisions, since the 1960s particularly, have interpreted the Constitution and First Amendment this way. Before that protection of freedom of speech was very limited, though not as bad as in contemporary France.

As much as the film focuses on L's doubt of the holocaust, it is coupled with his opinions concerning his opposition to the electric chair, hanging and the gas chamber. Leuchter has a preference instead for the lethal injection, on the grounds it is a more human method.

I don't understand your interest in L, and don't share it. I know nothing about him, and have no interest in learning more.

Now, what Derrida makes of this "odd character" in Leuchter is L's interest in killing w/"clean solutions." D., for his part, regards lethal injections as "truly terrifying," but perhaps more important is Derrida's preference for the overall approach that the documentary suggests itself to as a means of resistance both to the questionable science of disproving the holocaust and promotion of lethal injection.

Why Derrida is interested in this I haven't the slightest idea. That's for him to explain. I also don't know what you mean about the "questionable science of disproving the holocaust." There is no "science," questionable or not: just complete absurdity, which I see no reason to pay any attention to. Derrida apparently does, but you have to ask him why. I don't see any reason to. On "lethal injection," that issue does arise in the US, in connection with the death penalty, but very marginally: it is the right of the state to kill that should be challenged, not the particular methods used. Again, Derrida may have something else in mind, but I have no idea what.

Derrida says, "It's true in the United States, because of this supposed freedom of speech and expression, Nazi groups have the right to manifest themselves as such, and to demonstrate.

The phrase "supposed freedom" is interesting. I presume it is unnecessary to comment. At least it should be unnecessary, at least since the Enlightenment.

It's far more extreme than that. There is also freedom of speech for people who advocate, and carry out, mass murder. In fact, even explicit calls for genocide, leading to implementation, are not only protected but are not even criticized, often not even noticed, no matter how prominent they are—a fat that has no bearing on freedom of speech, but tells us a lot about the reigning intellectual and moral climate, and about ourselves in particular. For example, a few months ago the *NY Times* publishes some excerpts of recently released Nixon-Kissinger tapes, where Nixon tells Kissinger that he wants him to order bombing of Cambodia. Kissinger obediently transmits the orders, in these words: "A massive bombing campaign in Cambodia. Anything that flies on anything that moves." As an experiment, try to find some analogous call for what amounts to genocide in the archival record. And imagine how the prosecutors at the Milosevic trial would rejoice if they could find anything remotely comparable—thus ending the trial, sending him off to multiple life sentences, and if it was the US, probably to lethal injection. But in the reigning intellectual/moral climate, it is considered unproblematic when it is a US decision-maker. In fact, calls for use of nuclear weapons are not prevented, thought it might blow up the world. Hardly the only examples of how freedom of speech extends, properly, to vastly more dangerous actions than pro-Nazi manifestations.

But there are other ways of fighting (*FWT* 134).

What does that mean? That there is some problem dealing with pro-Nazi manifestations? Please

Such "other ways"—ways other than arguments solely on the level of arguing constitutional legality—are documentaries like ____Mr. Death____, wherein Leuchter, is given all the space in the world to express his views, all in what Derrida calls "hideous close-up." He calls this the "filmmaker's 'trap'" (–and such a 'trap', of course, that Michael Moore has been faulted for, and it may be interesting to get your take on Fahrenheit 9/11.

I don't see how my opinion about Moore's film is relevant here. The question is whether state power should be used to prevent documentaries that someone—maybe Derrida—doesn't like, whether it's Leuchter, Moore, or anyone else. And I'll repeat the familiar truism, once again: either we defend freedom of speech for views we detest, or we join Goebbels, Zhdanov, and other notables in defending freedom of speech for views we like.

What Derrida seems to be suggesting in all this is whether one might have approached the Faurisson case from this more.. could we say? . . . rhetorical angle. . . .???

I don't know what Derrida is suggesting, but what you quote—and I can't judge the context which I don't know—is just evasion of the issue of defense of the "supposed" right of freedom of speech, and implications that it is somehow problematic. Rhetoric has nothing to do with it in my opinion. The question is trivial, and the efforts to evade it with complex discourse should merit no comment.

Leuchter's documentary is, after all, strangely touching. To be sure, this is a chilling touch—all those close-ups of L's face and the juxtapositioning of arguments against the holocaust and for lethal injection—result in a viewer's revulsion. It's affective filmmaking. Leuchter is given space to have his say, and the combination of his science and preference for "clean solutions," I think, goes a long way to getting at what Agamben is exploring w/regards to Foucauldian 'biopower' and the politics of bodies (living and 'dead'), or what he calls the 'bare life' (see _Home Sacer_ 166-188).

As I mentioned, I know nothing about Leuchter and have no interest in the topic. I also don't understand what Agamben-Foucault have to do with this, but that my be my (very substantial) ignorance about them.

This latter connection w/Agamben-Foucault, of course, needs further unpacking, but the main idea here is how one might approach someone like Faurisson or Leuchter. It is clear from your response that "Faurisson" is just one of countless of freedom of expression cases, whereas Derrida sees something of a singularity both in Leuchter, but also in that style of argument.

Faurisson is not only one of countless such cases, but a particularly elementary one. From what you describe about L, I don't see that any freedom of speech issue arose. If this documentary were banned, that would be a different matter, and we should revert again to the truisms. As to how to approach F and L, the most sensible way, in my opinion, is to ignore them, in which case they will remain in deserved obscurity. Those who choose to offer them as much publicity as they can have some explaining to do. If state power is used to repress them, we should of course protest. Back to the truisms. There's nothing more involved, as far as I can see.

Perhaps D's approach approaches something that Susan Bachman gets at in her recent post to you that puts your approach to "concision" in contrast to her sense of "sketch". . . .

You've lost me. This is one case where concision is extremely easy; namely, the truism that I have now repeated several times.

Question:

A wider, less focused view from an onlooker who hasn't read the book. I hope I'm not being hopelessly Pollyanna. You decide. "Concision" sounds to me in at least two ways not so necessarily coercive but explanatory.

Human being communicate in shorthand or argument sketches, not always as Aristotle can be interpreted, because we want to conceal things or sneak in our conclusions, but because we can. We naturally do, it's fun, we have to, and it's efficient. The more a person knows and identifies with a group, the less he/she must say, and the more sketch/shorthand communicates because the tacit information lying behind it is filled in by a listener. The wider the differences, of course, the more an argument sketch can be analyzed unsympathetically or just erroneously. So a speaker outside his/her orbit, and especially one concerned not to risk misinterpretation, speaks less sketchily and fill in, unpeels, exposes, makes explicit.

Some people and some media are best suited to capturing only the shell of an argument. Yet even hostile or unknown territory, there may be merit to airing or revealing such argument sketches. You never know who's listening and might be intrigued to search out what lies behind. Does the whole deep story have to be said all this time? Other people and other media by design are better suited to analysis: Plato says the world of reasoning goes around by means of such "division and collection." It sounds to me as if Prof. Chomsky's preference is and gifts are in analysis, the specifying and laying out of the links in the reasoning, not merely in inviting people into the problem/dialog that a sketch leaves open. Perhaps after his track record, he's earned the right not to be in the evangelistic forefront suffering the slings and arrows of every misguided interpreter. He may be wise to say no to an interview to express an idea that details of which, by design, he can't clearly lay out and item by item defend. (But, as usual, you are damned if you do. Damned if you don't: people interpret silence in their own oblique ways too.) But neither does it mean that the media is limiting or forcing all discussion in one direction. I don't see media or the various brevity or concision genres as necessarily wielded agonistically. Consider poetry or song lyrics. Minds are changed by those. Why not the provocative sound byte?

What is poetry but often an idea/argument sketch or compressed image or suggestion. If people are intrigued, they unpack poetry. A good natured, suggestive argument sketch has its place, even if such an enthymeme plays to a minority or almost nonexistent (in that media) in-crowd. I don't want to sound either flip or naïve, but being "from Neptune" sounds to me funny, appealing almost, and also that it could be turned to Prof. Chomsky's own positive effect, regardless of its coiner's intention. Did you by chance play with/retort with that?

Finally, it's hard to be concise. Many of you will know this quote, but I enjoy it, and it's fun to remember. Goethe wrote to his sister (reportedly having gotten it originally from Pascal): Da ich keine Zeit habe, Die einen kurzen Brief zu schreiben, so schreibe ich Dir einen Langen. Because I don't have time to write you a short letter, I'll write a long one.

I'm learning a lot from this discussion, so thank you all.

Noam Chomsky:

Interesting comments, but I don't see what they have to do with "concision" in the sense of the earlier discussion. That had to do with the ways opinion is controlled by the mass media. Within the constraints of "concision," one can repeat orthodox doctrine (e.g., Libya is a terrorist state) or present far more important truths that depart from received doctrine (e.g., the U.S. is a terrorist state), and sound as though you are "from Neptune," because you are not permitted to explain, and listeners have a right to explanation of something that sounds controversial because they have rarely heard anything about it.

I'm not sure what book you are referring to.

I don't think that Professor Chomsky is making any philosophical statement about "concise" writing in whatever form it might take (e.g., a highly compressed poem, an efficiently written memo, etc.), but that he is objecting to a particular rhetorical tactic whereby a person is "allowed" to have her "say" insofar as what she says is kept so brief as to effectively regulate what can be said. One can, like Greenfield, euphemize the process as "concision" if one wishes, and it's no doubt rhetorically effective to do so. But this kind of "concision" has little to do with value of "concise" speaking or writing found in, for example, the work of disparate thinkers as Paul Grice, Herbert Spencer, or even Plato.

It seem to me that concision is not only a negative tactic that determines who may speak in a given forum, but that it is also a positive tactic one might use in order to prevent oneself from having to speak too long: consider the ludicrous (self-imposed) time-limits in presidential debates. How the candidates always seem so frustrated when interrupted by the hapless moderator, as if to say, "If only there were more time to clarify my position on X!"

And just as "concision" in Chomsky's sense can serve the interests of power, it seems to me than an opposing rhetorical tactic—perhaps euphemized under a technical-sound word like "diffusion"—could equally serve these interests. We can see this tactic at work when a person refuses to yield the floor; never provides a straight answer but hedges until doomsday (and, if interrupted, will always claim to be "misunderstood"); confounds a discussion with endless digressions, red herrings, procedural delays, etc. And just as concision may be mystified as a virtue instead of a self-serving tactic (even by the person who uses it), so may diffusion. Unless one has had one's" full say," one may (self-)righteously complain about being silenced, mischaracterized, whatever.

Context is inexhaustible, so no statement can be fully contextualized. Fortunately, full contextualization is not a necessary precondition for speech or writing. I suppose the most we can hope for is to be given an opportunity to contextualize what we say or write until we feel that we've said or written "enough."

Question: What is the "thief, thief technique," a phrase which crops in your writing from time to time? Any current examples?

Noam Chomsky: The first time I recall using the phrase in print is in *Year 501*, chap. 12 (1993). One subheading is entirely germane to the relevant passage:

The state-media complex has been resorting to a trick familiar to every petty crook and tenth-rate lawyer: When you're caught with your hand in someone's pocket, cry "Thief!, Thief!" Don't pretend to defend yourself, thus conceding the point or confront: rather, shift the onus to your accusers, who must then defend themselves against your accusations. It's a highly effective when control over the doctrinal system is assured. The device is familiar to propagandists for whom it is adopted unthinkingly.

A number of examples are discussed the most comical being the "anti-PC crusade," and the most important instances prove the dedication to effacing the memory of the Vietnam war. We're seeing more of that right now. A few weeks ago on a program on CNN called something like "America's Vietnam Obsession," moderated by *Washington Post* reporters with representatives from across what is considered "the spectrum." I was intrigued to see what they would say about the war of aggression, targeting mainly South Vietnam, which killed millions of people—many still dying from the Napalm campaign that was the least of the crimes—and destroyed three countries. Turns out that what was significant is that selectrics had a certain typeface in 1970, and whether Kerry might have strayed into Cambodia when Vietcong murder operations then in progress in the deep South, in the Mekong delta, at the height of US war crimes, about then, being a tiny footnote). That's an example. Don't even permit the thought that there might be any concern about this. Rather, focus laser-like on charges and counter-charges about trivialities.

I don't recall using it about Collier-Horowitz, but don't recall saying anything about them, apart maybe from *Znet* forum. It may be posted there.

Question:

In an essay entitled "The Role of Domestic Structure," Henry Kissinger writes: "In the traditional conception, international relations are conducted by political units treated almost as personalities. The domestic structure is taken as a given; foreign policy begins where domestic policy ends" (11).

Noam Chomsky: He's basically correct about the traditional conception of IR—the "realist" conception of IR—the "realist conception—though the more serious realist scholars, like Kenneth Walt, recognize the need to attend to the domestic structure of power, to what Walz calls the "internal dispositions" of states. Without that, the abstraction from the real world seems to me so extreme that the conception is severely flawed. How, for example, can one hope to understand US foreign policy without paying attention to the distribution of decision-making power internally, specifically, to the role of concentrated economic power, which of course has overwhelming impact on state policy? How could it be otherwise?

Question: In *H&S* and in many works before (*Toward a New Cold War, Deterring Democracy, American Power and the New Mandarins, For Reasons of State*, and the *Culture of Terrorism*), you consider how the rhetoric and implementation of U.S. militarization has deep connections to the domestic structure within the country. You've repeatedly claimed, that, since the public isn't going to do so freely, it has to be coerced into providing a subsidy to high-tech industry and the Pentagon system. You once told faculty and students at MIT that, if they didn't understand this concept, they needed to take a closer look at their paychecks. Hence, the rhetoric of militarization must cohere with the national vision, duping the paymasters into a false sense of security and well-being. In H&S, you quote a congressional official, who states that "the policy of the US toward Iraq and North Korea only gives more incentive for nations to get nuclear weapons. . . . If the US tests weapons, then China will test (and) there will be domestic pressure for India to test as well," then Pakistan: (As the official claims) "You're opening a can of worms." You go on to write:

> Defense analyst Harlan Ullman warned that a country that is specifically threatened, like Iran, "might hurry its nuclear weapons program after seeing the United States lead an assault on Iraq," providing the pretext for an invasion of Iran, in a self-fulfilling prophecy. Others expect that Pakistan, "felling pushed into desperation by India and its significant superiority in conventional forces, would feel freer to use significant superiority in conventional forces, would feel freer to use nuclear weapons in a first strike."
>
> Extension of the arms race to space has been a core program for some years; race is a misleading term, because the US is competing alone, for the moment. Militarization of space, including such programs as ballistic missile defense (BMD), increases the danger of destruction for the US, as for others. But that is nothing new: history provides many examples of the policy choices that increase security threats, consciously. More ominous is that the fact that the choices make some sense within prevailing value systems. Both topics merit some thought (H&S 223).

With this rhetoric of militarization of mind, could you point to specific aspects of the prevailing value systems within the U.S. that enhance the threat of worldwide terror? Value systems (even the "prevailing" one), in my understanding, are complex and can't be easily reduced to a formula. I think you're stated that it's impossible to fight a war on terror because fighting the war itself will only increase the terror. Are you saying, then, that increasing the terror is the real goal of imperial planners (in the hope of expanding the military-industrial base) or simply an effect of "compelling the domestic population to provide a subsidy to high-tech industry and the Pentagon system" for the benefit of U.S. corporations?

Noam Chomsky: You're of course right that value systems can't be reduced to a formula. There are many strands, and while there is a common core of concerns shared by most people, not just here, studies reveal considerable variation—cross-culturally in prevailing values. For example, studies of attitudes toward inequality show that Americans are quite unusual these days—not in the past, I believe, though I don't know of careful studies—in not finding it problematic. Notoriously, the US is entirely off the spectrum of industrial societies in religious commitment, often extremism, and religious beliefs regarded as astonishing in other societies—e.g., that the world was created 6000 years ago. I don't think glib answers are helpful. There are many dimensions, they vary over time, and it's important to determine the extent to which values are simply manipulated. It's hardly a secret that in the past century a huge industry has developed, the PR industry and its offshoots, dedicated to controlling the attitudes and beliefs—to achieve "off-job control" of people through immersion in consumerism and inducing passivity, alongside the "on-job control" of Taylorism in industry, as Michael Dawson describes the goals from the 1920s in his study of the development of the "consumer trap." And these efforts are greatly enhanced by state policies, not just inducing fear, jingoism, and militarist values and the like, but also by huge social engineering projects, such as the suburbanization of America, substantially planned by the state-corporate sector. As to what people's choices would be if they were given the options, we don't know. Suppose, for example, that in the 1950s, people had been given a choice as to whether to spend their tax dollars for research and development in what decades later became personal computers, and the internet, telecommunications, etc., or for decent schools and health care, a safe livable environment for their children, security for the elderly and disabled, etc. We don't know what they would have chosen. We do know that they weren't given much of a choice. The former choices were made by state-corporate power under the umbrella of "defense" against enemies about to overwhelm us. The issues were scarcely discussed, and are still largely unknown apart from some specialists and people engaged in dissenting activist movements, who find their own sources of information outside of conventional channels.

As for the "war on terror," there are a few problems. First, we can hardly be serious about it if we refuse to attend to the fact that it was not declared in 2001, but re-declared. It had been declared in 1981 by pretty much the same people or their mentors, with the much the same rhetoric as in 2001. We know the consequences of the first "war on terror": it was a murderous destructive terrorist war, with horrendous consequences. Many of those who conducted the terrorist war are in high places directing the renewed phase right now, with no concern whatsoever about their records, or about the whole history, almost entirely effaced—not for the victims, of course. Not only is this very relevant very recent history almost entirely suppressed, but so is the fact that the concept of "terror" is used in a highly distorted sense, restricted in principle to a subcategory of terror as it is officially defined: namely, THEIR terror against US AND OUR CLIENTS, whoever they happen to be—that varies with policy goals. Keeping just to this subcategory of terror, in what follows, the evidence is quite strong that combatting it is not a high priority among policy planners. They consistently undertake actions that they anticipate may—and often do—increase the likelihood of terror. I've written about it elsewhere, as have others, and won't try to review the current choices here. So it's hard to say with a straight face that there even is a war on terror. I wouldn't conclude that planners want to increase terror. It simply isn't a very high priority. If it is a side effect of achieving higher goals of power, domination, profits, then so be it.

You've called Israel and Turkey, for example, offshore U.S. military bases, pointing out that the domestic structure of both countries are beginning to mirror the domestic structure of its patron; more so in the case of Israel. Clearly, militarization is a threat to human survival. It seems, then, that the commitment to upholding the 'necessary illusions' of state has become extreme indeed; requires remarkable discipline on many fronts (media, intellectuals, etc.)."

Noam Chomsky: That's for sure.

In Chapter 6 of *H&S*, entitled "Cauldron of Animosities," while considering what you call the tripartite alliance between the U.S., Israel, and Turkey, you write: "The existing tripartite alliance (U.S.-Israel-Turkey) extends to parts of Central Asia and recently to India as well. Since its government came under the control of the Hindu right in 1998, India has shifted its international stance considerably, moving toward a closer military relationship with both the U.S. and its Israeli client. Indian political analyst Praful Bidwa writes that the ruling Hindu nationalist 'fascination' with Zionism is rooted in Islamophobia (and anti-Arabism) and hypernationalism. Its ideology is Sharon's machismo and ferocious jingoism. It sees Hindus and Jews (plus Christians) forming a 'strategic alliance' against Islam and Confucianism." Addressing the American Jewish Committee in Washington, India's national security adviser, Brajesh Mishra, called for development of a U.S.-Israel-India "triad" that will have "the political will and moral authority to make bold decisions" in combatting terror. According to Bidwai, "the growing Indo-Israel political-military contacts" are supplemented by coordination of the Hindu nationalist and Israel lobbies in the U.S.

India and Israel are both significant military powers, with nuclear weapons and delivery systems, and the emerging alliance system is another factor contributing to WMD proliferation, terror, and disorder in the unstable belt and beyond (160). You go on to discuss how these new alliances are relying upon Britain's historical example of using local management, in the form of an Arab façade of "weak compliant rulers, to suppress the demands of the local population, which is rightly angry about occupation, destruction of national cultures, etc. While the profits from the petroleum reserves flow Westward, fattening the pockets of the U.S. proxies, the native populations are left relatively helpless. Borrowing an *unfortunate* line from Lloyd George (former distinguished statesman from Britain), it appears we, the U.S., have, following Britain's historical example, "reserve[ed] the right to bomb niggers." (Lloyd George cited by V.G. Kiernan, European Empires from Conquest to Collapse (Fontana, 1982). In this case, "sand niggers," who don't comply with our (U.S.) plans for the region. The unfortunate quotation, and its extension into the present, is instructive with plenty of examples within the historical record—for those who can bear to look. Since nearly twenty percent of India is Muslim, as is most of Pakistan, India's commitment to nuclear proliferation could possibly lead to increased tensions among its Muslim neighbors, not to mention within its own national boundaries (presumably your point). With the example of British colonialism not too far removed from India's historical consciousness, why is it choosing an alliance that may escalate the rhetoric of colonial domination, with the not too unlikely 'tinder box' scenario, that Stephen Zunes and others have described, in the background?

Noam Chomsky: Indian elites had an ambiguous relationship with British imperialism. As nationalists, they opposed it. Nonetheless, they were part of the 'façade' that ruled the country (in Britain's imperial terminology) and as such they benefitted from the Raj, however the population may have suffered. In post-colonial states, nationalist elites quite commonly not only become brutal and oppressive, but are happy to subordinate themselves to the imperial powers, but are happy to subordinate themselves to the imperial powers, under the new "neo-colonial" relations. India in recent years is following the classic path. It is all extremely hazardous. Strobe Talbott—writing from special knowledge within the Clinton administration—recently wrote about a close encounter with nuclear war a few years ago during the conflict with Pakistan over Kargil. According to Talbott, it was only last minute US intervention that prevented the two countries from destroying

each other. History is replete with examples of leaders taking gambles on defeat—by now, even global destruction—for short-term gains of power and privilege. Many are discussed in the book you mention.

Toward the end of the last chapter of *H&S*, you discuss the emerging human rights culture here at home and throughout the world and the various peace movements that pose an immense threat to the concentration of state power and the latter's monopoly of violence. You mention, in a footnote (#39 in chapter 9), Rachel Corrie's example in Gaza. You write:

> Rachel Corrie was killed by Israeli forces in Gaza in March 2003 with a US-supplied bulldozer one of Israel's most destructive weapons; see p. 181. Murdered might be the more appropriate term, to judge by eyewitness reports. The killing of an American citizen by US clients using US equipment was no considered worthy of inquiry, even more than the barest report pointing out that she was in fact murdered.

Rachel, in her letters home, spoke of her recognition of her own white privilege that she viewed as protecting her against the abuses Palestinians suffer. It's really quite remarkable that the efforts of peace activists can represent such an immense threat (as you outline in the passages below):

Noam Chomsky: She was a courageous woman. We should be ashamed by the fact that she is not honored here.

It would be a great error to conclude that the prospects are uniformly bleak. Far from it. One very promising development is the slow evolution of a human rights culture among the general population, a tendency that accelerated in the 1960s, when popular activism had a notable civilizing effect in many domains, extending significantly in the years that followed. One encouraging feature has been a greatly heightened concern for civil and human rights, including rights of minorities, women, and future generations, the latter driving concern of the environmental movement, which has become a power force. For the first time in American history, there was some willingness to look honestly at the conquest of national territory and that fate of its inhabitants. The solidarity movements that developed in mainstream American in the 1980s, concerning Central America in particular, broke new ground in the history of imperialism; never before had substantial numbers of people from the imperial society gone to live with the victims of vicious attacks to help them and offer some measure of protection. The international solidarity organizations that evolved from these roots now function very effectively in many parts of the world, arousing fear and anger in repressive states and sometimes exposing participants to serious danger, even death. The global justice movements that have since taken shape, meeting at the World Social Forum annually, are an entirely new and unprecedented phenomenon in character and scale. The planet's "second superpower," which could no longer be ignored in early 2003, has deep roots in these developments.

Over the course of modern history, there have been significant gains in human rights and democratic control of some sectors of life. These have rarely been the gift of enlightened leaders. They have typically been imposed on states and other power centers by popular struggle. An optimist might hold, perhaps realistically that history reveals a deepening appreciation for human rights, as well as a broadening of their range—not without sharp reversals, but the general tendency seems real. The issues are very much alive today. The harmful effects of the corporate globalization project have led to mass popular protest and activism in the South, later joined by major sectors of the rich industrial societies, hence becoming harder to ignore. For the first time, concrete alliances have been taking shape in the grassroots level. These are impressive developments, rich in opportunity. And they have had effects, in rhetorical and sometimes policy changes. There has been at least a restraining influence on state violence, though nothing like the "human rights revolution" in state practice that has been proclaimed by intellectual opinion in the West.

These various developments could prove very important if momentum can be sustained in ways that deepen the emerging global bonds of sympathy and solidarity. It is fair to say, I think, that the future of the endangered species may be determined in no small measure by how these popular forces evolve (235-236).

Do you have any specific recommendations for how these global bonds of sympathy and solidarity might come together? Frequently, individuals who engage in peace and solidarity movements face the usual slanders: "You are naïve and idealistic; human conflict is a natural part of life. There's no point in trying to address these conflicts. The fault lies on every side." Or, in my case, "You are too close to the subject matter you are analyzing." Finally, Noam, what is it that has inspired you to live the life of a dissident for nearly fifty years when so much around you says your efforts may eventually be for naught, and that hegemony—not survival—is humankind's fate?

Noam Chomsky: The only specific recommendations I have are the ones we all know, the ones that have been followed in the past, often with considerable success which is why there has been a good deal of progress over the years including recent years—not without regression but in general in an upwards cycle. Rachel Corrie's choices are one example. Those taken by Turkish and Colombian intellectuals are another. For those of us who do not have that courage and commitment, there are many other options available to us, particularly those of us who have a fair share of privilege—thanks to the courageous struggles of those who brought these conditions about, over the centuries. The recommendations are the simple virtues: education, including

self-education; engagement over a wide range and it is indeed wide. That's how anything decent has happened in the past, and will again.

Here on this list and elsewhere you've expressed real contempt for the intellectual class in the U.S., France, and Britain.

Noam Chomsky: It's no different elsewhere, to my knowledge, with some exceptions that I've also written about.

The "secular priesthood" has, in your estimation, destroyed the historical record, ensured a systematic bias in academic scholarship, proved itself indispensable in sycophantically serving power, doesn't defend freedom of expression (except for itself and a few, favored, close associates) and ensures continued scholarly support for a favored Holy State. You've done battle over the years with the likes of Beth Elshtain, Michael Ignatieff, Michael Bérubé, Christopher Hitchens Jeffrey Issac, etc., demonstrating that the principle of universality eludes left-liberals, especially in the United States.

Noam Chomsky: I've barely mentioned them in print, as far as I can recall, except a few remarks about Elshtain's shocking apologetics, irrationality, and ignorance. In the past I've tried to consider much more serious writers, also highly critically. I've always been much more interested in the dominant intellectual culture mostly its more "liberal" extreme (in the US sense of that term).

You go to great lengths to document this in *H&S*. Universality (in evaluating military actions committed by one's own nation or favored client state, one applies the same or higher standards to the evaluation of the military action; in other words, we should evaluate our own crimes in the same way we evaluate the crimes of a loathed enemy). You urge those, who can't cope with the principle of universality, to at least demonstrate the decency to remain silent about the war on terror. In addition, you urge intellectuals to understand the military actions of a Holy State are to be assessed for the full range of their consequences, e.g. in 2002, you were severely criticized for quoting the *NY Times* and Amnesty International prior to the bombing of Afghanistan to the effect that we were about to engage in a sort of "silent genocide" faulted for your "hysteria and hauteur" and for claiming that "We're apparently about to starve 3-4 million people."

Noam Chomsky: Here I'd suggest an emendation. We assess actions in terms of the range of likely consequences. To take the example you mention, we condemn Khrushchev's placing of missiles in Cuba because of the possibility that it might lead to nuclear war, and do not exonerate him because fortunately the worst didn't happen. Precisely the same is true of the criminal decision to undertake the bombing of a half-devastated country over the strong objections of many of the leading and most respected anti-Taliban Afghan activists,

with the clear understanding that it put millions of people at grave risk of starvation, and the crime is not diminished by the fact that the worst didn't happen, exactly as in the case of the Cuban missiles. These should be truisms, and what is interesting is that although they are easily understood with regard to others, educated sectors cannot comprehend them with rare exceptions, when applied to their own actions. Nothing novel in history about that.

In response you cited that fact that we don't see people running out in the streets every October praising Khrushchev because he nearly brought the world global-thermal nuclear confrontation, but didn't AND we don't see the concomitant denunciation of those who warned that the missile buildup in Cuba was extremely dangerous. Why, then, were those who warned of the impending human rights catastrophe in Afghanistan the subject of similar denunciations?

Noam Chomsky: I assume the question is rhetorical. The answer is all too obvious—and familiar.

Through the principle of universality Nicaragua and Sudan have every right to bomb Washington and Boston. Since the Bush administration has invited the U.N. to go the way of a debating society, and as the World Court's security resolutions are ignored by the leading terrorist states, the rule of law apparently means nothing. These cases (mining of Nicaraguan harbors and the destruction of the Al-Shifa pharmaceutical facility in Sudan) remain, in your words, "uncontroversial." Those who don't know about these events are illiterates by choice since they can't plead fear. When Hitchens claimed the accidental bombing of the Sudan pharmaceutical factory paled in comparison to 9/11, you asserted that Hitchens failed to fathom the racist assumptions guiding his analysis since far more people would have died in Sudan, over a period of time, due to the absence of life-saving drugs.

Noam Chomsky: For the record, Hitchens is the only commentator I know who claims that the bombing of the Sudan pharmaceutical factor was far worse than 9-11. In his words, it had "appalling consequences for the economy and society" of Sudan. However awful 9-11 was, the bombing did not have anything like such consequences for the US. However, facts are irrelevant in these performances of the educated classes.

Using the now banal definition of the hypocrite (he who applies standards to others that he does not apply himself) isn't it fair to say that we are all total hypocrites on any element of the war on terror? "We," of course, being people like us who are lucky enough to have access to privilege, training, education, resources, position, books, time, etc.

Noam Chomsky: Unfortunately, yes, with the usual fringe exceptions one finds in just about any society—and not a fringe in some, like Turkey and

Colombia, to take two that I have discussed. It always strikes me as odd when Western intellectuals soberly discuss whether Turkey rises to the high standards of civilization of the West. There is plenty to criticize in Turkey— I've actually been under investigation by the State Security services, maybe still am, for running through some examples in talks in Turkey. But Western intellectual have a lot to learn from their Turkish counterparts, a fact that should not be easily overlooked.

In their new book, *Multitude: War and Democracy in an Age of Empire*, Michael Hardt and Antonio Negri take up some of the same questions you do in H&S about the difficulties posed in defining terrorism and a war on terror.

Noam Chomsky: I haven't read their book, but to clarify, I don't think it is difficult to define "terrorism." The official definitions seem to me quite good. It's also easy to define the term in its propagandistic usage (about 100% of total usage, and probably close to a historical universal): "Terrorism is the terrorism that *they* carry out against *us*." These definitions seem reasonably straightforward, at least as clear as those used for other terms of political discourse. It's true that no one wants to concede using the term in the propagandistic sense. But that's the problem, not a problem about defining the term.

You've stated that it is a serious analytical error to assume that terrorism is a weapon of the weak; like most methods of violence, it is overwhelmingly a weapon of the strong. It is universally condemned as a weapon of the weak because the strong control the doctrinal systems and their terror doesn't count as terror (a truism perhaps). Unlike you, however, Hardt and Negri consider how the U.S.'s overwhelming military force creates such asymmetries in first strike and response capabilities in comparison to non-nation enemies, that the asymmetries in power are themselves the problem. Hardt and Negri write:

> The technological advantage of the U.S. military not only raises social and political questions, but also poses practical military problems. Sometimes technological advantage turns out to be no advantage at all.

Noam Chomsky: The last sentence is correct. But it has no relation whatsoever to the sentence that precedes it. The fact that technological advantage may not be an advantage does not show that technological advantage poses practical military problems. That's just an error of logic. And the kind of reason why I find it hard to read their work.

Military strategists are constantly confronted by the fact that advanced technology weapons can only fulfill some specific tasks, whereas older, conventional weapons and strategies are necessary for most applications.

This is especially true in asymmetrical conflicts in which one combatant has incomparably greater means than the other or others. In a symmetrical conflict, such as that between the United States and Soviet Union during the cold war, technological advantages can be decisive—the nuclear arms race, for instance, played a major role—but in asymmetrical conflicts the application of advanced technologies are often undercut. In many cases the enemy simply does not have the kind of resources that can be threatened by the most advanced weapons; in other cases lethal force is inappropriate, and other forms of control are required.

Noam Chomsky: All correct and familiar, but so what? I don't see how this is some kind of disagreement with me. Or with just about anyone who writes on these topics. Sounds like truism.

> The fact that a dominant military power often finds itself at a disadvantage in asymmetrical conflicts has been the key to guerilla strategy at least since the bands of Spanish peasants tormented Napoleon's army: invert the relationship of military power and transform weakness into strength. The defeat of the United States in Vietnam and the Soviets in Afghanistan to incomparably inferior forces in terms of military might and technology can serve as symbols of the potential superiority of the weak in asymmetrical conflicts.

Noam Chomsky: It's true, familiar, and uncontroversial that military weakness can become strength. In Vietnam, for example, both sides recognized quite explicitly that the US was fighting a "military war" and the Vietnamese a "political war." Why is it interesting to be told this again 40 years later? Afghanistan was a quite different story. In the case of Vietnam, we may well disagree. I think it is a mistake to say, simply that the US was defeated, for reasons I discussed over 30 years ago. I tend to agree with the business world that the US had achieved its basic aims, and could easily pull out and abandon its more extreme aims. That's a partial victory not a defeat and if we look back at the early war aims as revealed in the documentary record, we see that it was a substantial victory. To call it a defeat is to assume that if the state does not achieve its maximal aims but only its basic aims, then it has been defeated. That stand, however, widespread it may be, deserves some reflection as to what it signifies.

> Guerilla attacks often rely on unpredictability: any member of the population could be a guerilla fighter and the attack can come from anywhere with unknown means. Guerillas thus force the dominant military power to live in a state of perpetual paranoia. The dominant power in such an asymmetrical conflict must adopt counterinsurgency strategies that seek not only to defeat the enemy through military means but also to control with social, political, and psychological weapons.

Noam Chomsky: This is familiar counterinsurgency doctrine from the 1950s. I don't see anything is added here.

> Today, the United States, the uncontested military superpower, has an asymmetrical relationship with all potential combatants, leaving it with vulnerable to guerilla or unconventional attacks from all quarters. The counterinsurgency strategies developed to combat and control weaker enemies in Southeast Asia and Latin America in the late twentieth century must therefore now be generalized and applied everywhere by the United States.

Noam Chomsky: Isn't this assumed almost universally? Why should we be interested?

> This situation is complicated by the fact that most of the current military engagements of the United States are unconventional conflicts or low-intensity conflicts that fall in the gray zone between war and peace. The tasks given the military alternate between making war and peacemaking, peacekeeping, peace enforcing or nation building—and indeed at times it is difficult to tell the differences between war and peace that we recognized earlier from a philosophical perspective reappears now as an element of military strategy.
> The gray zone is the zone in which counterinsurgency efforts must be effective, both combating and controlling the indefinite and often unknown enemy, but it is also the zone in which the dominant military power is most vulnerable to attack in an asymmetrical conflict. The U.S. occupation of Iraq for example, illustrates all the ambiguities of this gray zone (52-53).

Noam Chomsky: It's OK. It seems to me an inflated version of what has been conventional for many years.

2) Doesn't H and N's analysis suggest that the definition of terrorism ("the calculated use of violence or the threat of violence to attain political or religious goals through intimidation, coercion or instilling of fear") and the definition of counterterrorism/low-intensity conflict are nearly the same? If the two definitions do mirror each other what difference does it make? What implications, if any, would arise?

Noam Chomsky: That the definitions of terrorism and counterterrorism/ LIC are about the same has been pointed out a long time ago. By me, among others, in writings of the mid-80s, when the "war on terror" of the Reaganties was in full swing. The implications seem to me simple. Both are terrorism. It simply is a matter of whose ox is being gored.

In the chapter entitled "Imperial Grand Strategy," in the context of discussing Robert Kagan's concept of "anti-Americanism" you write:

> In such pronouncements, the term anti-American and its variants ("hating America," and the like) are regularly deployed to defame critics of state policy who may admire and respect the country, its culture, its achievements, indeed think it is the greatest place on earth. Nevertheless, they "hate America" and are "anti-American" on the tacit assumption that the society and its people are to be identified with state power. This usage is drawn directly from the lexicon of totalitarianism. In the former Russian empire dissidents were guilty of "anti-Sovietism." Perhaps critics of Brazil's military dictatorship were labeled "anti-Brazilian." Among people with some commitment to freedom and democracy, such attitudes are inconceivable. It would only arouse ridicule in Rome or Milan if a critic of Berlusconi's policies were condemned as "anti-Italian," though perhaps it would have passed in Mussolini's day (45-46).

The use of this rhetoric of anti-Americanism against critics of state policy is often accompanied by an invocation of Wilsonian idealism (a saintly glow of noble intent accompanying all that a powerful state does, even though clumsy execution of a particular military/policy objective may lead to some misgivings). These rhetorics drive sympathy, the core of human nature according to David Hume and Adam Smith (Rousseau too, perhaps), form the mind, replacing it with a hard-edged Real Politick. Do you have any thoughts on how education, particularly university education, aids or perhaps helps one resist the production of these rheorics? Is more "education" really the key to addressing these problematic rhetorics? Does it provide us with the means for intellectual self-defense? Or is education part of the problem? Isn't the university an important part of the Pentagon system? You've stated, for example, that the "consent" of the commissariat is crucial for the advancement of the state aim. Dissent, it would seem, must be weeded out.

Noam Chomsky: I don't feel I have anything useful to say about this. The answers to the problem can't be "more education," but rather only "decent education." More education may be harmful if it is deeper indoctrination. What's decent education? Here I can only go back to the Enlightenment and early classical liberalism, and to the modern variants of Russell, Dewey, the anarchist and workers education movements, etc. Can't try to amplify here what I've written about, mainly discussing these traditional/modern themes.

I'd be most interested, if you have a moment to explain and I haven't missed it by joining the discussion late, just what about your work with language/language structures has failed to capture your entire attention so that you have been moved to work so fully in the sphere of political activism?

Noam Chomsky: I was a political activist—that is, a concerned and engaged human being—long before I ever heard of linguistics. In fact, got into linguistics at age 17 when I was planning to drop out of college after a year because it was so boring. Someone I knew through political (that is, human) connections turned out to be a professional linguist teaching at the university that I was planning to leave—and as I later discovered, was one of the leading figures in the field. Political activism is just being a human being, I've always taken for granted, since early childhood. I've sometimes thought about how great it would be if the world would just away so I could spend all my time on intellectually challenging problems. But the world has an unpleasant way of staying there. So the question you raise has never arisen, for me at least.

I first heard your name and fame during a summer linguistics session in 1969 in Cambridge (the old one) where J. Fodor and his wife I think, were presenting all about you. It seemed to me then and now, you could have filled your whole life with that work.

Noam Chomsky: I was at the time the John Locke lecturer at Oxford, and was also giving constant talks in Oxford but university wide and at the colleges, on political issues (that is human affairs). So that was full-time commitment at Oxford, well beyond that of the faculty. I was also crossing the Atlantic four times a week because of the intensity of political activism (i.e., human affairs) here. I got to know the staff at Heathrow and Logan pretty well. I'd leave Oxford early in the morning arrive in time for afternoon and evening meetings and talks in Boston, running through the next day, take the overnight flight back to London-Oxford, and have seminars, give a Locke lecture, and meet with students in the evening at some political event they requested— because there were very few people on the faculty willing to do that.

I did fill my whole life, but with two parallel full-time careers. I've been doing it for a long time.

You have crusader/promotional energies in abundance: why not all in language?

Noam Chomsky: Because time is infinite, and the demands of being a human being seem to be too pressing just to abandon them for what is more intellectually challenging and more fun. We each make our own choices. Those have been mine.

Put another way: Some people find release from intellectual pressure in hobbies or aesthetic pleasures. But your work in political dissent is more than a mere distraction form your profession: it's a different whole additional career. Or are they linked for your specifically beyond feeling that intellectual freedom in general makes the other kind of research possible?

Noam Chomsky: Not in the least. Again, the demands of being a human being seem to me too pressing to ignore just for personal pleasure. I have never faced the questions you raise, and cannot answer for this reason.

Then extrapolating for us, is the polis for which the rest of us "intellectuals" have an obligation necessarily the global one? And who gets to keep score— or how will we know whether we've done enough?

Noam Chomsky: We will have never done enough, even if we devote our entire lives to engagement in human affairs.

I'll stop here.

The publication ("release" or "leaking" might be a better word) of the Pentagon Papers in the early 1970s provided rare insight into the mentality of those who you call the "backroom boys," a reference those who engineered the invasion and destruction of South Vietnam (McNamara, Rusk, Kissinger, etc.) You write, in *American Power and the New Mandarins*, that:

The Pentagon Papers do not deal with murder and destruction. They are not—and do not purport to be—a history of the war of the American involvement in Indochina. But they do provide much insight into the thinking and machinations of the backroom boys who bear the primary responsibility for a catastrophe of which they seem unaware. The study deals, not with war, but with the perception of the war in Washington, a rather different matter. The account is sometimes inaccurate and misleading, reflecting what the policy makers persuaded themselves to believe. The relative attention give to various phases of the conflict also reflects the perception of Washington, rather than the significance of the events themselves.

Noam Chomsky: The Pentagon Papers are of particular interest because they are not released officially, so they do not have omissions, deletions, etc. They are more like material taken from the archives of a conquered country, or like the archival material that Russia released after the Bolshevik revolution, causing a furor. Their release cause the government to release its own version, which is also quite valuable. It is rather interesting that they were rarely used or alluded to (apart from the *NY Times* extracts, far from the most revealing parts in my opinion), even in scholarship, despite their obviously unique significance and timeliness. Out of curiosity I checked with the publisher (Beacon) a few years later on sales of the fifth volume, which contained analytic essays and a detailed index. Anyone who intended to use the PP seriously would have had to have the index (this was long before electronic availability). I do not recall the exact numbers, but very few had been sold, so few that even university libraries were mostly not buying it, meaning the faculty was not asking the libraries to. By now they are supplemented with officially released material, under the standard 30-year rules.

Turning to the present, we find that the National Security Strategy gives the United States the right to preemptive attack against any nation that may conceivably, either now or in the future, be perceived as a threat to U.S. security. As you point out in *H&S*, "[t]he goal of the imperial grand strategy is to prevent any challenge to the power, position, and prestige of the United States." You were quoting, not Dick Cheney or Donald Rumsfeld but "the respected liberal elder statesman," Dean Acheson, in 1963. The basic principles of the imperial grand strategy go back to the early days of WW II.

The *Pentagon Papers* provide a retrospective on what decision-makers were thinking on Vietnam, while the government's public statements during the war were at stark odds with what's now been clearly documented. The NSS provides a window into the future: "Today the United States enjoys a position of unparalleled military strength and great economic and political influence. In keeping with our heritage and our principles, we do not use our strength to press for unilateral advantage. We seek instead to create a balance of power that favors human freedom: conditions in which all nations and societies can choose for themselves that rewards and challenges of political and economic liberty. In a world that is safe, people will be able to make their own lives better. We will defend the peace by fighting terrorists and tyrants. We will preserve the the peace by building good relations among the great powers. We will extend the peace by building good relations among the great powers. We will extend the peace by encouraging freed and open societies on every planet.

Noam Chomsky: This is the kind of boilerplate that every government, even the most grotesque, releases all the time. We should pay as much as attention to it as we did to the declarations of Stalin about protecting democracy and justice, in accord with the traditional practice of the Kremlin.

The NSS was released in September of 2002. I think it's fair to say, two years later, that the peace has not been secured either at home or abroad. For obvious reasons, the U.S. government tried to subject those who leaked the Pentagon Paper to criminal prosecution. The NSS, on the other hand, is widely distributed and promoted, a demonstration that Wilsonian idealism know no bounds.

Noam Chomsky: The NSS did in fact elicit harsh criticism, from right within the foreign policy elite—journals like *Foreign Affairs*, for example. But mostly on style, not substance, and on the brazenness of the pronouncements about the plan to dominate the world, by force if necessary. Fine doctrine, but it should be kept in the president's backpocket. I've written about the reaction in the "Afterword" to the paperback edition of *Hegemony or Survival*, and won't repeat. However, passages like the one you quote are just the routine self-praise that is reflexive in material released to the public.

Are today's Bush's, Cheney's, Rumsfelds, Powells, Perles, Wolfowitzs merely yesterday's Rusks McNamaras, and Kissingers? In other words doesn't an honest student of history tell us that the grand imperial strategy commitment to those principles stays the same. You've seemingly traced this sort of governmental rhetoric and course of action from American Power and that New Mandarins through *H&S*. Are you comfortable with what I've described here?

Noam Chomsky: The planning spectrum is fairly narrow. On this I agree with superhawks like Andrew Bacevich, who basically favors it because America is the "vanguard," etc. I think he goes a bit overboard, and it is not as narrow as he claims. Within the spectrum there are differences, in substance and style (which is not to be discounted), and in actions. I agree with mainstream critics who regard the Cheney-Rumsfeld-Wolfwitz-etc. crew as a radical reactionary minority, and dangerous one.

U.S. political, military, and economic support for Israel AFTER the 1967 Arab-Israeli war skyrocketed because Israel—by defeating Egypt's Nasser and the rising threat of Arab nationalism—proved itself to be a strategic asset in the Middle East region. You and Norman argue Israel's might and military performance in '67 not its weakness led to the creation of the "special relationship" between it and the U.S., i.e. Israel could be the U.S.'s "cop on the beat" in the region, receiving (in turn) vast political, military, and economic support; as it had done for the last thirty-seven years. Norman makes a curious statement in *The Holocaust Industry* about your and Hannah Arendt's pre-1967 relationship to Israel. He writes the following on p. 19 of *The Holocaust Industry*, in the context of discussing how "American Jewish intellectuals proved especially indifferent to Israel's fate" prior to 1967: "Telling irony: just about the only two public intellectuals who had forged a bond with Israel before June 1967 were Hannah Arendt and Noam Chomksy." Would you mind commenting on what appears to be a paradox? You and Arendt have been viewed and will be viewed as two of Israel's harshest critics; yet Norman states that this was far from the case thirty-seven years ago. Of course, one can be a critic of a state's policies, while admiring its people and cultural achievements. Trivial point, but often neglected. What was your intellectual stance toward Israel pre-1967 and why did you change it?

Noam Chomsky: Norman says we "forged a bond with Israel," not that we were supportive of the state's policies. In fact, part of the bond was that we (I think I can speak for Arendt in this respect) were critical of the state's policies, often harshly so. Neither of us, I suppose, was particularly critical of many states that we didn't care that much about.

My bond with the pre-state Yishuv goes back to early childhood, and though I was opposed to the idea of a Jewish state (as I still am), that was within the framework of the Zionist movement, pre-1948. I was very active in the Zionist youth movements, but associated with people and groups who favored a binationalist state, based on Arab-Jewish cooperation in a collective-based more or less libertarian socialist society. Maybe a dream, maybe not. Anyway, it was moot by 1948. My own personal bond with Israel remained and still does. My wife and I lived there briefly came close to staying on, maybe prematurely. I felt that once established Israel should have the same rights of any state within the international system, nothing more, nothing less—and certainly no unique right to be free from the kind of criticism that should be directed against any system of power, in the light of its own particular circumstances.

There's nothing paradoxical about having a bond to a country while being highly critical of state practices when they merit criticism, and even engaging in resistance to them when that is appropriate. That's also my relation to this country.

Of course, we should never succumb to the pathology of identifying the society, people, culture—the "country," loosely speaking—with the state authorities or even power systems. That's the totalitarian ideal, to be dismissed with contempt by free people. In fact, apart from the concept "anti-America" or "un-American," the concept is pretty well restricted to totalitarian states, military dictatorships, and the like. And as anyone with a bond to Jewish culture should know, the usage traces right back to the Bible, in the depraved sense.

Pretext's next reinterview is with Norman G. Finkelstein, author of *Image and Reality in the Israel-Palestine Conflict*, *The Holocaust Industry: A Personal Account of the Intifada Years*, and *A Nation on Trial: The Goldhagen Thesis and Historical Truth*. In an essay entitled "The Fate of an Honest Intellectual" (printed in *Understanding Power: The Indispensable Chomsky*, Peter R. Mitchell and John Schoeffel, Ed., p. 246-250) you describe the extraordinary circumstances that brought Finkelstein's name to your attention in 1984.

The publication of Joan Peters' *From Time Immemorial: The Origins of the Arab-Jewish Conflict over Palestine* in 1984 brought with it accolades from some leading figures on the U.S. intellectual scene.

Noam Chomsky: That's a bit misleading. It had hundreds of rave reviews from leading intellectuals, and scarcely a word of criticism—except in Israel. Finkelstein review the reaction to this work, which finally was published.

The book itself purported to demonstrate that Palestinians were recent immigrants around what is now present day Israel and were not in what was Palestine from time immemorial. As a consequence, Peters argues, the dispossession of the Palestinians wasn't really a dispossession but merely an unfortunate dislocation of recent arrivals who came to the area, hoping to benefit from Jewish prosperity; hence there should be no controversy about or moral issue around the current 3.5 million Palestinian refugees, who are "only the unfortunate victims of Arab propaganda that has used the Palestinian refugee problem as a political football."

Finkelstein, a careful researcher and at that time a graduate student at Princeton in Politics read through the book and found some surprising things about it. First of all, Peters badly mishandled the demographic evidence that formed the basis for her case. She misrepresented and mangled contentions of the historical documents (The Hope-Simpson Report among them), claiming that all of the "recent" Palestinian arrivals had not been adequately accounted for and that most of the 750,000 Palestinians that were expelled in 1948 were really recent arrivals. Finkelstein even raised questions about whether or not Peters actually wrote the book, or whether it was a bad agency job, because so much was clearly wrong with it. *From Time Immemorial* for example, places the 13-th century figure, Makrizi, in the 19th century (See Alexander Cockburn "From Lies Immemorial," *The Nation*, October 13th, 1984).

Well, Finkelstein—amazed that such a poorly written book was receiving such rave reviews—wrote to about thirty different scholars around the country about what he found in Peter' book. He heard back from one person: you, Noam Chomsky. You told him that he had, indeed, hit upon something pretty remarkable and that there was probably a lot more to the story. You also told him the issue, of whether or not a whole people could be relegated to the dustbin of history, as "recent immigrants" was probably a pretty important issue (there could, as a consequence, be no "Palestinian Question"), but that since so many luminaries had attached their names and reputations to Peters' book Finkelstein would only get himself into a lot of trouble by exposing some very important people as outright frauds. At that time, he didn't believe you; he just kept on and on, wondering why he couldn't get his findings published. Finally, he was able to get something published in *In These Times*, with your help. At that point, Finkelstein's professors stopped talking to him, wouldn't read his work, and refused even to meet with him. As you pointed out, "This is Princeton. Supposed to be a serious place."

You sent Finkelstein's findings to people you knew in England; they were ready when the book appeared there—it was just demolished. Well, the book was also demolished in Israel, and seen as a bad propaganda effort. Until last year, the book wasn't mentioned in polite company, especially among those in the know. Last September, Finkelstein had an interesting debate with a member of the Harvard Law School faculty that sort of went away. Sure enough, Joan Peters' *From Time Immemorial* found itself right back in the spotlight.

In this essay, "The Fate of an Honest Intellectual," you state that if Finkelstein had done what he was told (i.e. dropped the Peters' crusade and the Palestinian refugee question) he'd be a big professor somewhere today. In fact, in the middle of the whole affair, big professors called Finkelstein up and said, "Call off your crusade; we'll get you a job, we'll take care of you. A lot of books out there are frauds. No one really cares. Come on, just let it go." Well, he didn't let it go. Finkelstein, in his mid fifties, is currently an assistant professor of political science at DePaul University in Chicago with four internationally acclaimed books to his credit. Even graduate students who pursue Finkelstein's employment difficulties within the political science department at Hunter College (CUNY), even as a controversy to be studied, find themselves running into obstacles. What does the Finkelstein case tell us about how serious the left-liberal community in the United States is when it comes to confronting its complicity in affairs of state?

Noam Chomsky: I think it speaks for itself.

The whole controversy seems to give credence to Seville from the 17ᵗʰ century who wrote: "A man that should call everything by its right name would hardly pass the streets without being knocked down as a common enemy." The hatred and revulsion he arouses are very much to his credit. You conclude the essay, "The Fate of an Honest Intellectual," with the following

Still, in the universities or in any other institution, you can often find some dissident hanging around the woodwork—and they can survive in one fashion or another, particularly if they get community support. But if they become too disruptive or too obstreperous—or you know, too effective— they're likely to be kicked out. The standard thing, though, is that they won't make it within the mainstream institutions in the first place, particularly if they were that way when they were young—they'll simply be weeded out somewhere along the line. So in most cases, the people who make it through the institutions are able to remain in them have already internalized the right kinds of beliefs: it's not a problem for them to be obedient, they already are obedient, that's how they got here. And that's pretty much how the ideological control system perpetuates itself in the schools—that's the basic story of how it operates I think (247-248).

Noam Chomsky: Note that this is informal discussion, in a group that probably didn't even know it was being recorded. As such, it is oversimplified. I think the general drift is correct but if I were to write an article about it, I wouldn't put it just this way.

So, is this your message, then that honest intellectuals may make it in the university, but they are going to have a rough time of it?

Noam Chomsky: That there will be a tendency in that direction is only to be expected, particularly in the more ideological disciplines. But it isn't mechanical, and many have found it possible to survive with integrity.

Finkelstein Re/Interview Begins

Question: I guess it's only appropriate to being your reinterview where Noam's left off; so, let's begin with Joan Peters' book, *From Time Immemorial*. This book came to your attention in 1984 when you were working on your Ph.D. dissertation at Princeton on "Land and Zionism". Since I've already stated what basically happened to your academic career as a consequence of your exposure of the Peters' book, I won't repeat it here. If others have specific questions about what happened to you at Princeton and beyond, they can simply ask you directly. For those who want all the details on the Peters' book and your careful analysis of it, they can turn to chapter 2 of your *Image and Reality in the Israel-Palestine* conflict.

Last September, you engaged in an interesting exchange with Alan M. Dershowitz on Democracy Now, upon the publication of Dershowitz's new book, *The Case for Israel*. Amy Goodman found herself in the unenviable position of moderating a discussion between Jewish Americans who clearly hold starkly different views on the conflict. The debate can be found at http://www.democracynow.org/article.pl?sid=3/09/24/1730205. You alleged at that time, and still allege, that Dershowitz unabashedly plagiarized from Peters *From Time Immemorial*, becoming so confused in his massive borrowings from Peters, that he attributed Peters' phrase "turnspeak" to George Orwell, who, as all good readers of Orwell know, coined the phrase "Newspeak". In your estimation, the plagiarism isn't really the most telling issue, however; it as Dershowitz's "massive borrowings from a fraud to construct a fraud. Your specific allegations can be found at http:www.normanfinklestein.com/id141.htm.

Dershowitz's book contained specific attacks against Noam Chomsky and the late Edward Said, two of the most persistent critics of the Israeli occupation. Dershowitz, invoking the example of Robert Faurisson, claimed that professors such as Chomsky often commit a type of educational malpractice in the "fraudulent manufacturing of false anti-history," "deliberately misinforming, miseducating, and misdirecting the public" about the Middle East; actions "for which professors are rightly fired, not because their views are controversial, but because they are violating the most basic canons of historical scholarship," just as Faurisson committed educational malpractice in denying the existence of Nazi gas chambers. You claim, using Dershowitz's own standard, that *The Case for Israel* is "a collection of fraud, fabrication, and nonsense" and the he should be dismissed from Harvard Law School for "a hoax that he plagiarized from another fraud". You even went so far to suggest that Dershowitz may not have written the book and that the honorable thing for him to do is to say, "I didn't write it, I didn't have time to read it."

Norman Finkelstein: You have asked many questions, and it would be difficult to answer all, or even several, of them in a single response. Allow me

to then limit myself to the first question: What accounts for the determined effort to suppress exposure of the Peters fraud? The answer would seem to be quite straightforward. Peters herself was a nobody, and almost certainly didn't write *From Time Immemorial*. There was clearly no vested interest in protecting her. The real stakes were all those who had endorsed the book, protecting their reputations. Saul Bellow, Elie Wiesel, Barbara Tuchman, Lucy Dawidowicz all wrote breathless comments. When it was published the commentary reached comic heights. Probably the most memorable was Martin Peretz's claim in *The New Republic*, the magazine he published and edited, that Peters' book didn't contain a single factual error and that, if read, it would change the history of the future (whatever that means). So, now all these pundits were on record praising to high heaven a transparent fraud, which even some obscure graduate student was—without their vaunted expertise—able to detect. Actually, my own guess is that they really believed Peters's book, much like fellow-travelers of the Communist party believed Soviet Russia could do no wrong in the 1930s. The analogy is not quite right, however. The Communists and fellow-travelers had real ideals, however corrupted over time, and made real sacrifices. The likes of Peretz and Bellow, not to mention the execrable Wiesel, are just calculating charlatans.

Question: Why, in your estimation, did Dershowitz's book receive such generally positive reviews upon its publication in light of the serious questions raised about its scholarly apparatus? Why, in light of your documentation of how flimsy the scholarly apparatus of Dershowitz's book, is hasn't there been any strong criticism of Dershowitz of the book? Just last year, Dershowitz claimed, in an article in the *Congressional Monthly*, that the late Edward Said represented a more menacing threat to peace and the peace process than did Meir Kahane because the former was more influential, and had a wider audience, than the latter. Dershowitz also calls for the demolition of Palestinian villages in response to Palestinian suicide bombings; the village would be chosen at random by a computer and the inhabitants would have a short time in which to leave. His recommendation is in clear violation of international law and the Fourth Geneva Convention; all of this from a law professor. Did Larry Summers, Harvard University's President, ever respond to your criticisms of Dershowitz?

Norman Finkelstein: It's not altogether a coincidence that the Amazon.com website typically brackets *The Case for Israel* with Joan Peters's *From Time Immemorial*. Peters's book was published in 1984, after Israel invaded Lebanon and suffered its first public relations debacle. Dershowitz's book was published in 2003, after the start of the second intifada when Israel suffered another major p.r. disaster. Both books served the same basic purpose of shoring up morale among the Zionist faithful. Their *modus operandi* was likewise identical: in guise of a scholarly tract, each grossly falsified the documentary record. To be sure, in Dershowitz's case, this depiction only applies on those rare occasions when he adduces any evidence at all: while

Peters's forte was mangling primary documents. Dershowitz's is citing absurd "sources" or fabricating claims out of whole cloth. Leaning on his academic pedigree to wow readers and in lieu of any supporting evidence he typically clinches an argument with rhetorical flourishes like "This is a simple fact not subject to reasonable dispute" (p. 7), or "There can be no reasonable disagreement about the basic facts" (p. 8), or "This is simply historical fact" (p. 75), or "These are incontrovertible historical facts not subject to reasonable dispute" (p. 77), and on and on—invariably signalling that the assertion is sheer rubbish. Regarding his lecture tour for *The Case for Israel*, Dershowitz reports, "Whenever I make a speech, the most common phrase I hear from students afterward is, "We didn't know." One reason perhaps is that what he claims never happened. During a debate on his book, Dershowitz offered to "give $10,000 to the PLO" if his interlocutor (or anyone else) could "find a historical fact in my book that you can prove to be false." The genuine challenge is to unearth any historical fact in *The Case for Israel*.

Dershowitz will be protected from scrutiny just like Peters was, for the same reasons: it's for the cause; and for the cause, anything goes.

Question: I have admired the complexity of your arguments and the insistence with which you make them; you were kind to me as a graduate student (interested in writing your work in a chapter eventually excised from my dissertation).

I must ask a question about the forum for the kinds of arguments made in Holocaust studies.

Typically, academic ideas are floated as trial balloons in peer-reviewed journal articles, then revised and floated again as books. But much of the energy in recent Holocaust debates happen in non-peer-reviewed venues.

The classic example of this, in rhetorical studies, in the Searle-Derrida exchange, in which Searle's last "reply" to Derrida was not published in a peer reviewed journal, but instead in the *New York Review Books*. Similar moves happen in Holocaust debate.

When reflecting on responses to Goldhagen, we find two full volumes of responses republishing (almost entirely) book reviews which are not peer reviewed. Arguments are advanced in these book reviews that clearly go beyond the review of the actual book.

I am curious—Holocaust studies is by its nature interdisciplinary (the primary reason I stepped back from writing about it in my dissertation was fear of being unable to master the relevant disciplines). So perhaps the dynamic of peer review wouldn't work anyway. Perhaps the energy of the topic encourages writing for non-peer reviewed genres and publications.

But what role does publication through peer review have in advancing the issues you discuss, and what role does publication through non-peer-reviewed genres and publications have? As a rhetor reaching an audience and as one responding to the works of others, what do you see as the plusses and minuses of the different mechanisms for publication?

Norman Finkelstein: In my opinion this is an important question, and point up one of the egregious features of current academic life. To begin with, there's no academic discipline called Holocaust Studies. The very notion of it is preposterous: Imagine if the Irish proposed a discipline called "Potato Famine Studies," or even the Japanese proposing "Hiroshima Studies." They would immediately be seen as nonsensical. A single historical event, however horrific, cannot define a field: an area of inquiry, yes; a discipline, no. My goodness, it's impossible to conceive even an African-American Slavery Studies, and that lasted longer than the Nazi holocaust. Yet, nonsense has reached such summits that some universities actually give a Master's in Holocaust Studies. What can that possibly mean? Turning now to the peer review process, my own impression is that, even if this "quality control" mechanism were in place, it wouldn't help much; I have no doubt that Goldhagen's book would have passed through, even if it is the worst sort of Holo-porn. In fact, both in Holocaust Studies and Israel-Palestine Studies, the usual quality control mechanisms simply don't function. Consider the latest example. Alan Dershowitz claims to have written *The Case for Israel*. Assuming for argument's sake that he did (although it is easy to demonstrate that he didn't), the book is sheer rubbish from start to finish. This did not prevent it from excellent reviews in *The Times* and *The Boston Globe*. I'm sure it would have passed any peer review test. Here's the problem: these fields have been so corrupted by politics that the worst sorts of frauds get huge play in the media and the academy.

Question: Let me redirect, slightly away from the political—though I am persuaded by your arguments here, I am young enough an academic to hope for better in our academic institutions.

I agree with your statements about Holocaust Studies, but worry—the idea of "Holocaust Studies" as a discipline serves, to me, at least, one useful function. It yokes the literary-memoir aspects of writers about the Holocaust to the historical writers, and so provides a potential mechanism for checking the excesses of one against the other.

Too often, I see high school teachers teach "Holocaust Literature" with a background only in Holocaust Literature—not in historical writings about the Holocaust or anti-Semitism or German or Polish history. To learn about the Holocaust only from novels, and then to teach only the novels and memoirs troubles me. (An example to make my point, if not overstate it.

Everyone who teaches Wiesel should be forced to read Browning in other words, to enrich and to contextualize the novel in light of the historical research.

If there is no "Holocaust Studies," then our academic institutions leave us with "Holocaust Literature" and "Holocaust History," divorced, no?

Norman Finkelstein: Most history courses nowadays include the use of memoirs as a supplement to conventional research. That, to me, isn't the main problem. Rather, just like so much of the scholarship is trash, many of the memoirs are nonsense, and in a couple of cases, literally frauds. Generally speaking, the useful memoirs were those published right after the war, when there was no market for them, and people wrote only because they had something important to say and wanted the world to know. The memoirs I've found most affecting and insightful include Primo Levi's, which he wrote in 1946 (I think), and Ella Lingens-Reiner's *Prisoners of Fear*—long out of print, but a true classic.

Question: You've stated that only the son of Holocaust survivors could have written this book. *The Holocaust Industry: The Exploitation of Jewish Suffering.* Some claim you've inappropriately used your identity as a Jew and as the son of holocaust survivors to immunize yourself against criticism. In other words, you've wrapped yourself in your identity, making claims about the abuse of holocaust representation, Israel's treatment of the Palestinians, American-Jewish life, etc., that are wholly out of proportion to reality. The usual slanders, that you're a self-hating Jew and are anti-Semitic, can't stick to you as effectively as they might stick to others. If the "fan" mail on your website is an indication, some appreciate your efforts, while others wish you'd just disappear.

In her relatively recent book, *Precarious Life*, Judith Butler writes:

One is threatened with the label, "anti-Semitic," in the same way that within the U.S., to oppose the most recent US wars earns one the label of "traitor," or "terrorist sympathizer" or, indeed, "treasonous." These are threats with profound psychological consequences. They seek to control political behavior by imposing unbearable, stigmatized modes of identification, which most people will want more than anything to avoid identification with. Fearing the identification, they fail to speak out. But such threats of stigmatization can and must be weathered, and this can only be done with the support of other actors, other who speak with you, and against the threat that seeks to silence political speech (127).

Unprecedented efforts were made to block Holt's publication of your and Bettina Birn's book, *A Nation on Trial: The Goldhagen Thesis and Historical Truth*, a book that claims Goldhagen's thesis (that ordinary Germans were driven by an eliminationist anti-Semitism and were simply waiting for Hitler's rise to power to unleash it) is pure nonsense. When he intervened with Holt publishing company's president Michael Naumann, in an attempt to block the publication of *A Nation on Trial*, Leon Wieseltier, editor of *The New Republic*, claimed, "You don't know who Finkelstein is. He's poison, he's a disgusting self-hating Jew, he's something you find under a rock." Here is how Nauman and Segeve describe what transpired upon *A Nation on Trial*'s publication:

> I have never experienced, Nauman later recalled, "a similar attempt of interested parties to publicly cast a shadow over an upcoming publication." The prominent Israeli historian and journalist, Tom Segev observed *Haaretz* that the campaign verged on "cultural terrorism" (66).

ADL head, Abe Foxman, while calling on Holt to drop the publication of the book stated: "The issue . . . is not whether Goldhagen's thesis is right or wrong but what is 'legitimate criticism' and what goes beyond the pale" (66). However, Metropolitan associate publisher, Sara Bershtel replied, "Whether Goldhagen's thesis is right or wrong is precisely the issue" (*Holocaust Industry*, 66). You've claimed that Daniel Goldhagen is one of the poster boys of the Holocaust Industry, promoted by Elie Weisel and the *NY Times*, even though his work—in your, Birn's, and Hilberg's estimation—falls far short of a credible academic study.

You've claimed (as has Hilberg) that no one serving on Goldhagen's dissertation committee at Harvard's history department was an expert on the Holocaust. Despite this, the *NY Times* wrote this about *Hitler's Willing Executioners*:

> "Masterly . . . One of those rare new works that merit the appellation landmark."

In short, you and Hilberg have identified a quality-control problem. But is this really unique to Holocaust scholarship? Can't the same be said about many areas of academic work? Or are you claiming these are calculated efforts with clear political agendas/goals? If so, aren't you concocting a conspiracy theory and identifying evidence that suits your thesis? For example, you write:

> Consider, finally the pattern. Wiesel and Gutman (director of Yad Vashem) supported Goldhagen; Wiesel supported Kosinski (author of The *Painted Bird*: Gutman and Goldhagen supported Wilkominski (author of *Fragments*, later proven to be a hoaxer). Connect the players: this is Holocaust literature (65).

As my previous question intimated, you are describing what "you" (Hilberg has expressed similar concerns in less sweeping terms) see as a big pattern of scholarly, political, and economic abuse (you connect Goldhagen, Wiesel, Yad Vashem, the Clinton administration, George Pataki, Burt Neuborne, Israel Singer, Edgar Bronfman, Elie Wiesel, Alfonse D'Amato, Gerald Feldman, The *NY Times*, the *New Republic*, Harvard University, Holocaust reparations, swelling the numbers of holocaust survivors, sowing fears over the "new" anti-Semitism, etc. together) that, if I understand your arguments, has a single goal: the immunization of Israel against criticism in the repression of the Palestinians. Why did you choose the word, "industry," to describe all of these events/phenomena, which are possibly distinct and unrelated? Isn't your thesis reminiscent of the *Protocols of the Elders of Zion*? Is it all so simple? Perhaps I've oversimplified your arguments in *HI*.

Norman Finkelstein: The first question is a composite of multiple, not inherently related, sub-questions. I will try to answer a couple of them. It's uncontroversial among sane people that the epithets "anti-Semitic," "self-hating Jew" and "Holocaust denier" are flung with great abandon and little substance by Israel's apologists. Personally, I think Butler overdoes it in the kind of "hurt" these epithets inflict. Who could possibly give a moment's notice to what Anti-Defamation League national director Abraham Foxman thinks about anything—except perhaps breaking kneecaps, an area where he no doubt can claim real expertise? On a personal note again, the notion that I'm a Holocaust denier is so ludicrous as to deny belief. Not because both my parents survived the Nazi concentration camps—it's still conceivable for someone with that family genealogy to be so warped as to deny the Nazi holocaust—but rather because there's no topic I return to so frequently. As I told Amy Goodman, the host of *Democracy Now* and an old and dear friend, when she put a similar question to me, if anything I should be faulted for being a "Holocaust affirmer" since I never stop talking about the holocaust. Regarding the charge that I am a conspiracy theorist, it seems that a basic distinction needs to be made between being a conspiracy theorist on the one hand, and recognizing that people conspire on the other. Take for example Adam Smith's *The Wealth of Nations*. Smith writes at one point that capitalists "seldom meet together, even for merriment and diversion, but the conversation ends in a conspiracy against the public, or on some contrivance to raise prices." Does this make Smith a conspiracy theorist, or is he simply acknowledging a commonplace of business life? American Jews exercise a disproportionate influence in the film and publishing industries. No one, not even Foxman, denies this. It would be a surprise if they didn't use this power to advance an ethnic agenda. In fact, they always have. That's why Hollywood, largely a Jewish creation, depicted all the mobsters as Italian while many, perhaps most, were Jews! And the reason we're now so critical of what called American history is because WASPs wrote it in a way that privileged white males. Is this a conspiracy theory? It's hard to understand why, when you make these same elementary observations about the uses (and abuses) of ethnic Jewish power it's called a "conspiracy theory"—except as a desperate means to a discredit the obvious.

Question: A great deal of recent work in historiography (Hayden White) and critical theory (LaCapra, Leys, Laub, Caruth, Agamben, etc.) suggests that the Holocaust is an unrepresentable event, something outside of narrative and language, a trauma that needs a new language/idio for its recuperation and articulation (See, for example, *Probing the Limits of Representation*, Saul Friedlander, Ed.). You claim that the holocaust must be returned to as rational object of inquiry. How can something, which represents the epitome of irrational behavior, be approached rationally? As Chomsky has written, the Holocaust is "the greatest collective outburst of insanity." Aren't you privileging the concept of the "rational"? Do you have any use for the theoretical figures I mentioned in the first sentence?

You attack the concept of memory in the early chapters of *HI*, claiming that the obligatory academic nod toward Halbwachs, trauma, memory, transference has become somewhat obscene, a testament to the effectiveness of academic obfuscation. You also attack Elie Wiesel as the high priest of Holocaust memory, who for a handsome fee, will unlock the mysteries of the unrepresentable. The "shelves and shelves of schlock" you reference use "memory," "trauma," "transference," and "the differend" to unpack the inherent complexities of historical events. When addressing the motivations of actors and observers within a complex event such as the rise of the Third Reich and the commission of the holocaust, aren't these concepts necessary? Daniel Goldhagen, whose *Hitler's Willing Executioners* you've ridiculed in print, makes the distinction between eliminationist and functionalist anti-Semitism. The former focuses upon the motivations of individual actors, while latter zeroes in on the structural dimensions of institutions and the larger society. Goldhagen's "breakthrough" identified how the supposed pathological hatred or ordinary Germans, their eliminationist anti-Semitism awaited a proper moment to unleash itself upon the Jews of Central and Eastern Europe.

The eliminationist anti-Semitism is juxtaposed against the "bureaucratic efficiency" argument: The silence, complicity, and fear of those serving in German institutions (Eichmann, for example) led to the conditions of possibility for the Nazi genocide. This is essentially Hannah Arendt's "banality of evil argument"; something you apparently find much more convincing than the eliminationist argument.

Norman Finkelstein: Most acts of human iniquity are incomprehensible to me. This past week in Gaza a 12-year old girl carrying her book bag on her way to school was shot dead by Israeli soldiers. Lying dead (or wounded)

on the ground, the Israeli company commander came along and emptied his rifle of 20 more bullets into her skull. For some people this doesn't post any problem of "representation" (what that stupid word means); only the Holocaust does. Each year the atomic bombing of Hiroshima is reenacted in an American town (forgot the name) to much cheers and applause. This mentality poses not problems of "representation"; only the Holocaust does. Check out David Stannard's book entitled *American Holocaust*. There's a long chapter on the kinds of pathological brutalities inflicted on Native Americans by the likes of Andrew Jackson, who graces our currency.

To my mind, all this talk about the uniqueness of the Nazi holocaust is just ethnic chauvinism. What makes the brutality of the Nazi holocaust unique is that it was inflicted on Jews, who were so cultured. For the rest, folks like LaCapra are complete imbeciles who want to cash in on a ready market. He knows nothing about the Nazi holocaust, probably read four books on the subject and thinks he's an expert. Every grand tete is supposed to weigh in with pensées on the subject. It's a rite of passage to conferences, wine-and-cheese parties and the like. I once thumbed through the Saul Friedlander book you refer to. I've not seen so much gibberish since I read Althusser, squandering the flower of my youth. My advice is, Stay away from this nonsense. I don't know what it means to say that I am "privileging the concept of the rational." What should I be doing? Providing mental scribbles a la Wiesel and LaCapra and sighing in anguish? My late mother, may she rest in peace, used to call it, From empty to vacuum.

Question: I have been reading the posts from both Chomsky and Finkelstein with interest, and what strikes me the most is the paucity of participation in this particular PRETEXT interview. I'm assuming that most people out there are not responding for the same reason that I am. There is a great deal of truth to the arguments put forward by Finkelstein and Chomsky, but there's also a sort of glib self-righteousness that mars the quality of the argument. Whatever the logic of the Israeli commander who "finished off" the girl in Gaza, it comes in the context of a conflict that has seen escalating acts of terror on both sides. The bombings of Hiroshima and German cities like Hamburg and Dresden came in a similar context. Finkelstein is correct to critique those intellectuals that argue for the unrepresentable nature of the Holocaust but he downplays the uniqueness of the Holocaust (at least, in the text below). It was not just the Jews who were supposed to be so cultured, but the Germans, and thus the Holocaust strikes at the very notion of superiority of Western culture and the idea of progress. It is true that Andrew Jackson was guilty of ethnic cleansing and has not business gracing U.S. currency (except in some ironic and sick way) but Finkelstein's dismissal of "complete imbeciles" who write "gibberish" is just too facile for my taste, and I suspect, for most of the people on this list (even if he's right). Whatever happened to civil discourse?

I harbored the same feelings about Wiesel that Finkelstein does, but given the presence of Mel Gibson's dad and the *Journal of Historical Review*, why the tone? Who's the audience? Finkelstein, in his email, has brought up his mother again as ethos, but the Holocaust is a legitimate subject for intellectual inquiry, not merely something "owned" by the survivors or their children. I have taught Art Spiegleman's *MAUS* several times, and what strikes me as the genius of that work is its self-consciousness about representation and the complexity of its subject (since Vladek is in many ways the caricature of the economic Jew). The Holocaust may be no more evil than the Israelis in Gaza or the Trail of Tears, but the logic of it is far more complex, given the shared culture of the victims and victimizers. Representations of victimhood, like Wiesel's *Night*, are clearly inadequate, but how does one connect that work with something like Hillel Levin's *The Economic Origins of Anti-Semitism* in a coherent way? Instead of merely dissing Friedlander, can't we point to texts that adequately represent the Holocaust?

Norman Finkelstein: Several comments have been posted regarding my remarks. I can't address each issue individually, so I'll try to sort out the salient points of contention. ____ seems not to understand what's at issue in Holocaust industry claims about the Nazi holocaust. She compares the problems of "representation" regarding the atomic bombing of Hiroshima with those regarding the Nazi extermination. This truly is mixing apples and oranges. No one has ever claimed there are problems of representation regarding the atomic bombing; the problem is interpretation of the fact. I've never heard any historian claim that there's no language available to depict what happened—or any of the other literally nonsense formulations bandied about in Holocaust literature. She also seems to doubt that the atomic bombing could be celebrated in our culture. I suggest that she visit any of the numerous, and utterly respectable, Enola Gay websites where she can purchase handsome souvenirs of the plane and bomb used to annihilate Hiroshima. What would she think of a mainstream German website vending memorabilia paperweights of Treblinka? Next she tells us that "The Holocaust was unique" but provides no argument. She's free to her opinion, of course, but without a reasoned argument, I'm afraid it's worthless. Not to be faulted for political incorrectness, she adds that American slavery from 1830 to 1865 was unique. Why she never says, but it's also utterly irrelevant. Does any serious scholar make the uniqueness of American slavery a point de principe—or, rather the contrary, isn't the comparative study of American slavery a mainstay of the field? Consider Holocaust studies by comparison. The main journal of this ludicrous field is called Holocaust and Genocide Studies—i.e., there's the Holocaust and then there's everything else. She also finds shocking that cultured people should commit such heinous crimes. Jefferson, Adams, Madison, and Washington certainly didn't suffer from a lack of culture, which didn't prevent them from slaughtering the native population and enslaving the African one.

____ seems to suggest that pumping 20 bullets into a dying 13-year-old girl's skull is more understandable in the context of an ongoing terroristic war than what happened in the Nazi holocaust. So, let's look at the comparison. During the peacetime years of the Nazi regime (1933–9), the main legislative enactments were the Nuremberg laws, which denied Jews citizenship and prohibited miscegenation between Jewish and non-Jewish Germans. These laws pretty much resembled the laws on the books of the American South, which incidentally weren't overturned until the mid 1960s. The main outburst of violence against Jews in prewar Nazi Germany, Kristallnacht, was, according to all the data we have available, largely unpopular among Germans. Compare the lynchings in the American South (completely unthinkable in prewar Nazi Germany), which were public festivals, with schools and factories let out early, families organizing picnics to watch the bod mutilated and body parts subsequently sold to the highest bidder. (It bears recalling the obvious that those lynched shared a common culture with the lynchers, just as in Germany, nothing unique there.) The actual extermination of the Jews and attendant malignant indifference of the Germans began during the war, the terror bombings and privations, etc. So, does the German reaction become more "understandable"—but then what happens to all this talk of uniqueness? It takes an unusually paranoid imagination to believe that Mel Gibson's father and the *Journal of Historical Review* pose a significant political or intellectual threat in the U.S. Many Jews like to pretend that they are victims, always under the threat of another Holocaust—it's very convenient to turn yourself into a victim when the Palestinians are being brutally repressed. I do not know what this sentence, "Finkelstein.. has brought up his mother again as ethos," means? Why can't people write in English? Perhaps one reason my student papers are so awful is that their teachers can't write. I quoted a piece of Polish folk wisdom that my later mother frequently cited. Period. Full stop. Finally, it was among my most intellectually gratifying experiences to read all the excellent scholarship on the Nazi holocaust in preparation for my book (co-authored with Ruth Bettina Birn). *A Nation on Trial: The Goldhagen Thesis and Historical Truth*. It happened, however, that as Raul Hilberg has pointed out, this excellent scholarship is not most being produced by German scholars.

I have no idea what ____ is talking about—although it reminds me why a friend sent me an obituary for Derrida under the heading line—"Finally some good news."

Norman Finkelstein: One reason for the right-wing's ascendancy in the United States is that, at any rate, in some departments, and especially those where I can lay reasonable claim to personal and professional knowledge, what reactionaries have to say, however painful it might be to confess, contains a grain, and then some, of truth. It is frequently alleged in these right-wing quarters that universities have been effectively hijacked by semi-literate, politically correct blowhards spouting an incomprehensible and vacuous jargon, not to mention one with the tonal aesthetic of a tin can, which, rather than be a badge or shame, is for these post-whatevers a point of preening and, what's yet more a matter commanding consternation among those still preserving a jot of rationality, for them a signifier of superiority to the common herd who, God forbid, make themselves generally understood.

I am old enough to have passed through multiple of these epochs in non-thought. When I was coming of age politically, Althusser and his acolytes like Poulantzas were all the rage. Who can forget that prose that induced the same aesthetic effect as it was chewed over in the mind as tin foil does when chewed over in a mouth filled with cavities? This fashion passed expeditiously enough when Poulantzas jumped off a towering edifice (showing enough consideration for humanity by, reportedly, carrying his books with him as he plunged to eternity), quickly to be followed by Althusser strangling his wife to death, all in the fateful academic year 1979. (On a personal note, having been a student in Paris at the time, I still vividly recall these untimely deaths, attended by the almost simultaneous passings of Sartre and Roland Barthes, the latter run down by a car.) This lunatic craze however was almost immediately superseded by the Foucault cult, when every half-baked, ill-educated dimwit imagined him or herself a philosopher after having dabbed in (excerpts from, if even that much) Nietzsche, Heidegger and the Paris master-thinker himself.

Shortly thereafter began the Derrida fad with a fresh wagon-load of cliché and jargon unloaded at navel-contemplating conferences, pawned off as radical and cutting edge whereas it possessed all the intellectual and political content of marsh mellow topped with Redi-Whip; and – will the Lord ever forgive them for this sin- unloaded on unsuspecting students. I have on occasion, mostly for light amusement after a hard day's work, picked up some of these texts, and wonder how poor, unsuspecting, innocent, naive young people have borne such utter rubbish. To inflict it on them is – and here I write as a committed, if atheistic, educator – truly a sin beyond redemption. Fortunately adults such as myself, and not bound by the constraints, whether of political correctness or academic fashion, still preserve the liberty – which I, at any rate, do not intend to abdicate – of calling this what it is. For all I know he might have been the most decent fellow going, but as an influence on academic life Derrida was an abomination – or, more exactly, a too-long running joke. I do not in the least lament his passing, except in the sense of the truism that for those who knew him personally, his loss, like the loss of human life generally, must be source of sorrow. Beyond that, good riddens. The reactions to my posting on this listserv have fallen into three main categories: 1) studied disgust at my lack of academic couth – which is a useful pretext (if I might appropriate that word) for avoiding discussion of substantive issues; 2) incomprehensible gibberish about my "rhetoric," "representations," intermixed with words I've never heard of like "aporia" and "irenic" – or, to be precise, words I have heard of, but don't think it's worth the trouble of learning their definition, although I love dictionaries – my last great hope is that if reincarnation is yet a transcendental and temporal truth, I come back as a Webster's unabridged; and although reveling in the exquisite delights of learning new words: yet as a point of principle I refuse to invest the energy requisite for such lexicological investigation simply to satisfy the pitifully deformed ego of a pedant; and 3) factual points of difference. Almost none of the postings fit under the last head. I will limit my remarks here to two interrelated point.

I asserted that one evidence that Holocaust studies is a non-field is the sorts of questions it ponders: e.g. the fanatical insistence on proving the "uniqueness" of the Nazi holocaust. It was then asserted in response by one listserv member that this concern is hardly peculiar to Holocaust studies. Let's then, put forth a simple challenge. Consider this illustrative rendering from a leading light of this purported field. Professor Steven T. Katz has published the first of a projected three volume study (Oxford University Press) harnessing over 5,000 titles the purpose of which is to prove that "the Holocaust is phenomenologically unique by virtue of the fact that never before has a state set out, as a matter of intentional principle and actualized policy, to annihilate physically every man, woman and child belonging to a specific people." Clarifying his thesis, Katz explains: ""? is uniquely C. "? may share A, B, D, . . . X with?£ but not C. And again "may share A,B,D, . . . X with all £ but not C . . ."l lacking C is not ". . . . By definition, no exceptions to this rule are allowed.?£ sharing A,B,D, . . . X with "? may be like "? in these and other respects . . . but as regards our definition of uniqueness any or all?£ sharing A,B,D, . . . X with "? may be like "? in these and other respect . . . but as regards our definition of uniqueness any or all?£ lacking C are not "?. . . Of course, in its totality "? is more than C, but it is never "? without C." To avoid any confusion, Katz further elucidates that he uses the term phenomenological "in a non-Husserlian, non-Shutzean, non-Schelerian, non-Heideggerian, non-Merleau-Pontyian sense." Translation: the Katz enterprise, like Holocaust studies generally, is phenomenal non-sense. Now here's my question: Please cite even a single article in the vast output of scholarship on American slavery that even remotely echoes such insane preoccupations. Or, point to me a single article in the scholarly literature on American slavery making the claim that it "leads into darkness," "negates all answers," "lies outside, if not beyond, history," "defies both knowledge and description," "cannot be explained nor visualized," is "never to be comprehended or transmitted," marks a "destruction of history" and a "mutation on a cosmic scale," is "non-communicable" – "we cannot even talk about it." I am, or course, quoting here the high-priest of Holocaust studies, Elie Wiesel. Does this sound to anyone on the listserv like rational inquiry or is it, as I've suggested, a highly lucrative and politically useful mystery religion?

APPENDIX C

Chomsky-Dershowitz exchange of letters

Harvard Law School
1575 Massachusetts Avenue
Cambridge, Massachusetts 02138

Alan M. Dershowitz
Felix Frankfurter Professor of Law

January 7, 2005

Professor Noam A. Chomsky
Department of Linguistics and Philosophy
Massachusetts Institute of Technology
32-D840
77 Massachusetts Avenue
Cambridge, MA 02139-4307

Dear Noam:

I have received several emails from people to whom you have written claiming that the *Globe* ombudsman back in 1973, "finally told Dershowitz they wouldn't publish any more letters of his because he had been caught flat out lying." This is simply not true. The letters editor, not the ombudsman, told me that since each of us had published two letters, and I had published the first, Chomsky would get the last word. The ombudsman at the time was Charlie Whipple, whom I knew and got along with quite well. He would never—and never did—accuse me of "lying." Moreover, the *Globe* continued to publish more of my letters, columns, reviews, etc. over the years. I am asking you, respectfully, to stop spreading this false charge.

I also ask you, respectfully, to stop saying that I plagiarized "large parts" of *The Case for Israel*. As you well know, even Finkelstein claims only that I originally found a handful of quotations in Peters' book and cited them to their original sources, not to Peters. My research assistants tell me that you have done the same thing on numerous occasions. This is not plagiarism. It is a dispute over proper citation form regarding a small number of citations, about which I am correct, according to the best authorities. We can continue to disagree about a wide range of issues, but there is no reason for you to participate in Finkelstein's defamatory practices.

Sincerely,
Alan M. Dershowitz

January 13th, 2005

Mr. Alan Dershowitz
520 Hauser Hall
1575 Massachusetts Avenue
Cambridge, MA 02138

Dear Mr. Dershowitz,

I read your letter with interest, and more surprise. From the little I've been sent of your performances over the years, it had not really occurred to me that you might actually believe what you write. But from the fact that you sent the letter, I suppose I should assume otherwise. That is quite sad.

I'm afraid, however, that I cannot help you. On both of the matters that you mention, I feel that it is only appropriate to keep to honesty and truth when asked for reaction to what you write or are reported to have said. Unless asked—as the research assistants you refer to can doubtless inform you—I ignore it.

On the *Boston Globe*, I will continue, when asked, to tell the truth, which in the light of your letter, I have to assume you have managed to suppress. Perhaps not too surprising, given the contents. And I can even understand why my reluctant exposure of your mendacity with regard to Shahak, the Israeli courts, and the disgraceful behavior of the Labor government set off the personal jihad that seems to have been consuming you ever since, in quite comical ways, judging by what has been sent to me. But with all due sympathy, I'll have to continue as before, referring those who inquire to what is in print, and, if appropriate, to what followed, which I'll be glad to remind you of if you like.

On your second point, I think I can guess why you would like to believe that I would spend waste a moment on your liftings from Joan Peters. In the context of the lies, deceit, and apologetics for atrocities in this curious work, judging by the sample that has been sent to me, the plagiarism issue is too marginal even to mention—which is, I presume, why you bring it up.

I can only express my sympathies, but will have to keep to standard and proper practice.

Noam Chomsky

INDEX

Abu-Lughod, Ibrahim and Janet   110
Abunimah, Ali   121
Academic Bill of Rights   23
Adams, Michael   208n. 13
Afghanistan   63, 236n. 48, 303,
        342–3, 345
Ajami, Fouad   53
Alam, M. Shahid   25, 93–4, 210n. 45
Al-Arian, Sami   3
American Association of University
        Professors   7, 37, 86, 245n. 11
American-Israel Public Affairs
        Committee (AIPAC)   18,
        70, 74, 92–3, 112, 176, 196,
        208nn. 23, 26, 212
Amit, Zalman   29, 236n. 4
Amnesty International   61, 64, 71, 77,
        235n. 48, 298, 342
Anti-Defamation League   48, 83, 92,
        97, 112, 195, 261, 264, 361
Aruri, Naseer   72, 208n. 15
Association of American Universities
        37, 86
The Atlantic   57

Balakrishnan, Gopal   231n. 16
Battiste, John   21
Bauer, Yehuda   89
Begin, Menachem   191, 193
Bellow, Saul   94, 356
Bemis, Edward   12, 16
Ben-Ami, Schlomo   25–6
Ben-Cannan, Ari   18
Benda, Julian   113, 122, 211n. 2,
        231n. 21
Benevisti, Meron   76, 223n. 43
Bennett, William   104–5, 107–9,
        224n. 22
Berman, Paul   149, 231n. 18

Bérubé, Michael   143–4, 234n. 43, 342
Bhabha, Homi   106
Bichler, Shimshon   205, 210n. 51
Bickerton, Ian   97
Bilgrami, Akeel   85
Bindenagel, J. D.   218–19n. 6
Boyarin, Daniel   106, 228n. 56
Boyle, Francis   57
Brennan, Teresa   167
Brennan, Timothy   119, 129, 139,
        144, 199, 232n. 26, 235n. 49,
        245n. 2
Brohm, Schlomo   21
Bronfman, Edgar   62, 262, 361
Brunner, José   225nn. 26–7
B'tselem   71, 77, 270
Burg, Avraham   153, 176
Burke, Kenneth   154
Bush, George W.   19, 21, 131–2, 145–6,
        227n. 47, 234n. 46, 299–301,
        311, 313, 329, 343, 351
Butler, Judith   11, 218n. 2, 238n. 25,
        361, 363
Byrne, Peter   3, 207nn. 1, 5

Callahan, Patrick   85, 88
Campus Watch   23
Canaan   63
Carter, Jimmy   26, 57, 155, 179,
        194–6, 209n. 42, 236n. 4
Chaput, Cathy   7–8, 205, 230n. 13
Cheney, Richard   351
Chessler, Phyllis   68, 71
Chicago Manual of Style   65
Chinski, Sarah   106
Chomsky, Noam   1–2, 40, 55, 57, 64,
        72, 76, 81, 89, 94–5, 101,
        110–11, 113, 121, 125–50,
        293–354

Christison, Kathleen   48
Churchill, Ward   31, 220,
    230n. 14, 267
Clinton, Bill   26, 64, 140, 177,
    218n. 6, 234n. 41, 265, 298,
    300, 329, 349, 361
Cockburn, Alexander   65, 89, 112,
    121, 210n. 61, 216n. 23,
    238n. 24, 245n. 10
Cohn, Werner   235n. 54
Cole, Jonathan   82, 85
Cole, Juan   42, 85, 204
Cole, Tim   224n. 21
Common Good School   5, 9
Cook, Jonathan   187, 208n. 16,
    239n. 31, 240n. 3
Corrie, Cindy   2
Corrie, Craig   2
Corrie, Rachel   v, 1–2, 153–82,
    236nn. 6–7, 237nn. 10, 13,
    238nn. 14–15, 23, 261, 281,
    284, 292, 340–1
Counterpunch   17
Crossman, Richard   122
Cuomo, Mario   67

David Project   23
Davidson, Lawrence   48, 208n. 19,
    211n. 1
Dayan, Moshe   64, 186
*Declaration of Principles on Academic
    Freedom and Tenure,
    1915*   4, 10
De Genova, Nicolas   218n. 3
Deleuze, Gilles   106
Democracy Now   17, 36, 38, 59–61,
    81, 85, 95, 214n. 5, 218n. 1,
    355, 361
DePaul Political Science
    Department   218n. 5
DePaul University   35, 37, 60, 79–98,
    220, 230n. 11, 264, 266, 271,
    274, 279, 282, 284–5, 292–3,
    354
Derrida, Jacques   106
Dershowitz, Alan   1, 26–7, 36–98,
    178, 185, 210n. 49, 211nn. 5,
    14, 212n. 11, 215nn. 12–15,
    216nn. 20–4, 218n. 1,

219nn. 9–11, 221nn. 15, 19,
    226nn. 37–8, 240n. 4, 241n. 5
Dewey, John   9, 231n. 6, 347
Discover the Network   23
Dissident Voice   17

Ebban, Abba   89, 170, 239, 262
Eizenstat, Stuart   62, 89, 262
El-Asmar, Fouzi   1–2, 73, 76, 183–98,
    241n. 5
Ellis, Marc   163, 175–6
Emerson, Steve   53, 55, 121, 227n. 42
Enderlin, Charles   72
Engels, Frederick   20
Exodus   18, 67, 175, 195, 268

Feith, Douglas   21, 361
Feldman, Gerald   89
Findley, Peter   18, 34, 209n. 41,
    227n. 46
Finkelstein, Norman   1–2, 19, 25,
    30–1, 35–48, 59–98, 110,
    131, 137, 143, 149, 203–4,
    208n. 18, 210nn. 50, 57,
    212n. 14, 214n. 3, 215n. 13,
    216nn. 23, 27, 218nn. 2, 6,
    355–67
Finkin, Matthew   6
Fish, Stanley   4–5, 7, 81, 99–100,
    102–5, 108, 167, 207n. 4,
    222n. 1, 223n. 14
Flapan, Simha   28, 211n. 4
Foxman, Abraham   41, 62, 68, 71,
    178, 194, 211n. 6, 212n. 10,
    240n. 38, 262, 278, 360–1
Freedman, Robert O.   65
From Time Immemorial   11, 45, 59–61,
    64–6, 94–5, 216, 230n. 11

Galileo   12
Gates, Henry Louis Jr.   67, 220–1, 288
The German Ideology   20
Gide, André   122
Gilbert, Martin   89
Gilder, George   44
Ginsberg, Terri   3
Glenn, Cheryl   236n. 3
Gluzman, Michael   106
The God That Failed   122

Goldhagen, Daniel 81
Goldstone, Richard 41, 239n. 35
Goodman, Amy 81, 85
Gordon, Neve 218n. 1, 221n. 16,
    239n. 35
Gorny, Yosef 73, 188, 211n. 4, 240n. 1
Gouldner, Alvin 211n. 2
Gramsci, Antonio 22, 113–14
Grand Mufti of Jerusalem 23
Green, Stephen 34
Grose, Peter 48
Grunzweig, Emil 77

Haganah 53, 61, 63
Halper, Jeff 75, 217n. 42
Harper, William Rainey 6
Harrison, Bernard 44, 211,
    238n. 24
Harvard University 1, 24, 36, 39, 41,
    55–6, 60, 67, 75–6, 84, 196,
    218n. 1, 219n. 10, 220n. 11,
    226n. 37, 265, 268, 270,
    272–3, 275, 286, 292, 301,
    308, 353, 355–6, 360–1, 369
Haskell, Thomas 93, 225, 226n. 39
Herf, Jeffrey 44
Herzl, Theodor 188, 191, 239n. 29
Hever, Shir 210n. 51
Hilberg, Raul 79, 95, 216n. 27,
    220n. 11, 265, 286, 360–1,
    365
Hitler, Adolph 23, 175, 188–90, 324,
    360
Holtschneider, Dennis Rev. 82–7
Holy Land 63
Horowitz, David 26, 35, 53,
    230n. 15, 335
Human Rights Watch 71, 74, 77
Hunter College 40, 94, 104, 354

Indyk, Martin 26
Innocents Abroad 65
Iran 16, 21, 49, 53, 63, 86, 95, 113,
    116, 133, 146, 174, 203, 336
It's For Revolution School 5
It's Just a Job School 5

Jewish Institute for National Security
    Affairs (JINSA) 22, 43, 201

Kagan, Elena 219n. 10, 276
Kagan, Robert 347
Kahan Commission 77, 138
Kahane, Meir 356
Karsh, Ephraim 28
Kaspit, Ben 191, 242
Khalidi, Rashid 110, 117, 121,
    226n. 37
Kimmerling, Baruch 17, 106,
    208n. 22, 226n. 40,
    241nn. 7, 11, 242nn. 16,
    21, 244n. 46, 286
Klein, David 92
Koestler, Arthur 122
Kosinski, Jerry 41, 88–9, 360
Kovel, Joel 3, 42, 218n. 3
Krauthammer, Charles 53
Kuwait 53, 63

LaCapra, Dominick 102, 172,
    223n. 11, 224n. 21,
    238nn. 18, 27, 362–3
Lavon, Pinhas 77
Lemisch, Jess 127, 230nn. 7–8
Lerman, Miles 89
Levit, Daphna 30, 236n. 4
Lewis, Bernard 21, 53, 55, 94, 119,
    212n. 19
Lilienthal, Alfred 34, 55
Loar, Yitzak 176
Lochery, Neil 44
Lockman, Zachary 47, 211n. 1,
    212n. 12
London Review of Books 55–6, 196
Lovejoy, Arthur 6–7
Lustick, Ian 27, 238n. 22
Lyotard, Jean-Francois 106, 308

Makdisi, Saree 117
Ma'oz, Zeev 233n. 3
Martin, Bill 92
Marx, Karl 20
Massad, Joseph 3, 24, 30, 42,
    69, 178, 192, 196, 204n. 3,
    218, 231n. 22, 238n. 38,
    239nn. 28–9, 242nn. 17,
    19, 243nn. 31–4, 244n. 47,
    246n. 15
Mayhew, Christopher 208n. 13

McAlester, Melanie 211n. 1
Mearsheimer, John 18, 51, 56, 96,
 178, 209nn. 31, 40, 213n. 22,
 239n. 37
Megged, Ahron 107, 225n. 6
Meir, Golda 60, 191
Menetrez, Frank 86, 216n. 23
Michaels, John 199, 245n. 1
Middle East and Asian Languages
 and Cultures Department
 (MELAC), Columbia
 University 32
Miller, Aaron David 26
Morris, Benny 61, 73, 88–9, 111,
 188, 213n. 20, 216n. 22,
 227nn. 50–1, 228n. 51,
 241n. 14, 287

Nasser, Gamal Abdel 17, 70, 133, 351
Nearing, Scott 6, 12
Nelson, Carey 199, 207n. 8
Neuborne, Burt 89, 262, 361
New Historians 17, 27–8, 53, 61,
 107, 111, 173, 213n. 20,
 225nn. 26, 29
Nitzan, Jonathan 205, 210n. 51
Novick, Peter 224n. 20

Odom, William 21
Orientalism 52, 114–15, 193, 201,
 243n. 34

Palestine: Peace Not Apartheid 35,
 57, 179, 194, 196, 236n. 4,
 244nn. 39, 42
Pappe, Illan 61, 72, 96, 106, 173,
 213n. 20, 215n. 9, 243n. 28
Perle, Richard 351
Peters, Joan 1, 28, 45, 59–61, 64–6,
 94–5, 216n. 24, 230n. 11, 288,
 352, 355–7, 369, 371
Peterson-Overton, Kristofer 218n. 3
Pipes, Daniel 35, 53, 85, 121, 212n. 19
Plaut, Steven 53, 83, 85, 99, 214n. 2
Porath, Yehoshua 73, 188, 241n. 14,
 314
Post, Robert 6, 10, 218n. 2
Powell, Colin 351
Powell, Louis 3

Protocols of the Elders of Zion 43,
 73, 178, 240n. 38, 262–3,
 267, 361
Puccio, Paul 180

Rabin, Yitzhak 186
Ramal-Nankoe, Margo 218n. 3
Readings, Bill 199
Ridgen, D. 95
Roberts-Miller, Patricia 238n. 17
Robinson, Colin 62, 215n. 15,
 216n. 24
Robinson, William 3
Rosenbaum, Ron 71
Rosenfeld, Alvin 211n. 3
Ross, Dennis 26, 62
Ross, Edward 12
Rossier, N. 95
Rothstein, Edward 99–105, 107
Rumsfeld, Donald 351
Russell, Thaddeus 218n. 3

Sabban Center for Middle East
 Policy 43
Said, Edward 1, 2, 15, 52–3, 99–123
Salaita, Steven 93
Schmitt, Carl 22
Schoenfeld, Gabriel 68, 71, 211n. 6
Schrecker, Ellen 79–80, 84, 199,
 207n. 8
Schwarzenegger, Arnold 62, 74, 265
Seligman, Edwin 6–7
Shahak, Israel 57, 76, 137, 185,
 214n. 31, 276, 371
Shapira, Anita 107–9, 119,
 225nn. 28–30, 226n. 36
Sharett, Moshe 64, 77, 87, 304
Sharon, Ariel 76–7, 138, 186,
 217n. 43, 224n. 22, 329, 338
Sharrett, Yakov 77
Shatz, Adam 21, 209n. 33
Sheperd, Robin 44, 210n. 62
Sherman, Scott 57, 82, 214n. 33
Shils, Edward 211
Shor, Ira 181
Silberstein, Laurence 224n. 21
Silone, Ignazio 122
Simon, John 85
Singer, Israel 62

Socrates 12
Solway, David 44–5
Spender, Stephen 122
Spiegel, Charles 72
Spivak, Gayatri 116, 245n. 8
Stanford, Dorothy Leland 6
St Clair, Jeffrey 121
Stern Gang 53
Stone, Geoffrey 230
Suchar, Charles 95
Swisher, Clayton 26, 208n. 17

Tobin, Weinberg, Ferer 117
The Treason of the Intellectuals 122
Truman, Harry 18
Twain, Mark 65

United Arab Emirate 63
University of Chicago 6, 56, 90, 196, 218n. 6, 221n. 15, 262, 267
Uris, Leon 18

Vietnam 128, 142, 147, 150, 253, 299–300, 307, 335, 345, 349–50

Walt, Stephen 18, 51, 56, 96, 178, 209nn. 31, 40, 213n. 22, 239n. 37

War on Terror 19, 23, 104, 107, 121, 131, 137, 145–6, 175, 193–4, 294–5, 337–8, 342–4, 346
Washington Institute for Near East Policy (WINEP) 21, 43, 201
Webber, Mitch 275
Weizmann, Chaim 191
Wiesel, Elie 41, 62, 67–8, 81, 88–9, 91, 262, 268, 287, 292, 356, 359–64, 367
Wieseltier, Leon 71, 360
Wilshire, Bruce 199
Wilson, John K. 218n. 4
Winkler, Carol 233n. 31
Wistrich, Robert 44
Withey, Lynne 63
Wolfowitz, Paul 351
Worsham, Lynn 154

Yale University 204, 246n. 13
Yaniv, Avner 233
Yinon, Oded 57

Zakaria, Fareed 21
Zinni, Anthony 21
Žižek, Slavoj 136, 231n. 28, 310, 319–20

www.ingramcontent.com/pod-product-compliance
Lightning Source LLC
Chambersburg PA
CBHW060135280326
41932CB00012B/1525